I0374311

CENSORED

The News That Didn't Make the News—and Why

The 1994 Project Censored Yearbook

CARL JENSEN & PROJECT CENSORED

INTRODUCTION BY JESSICA MITFORD

CARTOONS BY TOM TOMORROW

FOUR WALLS EIGHT WINDOWS

NEW YORK

Censored: the news that didn't make the news and why
ISSN 1074-5998

10 9 8 7 6 5 4 3 2 1

FOUR WALLS EIGHT WINDOWS
39 West 14th Street, #503
New York, New York, 10011

Designed by Cindy LaBreacht

DEDICATION

To my Mother
Anna Håkansson Jensen
1902—1993
She gave me my first typewriter
when I was seven ...
and taught me to love America.

Table of Contents

Preface

CENSORED! The News That Didn't Make The News—And Why is published annually in response to a growing national demand for news and information not published nor broadcast by the mainstream media in America.

Originally self-published by Project Censored as a spiral bound resource book, the 1994 Project Censored Yearbook is now published by Four Walls Eight Windows of New York. As in the four previous Yearbooks (1990-1993), *CENSORED!* features the top 25 *Censored* stories of the year, background information about Project Censored, comments about the top 25 stories by the original authors and others, brief synopses of each of the stories, and a chapter on the top "junk food news" stories, with comments by the news ombudsmen who selected them.

This edition also includes a special introduction by Jessica Mitford; a déjà vu chapter of previously censored stories that finally have been "discovered" by the mainstream media; an updated eclectic chronology of censorship since 605 BC which attempts to put the whole issue into historical context; and a censored resource guide to alternative media organizations, electronic and print alternative media, and some selected mainstream media sources, which is updated annually.

A new addition to the 1994 Yearbook is the first Alternative Writer's Market which provides brief information about publications that are open to the work of alternative journalists. Since this is our first year publishing this writer's guide, it is limited in scope, but contains useful information about some of the leading alternative publications in America and is expected to expand in the future.

Also, like the 1993 Yearbook, this edition fulfills a goal I have had since launching Project Censored in 1976—it contains reprints of the original top 10 *Censored* articles wherever possible. You'll be able to review the brief synopsis of the story, see what the author has to say about the subject, and then read the original article in its entirety.

The synopses are originally written by Project Censored researchers participating in a seminar in news media censorship offered by the Communication Studies Department at Sonoma State University, a member of the California State University system. They are then edited for style and clarity. The synopses are not meant to replace the original articles upon which they are based, but rather to briefly summarize the major thrust of a much longer article or, in some cases, a brochure or book.

CENSORED! The News That Didn't Make The News—And Why is another effort by Project Censored to provide information on important issues the public should know about. I hope you will learn more about issues that touch your life, your community and, in a larger context, the global village of which we are all citizens.

I also hope that it will disturb you to discover that all this information was available to the press and that you will wonder why your local and national news media haven't already told you about these subjects.

Finally, I would like to invite you to join Project Censored as a scout or source for stories that deserve more attention from the mainstream media. Please see the postscript for information on how to nominate stories for the "Best Censored News Stories of 1994."

—Carl Jensen
Cotati, California

Acknowledgments

The first acknowledgment must go to all our *Censored* colleagues who contribute to the success of Project Censored by sending us stories as nominations. We receive some 700 nominations annually from journalists, educators, librarians, and many others who are concerned with the public's right to know. We truly are grateful to all of you who bring those stories to our attention.

Another group critical to the success of the project are the Sonoma State University students who participate as *Censored* researchers in the annual Project Censored seminar. It is their responsibility to analyze the hundreds of nominations received in order to determine whether they qualify as censored stories of the year. Following are the SSU students who evaluated the censored nominations of 1993:

PROJECT CENSORED RESEARCHERS OF 1993

Gerald Austin, Jesse Boggs, Paul Chambers,
Tamara Fresca, Tim Gordon, Bill Harding, Courteney Lunt,
Katie Maloney, Mark Papadopoulos, Kristen Rutledge,
Sunil Sharma, Laurie Turner

Many other groups and individuals contribute to the success of Project Censored, not the least of which are the publications, mostly from the alternative media, that publicize the annual results and the many radio and television news and talk show hosts who discuss the censored stories each year.

A special thanks goes to our colleagues at the Media Alliance in San Francisco, who are now into their fifth year of Bay Area Censored, and to Bill Doskoch, of the Canadian Association of Journalists, and Bob Hackett and Don Gutstein, of Simon Fraser University, who launched Project Censored Canada this year.

We also wish to acknowledge the support we receive from Sonoma State University, particularly from my colleagues in the Department of Communication Studies; Bill Babula, Dean of the School of Arts and Humanities; Alan Murray, General Manager of the SSU Academic Foundation; and Mark Resmer, Director of Computing, Media, and Telecommunications Services.

There are three other organizations that deserve special recognition. The interest, encouragement, and financial support from the C.S. Fund, of Freestone, California; Anita Roddick and the Body Shop Foundation, of England; and The John D. and Catherine T. MacArthur Foundation contribute significantly to the successful outreach of Project Censored.

Also, if it were not for support from these foundations, we would not have an assistant director, Mark Lowenthal, nor a research associate, Amy S. Cohen, working with us. Among many other activities, Mark is directly responsible for responding to the thousands of letters and phone calls we receive from people throughout the country and abroad each year. Amy is in charge of the new Censored outreach program designed to serve journalism professors and students across the country and she also compiled and updated this year's resource guide. I'm also grateful to both Mark and Amy for the time they spent reviewing and editing this manuscript.

I am indebted to Dan Simon, John Oakes and their colleagues at Four Walls Eight Windows for having the faith and fortitude to take on a subject that the conglomerate publishers rejected. For the same reasons, I appreciate the support and help of my literary agent, Michael Larson.

I want to especially thank my wife, Sandra Scott Jensen, for the many hours she spent reviewing early versions of this document and for all the support and encouragement she has given me and Project Censored since its start in 1976. Once again we celebrated Thanksgiving, Christmas, and New Year's Day working at the *Censored* computer.

JESSICA MITFORD—QUEEN OF THE MUCKRAKERS

Jessica Mitford, who was kind enough to share her wit and wisdom concerning the censorship of pornography in the introduction, was once appropriately named the "Queen of the Muckrakers" by *Time* magazine. The many deserving targets of her poison penmanship have ranged from

The American Way of Birth to *The American Way of Death* and also have included The Famous Writers' School, Elizabeth Arden's Maine Chance spa, the California State University system, NBC, and the prison system.

TOM TOMORROW—THE CARTOONIST

Tom Tomorrow's comic strip, "This Modern World," appears in more than 75 newspapers across the country. His first book collection, *Greetings From This Modern World*, is available from St. Martin's Press; he is currently putting together a second volume which will be published in September 1994. To communicate with Tom, write him at POB 170515, San Francisco, CA 94117.

PROJECT CENSORED JUDGES OF 1993

One of the most difficult challenges of Project Censored is to select the "Ten Best Censored" stories from among the 25 top nominations. This responsibility falls to our distinguished national panel of judges who volunteer their efforts. Perhaps one of the greatest tributes to the project is that some of our judges, identified with asterisks, have participated in Project Censored every year since selecting the first group of censored stories in 1976. (Ben Bagdikian sequestered himself in the years he also was a *Censored* author.) We are deeply indebted to the following judges who selected the top ten *Censored* stories of 1993.

DR. DONNA ALLEN, founding editor of Media Report to Women

BEN BAGDIKIAN,* professor emeritus, Graduate School of Journalism, UC-Berkeley

RICHARD BARNET, senior fellow, Institute for Policy Studies

NOAM CHOMSKY,* professor, Linguistics and Philosophy, Massachusetts Institute of Technology

HUGH DOWNS, host, ABC's "20/20"

SUSAN FALUDI, journalist/author

DR. GEORGE GERBNER, professor, Annenberg School of Communications, University of Pennsylvania

Introduction BY JESSICA MITFORD

I've been a Fervent Fan of Project Censored since its inception in 1976, and am honored to be asked to write an introduction to the 1994 Yearbook. The project's supreme contribution is, of course, its relentless exposure of mainstream media's suppression of vital day-to-day issues of concern to all of us. But I'd like to put in my two cents' worth on the subject of pornography, for the last decade a hot and divisive issue in the women's movement.

To ban or not to ban? The lines were drawn in 1984, when the city council of Indianapolis, at the behest of law professor Catherine MacKinnon and her ideological sidekick Andrea Dworkin, passed a sweeping anti-porn ordinance which must have surpassed the fondest hopes of Sen. Jesse Helms, Rev. Donald Wildmon and their many far-right adherents.

Eventually the statute was struck down by the courts, and a similar ordinance passed by the Minneapolis city council was vetoed by the mayor; but the debate rages on, fueled by the hyperbolic outpourings of MacKinnon and Dworkin. Here is an example of vintage Dworkin, in *Pornography: Men Possessing Women:*

> For men the right to abuse women is elemental, the first principle, with no beginning...and with no end plausibly in sight....Pornography is the holy corpus of men who would rather die than change. Dachau brought into the bedroom and celebrated....Pornography reveals that male pleasure is inextricably tied to victimizing, hurting, exploiting; that sexual fun and sexual passion in the privacy of the male imagination are inseparable from the brutality of male history.

There was more to come from that perfervid pen. In *Our Blood* she wrote: "I think that men will have to give up their precious erections and begin to make love as women do together...they will have to excise everything in them that they now value as distinctively 'male.'" Ooh-er, as the English say. More recently, Andrea Dworkin published a book starkly titled *Intercourse*, the theme of which is that all heterosexual intercourse is a form of rape.

Next, we have *Only Words* by Catherine MacKinnon, in which she declares that "Unwelcome sex talk is an unwelcome sex act... To say it is to do it, and to do it is to say it." How's that again? Carlin Romano begins his review in *The Nation* (November 15, 1993):

> Suppose I decide to rape Catherine MacKinnon before reviewing her book. Because I'm uncertain whether she understands the difference between being raped and being exposed to pornography, I consider it required research for my critique of her manifesto that pornography equals rape and should be banned.

O.K. folks, he's only kidding, as he soon makes clear. But he's dead serious when it comes to demolishing the MacKinnon thesis that words and deeds are one and the same.

The more traditional argument of the porn-bashers is not that words/deeds are the same, but that words (and pictures, objects, etc.) *incite* to deeds, the theory of cause-and-effect, which despite all efforts by the MacKinnon camp has never been shown to exist.

Those against legislation to ban pornography point out that there is no proof of a causal relationship between pornography and violence against women. They give the example of Amsterdam, capitol of Porn where you can't walk downtown without being assaulted on every side by filthy, absolutely revolting movie marquees offering everything the most rotten heart could desire in the way of dirty films, and sex shops, with God knows what for sale, porn bookshops and so on.

Yet Amsterdam claims to be freer of the crimes of assaults against women than any Western city. Why? One theory is that would-be rapists act out their fantasies by watching the dirty movies, reading the dirty books. I don't pretend to know if this is true—it has a sort of spurious-sounding logic, possibly dreamed up by the Amsterdam Chamber of Commerce.

The effort to supress indecent or obscene work has had a long and checquered history. Has anyone thought back to the famous trial of *Lady*

Chatterley's Lover (the book, that is, not the lover) in which the prose-cutor cautioned the jurors that surely they would agree that one wouldn't want one's children or servants to read such a book. Upon which some wag remarked: "...and certainly not one's gamekeeper." (In this case, the courts in both England and America lifted the ban on the ground that the book is a great work of literature, hence absolved. I should parenthetically confess here that I read a smuggled copy at the age of 12, purely out of a prurient interest in the fascinating information contained therein, and without regard for the excellence of the writing.)

Furthermore, has anyone reflected upon the implications of *The Rape of Lucrece* by W. Shakespeare which might easily inspire some modern-day Tarquin to go forth and do the same? Or what about the Holy Bible, full of s. & v., but a jolly good read nevertheless? Or the Kinsey Report which, as I recall, had fascinating tabulated data on the sexual habits of American males? For me, most intriguing in this catalogue was the revelation that one out of every eight American men has had intercourse with animals. At any large party, I can't help glancing around to try and guess which of the men present had done it—and with whom? Man's best friend? A sheep? A horse? The report was disappointingly reticent on this score. Have the animal rights advocates been heard from in this controversy? For is it not possible that a reader of the K. report might become so titillated as to have a go with a p g, just to see what it's like?

All jokes aside on this important subject, the radical feminist porn-bashers would do well to reflect on the motives of their strange bed-fellows on the far right. For example, the Moral Majority in a number of states, mostly Southern, have zeroed in on Maya Angelou's book, *I Know Why the Caged Bird Sings* and on Alice Walker's prize-winning *The Color Purple*, for their allegedly obscene content. This is a thinly-disguised effort to do in these best-selling Black authors along with such tried-&-true targets as J.D. Salinger, Kurt Vonnegut, and *Ms. Magazine*.

If vigilance is the price of liberty, let's all keep an eye on the guys and dolls, ladies and gentlemen, boys and girls—take your pick—who are out to protect us from our own baser selves.

"The only thing necessary
for the triumph of evil is for good men
to do nothing."—Edmund Burke

CHAPTER 1

Project Censored:
Raking Muck, Raising Hell

John Bunyan, a 17th Century English author, would be impressed if he knew the controversy a phrase of his would generate more than three centuries later.

In Part 2, of "The Pilgrim's Progress," 1684, Bunyan exhorted his readers to look upward for spiritual solace rather than always being concerned with the material world at their feet. Bunyan wrote disparagingly of "the man who could look no way but downward, with a muckrake in his hand; who was offered a celestial crown for his muckrake, but who would neither look up nor regard the crown he was offered, but continued to rake to himself the filth of the floor."

This catchy phrase did not escape the eyes of President Theodore Roosevelt who was seeking the appropriate words to excoriate journalists who were inciting social unrest with their investigations and revelations of corruption.

On April 14, 1906, while dedicating the cornerstone for the office building of the House of Representatives in Washington, Roosevelt, interpreting Bunyan in his own way, formally labeled such journalists as "muckrakers."

While acknowledging there was filth on the floor that needed to be scraped up with a muckrake, he warned of "the man who never does anything else, who never thinks or speaks or writes save of his feats with the muckrake, speedily becomes, not a help to society, not an incitement to good, but one of the potent forces of evil."

Thus, the term was institutionalized and the decade from 1902 to 1912 became known as the Golden Age of Muckraking. Despite Roosevelt's disparaging comments, it also may represent the most distinguished period of journalism in U.S. history. Media scholars Jay Black and Jennings Bryant said the "period may have been the highwater mark of journalistic ethics."

Some of the remarkable works of the period included David Graham Phillips' *The Treason of the Senate*, Ida Tarbell's *The History of Standard Oil*, Lincoln Steffens' *The Shame of the Cities*, and Upton Sinclair's novel, *The Jungle*, an exposé of the meat-packing industry that led to the passage of the first food inspection laws in the U.S.

Rejecting the derogatory connotation of muckrakers as described by Roosevelt, leaders of the genre instead wore it as a badge of honor. And not before, nor since, has journalism had as great an impact on society nor better fulfilled its role as society's watchdog.

Ironically, many of today's mainstream journalists reject recognition as muckrakers, apparently accepting the negative connotation intended by Roosevelt.

Such is not the case with Jessica Mitford. In her introduction to *Poison Penmanship: The Gentle Art of Muckraking*, which should be required reading wherever journalism is taught, Mitford wrote: "I first began to think of myself as a muckraker when *Time*...called me 'Queen of the Muckrakers.' I rushed to the dictionary to find out what I was queen of, and discovered that 'muckraker' was originally a pejorative coined by President Theodore Roosevelt to describe journalists like Lincoln Steffens and Ida Tarbell, who in his view had gone too far in exposing corruption in government and corporate enterprise. Thus the Oxford English Dictionary says 'muckrake...is often made to refer generally...to a depraved interest in what is morally 'unsavoury' or scandalous.' (I fear that does rather describe me.)"

Like her turn-of-the-century muckraker predecessors, Mitford's investigative work stirred the nation's psyche and led to social change. Her exposé of the funeral industry in 1963, *The American Way of Death*, led to significant beneficial changes, official and unofficial, in an industry which historically had profited by exploiting the bereaved.

Not unlike the first decade of the century, there are ample subjects for today's muckrakers to explore and expose, some of them hauntingly familiar to that earlier period. In what seemed to be a tragic reprise of Sinclair's *Jungle*, the U.S. Department of Agriculture was forced to undertake sophisticated new monitoring procedures at slaughterhouses and processing plants after several children died and hundreds of other people were poisoned in early 1993.

In fact, the warnings of Samuel Gompers, famed labor leader and head of the American Federation of Labor, are as relevant today as they were about a century ago: "We want more school houses and less jails, more books and less arsenals, more learning and less vice, more constant work and less greed, more justice and less revenge."

Project Censored agrees with that credo and has dedicated itself to help create a society that will bring about such change. We are flattered when the project is referred to as a muckraking organization. However, we hasten to point out that the true muckrakers are the individual journalists who are responsible for the articles cited as censored. Project Censored is better compared to the irritating grain of sand in an oyster.

Our role is to stimulate the journalism profession to support more muckraking investigative journalism. Unfortunately, despite a slight blip in the aftermath of Watergate, journalism has failed to fulfill its watchdog role as exemplified during the Golden Age of Muckraking.

Indeed, while the United States is without equal in terms of communications technology, it would appear that it has suffered a massive breakdown when it comes to communications content. While we may have a free press and the most sophisticated communications system in the world, unfortunately a free press and high technology do not guarantee a well-informed society.

As a society, we are exposed to more information now than ever before in history. Thanks to recent advances in communications technology followed by the current explosion in computer sciences, the average citizen today is exposed to more information, at a greater speed, from throughout the world, than was available to our country's leaders not too many years ago. CNN viewers in Keokuk, Iowa, were probably more quickly informed of what was happening during the Gulf War than the President of the United States was of events in Vietnam during that conflict.

Like the horse and buggy, the agricultural and industrial ages are far behind us; we are hurtling headlong into the information age. All indicators support this thesis—from the diversity of information sources to the sophistication of communications technology to the amount of time people spend with the media.

In 1992 it was estimated that an average person spends some 3,256 hours a year with the media—nearly nine hours a day—the largest amount of time devoted to any one activity, including sleep and work. TV news buffs are given hourly updates on the networks, round the clock news on CNN, and special coverage on channels like C-SPAN.

But the problem is not with the quantity of information available in our society, which sometimes seems to reach an overload level, but rather with the quality of that information.

For example, when something starts to go wrong in your personal life, there generally are some warning signals that alert you to the problem. If you are a rational person, you normally act upon that information in an effort to solve the problem.

So too, it is with a society. When a problem arises, there should be a warning signal—information—that alerts citizens that something is wrong which needs attention and resolution. An aware and informed populace could then influence its leaders to act upon that information in an effort to solve the problem. This, unfortunately, is not the case in the United States as we are discovering during these difficult times.

I suspect there are few people who do not believe that the United States has serious problems that need to be resolved if we are to succeed and survive in the future. Yet, how many of us are fully aware of the scope of these problems and how many of us have all the information we need to deal with them?

Despite the quantity of news and information being disseminated around the clock, you and some 250 million other Americans are not being told everything you have a need and right to know. And, without full information about the affairs of our society, we cannot function as good citizens.

THIS MODERN WORLD by TOM TOMORROW

It is not realistic to expect anything to change, in America or in your community, until enough people lean out their windows and shout: "I'm mad as hell and I'm not going to take it any more."

But, for that to happen, we need someone out there raking muck and raising hell. This of course should be the role of a free press—but the media are selling us short. Instead they have become the willing tools of the propagandists that Jacques Ellul warned us about in *Propaganda: The Formation of Men's Attitudes,* in 1965.

The point is that our primary sources of news and information are increasingly being controlled by a very small group of men—supporting the thesis that an elite group has gained control over the information industry in the United States. As media scholar Ben Bagdikian points out in the latest edition (1993) of *The Media Monopoly,* his classic critique of corporate media control, fewer than 20 corporations now control most of the nation's mass media.

The next step in the information control process in America is to use this control to effectively exploit our minds. This, also, it seems, has been accomplished. The mind manipulators are well aware of the first principle of successful mind control—repetition.

To be successful, as Jacques Ellul wrote, propaganda must be continuous and lasting—continuous in that it must not leave any gaps, but must fill the citizen's whole day and all his days; lasting in that it must function over a long period of time.

Today's information industry learned this lesson well from Adolph Hitler who so successfully used propaganda in his quest for power. It was about a half century ago when Hitler said the masses take a long time to under-

stand and remember, thus it is necessary to repeat the message time and time and time again—the public must be conditioned to accept the claims that are made...no matter how outrageous or false those claims might be.

We, as a society, appear to have been well-conditioned to accept any number of claims regardless of how detrimental they may be to our environment or to our own well-being.

The Madison Avenue propagandists use the same techniques to sell us products and services we don't need and often can't afford. Repetition is also the key to success on Madison Avenue.

Propaganda tends to make an individual live in a separate world, a world lacking outside points of reference. You must not be allowed time for meditation or reflection in which to see or define yourself as might happen when the propaganda is not continuous. For if propaganda is not continuous, you might have a moment or two when you can emerge from its grip and realize you have been manipulated.

Meanwhile, our children are walking billboards for products—Coca Cola, Mickey Mouse, Barbie, MTV, Teenage Mutant Ninja Turtles, Nintendo, and others. Even worse, these products are selling us a way of life and conditioning us to accept it, along with other messages, including messages from political propagandists. Indeed, successful propaganda must occupy every waking moment of your life—and it does. Yet too few of us are aware of what is happening to us since the conditioning starts at such an early age.

In 1992, *Consumer Reports* magazine noted that children between the ages of four and 15 spend more than $18 billion annually and reported

THIS MODERN WORLD by TOM TOMORROW

HEY, CITIZENS! HAVE YOU EVER THOUGHT ABOUT THE ENORMOUS DEBT WE ALL OWE THE MEN AND WOMEN OF THE *ADVERTISING PROFESSION?* AFTER ALL, IF NOT FOR THEIR TIRELESS EFFORTS, HOW WOULD WE *EVER* BE ABLE TO CHOOSE THE MASS-PRODUCED CONSUMER ITEMS BEST SUITED TO OUR *INDIVIDUAL LIFESTYLES?*

IF NOT FOR BIG-BUDGET *COLA ADS,* HOW COULD WE POSSIBLY SELECT THE CARBONATED, CHEMICALLY-ENHANCED BEVERAGE THAT'S RIGHT FOR *US?*

I SEE FROM THE BRAND OF SODA YOU'RE DRINKING THAT YOU'RE A *FUN-LOVING PERSON!*

THAT'S *TRUE*-- I AM!

how one New York ad executive sold the youth market: "It isn't enough to just advertise on television....You've got to reach kids throughout their day—in school, as they're shopping in the mall...or at the movies. You've got to become part of the fabric of their lives."

By 1993, Madison Avenue's child exploiters had broadened their market to include three-year-olds, as reported by author Karen Stabiner in the *Los Angeles Times Magazine*. Noting that the business community believes it is hardly ever too soon to start building allegiances, Stabiner quotes Deyna Vessey, creative director of Kidvertisers agency in New York: "Every kid is different...But the general rule of thumb is that when a kid is three, you can go after them on television."

And Madison Avenue isn't just selling goodies to the $18 billion kids' market, it's conditioning those budding consumers to accept the commercial and political propaganda yet to come in their lives. Indeed, the hidden persuaders have become part of the fabric of our lives.

Finally, to assure complete compliance with the propagandistic techniques, to close the information control loop, to prevent you from finding external points of reference which might cause you to question the propagandists' messages, the information industry insulates you by censoring anything contradictory, any dissonant messages that might come in from the outside.

Since 1976, I have been conducting a national media research project which seeks to locate and publicize those dissonant messages, messages the media elite don't want the rest of us to know about.

PROJECT CENSORED LAUNCHED

Concerned about increasing social problems and apparent public apathy, I launched a national research effort in 1976, called Project Censored, to explore whether there really is a systematic omission of certain issues in our national news media. My concern was specifically stimulated by personal bewilderment over how the American people could elect Richard Nixon by a landslide more than four months *after* Watergate, one of the most sensational political crimes of the century. (For an insight into how the mass media failed the electorate in that election, see the 1972 Watergate reference in Appendix A—"An Eclectic Chronology of Censorship From 605 B.C. to 1994.")

Project Censored is now an international media research project in its 18th year. By exploring and publicizing stories of national importance on issues that have been overlooked or under-reported by the mainstream news media, the project seeks to stimulate journalists and editors to provide more mass media coverage of those issues. It also hopes to encourage the general public to seek out and demand more information on important issues.

Since its start, the research effort has generated queries for more information about the project as well as about individual stories from journalists, scholars, and concerned people throughout the world. It has been described as a tip sheet for investigative television programs like "60 Minutes" and "20/20," as a distant early warning system for society's problems, and even as a "moral force" in American media, as cited by media columnist David Armstrong in the *Washington Journalism Review*, July 1983. The national Association for Education in Journalism and Mass Communication cited the project for "providing a new model for media criticism for journalism education."

Concerned with the increasing attempts at censorship in our public schools and on college campuses since the Supreme Court's 1988 Hazelwood decision, Project Censored launched an educational outreach program in 1993 specifically developed for journalism teachers, advisors, and students. The objective of this program is to offer stimulating materials to student journalists in an effort to broaden discussion, understanding, and response to the threat of news media self-censorship.

Also, in late 1993, in response to the many tips and suggestions the Project receives concerning issues that might well be of interest to investigative journalists, we developed a "CENSORED TIPS" program. As news tips are received, they are summarized and sent out to media and journalism organizations who have the resources to investigate them. Some of the "tips" sent out in 1993 included information on the nation's AIDS-tainted blood supply, the mysterious death of a journalist investigating the INSLAW case, a whistleblower's report on discrimination at the U.S. Department of the Treasury, and the ironic censorship of *Bury My Heart At Wounded Knee* at the Little Bighorn National Monument bookstore.

1993 also saw the development of Project Censored Canada. The Canadian Association of Journalists, located in Ottawa, Ontario, and the communication department at Simon Fraser University, in Burnaby, British Columbia, jointly launched Project Censored Canada. The project will explore issues and events that do not receive the coverage they deserve in the Canadian media.

The Canadian effort originated with Bill Doskoch, a journalist with the *Leader-Post*, in Regina, Saskatchewan, and will be coordinated by Dr. Bob Hackett, associate professor, and Don Gutstein, lecturer, both with the Department of Communication at Simon Fraser University.

In announcing the project, Doskoch pointed out some differences in the media culture between the United States and Canada. "We have had the benefit of a strong, independent public broadcaster and a culture that has, in the past, permitted a slightly wider range of debate in the mass media than the U.S. However, their alternative media are more developed. And it's the alternative media that have provided the grist for Project Censored's mill in the U.S."

"If the world was perfect, Project Censored Canada wouldn't be needed, because Canadians would be fully informed about issues that affect them," Doskoch added, "but we feel that likely won't be the case."

Another Project Censored-inspired effort is Bay Area Censored, a regional project sponsored by the Media Alliance, an association of more than 2,000 media professionals in San Francisco. It has successfully exposed and explored scores of undercovered stories in the Bay Area and will conduct its fifth annual research effort in 1994.

THE CENSORED RESEARCH PROCESS

Researchers who participate in the censorship seminar (taught each fall semester at Sonoma State University, in Rohnert Park, California) have reviewed thousands of stories over the past 18 years that many Americans have not seen or heard about—but should have. The stories are nominated annually by journalists, scholars, librarians, and the general public from across the United States and abroad.

From the hundreds of articles submitted, the seminar researchers select the top 25 stories according to a number of criteria including the amount of coverage the story received, the national or international importance of the issue, the reliability of the source, and the potential impact the story may have. Next, the top 25 *Censored* stories are submitted in synopsis form to a panel of judges who select the top ten stories of the year.

Some of the judges who have participated in the project in the past, in addition to those cited earlier in the preface, include Hodding Carter, Shirley Chisholm, John Kenneth Galbraith, Charlayne Hunter-Gault, James J. Kilpatrick, Robert MacNeil, Mary McGrory, John McLaughlin, Jessica Mitford, Bill Moyers, George Seldes, Susan Sontag, Alvin Toffler, and Mike Wallace.

A review of the project to date reveals that the major news media do systematically overlook, ignore, or distort certain subjects. In the first four years, the most under-reported category of ignored subjects dealt with business and economic issues, what some call "corporate crime." Since 1980, coincidental with the start of the Reagan presidency, the leading category of ignored subjects has dealt with political or governmental corruption ranging from regulatory agencies to foreign political/military involvement to the presidency. Corporate crime dropped to second place. The third-ranked subject area concerns dangers to an individual's health, whether from poisonous agricultural pesticides, pharmaceutical malfeasance, low-level radiation, or hazardous consumer products. Other leading subjects often undercovered by the mainstream press include civil and human rights, the military, and the environment.

Before examining why some issues are overlooked—what we call censored—and why other issues are over-covered—what we call "junk food news"—we must define what we mean by censored.

WHAT IS CENSORSHIP?

Censorship has a long and scurrilous history which started at least two millennia before the invention of the printing press as noted in the chronology found in Appendix A.

A brief review of definitions offered by more traditional sources provides an insight into the problems surrounding the censorship issue. The definitions seem to be as varied and numerous as there are scholars, politicians, and lexicographers eager to address the subject.

When I started Project Censored in 1976, I developed an alternative definition of censorship. Rather than starting with the source of censorship as traditionally defined—with the obligation of an elite to protect the masses (the classic "we know what's best for the people and they're better off without this information" syndrome)—my definition starts at the other end—with the failure of information to reach the people.

Expanding on this foundation, following is our alternative definition of censorship as originally put forth in 1976:

First, we assume that real and meaningful public involvement in societal decisions is possible only if a wide array of ideas are allowed to compete daily in the media marketplace for public awareness, acceptance, and understanding.

Next, we realize that the mass media, particularly the network TV evening news programs, are the public's primary sources of information on what is happening in the world.

If, however, the public does not receive all the information it needs to make informed decisions, then some form of news blackout is taking place.

In brief, then, for the purposes of this project, censorship is defined as the suppression of information, whether purposeful or not, by any method—including bias, omission, under-reporting, or self-censorship—which prevents the public from fully knowing what is happening in the world.

WHY ARE SOME ISSUES OVERLOOKED?

One of the questions often asked of Project Censored is why doesn't the press cover the issues raised by the research. The failure of the news media to cover critical and sometimes controversial issues consistently and in depth is not, as some say, a conspiracy on the part of the media elite. News is too diverse, fast-breaking, and unpredictable to be controlled by some sinister conservative Eastern establishment media cabal.

However, there are a variety of factors operating that, when combined, lead to the systematic failure of the news media to fully inform the public. While it is not an overt form of censorship, such as the kind we observe in some other societies, it is nonetheless real and often equally dangerous.

The traditional explanations for censorship are plentiful. Sometimes a source for a story isn't considered to be reliable; other times the story doesn't have an easily identifiable "beginning, middle, and end;" some stories are considered to be "too complex" for the general public; on occasion stories are ignored because they haven't been "blessed" by *The New York Times* or *The Washington Post*. (Reporters and editors at most of the other 1650 daily newspapers know their news judgment isn't going to be challenged when they produce and publish fashionable "follow-the-leader" stories, a practice which leads to the "pack" or "herd" phenomenon in journalism.)

Another major factor contributing to media self-censorship is that the story is considered potentially libelous. There is no question that long and costly jury trials, and sometimes multi-million-dollar judgments against the media, have produced a massive chilling effect on the press and replaced copy editors with copy attorneys.

Nonetheless, the bottom line explanation for much of the censorship found in the mainstream media is the media's own bottom line. Corporate media executives perceive their primary, and often sole, responsibility to be the need to maximize profits, not, as some would have it, to inform the public. Many of the stories cited by Project Censored are not in the best financial interests of publishers, owners, stockholders, or advertisers. Equally important, investigative journalism is more expensive than the "public stenography" school of journalism. And, of course, there is always the "don't rock the boat" mentality which pervades corporate media boardrooms and filters on down to the newsroom.

Real news is not repetitive, sensationalistic coverage of events such as Bill Clinton's haircut, the Amy Fisher/Joey Buttafuoco case, or John Wayne Bobbitt's severed penis. These are examples of what I call "Junk Food News" as described in Chapter 5.

By contrast, real news is objective and reliable information about important events occurring in a society. The widespread dissemination of such information helps people become better informed, and a better informed public can elect politicians who are more responsive to its needs.

WOULD IT MAKE ANY DIFFERENCE?

Finally, there is yet another question that is often asked about the project. Would it really make any difference if the press were to provide more coverage of the kinds of stories cited by Project Censored?

The answer is very simple: yes.

First, we must address the issue of public apathy. Critics of Project Censored say that the media give the public what it wants, i.e. "junk food news," because people are not interested in reading about the issues raised by Project Censored. We counter that by suggesting that the public is not given the opportunity to read those stories in the mainstream media and thus, unfortunately, will read or watch what the mass media do offer.

However, we suggest that it is the media's responsibility, as watchdogs of society, to explore, compile, and present information that people should be aware of in a way that will attract their attention and be relevant to their everyday lives. And, when the media do this, people will read and respond to the issues raised. There is, indeed, a genuine desire on the part of the public to know more about issues that affect them. Your interest in this book confirms that.

But then, the next question is, would it make any difference if people were better informed?

Hunger in Africa was consistently nominated as a "censored" subject during the early 1980s. When I would ask journalists why they did not cover the tragedy unfolding there, they would say: "It is not news," or, "Everyone already knows about starving Africans," or "Nothing can be done about it anyway."

Early in 1984, an ABC-TV News correspondent in Rome came upon information that led him to believe that millions of lives were being threatened by drought and famine in Africa. He asked the home office in New York for permission to take his crew to Africa to get the story. The answer, based on costs, was no.

ABC-TV News was not the only, nor even the first, television network to reject the tragic story of starving children in Ethiopia. In October, 1983, David Kline, a free-lance journalist and news producer in San Francisco, shot film on assignment for CBS showing emaciated adults and children near death. According to a *Columbia Journalism Review* article, one of the children in Kline's footage was so thin that its heart could be seen beating through the chest wall. Nonetheless, Kline was told *the footage was not strong enough.* After being rejected by CBS, Kline offered to do the story for NBC and PBS and they both turned him down. Nor were the television networks the only media not interested in a story about millions of people facing death. Kline also offered the story to a number of magazines including *Life, Playboy, The New Yorker, Esquire, Harper's,* and *Mother Jones,* all of whom rejected it. Only the *Christian Science Monitor* ran Kline's piece.

Later, a BBC television crew traveling through Ethiopia, captured the stark reality of children starving to death. People throughout the world saw the coverage and responded. Overnight, it sparked a world-wide reaction that reportedly saved the lives of seven million Ethiopians. Indeed, the media can make a difference.

The press has the power to stimulate people to clean up the environment; to prevent nuclear proliferation; to force corrupt politicians out of office; to reduce poverty; to provide quality health care for all people; to create a truly equitable society; and, as we have seen, to literally save the lives of millions of human beings.

And this is why we must look to, prod, and support a free, open, and aggressive press. We have a constitutionally guaranteed free press in the United States and we have the best communications technology in the world. Now let us seek a more responsible and responsive press—a press that truly earns its First Amendment rights. Indeed, a press not afraid to do a little muckraking. Then, and only then, will we all have the information we need to build a more enlightened and responsive society.

In November 1969, Vice President Spiro Agnew
sparked a national controversy over media bias
by accusing the press of favoring liberals.

In November 1993, President Bill Clinton
continued the controversy by whining about
"the knee-jerk liberal press "

CHAPTER 2

U.S. Censorship in 1993

Some observers of the national media scene foresee a more open political
system and fewer examples of censorship now that we have a Democrat in
the White House.

However, even a cursory review of the *Censored Yearbook*, with its litany
of censored examples from 1993, should dissuade anyone from that thesis.
1993, like many other years, was just another growth year for censorship.
While there was some cause for optimism, as cited below and in Chapter
4, "Censored Déjà Vu," there were far more examples of continuing censorship—as well as some ominous warning signs for the future.

Indeed, 1993 serves to emphasize one of the underlying themes of
Project Censored—censorship in a democracy such as the United States is
far more insidious and dangerous than censorship in a totalitarian society.
In a totalitarian society, people know they are being propagandized and
thus live their lives accordingly; but in a democratic society, citizens
believe they are being given a full range of information and thus are more
easily gulled.

One of the *Censored* stories of 1993 deals directly with this issue.
"Public Relations: Legalized Manipulation and Deceit" (#14), is a stri-

dent warning of how the Madison Avenue flacks work with America's corporate and political elite to mold and manipulate public opinion.

Thus, and perhaps *because* we have a Democrat in the White House, we should be ever more alert to what is happening on the media front in America. Let us not forget what President Bill Clinton told investigative journalist William Grieder while being interviewed for a *Rolling Stone* article. While defending his record in office, Clinton complained that he fought more battles for more issues..."and not gotten one damn bit of credit from the knee-jerk liberal press, and I am sick and tired of it, and you can put that in the damn article."

Following are the major categories of *Censored* subjects of 1993 and a brief overview of the 1993 media year.

THE CENSORED SUBJECTS OF 1993

For the first time since another Democrat, Jimmy Carter, was in the White House, underreported corporate issues was the top category of censored stories for the year. Political corruption, which had dominated our censored lists since Ronald Reagan's election, dropped to sixth place. Environmental issues ranked number two in 1993, followed by international issues.

On the surface, the top-ranked *Censored* story of 1993, which deals with the murder rate of our young people, would appear to be an anomalous one since the subject of murdered children had captured the media's interest and the public's attention by the end of the year.

The #1 *Censored* story, by Gayle Reaves, of the *Dallas Morning News*, deals with an underreported study by the United Nations Children's Fund. That study revealed that our young people were subject to a rate of violence not known in the rest of the world. As Reaves said, we should know that the rest of the world does not have the same problems with murdered young people that we do. It was a warning that the nation should have been given much earlier.

THE TOP CENSORED CATEGORIES

Following are the top 25 stories of 1993 separated by category:

CORPORATE
    #4— America's Corporate Welfare Cheats
    #9— Poverty Can Be Profitable

COMMENTS BY THE JUDGES

Following are reflections on this year's *Censored* selections by some of the judges who helped select the top ten stories of 1993:

DONNA ALLEN, founding editor of *Media Report to Women* and a *Censored* judge since 1980, is concerned with the increasing power of public relations practitioners to influence public opinion, the subject of our #14 ranked story—"Public Relations: Legalized Manipulation and Deceit."

"The use by mass media of press releases as the base, sometimes the entirety, of most news stories puts news judgments in the hands of those wealthy enough to hire public relations firms, instead of coming from the people, as it should in a democracy.

"This 'news' source practice belies the mass media claim that they mirror the public interest and makes a travesty of their claim that they give the public the information it 'needs to know.' They give the public *what they want it to know.*

"While they choose to accept these p.r. firms' releases, the mass media do not accept the press releases of those trying to reach the public with other information. Thus, we have such 'censored stories' as Somalia, Haiti, biowarfare testing, Cuba, Chernobyl, to mention only a few.

"Those wealthy enough to own mass media have a right to say their side of all issues but not, in a democracy, to have a *monopoly on the means of reaching the majority of the public.*

"This makes the First Amendment a right based on wealth, not a citizenship right as was intended (and we all profess to believe it is), and which it must be in a democracy. The result is that even the smaller press, such as that trying to report the grand jury findings in the case of Rockwell International's Rocky Flats nuclear weapons plant, cannot be heard by enough of the public to affect public policy on this issue—which is then determined by default, by the censorship silence controlled by the mass media."

BEN BAGDIKIAN, professor emeritus, of the Graduate School of Journalism, University of California, Berkeley, and a *Censored* judge since 1976, is concerned with the selective process with which some major issues are treated. "Striking to me was the continued silence by most of the media about major factors at work in crises that get a high level of other kinds of media attention—Somalia, Haiti, Cuba, etc."

RICHARD BARNET, senior fellow, at the Institute for Policy Studies, feels that all entries for 1993 deserved much more national attention than they received. "Stories about the continuing effects of the Cold War—Stinger missiles, Chernobyl—are still neglected."

NOAM CHOMSKY, professor, Linguistics and Philosophy, at the Massachusetts Institute of Technology, and a *Censored* judge since 1976, feels there were too few stories on international affairs on this year's list.

"In my opinion, the biggest story of 1993 that was completely suppressed, as it has been for many years, was what really happened in the Middle East peace agreements.

"In brief, the world capitulated, and accepted the U.S. demands that had blocked every diplomatic initiative for about 20 years: namely, U.S. rejection of Palestinian national rights, U.S. rejection of Israeli withdrawal to the international borders, and U.S. rejection of the right to resist military occupation.

"On these three issues, the United States has been essentially alone. The U.N. record (always suppressed) reveals the basic facts. The Security Council has been eliminated by U.S. veto; General Assembly votes are roughly 150-2 (U.S. and Israel), year after year. The agreements accept the U.S. position on all three issues.

"The media reaction is close to 100 percent euphoric—exactly as the Belgrade press will be when Bosnian Muslims capitulate.

"The facts have been so deeply buried that I would bet the [*Censored*] judges wouldn't believe them. The U.S. media approach totalitarianism on this topic."

HUGH DOWNS, host of ABC-TV's "20/20" and longtime advocate for the public's right to know, submitted his selections in order of importance ("or urgency or infuriation"), adding, "Many of these stories are connected by the ominous thread that political parties make little difference in the larger workings of business-government-military-industry. A change of administration is not as likely to correct the things that worry us as we would like.

"On rare occasions (such as the publication of Upton Sinclair's *The Jungle*, where the surprised author said he had aimed at America's heart and hit it in the stomach), government action is speedily taken to clean up a ghastly health problem—the meat packing industry. But often, solid efforts to call attention to a dangerous or unjust situation spurs a government to exert effort in covering up.

"These are important under-reported stories. Maybe 'Project Censored' will prove to be another *Jungle* and trigger some genuine corrective activity on the part of government."

SUSAN FALUDI, author of *Backlash: The Undeclared War Against American Women* and a Pulitzer Prize winning journalist, shared Donna Allen's concern over the power of publicists (#14).

"The failure by the media to cover the vice-like and sophisticated grip of public relations firms in no small measure explains the media's failure to cover or discover many of the other 'censored' stories on the list this year.

"Whether it's tropical rainforests or public education or Somalia, we are getting our news filtered through the distorting lenses of spin doctors, image makers and p.r. professionals—all people with an agenda and a hefty war chest to see to it that the public gets only the version of the story that serves the ends of the governments or corporations paying them to get the twisted word out.

"Until the media start relying on their own shoe-leather reporting—rather than the Gucci-footed fast stepping of the Hill & Knowlton crowd—we'll continue to see more and more 'news' generated by the p.r. machine."

EDWARD S. HERMAN, professor emeritus at the Wharton School, University of Pennsylvania, and a first-time *Censored* judge, identifies several principles to help explain why these stories are censored by the mainstream media.

"This year's Project Censored selections point up several considerations that cause the mainstream media to ignore or downplay seemingly important stories.

"One is the media's valuation of people. The media attend closely to superstars, have little interest in ordinary U.S. citizens, and couldn't care less about ordinary citizens in faraway places. This helps explain their disinterest in the slaughter of a large number of hill tribes people in Bangladesh, and even in the victimization of Ohioans in the vicinity of an illegal incinerator.

"A second principle is that facts, opinions, and even detailed studies that contradict conventional wisdom have a hard time penetrating the media, as evidenced by their treatment of the Sandia report on education or the report on the biggest drug bust (DARE).

"A third consideration is that the media don't like to pursue stories that will offend powerful people and groups, as in the case of the Anti-Defamation League scandal or the story on corporations as welfare cheats.

"Finally, the media often fail where the real issues escape them by their complexity and reportorial and editorial ignorance and lack of investigative zeal, as with the story on Clinton's Option 9 plan for the ancient forests.

"The mainstream media often touch on many of these stories, but frequently miss the real issues and underplay their importance, thereby failing to make them salient public issues."

SUT JHALLY, professor of communications at the University of Massachusetts and also a first time judge, suggests that a close look at the *Censored* stories dispels the myth of the "liberal media."

"Looking at the range of issues and subjects covered in the 25 nominations for censored stories (from exposé of corporate abuses, environmental hazard cover-ups, suppression of public reports, to the highly skewed reporting of American foreign policy), it becomes clear that the biggest censored story is the continued allegiance by journalists and editors to the myth of 'the liberal media.'

"The censored stories are, without exception, concerned with revealing in a negative public light the interests of private wealth or state power. There could be no clearer indication that the idea of 'the liberal media' is a cruel lie that is meant to deflect attention away from the reality of our media system—its systematic coupling with established corporate/state power.

"The continuing work of the SSU Project Censored team is a much needed counter-voice to the all-prevailing structure of ideology and hegemony built into our present structures."

RHODA H. KARPATKIN, president of the Consumers Union and a *Censored* judge since 1988, passed along some of her thoughts on censorship.

"Everyone agrees that Americans need good information to participate effectively in the political process. But all too often, the important facts that Americans need to know are hidden, covered up, or just not reported at all.

"Investigative journalism digs out the facts and gets them to the public. It is a vital force for political and social accountability. Unfortunately, the press hasn't shown enough zeal to serve as a watchdog for the public interest.

"Many of the stories nominated for selection this year illustrate how community interests can be undermined when the press and the public isn't informed. For our democracy to work, news organizations have to go after the tough stories, even when doing that raises the hackles of powerful interests.

"Presenting the news effectively also means that the public's attention must be truly engaged. Sometimes, important facts are reported somewhere in the media, but they're banished to unimportant parts of the paper or dealt with in a skimpy way.

"As this year's nominations show, serious information failures are taking place. As a society, we can't afford to be complacent about that."

FRANCES MOORE LAPPÉ, co-director of the Center for Living Democracy, said that although she reads *The New York Times* and many other news publications regularly, most of these vitally important *Censored* nominations were unknown to her.

WILLIAM LUTZ, a professor of English at Rutgers University and editor of *The Quarterly Review of Doublespeak*, stresses the need for a well-informed electorate.

"Every one of these stories (and not just the top 10) needs wide publication, because only an *informed* electorate can make the hard decisions in a democracy. Without information, voters make uninformed choices that set public policy, and when that happens we all suffer.

"These nominations again prove that there is vital information we *need* to know, and the media are failing in their duty to keep us informed."

JACK L. NELSON, a professor in the Graduate School of Education at Rutgers University, has been a *Censored* judge since 1976.

"We have some new topics this year, but there are far too many repeats: environmental coverups, corporate corruption, government collusion.

"Once again the list celebrates the dark side of unreported abuse of public confidence by agencies intended to protect or service us.

"Bertrand Russell counsels skepticism and the ACLU suggests vigilance. Since these are two of my favorite sources of ideas and views, I proposed the slogan 'skeptical vigilance' for Project Censored.

"It is interesting to note that education-bashing continues despite the Sandia report—this shows the impact of censorship. And the ADL story of secret files, although not enough to compete with those in my top 10, also was a new topic in the group."

MICHAEL PARENTI is a political scientist and author as well as a new judge. "[Censored is] an important collection of censored stories that raise basic questions about social justice, environmental devastation, U.S. domestic and foreign policy, and corporate power. Democracy becomes a charade when its citizenry is denied the ability to defend itself because vital information is suppressed by the media. Project Censored does its part to fight back."

HERBERT I. SCHILLER, visiting professor of communication at New York University, said, "These nominations vividly indicate the sweeping takeover, and destruction, of American democracy by a corporate business system almost totally indifferent to the public's interest and welfare."

SHEILA RABB WEIDENFELD, president of D.C. Productions and a founding member of the Censored panel of judges in 1976, comments on the paradox of censorship in a media-rich society.

"With all the information we receive from the news today, it is remarkable that we need Project Censored to bring to our attention important stories that affect our health, well-being, and economic security.

"To choose a few examples from this year's nominations—it is shocking that nine out of ten young people murdered in the industrialized world are slain in the United States. Considering the media exposure given NAFTA, it is bewildering that the huge lobbying expenditures of the Mexican government and various Mexican corporate groups were not reported. One would also think that a story dealing with incompetent, poorly trained and mentally impaired doctors killing or injuring tens of thousands of Americans each year would receive wide coverage. Incredibly, it also did not.

"These and other important stories were ignored by the national media. Project Censored makes it possible for such stories to receive the coverage they deserve."

COMPARING PROJECT CENSORED
WITH THE ASSOCIATED PRESS

Let's compare Project Censored's top ten *Censored* stories of 1993 with the Associated Press's top ten "biggest" stories of the year:

PROJECT CENSORED	ASSOCIATED PRESS
1. U.S. Is Killing Its Young	1. The Flood of 1993
2. Why Are We In Somalia?	2. Cult Inferno in Waco, Texas
3. Censored Sandia Report	3. Clinton's Presidency
4. Corporate Welfare Cheats	4. World Trade Center Bombing
5. Censored Tragedy of Chernobyl	5. Somalia: Mission Gone Wrong
6. Biowarfare Testing Resumed	6. Mideast Peace
7. Selenium Ecological Disaster	7. NAFTA
8. America's Deadly Doctors	8. Health Care Reforms
9. Poverty is Profitable	9. Turmoil in Russia
10. Haiti: Drugs, Thugs, CIA	10. Bosnian Bloodshed

The most obvious distinction between the two lists is the mainstream media's emphasis on reporting events, as cited in the Associated Press list, *after* they occur. On the other hand, the Project Censored list reflects a concern with issues *before* they become media events. This distinction once again exposes the mass media's failure to fulfill its role as a watchdog of society.

While Somalia is cited on both lists, the mainstream media's concern was why the mission went wrong, while the alternative press concern focused on why we went to Somalia in the first place. If securing the country for its oil resources was the original objective, perhaps the mission didn't go wrong.

Another distinction between the two lists is that the *Censored* list reflects more of an investigative approach to journalism, while the AP list reflects more of what could be called the public stenographer's school of journalism where one merely records and reports what has already been said or done.

If journalism is to provide a warning signal for society, and we would argue that is an obligation of a responsible press, then it is obvious that the media are failing us. Following are additional insights into this and other media issues of 1993.

1993 MEDIA YEAR IN REVIEW

MEDIA MERGER MANIA—It is doubtful that even Ben Bagdikian, who has repeatedly warned of the dangers of media monopolization, could have foreseen such a single blockbuster year for high-financed media power-mergers.

In a dramatic, immediate reaction to the 1993 Supreme Court decision which struck down the historical barriers between their respective industries, the nation's telephone companies rapidly began merging with cable television and the video age.

In terms of dollars, the proposed $33 billion merger between Bell Atlantic and Telecommunications Inc. paced the phone companies' media-merger itch. The Bell Atlantic-TCI merger would make the much ballyhooed 1989 Time Inc. $14 billion-takeover of Warner Communications look like small change.

Other phone companies on the prowl in 1993 included US West, which invested $2.5 billion in Time Warner's cable division; NYNEX, which invested $1.2 billion in Viacom; Bellsouth, which bought a 22.5 percent stake in Prime Management, which manages cable companies; and Southwestern Bell, which bought Hauser Communications, a cable firm, for $650 million. Another major player, Pacific Telesis, announced in November that it would eschew the merger route but would invest $15 billion to build its own information network to deliver TV and high-speed data services in California.

In another high-tech, high-finance deal, AT&T bought McCaw Cellular Communications, Inc., the nation's largest cellular company, for $12.6 billion. Observers predicted the buyout would render existing phone regulations obsolete.

Wall Street had barely digested the Bell Atlantic/TCI news when the hunt was on for Paramount Communications, with Viacom and QVC in hot pursuit. It would surely be ironic if a television shopping channel were to end up owning the nation's largest book publisher.

While there were a number of other media mergers during the year, a few of them deserve special recognition.

Even while it was being targeted for takeover, Paramount Communications bought book publisher Macmillan, adding to its publishing operations which already included Simon & Schuster and Prentice Hall.

The New York Times bought the Boston Globe, one of the few large American newspapers still under family control, for $1.1 billion, the highest sum ever paid for an American newspaper.

On a smaller, but still interesting, media-merger scale, televangelist Pat Robertson's Christian Broadcasting Network (CBN) bought Zapnews, a news agency serving small broadcasters and a few newspapers. In response to the expected question, a CBN spokesperson said Zapnews would be a secular, editorially independent news organization, and that Robertson's religious and political views would "have no influence" on news.

And in another sign of the times, the Times Mirror Co. and Prodigy Service Co. said they plan to combine the nationwide Prodigy information service with regional interactive services offering news, advertising, and other information.

If one is impressed by the sheer magnitude of the dollars involved in these financial transactions, one should be even more concerned by the impression they had on Ben Bagdikian.

In briefly looking back over the year, Bagdikian told us: "The mergers and planned mergers for 1993 reached a new height of placing in the same hands, both the channels into the homes of Americans and the control over the cultural and political content people will be able to receive over those channels."

It would appear that we have reached a new level of media control in America where many of the same mega-media corporations that own the technology also determine the content to be transmitted over that technology.

THIS MODERN WORLD by TOM TOMORROW

SO FAR, THE DISCUSSION OF THE FORTHCOMING "INFORMATION HIGHWAY" HAS NOT STRAYED MUCH BEYOND THE PAINFULLY OVER-EXTENDED METAPHORS OF BUSINESS WRITERS AND COMMENTATORS...

...WILL THERE BE ROAD-KILL ON THE INFORMATION HIGHWAY? WILL THERE BE LITTERING LAWS? AND WHEN WE PULL OVER TO THE INFORMATION GAS STATION, WILL THE REST ROOMS BE CLEAN AND SANITARY?

THE HYPE HAS BEEN EAGERLY EMBRACED BY THAT SEGMENT OF THE POPULATION WHICH REFUSES TO ADMIT THAT NEW TECHNOLOGIES CAN BE ANYTHING BUT BENEFICIAL...OF COURSE, EVERY ERA HAS SUCH--ER--VISIONARIES--

SOMEDAY EVERYONE WILL OWN A "TELEVISION"...AND IGNORANCE WILL BE ERADICATED!

JUNE 1938

THE INFORMATION SUPERHIGHWAY—The good news is that the map has been drawn for the long-awaited Information Superhighway which promises to be an educational and informational tool, as well as a rich source of interactive entertainment. The bad news is that the content that will be transmitted over the promised 500 channels will be controlled by the same bottom-line-driven mega-corporations cited above.

MEDIA GAFFES OF 1993—The conservative *National Review* brought out its big guns (6/21/93) to announce the "decline of American journalism," and, not surprisingly, discovered the problem was because the media are too liberal. Following are some of the *true* symptoms of an ailing institution:

"Dateline NBC" rigged a broadcast showing a General Motors truck bursting into flames during a collision; CBS News, in a two hour special titled "The Incredible Discovery of Noah's Ark," described a doctored chunk of California pine as a piece of Noah's ark; ABC's "PrimeTime Live" was found guilty of defaming a Virginia electronics store in an investigative piece on repair shops; the news director at Fox Broadcasting's Washington, D.C., TV station quit after it was found that he had pledged to consult prominent conservatives before making staff changes.

CBS's "Street Stories" settled an invasion of privacy suit with an Oakland woman; a lawsuit by an eye clinic against "Dateline NBC" was dropped after the network acknowledged it had found no wrongdoing at the clinic; *Time* magazine admitted that a series of photographs reportedly showing child prostitutes in Moscow was staged; one of the largest makers of 30-minute television "infomercials" was found guilty of making false advertising claims and fined $3.5 million by the Federal Trade Commission.

The *Los Angeles Times* was charged with forcing a youth paper it prints to kill part of a story involving AIDS prevention in oral sex; ethical questions about high-powered lobbying for the Pulitzer Prize were raised after *The New York Times* was awarded a Pulitzer even though it was not a finalist.

Author Janet Malcolm was found guilty of libeling Jeffrey Masson by knowingly using false quotes in a profile piece she wrote for *The New Yorker*; author Joe McGinnis and his publisher Simon & Schuster defended the presentation of fiction as fact in his biography of Sen. Edward Kennedy, *The Last Brother*.

TV NEWS VS SITCOMS—The increasing appeal of television news magazines, albeit sometimes flawed as noted above, was most evident during the week of August 16, 1993, when five of them were cited in the top six slots in the ratings race. "60 Minutes," "Dateline NBC," "PrimeTime Live," "20/20," and "Now," beat out ratings leaders like "Seinfeld," "Roseanne," and "Full House."

PC--RIP--1993—No less an authority than *The New York Times* declared that the term "politically correct" has run its course and should be retired (12/7/93). Noting the explosion of PC references (103 print mentions in 1988 and nearly 10,000 in 1993), the *Times* noted that journalists had been caught up in the tide and that it was now "time to bid the bogeyman farewell." The death knell probably was sounded on November 16 when the University of Pennsylvania announced it was scrapping its controversial ban on hate speech. The University's speech code ignited national discussion after a white student was charged with racial harassment for calling five black sorority sisters "water buffalo."

CENSORSHIP ON CAMPUS—While one would expect academic institutions to be in the vanguard in the fight against censorship, this was not the case. Rather, in 1993, censorship took its ugliest form—by theft and burning—on campuses across the country. The Student Press Law Center reported in November that 29 campuses were hit by newspaper thefts in the previous 14 months compared to a normal average of five or six a year. Meanwhile, reports of censorship in America's public schools continued to mount during the 1992-93 school year, according to the annual survey of "Attacks on the Freedom to Learn," by People for the American Way.

SECRETS THAT LASTED FOUR DECADES—Critics of Project Censored sometimes say a story couldn't be true because too many people knew about it and someone would have talked. The fallacy of this argument was revealed in 1993 when the government finally started to release cold war documents about nuclear research performed on civilians. Dating back to the '40s, the United States government conducted some of the vilest experiments on its own citizens, often the poor or minorities. Radioactive pills were given to hundreds of pregnant women, radioactive materials were released from aircraft, and, in the cruelest of all tests, more than 200 newborn infants were injected with radioactive iodine. No one knows how many hundreds, or thousands, of people were involved in these tests either as subjects or experimenters, including scientists at some of our most prestigious universities. But we do know that while these tests were conducted from the '40s up until the '60s, this incredible story was not revealed until late 1993.

THE JUNK FOOD NEWS NETWORK—Finally, we must acknowledge a new player in the Junk Food News Game. It is the Splash News Service formed in Los Angeles by British-tabloid-journalism veterans Kevin Smith and Gary Morgan. In an article by Maureen Orth, published in *Vanity Fair*, January 1994, Orth described Splash as "Los Angeles's first official tabloid brokers—a clearing house for anyone with inside dirt or otherwise about the stars." In discussing the ethics of paying for news, Smith said, "I don't have any great moral problems paying for stories. If that's what it takes, so be it. If you don't pay for stories, there's no incentive for people to come forward. That's a form of censorship, because the news doesn't get out." America's alternative press can be thankful that the many legitimate whistleblowers in our society are more motivated by truth and justice than by money.

MEDIA HEROES—Before leaving this review of the media's performance in 1993, we should recognize that there are some "muckrakers"— socially responsible journalists—as well as a few fearless publishers. After all, each of the stories cited by Project Censored have been published somewhere, albeit most often in the alternative press.

Don Hazen, executive director of the Institute for Alternative Journalism (IAJ) in Washington, D.C., reminds us that it is important to honor and support those individuals and organizations devoted to keeping critical and truthful information alive and well in the body politic. Don sent along his selection of "Ten Media Heroes" of 1993 who are "especially brave at promoting information in the public interest."

1. THE TV SHOW, "RIGHTS AND WRONGS"—Producers Danny Shechter and Rory O'Connor and anchorperson Charlayne Hunter-Gault. "Rights and Wrongs" is a high quality, thought-provoking series on international human rights.

2. ANGUS MACKENZIE—a longtime journalist for The Center for Investigative Reporting and the nation's top authority on government secrecy. Mackenzie has dedicated his life to the investigation of information privacy in the federal government.

3. LANI GUINIER—after being nominated for the position of Assistant Attorney General for the Civil Rights Division, Lani Guinier was attacked by the media whose mob mentality, in concert with a well-organized political lynching, forced President Clinton to withdraw her nomination. But Guinier refused to be intimidated by the headline-generating hysteria and confronted the hypocrisy in the American media.

4. THE SAN FRANCISCO MIME TROUPE—for the past 30 years this group of minstrels has effectively addressed social issues in their fearless satirical performances that confront local, national, and international issues in a unique and poignant way.

5. GAY AND LESBIAN ALLIANCE AGAINST DEFAMATION (GLAAD)—a group of activists determined to redress inaccurate coverage and stereotyping of lesbians, gays, and bisexuals in the media, in classrooms, and in boardrooms. GLAAD's nine chapters respond to attacks on gays and lesbians both locally and nationally, be it demonstrations against Hollywood's depictions of lesbians and bisexuals in "Basic Instinct," the rabid homophobia of Rush Limbaugh, or the wall of silence around gay and lesbian issues in public schools.

6. HIGHTOWER RADIO—Jim Hightower, a modern-day Will Rogers of the airwaves, combines his acerbic humor with outspoken views on who's zooming whom to create a unique form of media commentary. Whether it's cereal price gouging, the congressional revolving door, drug companies' profits, or the health care lobby, Jim Hightower tells it like it is.

7. DETROIT METRO TIMES AND EDITOR/PUBLISHER RON WILLIAMS—while the alternative press is criticized for losing its investigative zeal and the mainstream press rarely displays it, the Detroit Metro Times, under the direction of Editor/Publisher Ron Williams, significantly increased its investigative efforts. Williams reasoned that investing resources in in-depth journalism was a good business decision and his efforts increased the visibility and credibility of his paper, as well as its revenue.

8. THE NEIGHBORHOOD WORKS—in its 15 years of publication, The Neighborhood Works has fostered a holistic attitude toward community activism by relating national issues to local neighborhood movements. The three people responsible for its production, Patti Wolter, Karl Vogel, and Bridget Torres, are dedicated to writing about what real people are doing to make a difference in their communities.

9. GREG RUGGIERO, STUART SAHULKA, AND THE OPEN MAGAZINE PAMPHLET SERIES—Ruggiero and Sahulka have set new standards for provocative journalism by providing a forum for variant viewpoints on political events in their Open Magazine Pamphlet Series. It is an effective response to the lack of intelligent information made available to the public and has included essays, lectures, and commentaries on important issues like the L.A. riots and the Gulf War.

10. UNPLUG—a group of young women who have joined to fight the growing tide of commercialism in America's schoolrooms. The initial focus of Unplug's ire has been Channel One, a product of Whittle Communications. Unplug was started "by youth, for youth" and finds the increasing presence of commercial exploitation in the classroom to be offensive and harmful.

(PLEASE NOTE: Ten Media Heroes was excerpted with permission from Don Hazen and the AlterNet News Service as released on 12/22/93.)

> "We are a democracy, and there is only one way
> to get a democracy on its feet in the matter of its individual,
> its social, its municipal, its State, its National conduct,
> and that is by keeping the public informed about what is going on.
> There is not a crime, there is not a swindle, there is not a vice
> which does not live by secrecy. Get these things out in the open,
> describe them, attack them, ridicule them in the press
> and sooner or later public opinion will sweep them away."
> —Joseph Pulitzer

CHAPTER 3

The Top 25 Censored News Stories of 1993

Following is a detailed analysis of each of the top 25 *Censored* subjects of 1993. Each segment starts with the publication source and author of the original article (or articles). A brief synopsis by the Sonoma State University *Censored* researcher of the nominated article follows. The segment concludes with comments about the issue and article, in most cases by the author of the original source article. An asterisk (*) following an article title indicates it is reprinted in Appendix D, "CENSORED Reprints."

1

The U.S. Is Killing Its Young

Sources:

DALLAS MORNING NEWS
Date: 9/25/93
Title: "U.N. Says U.S. Dangerous for Children"*
Author: Gayle Reaves

USA TODAY
Date: 6/16/93
Title: "Report: 12M kids go hungry in USA"

SYNOPSIS: While politicians and the media play their adult games, the United States has become one of the most dangerous places in the world for young people—and it is getting worse.

An alarming report issued in mid-September by the United Nations Children's Fund should have been a lead item on the network evening news programs, but wasn't. In fact, according to the *Tyndall Report*, which monitors the evening network news programs, the report did not even make the top ten list of news subjects on the networks during the period from September 13 to October 1, 1993.

According to the United Nations Children's Fund:

- Nine out of ten young people murdered in industrialized countries are slain in the United States.
- The U.S. homicide rate for young people ages 15 to 24 is five times greater than that of Canada, its nearest competitor.
- The U.S. poverty rate for children is more than double that of any other major industrialized nation.
- Over the past 20 years, while other industrialized nations were bringing children out of poverty, only the United States and Britain slipped backward.

An earlier report by researchers at Tufts University revealed that nearly 12 million children are going hungry in the United States now.

The plight of our children does not appear to be a function of our recent declining economy but rather one of misguided priorities. The economic problems that have affected the United States in the last decade have affected much of the rest of the world too. Other countries have used taxes and other government policies to help address the situation; this has not happened in the United States.

Arloc Sherman, a Children's Fund research analyst, noted that children have been hurt by failing economies throughout the world. "What really distinguishes the United States from all these countries is that we started off with less generous benefits, and as we went through the 1930s other nations got more generous," Sherman says, but "we got even less generous."

Journalist Gayle Reaves, who reported on the findings by the Children's Fund, noted, "Unlike every other industrialized nation, the United States has not signed or ratified the Convention on the Rights of the Child, a set of principles adopted by the U.N. General Assembly in 1989."

Now that the United States is one of the most dangerous places in the world for young people to live, it would seem that the time has come for the mass media to alert the public to this growing tragedy.

SSU Censored Researcher:
Mark Papadopoulos

COMMENTS: An alarming report by the United Nations Children's Fund, released in late September 1993, should have been widely publicized in the mass media. It was a strident warning to the American people that our young people were in mortal danger for their lives. It also revealed how out of step we were with the rest of the industrialized world in the way we treat our youth. And yet, this alarming story was not put on the national agenda by the mass media.

Gayle Reaves, a reporter with the *Dallas Morning News*, recognized how important the issue was and her story was published on the front page of the *Dallas Morning News*. But that was an exception. Reaves felt it was important to tell the story since "It probably would benefit the public to understand that the rest of the world does not have the problems with societal, peacetime violence that the United States has It is important for people to know that we are not the norm, by far."

Ironically, a series of events in late 1993 forced the mass media to put the issue on the national agenda.

In Northern California, Polly Klaas, a 12-year-old girl from Petaluma, was kidnapped and later found murdered; in St. Louis, Missouri, two young girls, Angie Housman, 9, and Cassidy Senter, 10, were abducted at separate times and both found murdered; and in Southern California, the search for a serial child molester, tied to 32 attacks in the suburban San Fernando Valley, continued.

Tragically, America's young people tried to tell the story which the mass media had ignored. The Children's Express, a news program produced by and for young people, held a two-day conference on violence against youth in Washington, DC, in late October.

George Zimay, president of the National Head Injury Foundation in Washington, told a panel of Children's Express reporters, aged from 10 to 14, that "In the nation's capital, it is not uncommon for children to attend two or three funerals a week for friends who have been shot. This is a national epidemic."

Even though it *is* a national epidemic, it took the senseless deaths of Polly Klaas, Angie Housman, and Cassidy Senter, before the news media focused national attention on this tragic problem.

Why Are We Really In Somalia?

Sources:

LOS ANGELES TIMES
Date: 1/18/93
Title: "The Oil Factor In Somalia"*
Author: Mark Fineman

PROPAGANDA REVIEW
Date: No. 10, 1993
Title: "Somoilia?"*
Author: Rory Cox

EXTRA!
Date: March 1993
Title: "The Somalia Intervention: Tragedy Made Simple"
Author: Jim Naureckas

SYNOPSIS: There was little question about the influence of oil on our decision to send troops to the Persian Gulf on behalf of Kuwait. But Somalia was strictly a matter of humanitarian aid. Right?

Or was the preponderance of tragic images of starving Somalis all over the major media outlets during the end of 1992 and the first half of 1993 merely a more refined and cynical method of selling yet another war for oil, asked Rory Cox in *Propaganda Review.*

Or, as Jim Naureckas asked in *EXTRA!,* "If the U.S. has not con-

sistently acted in an altruistic manner toward starving people in Africa, why did it dispatch troops to Somalia at this point? There have been frequent media denials that geopolitical considerations might have entered into the decision. The *Washington Post* reported (12/6/92) that 'Unlike previous large-scale operations, there is no U.S. strategic or economic interest in the Somalia deployments.'"

Oddly enough, while the U.S./U.N. military involvement in Somalia began in mid-November, it wasn't until January 18, two days before George Bush left office, that a major media outlet, the *Los Angeles Times*, published an article that revealed America's oil connection with Somalia.

Times staff writer Mark Fineman started his Mogadishu-datelined article with, "Far beneath the surface of the tragic drama of Somalia, four major U.S. oil companies are quietly sitting on a prospective for-tune in exclusive concessions to explore and exploit tens of millions of acres of the Somali countryside. That land, in the opinion of geologists and industry sources, could yield significant amounts of oil and natural gas if the U.S.-led military mission can restore peace to the impoverished East African nation."

According to Fineman, nearly two-thirds of Somalia was allocated to the American oil giants Conoco, Amoco, Chevron and Phillips before Somalia's pro-U.S. President Mohamed Siad Barre was overthrown. The U.S. oil companies are "well positioned to pursue Somalia's most promising potential oil reserves the moment the nation is pacified."

While oil industry spokesmen, along with Bush/Clinton administration spokespersons, deny these allegations as "absurd" and "nonsense," Thomas E. O'Connor, the principal petroleum engineer for the World Bank, who headed an in-

THE SUBSEQUENT FAMINE IS NOT ONLY *TRAGIC*, IT IS *OBSCENE*... PARTICULARLY WHEN ONE CONSIDERS THAT ENOUGH GRAIN IS ACTUALLY GROWN EACH YEAR TO *EASILY* FEED EVERY HUMAN ON THE *PLANET*...BUT UNFORTUNATELY, MUCH OF THAT GRAIN IS INSTEAD USED TO FATTEN *LIVESTOCK* SO THAT CITIZENS OF THE DEVELOPED WORLD CAN CONTINUE TO ENJOY THEIR *BIG MACS*...

UM... SO WHAT'S YOUR *POINT*?

STILL... EVEN IF NONE OF THESE UNDERLYING FACTORS ARE ADDRESSED, THE FACT REMAINS THAT THIS INTERVENTION *WILL* SAVE SOME LIVES...TO HELP US SORT OUT THIS CONFUSING SITUATION, LET'S SEE WHAT OUR RESIDENT PUNDIT *SPARKY* HAS TO SAY...

WELL...THOSE OF US WHO GET PAID TO HAVE DEFINITIVE OPINIONS ON EVERY SUBJECT AREN'T EVER SUPPOSED TO ADMIT THIS... BUT FRANKLY, I JUST DON'T KNOW *WHAT* TO THINK...

GASP!

OH MY GOD!

TOM TOMORROW 12-29-92

depth three-year study of oil prospects off Somalia's northern coast, said, "There's no doubt there's oil there....It's got high (commercial) potential...once the Somalis get their act together."

Meanwhile, Conoco is playing an intimate part in the U.S. government's role with the humanitarian effort in Somalia. Conoco agreed to "rent" its Mogadishu corporate compound to U.S. envoy Robert B. Oakley, who transformed it into a temporary U.S. embassy.

One Conoco executive said, "With America, there is a genuine humanitarian streak in us...that many other countries and cultures cannot understand." Nonetheless, the cozy relationship between Conoco and the U.S. intervention force, coupled with America's well-known need for oil, has left many Somalis and foreign development experts disturbed.

It may well be that the Operation Restore Hope slogan was less representative than Operation Restore Oil.

SSU Censored Researcher: Kristen Rutledge

COMMENTS: Jim Naureckas, investigative journalist and editor of *EXTRA!*, noted that Somalia has received two intense bursts of coverage in the media. "The second burst, obviously, corrected some of the simplistic assumptions of the first—but in many cases simply replaced them with new stereotypes. Some information, like the role of oil companies in the Somalian intervention, has never gotten adequate attention. And there has still not been the sustained discussion of the causes of famine that we (*EXTRA!*) called for.

The general public would benefit from wider exposure of this subject since it was given minimal information on which to base a judgment on the Somalian intervention, Naureckas added. The limited amount of information "led to shock and disillusionment when it turned out military intervention was not the easy solution it had been sold as. U.S. citizens need realistic discussions of the real causes of famine if humanitarian efforts are to have real success."

Naureckas charged that the primary beneficiaries of the flawed coverage of Somalia are "the U.S. military and foreign policy apparatus, who treated Somalia as an opportunity for a p.r. victory, while treating Somalis as a conquered people. The oil companies with stakes in Somalia are secondary beneficiaries."

Author Rory Cox, who examined the influence of oil on our Somalian policy for *Propaganda Review*, said that "While U.S./U.N. involvement in Somalia has been covered widely, scant information is available on the oil-producing potential of the region. This was the gist of my piece, and since I wrote it the story has continued to be virtually ignored, though strangely enough I've heard a few talk-radio hosts rant about it."

Cox feels the public should be aware of the oil potential since "there seems to be a general sense of confusion about the mission in Somalia and its changing nature, i.e. from feeding the starving to chasing a warlord. If the public knew about the oil angle on all of this, they/we would have a clearer picture of the situation, and that there is potentially a resource for us to use (or for oil companies to profit from)."

Cox adds a caveat to his comments, noting that he has not personally been to Somalia, nor is he an expert on the region, but "regardless of what role oil plays, it's potential in Somalia is a well-documented fact, and one that should be considered in any debate on the subject."

Mark Fineman, staff writer with the *Los Angeles Times*, who examined the "oil factor in Somalia," was on assignment in Cypress and not available to comment on his story.

Clarence Page, a syndicated columnist in Chicago, raised another little known fact about our Somalia involvement in his column published October 14, 1993. In trying to understand how we got into the mess in Somalia, Page said

"one comes across an ominously familiar name from the past: April Glaspie. Yes, the same former ambassador to Iraq who many believe inadvertently signaled during a meeting with Saddam Hussein that the Bush administration would not get all that upset if he invaded Kuwait.

"Glaspie has re-emerged like the Typhoid Mary of American diplomacy as a senior adviser to the United Nations in Somalia, our latest disaster," Page said.

Page reports that Glaspie may have played a key role in turning Aidid against the U.N. and the United States at a time when he was cooperating with peacemaking efforts.

3

The Sandia Report On Education: A Perfect Lesson In Censorship

Sources:

PHI DELTA KAPPAN
Date: May 1993
Title: "Perspective on Education In America"*
Author: Robert M. Huelskamp

THE EDUCATION DIGEST
Date: September 1993
Title: "The Second Coming of the
Sandia Report" reprinted from
Phi Delta Kappan

U.S. NEWS & WORLD REPORT
Date: 10/18/93
Title: "School choice: Its time has
come"
Author: Michael Barone

SYNOPSIS: One of the most thorough investigations into public education did not produce the expected results and instead, ended up being censored.

When state governors and President George Bush set national education goals after the 1989 education summit, the administration charged Sandia National Laboratories, a scientific research organization, with investigating the state of public education.

In 1991, Sandia presented its first findings to the U.S. Department of Education and the National Science Foundation. While the response from these government agencies should have been one of some celebration, instead it was one of silence—a silence compounded by the national media. The results did not reveal a seriously deficient educational system in dire need of profound changes such as a nationwide voucher program. And the report was suppressed.

Briefly, the Sandia Report did find the following: on nearly every measure employed in the survey, a steady or slightly improving trend was identified in public education. Overall, the high school completion rate in the U.S. at 85 percent ranks as one of the highest in the world. The dropout rate is inflated by a growing immigrant school population. SAT results often reported as falling do so not because of decreasing student performance but because of increased participation from students in the lower percentiles, a factor not always found when comparing results to other countries. One quarter of young people will achieve a bachelor's degree. Spending on education, often characterized as out of control, has risen by 30 percent but this has gone into special education programs, not the "regular" classroom.

Areas of concern raised by the report focused on the performance of minorities who were still lagging behind whites. Also, it suggested that a cycle of low esteem among educators posed a threat to future educational progress. And a lack of training in the workplace, compared to countries such as Japan and Germany, threatens productivity.

Given the range and insights that the Sandia Report produced, it was remarkable this information did not form the basis for the 1992 education debate. The lack of coverage of the report, and the rancor with which the report was met from government departments and, more importantly, from the "Education President," George Bush, was astounding. Clearly, the findings of the report contradicted the political philosophy of "deregulating" public education and would have seriously weakened the "choice movement." The fact that eight of the 10 Nobel winners announced this year in economics, medicine, physics, chemistry, and literature were Americans similarly failed to give the anti-public school group much ammunition.

The Sandia Report is so threatening to the anti-public-school-lobby that those supporting school choice initiatives still refuse to acknowledge its existence. In an impassioned plea for "school choice," published in *US News & World Report*, writer Michael Barone cites the 1983 "Nation at Risk" Report while ignoring the more recent Sandia Report.

While the appeal by Sandia researcher Robert M. Huelskamp for a "Second Coming of the Sandia Report" may be ignored, the deliberate withholding of the Sandia Report for political ends surely deserves the public's attention.

SSU Censored Researcher:
Gerald Austin

COMMENTS: Given the reception Project Censored received

when we contacted Sandia National Laboratories for follow-up information (as we do with all original sources), we are hardly surprised that the media have not given the Sandia study more coverage. At best, we can say that Sandia doesn't want to discuss the study in any way.

When we contacted Bob Huelskamp, author of the *Phi Delta Kappan* article, he said that Sandia was not interested in replying to our questionnaire and that all further inquiries should be directed to a public information official by the name of Al Stotts.

When Mr. Stotts didn't return our call of December 13, we tried again on the 16th and were told that he was on vacation until after New Year's day. But we were told to contact Jerry Langheim who would be able to help us. As it turned out, Mr. Langheim was out ill and wouldn't be back until after the first of the new year. But we were told to contact Rod Geer who would be able to help us.

We were finally able to reach Mr. Geer on December 17.

When I explained the Project to Geer, he responded, "We're not going to fill out the form and send it back to you....It was published in the *Phi Delta Kappan*...and we consider ourselves finished with that business."

Geer then went into some background on how the study came

about. In brief, he said that the report did not originate from a Department of Energy grant to do a study on education in America, but was primarily an in-house effort to help Sandia improve its own educational outreach. Geer suggested that the media had overblown the importance of the study.

When it became obvious that Geer was not going to comment further on the study—"The study now has been published in the *Kappan* and that finished it."—we asked whether this indicated that Sandia is repudiating the results of its study.

Geer said, "We continue to support what the article says."

After further non-productive jousting, Geer said it was "fine" for us to reprint the *Kappan* article; thus it appears in Appendix D.

Given the potential significance of the Sandia study in terms of a national debate on educational policy, one has to wonder why the study is being handled so delicately by Sandia personnel. Regardless of what Geer says, the research study was performed at Sandia National Laboratories and was supported by taxpayer dollars from the U.S. Department of Energy. It would appear that there is still more to this story deserving of media attention.

4 CENSORED

The Real Welfare Cheats: America's Corporations

Source:

MULTINATIONAL MONITOR
Date: January/February 1993
Title: "Public Assets, Private Profits: The U.S. Corporate Welfare Rolls" (Editorial introduction to special issue reprinted.)*
Authors: Chris Lewis, Laurence H. Kallen, Jonathan Dushoff, David Lapp, Randal O'Toole

SYNOPSIS: In his presidential campaign, Bill Clinton called for welfare reform, decried welfare cheats, and emphasized workfare. But he failed to mention the largest recipients of taxpayer largesse: U.S. corporations. Ralph Nader's magazine, *Multinational Monitor*, documents five major areas of government giveaways to corporations.

1. "Public Assets, Private Profits" by Chris Lewis: In 1980, the Government Patent Policy Act opened a floodgate of government research and development money to universities and private firms, then allowed these recipients to

keep the patents and the profits on products developed. Amendments in 1984 and 1986 amounted to a giveaway on patents developed with public funds. One glaring example is the AIDS-fighting drug AZT. While AZT was developed with public funds and was in the public domain since 1964, the FDA gave the patent away to Burroughs Wellcome Corp., which has earned over $300 million in sales over the last two years with no royalties going to U.S. taxpayers.

2. "Bankruptcy Bailouts" by Laurence H. Kallen: In 1986, the new bankruptcy code was established. Chapter 11 of this code, known as business reorganization under protection and supervision of a bankruptcy court, has allowed corporations, many of them solvent, to jettison debts. These "debts" have included EPA-required toxic site clean-up costs, personal injury judgments, union contracts, and even retirement benefits. Some businesses have remained under Chapter 11 for years while continuing to run business as usual and even get bank loans.

3. "Gold-Plated Giveaways" by Jonathan Dushoff: Under the Mining Act of 1872, companies can mine valuable minerals and metals from federal lands without paying a cent in royalties and they can buy federal lands for five dollars an acre or less. One example of U.S.

largesse is the Goldstrike mine in Nevada, the largest single known gold deposit in the U.S. with a gross value estimated at more than seven billion dollars. While the land and mineral deposits are federally owned, the mine has been claimed under the Mining Act by American Barrick Resources, a Canadian controlled company. Barrick is free to mine the gold without paying a royalty fee to the government and has now applied to purchase the seven billion dollars deposit site for five dollars an acre.

4. "The Price of Power" by David Lapp: The 1992 Energy Policy Act guarantees our government will continue to subsidize the nuclear power industry. These taxpayer dollars go to an industry with a dismal record on safety and efficiency. The Congressional Research Service estimates R&D support to the nuclear industry at $39.8 billion (in constant 1982 dollars) between 1948 and 1990. The DOE has failed to collect over $11 billion in past costs due to underselling of its enriched uranium, according to a 1989 General Accounting Office (GAO) study.

5. "Last Stand" by Randal O'Toole: U.S. taxpayers own more than 192 million acres of forest lands that are managed by the U.S. Forest Service and Department of Agriculture. Over the past 15 years, the Forest Service has lost between one and two billion dollars annually

in undervalued timber sales. The largest recipient of these subsidies is Louisiana-Pacific. It owns very little of its own timber lands and often pays as little as five dollars per thousand board feet for timber that costs the U.S. taxpayer over $50 per thousand board feet to sell. Yet this financial loss is still small compared to the losses to the public in recreation sites, watershed, and wildlife preservation.

**SSU Censored Researcher:
Paul Chambers**

COMMENTS: "Bankruptcy Bailouts"—Laurence H. Kallen, author of *Corporate Welfare: The Megabankruptcies of the 80s and 90s*, said the subject of his article in the *Multinational Monitor* received no other exposure. Kallen feels the topic deserves greater coverage since "A good number of the largest corporations in this country have taken advantage of the bankruptcy law...to chisel their suppliers (many of whom are small companies), bust unions, and clean up their balance sheets, with little actual risk. They have gained billions of dollars of benefits through their use and abuse of the Bankruptcy Code—a form of hidden welfare that we all pay indirectly."

"Gold-Plated Giveaways"— Author Jonathan Dushoff reports that there have been only one or two brief newspaper stories on mining on public lands, and the stories about the legislation in Congress merely gave the typical summary of "both sides" without going into any substantive detail on the issues. Dushoff says the public would benefit from more exposure of the issue since it could help bring about reforms that could save taxpayers tens of billions of dollars. He notes that the primary beneficiaries of the lack of coverage to the issue are "large American and foreign mining companies who benefit from a vested right to mine federal minerals for free." Dushoff concludes "As I write (11/24/93), both houses of Congress have passed legislation to reform the Mining Act that was the focus of my article. The Senate's bill is what ardent reformers call 'sham reform' intended to cure some of the most glaring abuses of the Act (such as land sales for $2.50 an acre) while leaving the mining industry's power over the federal lands intact. The House bill, on the other hand, would give federal regulators the power they need to make miners follow environmentally sound operation and cleanup practices. The bill is now headed to conference. The battle is far from over."

"The Price of Power"—David Lapp reports that the huge subsidies given the nuclear energy industry, about $100 billion since 1950, have "not even entered the realm of public debate, largely due to the lack of attention given the subject by the mainstream media." He also charges that the "Clinton administration has reneged on its commitment to eliminate funding for nuclear R&D; it now supports funding breeder reactor technology, a technology rife with uncertainties and the dangers of nuclear weapons proliferation." Lapp strongly feels the public should know more about this issue because "If people knew that for Fiscal Year '93, nuclear energy received $1,012,000,000 in funding compared to $210,000,000 for renewable energy—about 25 percent of what nuclear energy gets—they would be justifiably outraged."

"Last Stand"—Author Randal O'Toole charges that while many people know that the government loses money on sales of public timber and other natural resources, "few realize that the reason for this is that agencies like the Forest Service are rewarded for losing money on environmentally destructive activities. Media coverage on this fact has been almost non-existent." He believes that people need to know how their tax dollars are being spent and that changes in the budgetary process are required. O'Toole concludes that problems with the Forest Service are symptomatic of the entire federal government and that taxpayers face a multi-trillion-dollar debt "because Congress, bureaucrats, and special interest groups all benefit from wasteful and environmentally destructive activities. The public in general and environmentalists in particular must stop seeing the federal government as their saviors and return instead to the principle of Henry David Thoreau: 'That government is best which governs least.'"

5 | CENSORED

The Hidden Tragedy of Chernobyl Has Worldwide Implications

Source:

THE NATION
Date: 3/15/93
Title: "Chernobyl—The Hidden Tragedy"*
Author: Jay M. Gould

SYNOPSIS: A devastating book on the far-reaching dimensions of the 1986 Chernobyl disaster, written by Vladimir Chernousenko, a Ukrainian nuclear physicist involved in the emergency cleanup, has not received the media attention it deserves. Chernousenko, fired from his post at the Ukrainian Academy of Science for telling the truth about the catastrophic effects of the disaster, is, himself, now dying of radiation poisoning. His book, *Chernobyl: Insight From the Inside*, may never be published in Ukraine or Russia.

Chernousenko explodes many of the Chernobyl myths propagated by the Soviet authorities and eagerly accepted by the international nuclear establishment.

He points out that the accident was not the result of operator error but was caused by major flaws of design present in 15 other Soviet reactors that are still in operation.

In contrast to the widely accepted belief that only 31 people died from exposure to radiation in the effort to contain the emissions, Chernousenko asserts that between 7,000 and 10,000 volunteers were killed.

But according to author Jay M. Gould, the most serious charge made by Chernousenko is that the accident released the lethal contents of 80 percent of the reactor core rather than the three percent figure announced to the world. "Chernousenko estimates that the radioactivity released was equivalent to more than one curie for every person on earth, i.e. more than 1 trillion picocuries per capita, to use the unit in which radioactive concentrations in milk and water are customarily measured. The radiation released was roughly equivalent to the explosion of 1,000 Hiroshima bombs."

While the fallout was concentrated mainly in the three Soviet republics of Belarus, Ukraine, and Russia, the reluctance of the Soviet authorities to recognize the true extent of the contamination of farmland resulted in the shipment of contaminated food and grain to all the former Soviet republics, thus spreading radiation illness.

Chernousenko reported that public health surveys in which he participated revealed that there is hardly a child in Belarus, which was hardest hit, who is not suffering from some immune deficiency disease, either cardiovascular, lymphoid or oncological. Most of these children are unable to attend a full day in school.

A 1989 public health survey reported that every second adult in the three biggest provinces of Ukraine was ill.

In Ukraine and Belarus, the incidence of the immune deficiency diseases has doubled or tripled since 1985 and is now spreading to all other areas that have been consuming radioactive food. This disturbing statistic was confirmed by the World Health Organization in a letter published in *Nature* magazine. The letter reported the incidence of thyroid cancer cases among children in Belarus rose from two in 1986 to 55 in 1991; similar extraordinary increases in children's thyroid cancer were reported in Gdansk, Poland.

A study by Gould, a former member of the EPA's Science Advisory Board, and Dr. Ernest Sternglass, published by the American Chemical Society in January 1989, charged that the effects of the Chernobyl accident were even apparent in the small but statistically significant excess mortality in the U.S. in May 1986. The disturbing results, which were not widely publicized, have yet to be challenged.

SSU Censored Researcher:
Courteney Lunt

COMMENTS: The author, Jay M. Gould, co-author of *Deadly Deceit: Low-Level Radiation, High-Level Cover-up*, says that despite the overwhelming significance of the issue, it has received no exposure at all. He adds that this lack of exposure benefits "the international atomic energy industry and its two trillion dollar investment in this universally unpopular, expensive and dangerous way of boiling water." In November, Gould updated the current health conditions with data provided by Dr. Chernousenko in late October. "As of 1993, some 15,000 of the 30,000 young conscripts who were unnecessarily exposed to incredibly high radiation levels in order to permit the other three Chernobyl reactors to continue operations...have died since 1986. Because 100,000 square kilometers of productive land has become permanently uninhabitable, contaminated food from these areas has been widely shipped to other areas of the former Soviet Union and consumed by an estimated 65 million persons, with varying degrees of consequent damage to their immune response." Gould also noted that while Chernousenko received five commendations from Mikhail Gorbachev for heroism, his final report on the true radiation levels was never published.

6 CENSORED

U.S. Army Quietly Resumes Biowarfare Testing After Ten-year Hiatus

Sources:

THE SALT LAKE TRIBUNE
Dates: 1/27/93; 7/28/93
Titles: "Army Resumes Biological-Agent Tests At Dugway After 10-Year Cessation;"* "Dugway to test disease-causing agents at remote lab"
Author: Jim Woolf

Date: 9/21/93
Title: "Dugway Base Cited for 22
   Waste Violations"
Author: Laurie Sullivan

HIGH COUNTRY NEWS
Date: 8/9/93
Title: "Biowarfare is back"*
Author: Jon Christensen

HIGH DESERT ADVOCATE
Date: 9/15/93
Title: "Utah biowarfare oversight
   group wants to do its work
   behind closed doors"

SYNOPSIS: Although few people
outside of Dugway, Utah, are aware
of it, the U.S. Army has brought biological warfare testing back to a site
it declared unsafe a decade earlier.

Ten years ago, residents of
western Utah breathed a healthy
sigh of relief when the Army discontinued testing biological warfare
agents at its Dugway Proving
Ground. The reason given was that
the Army's testing facility was getting old, and its safety—its ability
to prevent potentially deadly diseases from escaping into the air
outside the facility and thence to
the rest of the world—could no
longer be guaranteed. Now the
deadly bugs are back.

Military scientists are testing a
device called the Biological
Integrated Detection System
(BIDS) at the renovated Dugway
facility. BIDS is described as a

defensive weapon, designed to
detect the presence of biological
agents in time to allow soldiers to
put on protective clothing.

A Dugway representative said the
tests, which include organisms such
as anthrax, botulism, and the
plague, would initially be liquid, not
aerosol, tests. Aerosol tests are the
most hazardous form of testing
because they involve spraying biological agents into the air inside a
sealed chamber. One tiny air leak
could result in a catastrophic release
of deadly diseases. It was precisely
this hazard that led to the closing of
the Dugway facility in 1983. The
biowarfare lab has been renovated
since then and Army experts claim
their elaborate safety precautions
will prevent such a leak.

Nonetheless, new safety concerns were raised in September
1993, when the Dugway Proving
Ground was cited for 22 violations
of state hazardous-waste regulations, ranging from inadequate
record-keeping to improper
dumping of poisonous chemicals.
Notices of violation and orders for
compliance were issued to the
Army base by the Utah
Department of Environmental
Quality.

Critics also point out that it was
the Army that denied for a year
that it was responsible for the 1968
accidental release of nerve gas from
Dugway that killed some 6,000
sheep in the area.

Finally, public information about what was happening at Dugway suffered a serious setback in September 1993, when the biowarfare oversight committee that advises the governor of Utah on biological defense testing matters at Dugway voted to make itself off-limits to the public. Reasoning that they could obtain more information from the Army if confidentiality could be assured, the oversight group also voted to disengage from its parent organization, the State Advisory Council on Science and Technology. The committee had been frustrated by its inability to get timely information from Dugway.

Critics doubt the committee will have access to any more information than it has received in the past and that the net result only further distances the Army from accountability and the public from the truth.

SSU Censored Researcher:
Jesse Boggs

COMMENTS: Jim Woolf, environmental writer for *The Salt Lake Tribune*, said he was surprised by the lack of attention this story generated. "It was treated as a local story that had little significance to the general public," Woolf said, adding, "I disagree."

Woolf felt the general public should know more about this story for at least three reasons:

"1. This is an important local story. Military scientists near my home are conducting tests with some of the most deadly disease causing organisms and natural toxins ever identified. What if some of these 'bugs' escape into the environment or are carried by workers into my community? Are local doctors trained to recognize and deal with this threat? Has the Army taken all prudent steps to reduce the risk? Has the public been told the full scope of testing being carried out by the Army?

"2. Biological and chemical weapons have been described as the 'poor man's atomic bomb.' They are relatively easy to produce and could have devastating consequences in battle. Several of our enemies are known or suspected to have these weapons. All announced testing at Dugway focuses on developing systems to protect American troops from these weapons. (The development or testing of OFFENSIVE biological or chemical systems is prohibited under international treaties.) Work in this field would be of general interest to military families and others who may feel threatened by this category of weapon.

"3. The resumption of testing and plans to build an upgraded research laboratory at Dugway could have important consequences for America's international relations. Critics claim there is no clear line dividing defensive from offensive testing —the scientific knowledge gained at Dugway can be used for either good or bad. Does the resumption of this testing send a message to other countries that the United States is interested in bio-chem warfare? Will it prompt other countries to upgrade their test facilities and lead to an escalation in the race to produce ever-more-deadly weapons?"

Woolf felt that the interests of several groups were served by the limited coverage given the resumption of biowarfare testing.

"The Army was pleased. Military scientists want freedom to study whatever they want, no matter how dangerous or far-fetched the potential threat may be. The last thing they want are questions from the public or elected officials.

"Congress was served because members were not required to confront another potentially controversial issue. A handful of members interested in military issues are responsible for most of the funding decisions in this area. If there is no controversy, no one else has to confront the difficult questions surrounding this topic.

"Certain economic interests in Utah and elsewhere were served. Dugway provides jobs in a remote area of the state. If biological testing were eliminated or scaled back, the Army would have fewer reasons to maintain the base. Also,

a handful of companies are developing products and services related to biological-defense. None would like to see their income potential reduced."

Woolf notes that the resumption of biological testing has been a difficult issue in Utah and concludes with a chilling question.

"The presence of these deadly agents so close to our community is a source of concern, but we watched on CNN the terror in Israel during the Iraq war when no one knew whether the bombs that were falling contained chemical or biological weapons. We understand the need to improve our defenses, but wonder why it has to be done in our backyard, whether there are safer alternatives, and whether all safety precautions have been taken.

"We're also frightened that the Army may not be telling the whole truth—that in times of emergency they will cover their operations with the national security veil and do whatever they think is right, regardless of the threat to their neighbors. Utahns learned this lesson living downwind from the nuclear-weapons tests at the Nevada Test Site.

"Will the clouds of radioactive material be followed by the plague?"

Jon Christensen, Great Basin Regional Editor for the *High Country News*, agreed that there hasn't been sufficient coverage of this issue. "The only papers to cover the story adequately were *The Salt Lake Tribune* and the *High Desert Advocate*, in Wendover, Nevada." Without their coverage, Christensen felt that we all might have missed this story about the resumption of biowarfare testing at Dugway, Utah. He feels it is important for people to know about this issue since they "might better understand the domestic costs and risks of preparing for war, many of which are borne by remote, rural Western communities (among others). Also, our stockpile of dangerous chemical weapons and biological agents must be stored and destroyed safely. The public needs to know how." Christensen emphasized that "The regional media deserve credit for following this story. Without them, we would all be in the dark about this."

7

The Ecological Disaster That Challenges The Exxon Valdez

Source:

SPORTS ILLUSTRATED
Date: 3/22/93
Title: "The Killing Fields"*
Author: Robert H. Boyle

SYNOPSIS: "It's hard to believe, but the ecological disasters caused by the oil spills from the Exxon Valdez, in Prince William Sound, Alaska, in 1989 and the Braer, off Scotland's Shetland Island, in 1993 seem to pale when compared with the chronic environmental nightmare being wrought by selenium-contaminated drainwater flowing from irrigated lands in California and 13 other Western states." The strident warning comes from environmental writer Robert H. Boyle, president of the Hudson River-keeper Fund

"Although selenium runoff is also a problem in Arizona, Colorado, Idaho, Kansas, Montana, Nebraska, Nevada, New Mexico, Oregon, South Dakota, Utah, Washington, and Wyoming, no state has been hit as hard as California, where agricultural interests wield clout out of all proportion to their importance to the state economy."

Ironically, selenium is not a new problem; poisoned water holes and sinks have existed for years in the West. The first recorded case of selenium poisoning was in 1857, in Nebraska. A mysterious livestock disease in Mississippi in 1933 was found to be selenium poisoning. Now, however, man-made "lakes" and ponds saturated with selenium from agricultural run-off are threatening our drinking water and wildlife.

In the 1960s, at the cost of $1.4 billion, the U.S. Interior Department began constructing a canal to carry off drainwater in the San Joaquin Valley, but for lack of funds the project only got as far as the old Kesterson Ranch, a tract of land that contains 1,280 acres of gouged-out ponds, now called the Kesterson National Wildlife Refuge. All was well until 1978 when drainwater began flowing into the ponds. By 1982, the hardy mosquito fish, the only fish still living in Kesterson, was found to contain the highest selenium levels ever found in any fish anywhere.

In 1983, Harry M. Ohlendorf, a wildlife research biologist, studying nesting birds at Kesterson, found a high incidence of dead adults, dead embryos, deformed embryos and deformed young coots, ducks, eared grebes, black-necked stilt and killdeers. When he reported these findings to the regional deputy director at the U.S. Fish and Wildlife Service, he was told to delete those references in his report since the subject was "totally out of context—does not lend anything but a red flag to people." In 1984, virtually no nesting birds were seen at Kesterson; instead, 16,000 adult birds died from selenium poisoning.

Boyle estimates that tens of thousands—some say hundreds of thousands—of birds have died or have been born dead or with grotesque deformities. But the calamity has not attracted the media or even the environmental group attention it demands. Lloyd Carter, an environmental activist who has been trying to sound the alarm about selenium for years now, said, "It amazes me that not a single major environmental group has done anything to stop the killing."

However, Carter also points out the hazards of blowing the whistle. "Anyone in Interior who dares speak the truth about what is really happening will be swiftly punished or driven from government service. The people in charge have abdicated their responsibilities to protect wildlife in favor of careerism, big agribusiness, and political expediency." While the selenium crisis has now grown to extraordinary proportions—in California alone, the selenium runoff now threatens the entire 500-mile-long Central Valley as well as the water supply for Los Angeles—it has yet to attract the mainstream media.

SSU Censored Researcher:
Paul Chambers

COMMENTS: Author Robert Boyle said, "In no way has the calamity of toxic drainwater, which involves criminal violations of federal law, received anywhere near sufficient exposure in the mass media, be it in the last year or the several years before that. In point of fact, drainwater has received next to no exposure, aside from the reporting of Lloyd Carter, (formerly) of UPI's Fresno bureau, Russell Clemmings of the *Fresno Bee*, and Tom Harris, recently retired from the *Sacramento Bee*. Their readership, alas, is pretty much limited to the San Joaquin Valley." Boyle believes that if the "general public knew the extent of the damage and threats posed by toxic drainwater...thinking people would demand that the federal government end the problem, prosecute those responsible, and reform, if not cauterize, the government agencies involved." He also noted that those who benefit from the lack of coverage include "agribusiness interests who get a free ride from subsidized water, the politicians who lustily suck upon the teats of agribusiness (among them some of the biggest names in both parties), and the ass-kissing bureaucrats in the federal government who get ahead by denying that problems exist and by harassing and punishing scientists who attempt to come up with the facts."

When I asked Boyle whether he had any additional comments to make about his efforts to get his story published, he said, "You bet." Given the extraordinary experiences Boyle had in getting his toxic drainwater story printed, and the insights they provide into the media's "selection process," his comments are reprinted in full.

Robert H. Boyle: "A bit of background that may be pertinent: I went to work for *Sports Illustrated* (SI) in 1954 when the magazine was only four issues old, and in 1986, 32 years later, I took early retirement as a Senior Writer and accepted a contract with the magazine as a Special Contributor.

"While on staff, one of my fortes was environmental reporting, which I pioneered for the magazine starting in 1959 with a story that foiled the attempted rape of Tule Lake in Northern California, the single greatest gathering spot in the world for migratory waterfowl, by a bunch of farmers and a schemer in the U.S. Bureau of Reclamation.

"For years afterwards, SI ran hard-hitting environmental pieces from time to time because the magazine covered participant sports, such as fishing, hiking, mountain climbing, sailing, hunting, camping, etc., along with spectator sports, and the editors figured that if someone was messing up a trout stream, or a mountain, or an ecosystem, the readers ought to know. This editorial stance started to change 10 years ago as the magazine became more and more jock-oriented, and that's the major reason I chose early retirement.

"Mind you, in the old days we didn't preach about the environment every week—it's easy to turn people off—but we did run anywhere from three to six compelling articles a year. I think of Jack Olsen's articles on the deadly 1080 "coyote-getter" poison, and pieces by Robert Cantwell and Bill Gilbert. A piece I did in 1970 first reported the presence of PCBs in fish in North America (I collected or arranged for correspondents to collect fish that I then had tested by the leading analytical laboratory in the country), and this was five years before the federal government finally owned up to a pervasive PCB problem. In a 1984 piece I offered the hypothesis, based on chemical evidence that I had gathered, that acid rain was largely responsible for the lack of reproductive success by striped bass and five other important Atlantic Coast species of fish that spawned in rivers tributary to Chesapeake Bay. This hypothesis, since proven, prompted a scientific conference, and the papers presented were published in a special issue of the peer-review international scientific journal, *Water, Air & Soil Pollution*.

"I first offered the drainwater story to *Sports Illustrated* in July of 1991. After five months of batting it around, editors, off into deep jockdom, rejected it.

"In February of 1992, I offered the article to *Audubon* magazine. The editor, Michael Robbins, said he would publish it as soon as pos-

sible, which I took to mean at once.

"In the meanwhile, I offered *Audubon* another article, this one on edible insects that were to be served at the banquet celebrating the 100th anniversary of the New York Entomological Society, to which I belong. Robbins published the edible insects article immediately after I turned it in, but he kept postponing publication of the drainwater article even after researchers called me up to check and double-check the facts.

"Finally, Bruce Stutz, an editor at *Audubon* and an old friend, phoned to say that the drainwater article would be in the November-December 1992 issue. Then, at the last minute, Stutz called again to say that the article was being yanked in favor of an article on Roger Tory Peterson, but that it would finally appear in the January-February 1993 issue. I said, 'Bruce, you are a dear fellow, but I want my article back. *NOW!* Go tell Michael Robbins that he has turned *Audubon* into the *People Magazine* of the environment. What is *Audubon* going to tell us that's new about Roger Tory Peterson??? How the penguins hop up and down with joy when Peterson, binoculars at the ready, sets foot on Antarctica once again with a troupe of blue-haired ladies from a Lindblad cruise ship??? The National Audubon Society was founded specifically for the protection of birds. By the way, *Audubon* still owes me anywhere from $500 to $1,500 for the extra reporting Robbins asked me to do. Don't bother to send it. I don't want *Audubon's* goddamned money.'

"I got the article back, but not, of course, the money due me. What to do now? I had a world-class scoop and nowhere to place it. I decided to send the article to an editor I knew at *The New Yorker* because the magazine had recently run two 'Talk of the Town' pieces I'd written. I got two responses from *The New Yorker*. One was that Tina Brown, who had just taken over the editorship, wasn't interested, and the other was that my drainwater article conflicted with a piece the magazine was going to run.

"I tried *Harper's*. The magazine rejected it because the article was too regional. By this time my wife was saying 'Do you have to devote your life to an article about drainwater?'

"My wife and I then went to SI's Christmas party at the Hard Rock Cafe on Manhattan's West 57th Street. We had a good time, and just as we were leaving, Mark Mulvoy, who had returned from being publisher to managing editor, stopped me and said, 'I want you to see me after the holidays.'

"We met in Mulvoy's office in the Time-Life Building after the holidays. 'I want a strong environmental piece for the March 22nd issue,' he said.

"Mark, I sent one in a year and a half ago. The magazine turned it down. My wife says I'm ruining my life making a career about it, but it deals with toxic drainwater in the West, selenium poisoning in California in particular.

"'Never heard about it, but it sounds great,' Mulvoy said. Turning to subordinates, he announced, 'March 22nd issue, 400 lines, close it two weeks ahead.' Turning to me, he said, 'Okay, Bob?'

"'Mark, you'll have it,' I replied.

"And thus *Sports Illustrated* finally published it."

8 | CENSORED |

America's Deadly Doctors

Source:

WOMAN'S DAY
Date: 10/12/93
Title: "Deadly Doctors"*
Author: Sue Browder

SYNOPSIS: The trust Americans put into their doctors may be sorely misplaced. According to estimates, five percent to 10 percent of doctors—some 30,000 to 60,000—could be hazardous to your health. A study by Public Citizen's Health Research Group concluded that medical negligence in hospitals alone injures or kills 150,000 to 300,000 Americans each year. Experts cite two major reasons why some doctors are dangerous: They've become physically or mentally impaired, or they were poorly trained or incompetent to start with.

Charles Inlander, president of the People's Medical Society, said that impairment is the number one reason doctors are dangerous.

Impairment takes many forms including alcoholism (10 percent of all physicians) and drug addiction (three percent), which accounts for some 78,000 doctors nationwide. Another impairment is mental illness; a 1989 New Jersey report on incompetent physicians revealed that one percent, or about 6,000 doctors, are mentally unbalanced. Senility is another problem with many doctors continuing to practice after growing too old to do so. A final reason is ignorance—doctors, who are otherwise mentally and physically healthy, may fail to keep up with medical research.

The second main reason doctors can be deadly is simple incompetence and poor training.

Students who could not qualify for admission to American medical schools often attend unaccredited schools in the Caribbean. "A school in the Dominican Republic was selling medical degrees several years ago," said Dale Breaden, asso-

ciate executive vice president of the Federation of State Medical Boards. Sometimes those who can't get a medical license simply practice without one or use a fraudulent degree. Some doctors also lack the appropriate skills when they practice beyond their area of expertise. Finally, there are doctors who are driven by greed. One New Jersey doctor did so many needless surgeries he lost his malpractice insurance, yet he kept treating patients.

So, why aren't these deadly doctors stopped? According to Arthur Levin, director of the Center for Medical Consumers, thousands of doctors who have lost their licenses or gotten in trouble for being drug addicted, senile, or otherwise incompetent simply move across state lines. Others just continue to practice without a license. Also, state medical boards set up to police bad doctors offer far too little protection. A survey by the Health Research Group indicated that only 3,034 disciplinary actions were taken against some 585,000 doctors in 1991. State medical boards move at such a slow pace that even after abuses have been proven in court, hearings on lifting a doctor's license can drag on for years. Bad doctors also stay in business because their colleagues refuse to expose them.

Ultimately, however, the lack of media coverage on the misconduct of doctors is a major reason deadly doctors continue to take their toll on a trusting American public.

SSU Student Researcher:
Laurie Turner

COMMENTS: Sue Browder, a freelance magazine journalist and author of the article in *Woman's Day*, feels that the issue of deadly doctors in America never has received the mass media exposure it deserves. "National magazines frequently shy from the topic (perhaps for fear they'll be sued)," Browder said, "whereas daily newspapers tend to report such stories *only* after an injured patient has just won a multi-million dollar lawsuit and the damage has been done. The *Hartford Courant* did a fine reporting job once it became publicly known that Dr. Steven Weber had given one Connecticut woman an abortion without her knowledge. But no stories were done on Weber before he committed this atrocity—even though he had lost his license in New York the previous year for his inept care of 10 other women. The *Boston Globe's* New Hampshire edition also covered the Dr. Stephen Dell case after Dell's license had been temporarily suspended in New Hampshire. Yet the investigating reporter could not persuade the *Globe* to publish the story in their Boston edition, even though Dr.

Dell was still practicing on—and possibly hurting—people in Massachusetts."

"It's not that this subject needs *wider* exposure so much as it needs *earlier* exposure," Browder continued. "Since deadly doctors who have lost their licenses in one state often simply move across state lines, reporters need to keep a closer eye on doctors coming into their states and keep checking their track records. Since this is such a vital public health issue, we need more stories exposing dangerous doctors before they hurt or kill innocent people."

Browder believes it is not just the interests of the American Medical Association that benefit from the limited coverage given this issue. "But the whole medical establishment benefits by keeping this issue under wraps. Politicians and lawmakers also benefit: when stories about deadly doctors continually get swept under the rug, the public knows too little about the hazards to demand reform."

Although Browder has repeatedly tried to get articles about dangerous doctors published during her 20-years-experience as a freelance magazine journalist, she has had only limited success.

"Many of my magazine markets want only 'upbeat, happy' stories that won't disturb their readers. And even those willing to tackle more serious subjects often seem to regard doctors as sacred cows too highly respected to criticize.

"I once wrote a story about a Connecticut 'psychologist' (he claimed to be licensed when he was not) who had had sex with several of his patients. He claimed to have graduated from Yale (again, he had not) and was guilty of countless other deceptions. I had the guy lying to me on tape, I had several of his victims willing to talk, and I even had written proof that he'd lied about his credentials. Yet the editors at the magazine for which I was freelancing at the time killed the story because it was too 'controversial' (translation: the doctor had a lot of money and a team of lawyers, and the editors didn't want to publish anything they might have to defend in court).

"Just as doctors refuse to blow the whistle on inept colleagues because they don't want to ruin a friend's career or fear they'll be sued for slander, I think the media often shy from this subject because they fear doctors' clout. As a result, the public suffers. Certainly, *Woman's Day* deserves a great deal of credit for suggesting that I write this story and for backing me so completely throughout my investigation."

In November, the Public Citizen's Health Research Group released the third edition of its listing of doctors who have been sanctioned by state medical boards of the federal government.

The latest data cites 10,289 questionable doctors who have been disciplined a total of 14,574 times by state and federal government agencies—an *increase of 3,453 new doctors* from the prior study released more than two years earlier. The reasons for the actions against the doctors include at least 1,346 criminal convictions, 1,130 instances of overprescribing or misprescribing of drugs, 1,070 cases of substandard care or negligence, 817 instances of alcohol or drug abuse, and 173 instances of sexual abuse of or sexual misconduct with a patient, including rape.

There's A Lot Of Money To Be Made In Poverty

Source:

SOUTHERN EXPOSURE
Date: Fall 1993
Title: "Poverty, Inc. Why the poor pay more—and who really profits."*
Authors: Mike Hudson, Eric Bates, Barry Yeoman, Adam Feuerstein

SYNOPSIS: Want to know what is the hottest new profit center for big blue-chip corporations like ITT, General Motors, American Express, and others? The acceptable term is "fringe banking;" the less acceptable, but more accurate, term is "loan sharking."

Fringe banks are pawn shops and check cashing outlets—operations that serve low-income people, usually in urban ghettos, who don't fit into the picture at mainstream banks. Interest on pawn shop loans typically runs over 200 percent, and check cashers charge two to 10 percent of a check's value for cashing it. These are just two examples of the ways some large U.S. corporations are profiting from the cycle of poverty, particularly in the South.

The Fall 1993 cover article of *Southern Exposure* magazine documents how huge national and international corporations own and finance a growing "poverty industry" that targets low-income, blue-collar, and minority consumers for fraud, exploitation, and price gouging.

In addition to "fringe banks," other money-making endeavors include:

■ Second-mortgage companies—making loans with 30 percent interest to pay off bills or make repairs

■ Used-car dealers—working in tandem with banks and finance companies to bilk people with "bad credit"

■ Finance companies (ITT is a standout here)—charging huge interest rates by acting as a lender of last resort for borrowers with limited incomes

■ Rent-to-own stores—which constitute a $3.7-billion-a-year business, charging customers about five times what they'd pay at traditional retailers

■ Trade schools—lending out federal loan money on the promise of giving usable skills to low-income students, then leaving them with no skills and a big debt

■ Debt collectors—the not-so-friendly people who badger, threaten, and coerce low-income borrowers to pay back funds regardless of their circumstances

It is a normal practice for companies engaged in these activities to entice low-income people into deeper and deeper debt, at interest rates many times higher than those paid by middle-class Americans. A typical example: a 66-year-old Atlanta man pawned his car for $300. He agreed to pay back $545 over twelve weeks, but fell behind in his payments. The pawn broker tacked on late charges and threatened to have the man arrested. When the borrower went to Legal Aid for help, the attorney discovered that the loan contract listed the annual interest rate as 24 percent; the real rate was 550 percent.

Unlike banks and S&Ls, huge financial service businesses—part of such mega-corporations as American Express, Sears, General Electric, General Motors, and Westinghouse—are not subject to federal regulations that require financial disclosures, limit wheeling-and-dealing, combat racial discrimination in lending, and put caps on interest rates. Ironically, banks are crying foul, while simultaneously extending huge lines of credit to the very companies they're accusing of undermining them.

**SSU Censored Researcher:
Jesse Boggs**

COMMENTS: This is an extraordinary untold story of how some of America's biggest corporations are making billions of dollars by targeting the poor for profit. In the introduction to the special 28-page section on "Poverty, Inc." published in *Southern Exposure*, Mike Hudson, a reporter with the *Roanoke Times & World-News*, and Eric Bates, editor of *Southern Exposure*, describe this feature as an explanation of how the poverty industry really works—and how average citizens are fighting back. Support for the extensive investigative project was provided by the Alicia Patterson Foundation, the Fund for Investigative Journalism, and the Dick Goldensohn Fund. Mike Hudson, who spent two years investigating the poverty industry, provides the background on this story.

"The nation's news media have largely ignored the story and its ramifications. To our knowledge, no major news outlet—or small one for that matter—has identified the broad scope of corporate America's role in profiteering from the poor via credit fraud and usury. No one has called the 'poverty industry' what it is—a huge, multi-billion-dollar collection of companies fueled by Wall Street funding and propped up by a

THIS MODERN WORLD by TOM TOMORROW

FROM *WASHINGTON*-- IT'S *CROSSFIRE!* WATCH THE NEVER-ENDING IDEOLOGICAL BATTLE BETWEEN THOSE WHO FEEL CORPORATE POWER SHOULD GO *UNCHECKED*, REGARDLESS OF THE HUMAN CONSEQUENCES --

IF BUSINESS IS NOT ALLOWED TO DUMP TOXIC SEWAGE INTO THE NATION'S DRINKING WATER, ECONOMIC GROWTH WILL BE *STIFLED!*

--AND THOSE WHO FEEL THAT MINOR, INCONSEQUENTIAL RESTRICTIONS SHOULD *OCCASIONALLY* BE ENFORCED, IF ONLY FOR THE SAKE OF APPEARANCES!

WELL, OF COURSE ECONOMIC GROWTH *SHOULD* BE OUR FIRST PRIORITY... BUT SHOULDN'T BUSINESS AT LEAST BE REQUIRED TO FILTER OUT A FEW OF THE *DEADLIEST* TOXINS?

new veneer of corporate respectability. Nor have the media reported in a comprehensive way on how these businesses are using their polish and resources to engineer legislative 'deregulation' in nearly every state—gutting laws that had once given low-income and minority consumers a measure of protection from predatory lending.

"There have been a few notable exceptions to this rule of media inattention. These including reporting by the *Boston Globe* and the Atlanta newspapers on second-mortgage fraud against minority homeowners, Mary Kane's excellent coverage of inner-city economics for Newhouse News Service, and a *Wall Street Journal* story by Alix Freedman on how the nation's largest rent-to-own chain takes advantage of the poor.

"But, once again, these stories are the exceptions. The major media have missed the big picture either by ignoring the story altogether, or by limiting their critical scrutiny to narrow segments of the poverty industry (or specific companies such as Fleet Finance) and failing to make connections between the various businesses that market to the poor.

"And, to make matters worse, national business magazines and major daily newspapers have quite frequently produced stories that read like press releases from these businesses.

"A typical example: a business-page article in one major midwest newspaper ('Pssst! Hocking your VCR has gotten respectable'), which trumpeted the arrival of a national pawn chain but failed to point out that a loan at a 'respectable' pawn broker in the state could carry an annual interest rate of 276 percent.

"The general public would benefit in a number of ways from greater exposure to this subject. Such exposure would:

- alert the public to a silent but devastating crisis that is pushing people deeper into poverty and destabilizing neighborhoods.
- warn individual consumers so that they could protect themselves from being preyed upon and seek redress for past exploitation.
- provide citizens and activists the information they need to fight for tougher legislation and law enforcement efforts aimed at reining in these practices.
- offer investors and stockholders in these companies a clearer picture of how their money is being used, and who is being hurt by their investments.
- give citizens a fuller understanding of the nature of poverty and economics in disadvantaged neighborhoods, thus fueling the debate about welfare, inner-city blight and related issues.

"The primary beneficiaries of limited coverage are the corporations that profit from these practices, along with their stockholders and investors. The less scrutiny they receive, the more effective they can be in attracting investment capital and in cultivating positive images with legislators and consumers. The profits they make from these ventures, as our stories show, are huge.

"Others who benefit include legislators who receive campaign contributions from these companies (and in the case of many lawyer/legislators, lucrative private legal work). Likewise, corporate news media benefit from the advertising that these businesses buy from them.

"When the [*Southern Exposure*] issue came out, we sent out press releases to a number of other publications, but have received limited response. The Associated Press wrote a story on our study, but distribution of the article was limited to North Carolina and was picked up only by a few papers.

"We are trying to get the article reprinted in other alternative publications and are encouraging other journalists to pursue the story. In addition, the publisher of *Southern Exposure*, the Institute for Southern Studies, is in the process of creating a quarterly newsletter, *Poverty, Inc.*, which will continue to track these issues and serve as a networking vehicle for journalists, activists, attorneys, and others concerned about the subject.

"Since the *Southern Exposure* issue came out, Rep. Henry Gonzalez, D-Texas, has introduced legislation that would put tough federal limits on the rent-to-own industry."

Meanwhile, on December 16, it was announced that the State Attorney General of Georgia and Fleet Finance have agreed on a settlement of the state's criminal investigation for a sum of $115 million (the equivalent of about two year's profits for Fleet Finance in the early 1990s.)

10

Haiti: Drugs, Thugs, the CIA, and the Deterrence of Democracy

Sources:

THE NEW YORK TIMES
Date: 11/1/93
Title: "Key Haiti Leaders Said To
    Have Been In The C.I.A.'s Pay"
Author: Tim Weiner

PACIFIC NEWS SERVICE
Dates: 10/20/93; 11/2/93
Titles: "What's Behind
    Washington's Silence on Haiti
    Drug Connection?;"* "A Haitian
    Call to Arms"
Author: Dennis Bernstein

SAN FRANCISCO BAY
    GUARDIAN
Date: 11/3/93
Title: "The CIA's Haitian
    Connection"*
Authors: Dennis Bernstein and
    Howard Levine

LOS ANGELES TIMES
Date: 10/31/93
Title: "CIA's Aid Plan Would Have
    Undercut Aristide in '87-88"
Author: Jim Mann

SYNOPSIS: After the October 30, 1993 deadline to restore duly-elected President Jean-Bertrand Aristide passed unrealized, observers reported an increasing sense of fear and despair. More than 4,000 civilians have been killed since the 1991 bloody military coup which ousted Aristide. Few Americans are aware of our secret involvement in Haitian politics, nor the impact those policies have had on the U.S.

Some of the high military officials involved in the coup have been on the CIA's payroll from "the mid-1980s at least until the 1991 coup...." According to one government official, "Several of the principal players of the current situation were compensated by the U.S. government."

Further, the CIA "tried to intervene in Haiti's election with a covert-action program that would have undercut the political strength" of Aristide. The aborted attempt to influence the 1988 election was authorized by then-President Ronald Reagan and the National Security Council. The program was blocked by the Senate Select Committee on Intelligence in a rare move.

Next, a confidential Drug Enforcement Agency (DEA) report revealed that Haiti is "a major transshipment point for cocaine traffickers" who are funneling drugs from Colombia and the Dominican

Republic into the United States. The DEA report also revealed that the drug trafficking, which is bringing one to four tons of cocaine per month into the U.S., worth $300-$500 million annually, is taking place with "the knowledge and active involvement of high military officials and business elites."

According to Patrick Elie, who was Aristide's anti-drug czar, Haitian police chief Lt. Col. Michel Francois is at the center of the drug trade. Francois' "attachés" reportedly have been responsible for a large number of murders and violence since the coup.

The revelations offer a disturbing look into CIA and State Department policy toward Haiti. Elie stated that he was constantly rebuffed by the CIA when he tried to alert it to the military's drug trafficking: "All we were met with was stonewalling, and in fact we were told there was going to be no more cooperation between the U.S. and Haiti, but at the same time... the CIA continued to cooperate with the Haitian military." Elie reported how the CIA-created Haitian National Intelligence Service (NIS)—supposedly created to combat drugs—was actually involved with narcotics-trafficking, and "functioned as a political intimidation and assassination squad."

The Clinton administration's silence on the Haitian drug flow has led some congressional critics, such as John Conyers (D-MI), to suggest that this silence reflects de facto support for the drug-trafficking Haitian military and a reluctance to substantively support the democratically-elected Aristide.

SSU Censored Researcher: Sunil Sharma

COMMENTS: Investigative author Dennis Bernstein charges that the U.S. government's ongoing relationship with drug-trafficking dictators and their associated henchmen is perhaps one of the most important and under-reported stories of our time.

"President Clinton's continuing silence on the Haitian military's involvement in a one-billion-dollar a year illegal cocaine operation—and the mainstream media's acceptance of this silence—is causing untold suffering in Haiti and the U.S.," Bernstein said. "In fact," he continued, "it is this silence about the drugs that allows the military to continue to skirt the embargo with massive amounts of drug-money, to torture and assassinate thousands of Haitians, and to wreak havoc in this country by continuing to import tons of cocaine onto U.S. soil. The U.S. created, funded, and trained Haiti's drug-dealing death-squad—the National Intelligence Service—which apparently was conceived to destabilize President Aristide.

"Democracy doesn't exist without a free and unfettered press that isn't afraid to ask the difficult questions and then to publish the answers to those questions without checking informally with the state department and the CIA. The press's continuing failure to report adequately on illegal intelligence operations and CIA-sponsored drug-running and assassination coup teams may ultimately lead to the death of democracy, not only in Haiti but in the U.S.

"The only people to gain from the press's limited reporting of the Haiti drug story and related U.S. complicit silence are drug-traffickers and their supporting death-squads and dictators, as well as collaborating smugglers and related criminals involved in a billion-dollar-drug operation."

Bernstein concludes that "The soaring number of crack addicts in the U.S. and Haiti—and their families—and the victims of addict robberies and murders will definitely not benefit from the silence...and lack of good reporting."

PBS's "Frontline," one of the nation's most acclaimed investigative television programs, produced a well-documented, hour-long special, on November 9, titled "Showdown in Haiti," which examined President Clinton's foreign-policy initiative in Haiti. Ironically, the otherwise hard-hitting documentary didn't mention drugs or the CIA.

11 | CENSORED

Maquiladoras In Silicon Valley

Source:

THE NATION
Date: 4/19/93
Title: "Silicon Valley Sweatshops:
   High-Tech's Dirty Little Secret"
Author: Elizabeth Kadetsky

SYNOPSIS: In two high-profile visits to Silicon Valley, California's high-tech "paradise," President Bill Clinton has praised that industry as a model for America's economic future, which "will move America forward to a stronger economy, a cleaner environment and technological leadership."

Unfortunately, it is a model with some poor-fitting and missing parts. In reality, Silicon Valley is home to some of the nation's dirtiest, most dangerous jobs—a fact that has been virtually buried in the rush to embrace our technological future.

The people who work on the assembly lines, making printed circuit boards and other electronic components for companies like IBM and Digital Microwave Corporation, earn about six dollars per hour, have no health benefits, and routinely have to handle highly toxic substances without even the most rudimentary safety equipment, such as gloves and goggles.

If they protest their conditions, as Joselito Muñoz did last October, they are fired. More than 60 percent of the 80,000-plus workers in this environment are female, and 70 percent of them are Asian or Latino.

A large part of the problem is that these workers aren't actually employed by major companies like IBM or Digital Microwave. Instead, they work for small components contractors like Versatronex—the company that fired Joselito Muñoz. The week after Muñoz was fired, 85 of his fellow workers walked out in protest and called the United Electrical, Radio and Machine Workers Union. Within a few months, the National Labor Relations Board ordered Versatronex to recognize the union. The company's response was to file for bankruptcy and shut down its Sunnyvale plant. The message was not lost on other workers.

This is not an atypical scenario. The big *Fortune* 500 dynamos of Silicon Valley, whose employees enjoy flextime, elder and child care, sabbaticals, paternal leave, profit-sharing, employee swimming pools, and fitness centers, benefit enormously from this system of Maquiladora-like subcontractors who can supply them with cheap parts because their wages and standards are so low.

When approached about the issue, these companies take a "hands-off" attitude. When asked about conditions at companies like Versatronex, the American Electronic Association's "director of workforce excellence" responded, "We try to build consensus and not pick issues that are divisive. So we don't have any policy statement on it."

President Clinton, meanwhile, has laid out a plan for subsidies to small business and emerging technologies that promises government windfalls to Silicon Valley—and appears destined to reinforce—existing conditions.

In the words of University of California economist Marshall Pomer, "Insofar as he allows Silicon Valley's desperate immigrants to work in terrible conditions with no chance of advancement and no chance of collecting disability, Clinton is furthering the Reagan agenda."

**SSU Censored Researcher:
Jesse Boggs**

COMMENTS: Investigative author Elizabeth Kadetsky, who wrote about the Silicon Valley sweatshops for *The Nation*, pointed out the critical need for local coverage of issues that also have a national impact.

Pointing out how the Silicon Valley has benefited enormously from its high-tech image, Kadetsky notes that "Even local newspapers have a tremendous stake in preserving Central California's relatively newfound national prominence. Twenty years ago a job at the *San Jose Mercury News* would never have landed reporter or editor work on a top metropolitan newspaper; today and thanks expressly to high tech, the *Mercury* itself is one of those coveted journalistic venues.

"As in many company towns, in Silicon Valley there is a feeling of living with a Big Lie—read even the alternative press and you'll learn a lot about big boss's paternalism and benevolence, but nothing of his shortcomings. With boomtown boosterism so ingrained in the local psyche, it's not surprising few have been willing to rip the curtain from this Emerald City. And without the local press's lead, national news has nothing to steal.

"My piece went the way of many *Nation* stories: *The New York Times* ran an article within the month that was essentially a rip-off of mine—down to passages extremely reminiscent of my own wording—of course never citing me or *The Nation*. Then, surprise, the *Times* dropped the story, failing to mention conditions for Silicon Valley's immigrant workers and the persistence of grassroots labor organizing in the paper's myriad encomia on Clinton's visits and other flirtations with Silicon Valley's Republican *patróns*.

"I believe negligence rather than occult machinations explains the mainstream press's blithe omission of stories on immigrant labor. Like many Americans, a lot of journalists and editors are skeptical of unions and still don't understand the difference between a don from the Carpenters Union going to jail and a barrio Chicano going out to speak Spanish with workers who could well be his or her relations. The increasingly professionalized and educated journalism establishment goes to parties where they drink white wine with other professionals. In Silicon Valley at least, they come to idealize the fancy cars and beautiful homes of high-tech's most successful entrepreneurs. The janitor from Acapulco who had a miscarriage while breathing toxic cleanser fumes is just not someone a $50,000-a-year editor cares to understand."

Nonetheless, Kadetsky said she feels that coverage of immigrants is improving and cited several articles that recently appeared in the *San Francisco Examiner*, *The New York Times*, and the *Los Angeles Times*.

12 CENSORED

The Grand Jury That Wouldn't Take It Any More

Sources:

DENVER WESTWORD
Date: 9/30/92+
Title: "Rocky Flats Grand Jury" series
Authors: Bryan Abas and Patricia Calhoun

HARPER'S MAGAZINE
Date: 12/92
Title: "Readings: The Grand Jury Report"

THE DENVER POST
Date: 1/5/93
Title: "Panel: Flats probe thwarted"
Authors: Kelly Richmond and Robert Kowalski

THE WASHINGTON POST
Date: 8/11/93
Title: "Free the Rocky Flats 23"
Author: Jonathan Turley

SYNOPSIS: "For forty years, federal, Coloradan, and local regulators and elected officials have been unable to make the Department of Energy (DOE) and the plant's corporate operators obey the law. Indeed the plant has been, and continues to be, operated by gov-

ernment and corporate employees who have placed themselves above the law and who have hidden their illegal conduct behind the cloak of 'national security'."—from sealed report of the special grand jury impaneled in Denver in August 1989, and submitted to the court in March 1992.

But all that seemed to end on March 26, 1992, when a U.S. prosecuting attorney announced that Rockwell International, the company that operated the Rocky Flats nuclear-weapons plant in Colorado for 14 years, had pled guilty to ten charges of violating federal hazardous waste disposal and clean water laws. The plea bargain called for an $18.5 million fine which Rockwell agreed to pay. All that remained was for the court to approve the settlement.

That might have been the end of this environmental crime if it had not been for a grand jury of 23 citizens who refused to participate in a cover-up and an aggressive alternative weekly newspaper, the Denver-based *Westword*, which believed in the public's right to know.

While the prosecuting attorney announced that Rockwell's fine would be the largest ever collected by the federal government for violations of hazardous waste disposal laws, critics pointed out that the $18.5 million fine was less than the $22.6 million in bonus fees awarded Rockwell from 1987 to 1989.

On September 30, 1992, *Westword* started publishing a remarkable series of articles by Bryan Abas and *Westword* editor Patricia Calhoun about the jury investigation—including incriminating court documents and charges of an official cover-up.

On November 20, 1992, the grand jurors went public charging that the Justice Department prevented them from fulfilling their oaths to pursue wrongdoing regardless of the consequences. In turn, the Justice Department threatened them with criminal charges for revealing information on the case.

Jonathan Turley, an environmental law professor at George Washington University, who also is representing the jurors on a pro bono basis, cited the "Rocky Flats 23" for being the first grand jury in history to risk possible personal incarceration for revealing information critical of the Justice Department.

By August 1993, the Justice Department's environmental crimes section was being investigated by the department itself and by a House oversight subcommittee to determine whether the Bush administration allowed corporations and corporate officials to escape punishment for serious environmental crimes.

Turley reported, "House investigators, while facing what one of them called 'extreme' resistance from the department, uncovered evidence of high-level intervention by Justice Department officials to reduce both charges and fines against Rockwell." Oversight subcommittee chairman Howard Wolpe and other lawmakers have asked President Bill Clinton to pardon the grand jurors.

SSU Censored Researcher: Kristen Rutledge

COMMENTS: The Rocky Flats case is a classic example of how a small but aggressive weekly paper can bring an issue to national attention through its own persistent coverage. While the Rocky Flats Grand Jury story started in mid-1989, it wasn't until late 1992 that it started to attract media attention, as reported by Amy Asch, promotion manager for *Harper's Magazine*.

The Denver *Westword* started covering the story on September 30, 1992, when it published the first in a series of articles about the Rocky Flats Grand Jury by reporter Bryan Abas and *Westword* editor Patricia Calhoun. Abas had obtained a draft copy of the grand jury's report, which had been sealed by the judge, and, according to Asch, "*Harper's Magazine* brought the story to the national press, by printing the first lengthy extract from the document in the December 1992 issue. This resulted in news stories being written by *The New York Times*, the *Washington Post, Chicago Tribune, Rocky Mountain News, Sacramento Bee,* and other newspapers."

Westword editor Calhoun pointed out that if *Westword* had "not broken the original story—and like the grand jurors, risked contempt of court in doing so—it's unlikely that the subject would have ever seen the light of day."

Calhoun said the general public would benefit from even wider exposure of this story since "Rocky Flats is only one instance of the justice department dragging its heels on the issue of environmental crimes at federal facilities. A Congressional subcommittee is currently considering thirty other cases in which Justice may have willfully failed to prosecute such crimes. Certainly, wider exposure of the Rocky Flats story would illuminate these other cases."

Calhoun noted that the primary beneficiaries of the lack of coverage given the issue include the Justice Department, Department of Defense, Department of Energy, and Rockwell International.

Harper's Asch notes that the magazine "believes strongly in providing the facts and letting readers make their own decisions. The Rocky Flats cover-up...is not only an environmental issue, but also concerns the negligent behavior of the DOE, and what seems to be an attempt by the Justice Department to cover up the DOE's cover-up of its environmental abuses."

Ironically, more than four years after this story started, it still has not received the coverage necessary to prod the administration to resolve it. On November 1, 1993, Dick Thomas, associate editor of *The Oregonian,* in Portland, reported that the Rocky Flats grand jurors still haven't received justice and "remain unanimous in their commitment to disclosing what they know about the crimes committed at Rocky Flats."

13

Public Input and Congressional Oversight Locked Out of NAFTA

Sources:

THE PROGRESSIVE
Date: January 1993
Title: "Citizens Shut Out"
Author: Jeremy Weintraub

ROLLING STONE
Date: 10/28/93
Title: "Congress: Kill NAFTA—The free-trade agreement is a bad deal"
Author: William Grieder

THE TEXAS OBSERVER
Date: 6/18/93
Title: "Mexico Buys Free Trade"
Author: Don Hazen

SYNOPSIS: The North American Free Trade Agreement (NAFTA) with Canada and Mexico, cited as perhaps one of the most important international trade policies in history, was created in what one member of Congress called "fifteen months of the most secretive trade negotiations I've ever monitored."

Researcher and author Jeremy Weintraub reports, "From the beginning, negotiations were conducted clandestinely, documents classified, and statements veiled, all because, according to Administration officials, NAFTA was far too complex, too dense for the average member of Congress."

Nonetheless, those same members of Congress were given ninety days to make a decision on whether to support or reject the treaty. It makes sense to ask, if NAFTA is as wide-ranging and complex as touted, how can the "average member of Congress," let alone his or her constituents, make a reasonable, let alone intelligent, decision on the agreement.

Of course, most constituents won't have a chance to read the treaty, Weintraub writes, "When NAFTA was completed...the U.S. trade representative's office began allowing interested citizens to view the 2,000-page document—for one hour." And while public participation was barred from the negotiation process, one industry expert after another was called in to comment or participate.

Critics also suggest that NAFTA is beginning to look a lot like the Reagan/Bush era's final *coup de grâce* for the labor movement and manufacturing in the U.S. and Canada. The flow of jobs to Mexico, already a major concern, is expected to increase with NAFTA, creating a long-term downward pressure on wages in the U.S. Meanwhile, labor in Mexico is also suffering. In a well-documented *Rolling Stone* article, author William Greider describes how American corporations already are trying to break the labor movement in Mexico.

Meanwhile, opponents charge that environmental oversight and standards are expected to devolve to the lowest common denominator under NAFTA, exacerbating the problems of toxic dumping and environmental abuse already evident in the *maquiladora* zone along the border. While the Mexican government has promised reforms, and has some highly paid public relations firms working to sell the American people on those promises, it has a long history of empty rhetoric.

In an interview published in *The Texas Observer*, Chuck Lewis, executive director of the Center for Public Integrity and the "scourge of the lobbying world," said, "Since 1989, the Mexican government and the various Mexican corporate groups tied to the government such as COESCE [the Mexican Chamber of Commerce] have spent from $25 to $30 million for trade lobbying." For perspective, that is more than twice what Kuwait spent to persuade Congress to attack Iraq.

While NAFTA has received considerable media coverage and will no doubt be one of the top 10 news stories on the Associated Press list for 1993, this nomination deals with the lack of information regarding the secretive trade negotiations that went into the development of the treaty and the lack of public input and congressional oversight.

SSU Censored Researcher:
Paul Chambers

Comments: Given the lack of public input and congressional oversight, it was not surprising when NAFTA passed both houses with ease and turned North America into one of the world's largest free trade zones. The highly touted Al Gore/Ross Perot "debate" didn't hurt either.

Jeremy Weintraub, an author and researcher for the Global Economy Project at the Institute for Policy Studies in Washington, DC, provides an interesting insight into the media's machinations behind the NAFTA vote.

"To most Americans," Weintraub wrote, "NAFTA coverage in the mainstream media was probably excessive; yet NAFTA suffered an alarming degree of censorship, albeit unconventional. Rather than question the administration's assumptions concerning the global economy, reporters seemed to accept tacitly the idea that public debate is an anathema to a healthy

THIS MODERN WORLD by TOM TOMORROW

NAFTA; as a result, NAFTA coverage was largely obfuscating or, at best, superfluous.

"NAFTA hibernated long in the business pages of dailies, safe from public scrutiny—until the House vote neared. Suddenly, NAFTA was headline news and mass media outlets gave business executives and pro-NAFTA government officials limitless room to explain its significance. In contrast, the environmental, labor, and consumer groups who campaigned tirelessly to highlight NAFTA's shortcomings couldn't get a word in edgewise. Television coverage of NAFTA lacked analysis but provided one of the most entertaining debates in recent history: Ross Perot versus Vice President Al Gore. The two combatants fired from their machine-gun-mouths invectives and accusations; and, while little of substance was said, Gore came across better, and the polls reflected an increase in NAFTA support.

"If mainstream coverage had extended beyond the jobs-environment debate and included reports on the lack of citizen input and oversight in creating NAFTA, the public would likely have rejected NAFTA early on as an affront to democracy. With the end of the Cold War, there is now even less justification for closed-door deals.

"Through its irresponsible coverage of one issue—NAFTA—the mass media abetted or supported: (a) The conviction, held by reactionary government officials, that government knows best what the public needs—thereby entrenching an outmoded, unacceptable relationship between the federal government and its citizens. Ironically, the U.S. press repeatedly highlighted the lack of democratic participation in ratifying NAFTA in Mexico, while somehow alluding to a contrast in America. (b) Profit-minded business executives who admitted freely to the *Wall Street*

UNDERLYING THE DEBATE ARE CONCERNS THAT NAFTA WILL ENCOURAGE U.S. JOB FLIGHT TO MEXICO... HOWEVER, ECONOMISTS INSIST THAT THERE'S *NO CAUSE FOR ALARM*...

THAT'S *RIGHT!* HECK, WE MAY LOSE A FEW *MANUFACTURING* JOBS--BUT THERE'LL BE PLENTY OF GROWTH IN *HIGH TECH!*

HMM...SO THE UN-EMPLOYED *FACTORY WORKERS*...SIMPLY HAVE TO BECOME HIGHLY SKILLED *COMPUTER PROFESSIONALS*..?

UH...SOMETHING LIKE THAT...

IT IS A COMPLEX ISSUE, WITH WHICH SOCIETY MUST GRAPPLE...THOUGH AT THIS POINT, MANY AMERICANS ARE NOT ONLY *UNDECIDED* ABOUT NAFTA--THEY DON'T EVEN KNOW WHAT IT *IS*...

NAFTA? ISN'T THAT SOME KIND OF *DISEASE?*

NO--IT'S A NEW *RAP GROUP!*

I THOUGHT IT HAD SOMETHING TO DO WITH *FREE TRAINS!*

Journal their plans to move operations to Mexico. These same executives run corporations like DuPont, ranked toxic offender number one by the EPA; and General Electric, a notorious violator of worker rights in Mexico; and they crafted NAFTA with a single goal: global market domination, with no regard for communities, jobs, the environment, or democracy. As a result NAFTA contains many provisions for investment rights but few rights for citizens affected by the 'fruits' of free-trade.

"Many examples illustrate the dour effects of mainstream media's unprovocative, tired reporting. The most striking indictment is that NAFTA remains obscure in the public's mind: few know what N-A-F-T-A stands for, let alone what it stands to do....Reactions to NAFTA's passage ranged from 'I've seen it on TV and listened to them talk about it. But I'm not really aware of what it's about,' to 'Does it have something to do with Africa,' to 'I don't know anything about it and I've never heard of it,' the last being a candid admission by a university student.

"Moreover, Congressional integrity was compromised by the Administration's pro-NAFTA strong-arm tactics. The *Wall Street Journal* reported strategic meetings between the White House and pro-NAFTA corporations in the weeks preceding the House vote; these corporations were told to pressure, with the threat of withholding campaign contributions, undecided lawmakers into voting for NAFTA. Similarly, the Administration cut various deals to assure passage of NAFTA....

"In all cases, if the mass media had reported NAFTA's secrecy and resultant narrow agenda, thoughtful members of Congress would not have felt pressured to sign into law an agreement they know to be undemocratic; and their constituents would have balked."

Investigative author Don Hazen interviewed Chuck Lewis, executive director of the Center for Public Integrity, just prior to the release of the Center's study, "The Trading Game: Inside Lobbying for the North American Free Trade Agreement." The study was presented at a news conference in Washington, DC, on May 27, 1993.

While the study received limited print media coverage and some coverage on NPR and cable television (CNN, C-Span, and CNBC), Hazen speculated as to why it received no network television coverage.

"ABC, NBC and CBS all brought their cameras to the news conference but never aired anything. Apparently, the chief attorney for Mexico sent a letter raising questions about the Center's forthcoming study to ABC executives *prior to May 27th*, the date of the press conference.

"The networks snub of this extremely important and comprehensive study generated considerable speculation about what really happened. At this point, no one has the answers, but some possible related issues are: 1. In April, Capital Cities/ABC made an offer to buy a recently-privatized television network in Mexico, which would presumably require some sort of Mexican government approval. 2. CBS, through Chairman Lawrence Tisch's Loew's company, has financial ties to Mexico. 3. General Electric, which owns NBC and also has holding in Mexico, was one of the most aggressive pro-NAFTA companies.

"In a related event, Fox Television retained the Center as a paid consultant for a 'Front Page' segment on NAFTA lobbying, but after taped interviews were done in several cities, and the piece was produced, it never aired and no reason was given. Rupert Murdoch, who owns Fox, signed newspaper advertisements pushing for NAFTA in the days prior to the vote."

Finally, now that the dust has settled on NAFTA, the push is on for GATT. And, once again, as was the case with NAFTA, few in the public know what G-A-T-T stands for, let alone what it stands to do.

14

Public Relations: Legalized Manipulation and Deceit

Source:

COVERTACTION
Date: Spring 1993
Title: "Public Relationships: Hill & Knowlton, Robert Gray, and the CIA"
Author: Johan Carlisle

SYNOPSIS: Edmund Burke said there were Three Estates in Parliament; but, in the Reporters' Gallery yonder, there sat a Fourth Estate more important by far than them all. So it once may have been. Today it would appear that journalism and the reporters of the Fourth Estate have been replaced by the public relations flacks of Madison Avenue.

Few Americans have ever heard of Hill and Knowlton (H&K). Yet it is one of the world's most influential corporations with virtually unregulated status, long-standing connections to intelligence agencies, and the power to shape national, if not international, policy. But H&K is just the jewel on the gaudy crown of the propagandists. Altogether, in 1991, the top

50 U.S.-based PR firms charged more than $1,700,000,000 for manipulating public opinion.

As Johan Carlisle noted in *CovertAction*, "One of the most important ways public relations firms influence what we think is through the massive distribution of press releases to newspapers and TV newsrooms." A study by Scott M. Culip, ex-dean of the School of Journalism at the University of Georgia, revealed that 40 percent of the news content in a typical U.S. newspaper originated with public relations press releases, story memos, or suggestions.

An analysis of a typical issue of the *Wall Street Journal* by the *Columbia Journalism Review* once found that more than half the *Journal's* news stories "were based solely on press releases." And while the releases were reprinted "almost verbatim," many of the articles were given a *Wall Street Journal* staff reporter byline.

Hill & Knowlton's clients include Turkey, China, Peru, Israel, Egypt, and Indonesia, all well-known chronic human rights abusers. H&K's executives, such as former Vice President George Bush's Chief of Staff Craig Fuller, and Democratic power broker Frank Mankiewicz, have run campaigns against abortion for the Catholic Church; represented the Church of Scientology and the Moonies; made sure gasoline taxes were kept low for the American Petroleum Institute; handled the critics of Three Mile Island's near-catastrophe; and mishandled the apple growers' assertion that Alar was safe.

One of H&K's better known propaganda coups was on behalf of Kuwait. H&K was hired by Citizens for a Free Kuwait and eventually received nearly $10.8 million to conduct one of the largest and most effective public relations campaigns in history.

Perhaps its most stunning promotion was when it presented 15-year-old "Nayirah" before the House Human Rights Caucus to tearfully testify about Iraqi soldiers taking Kuwaiti babies out of incubators at the al-Addan hospital and leaving them on the cold floor to die. As it turned out, "Nayirah" was the daughter of Sheikh Saud Nasir al-Sabah, Kuwait's ambassador to the U.S. Her story, which was impossible to corroborate, was neatly orchestrated by H&K and coordinated with the White House on behalf of the government of Kuwait.

The problem did not end with the Reagan/Bush administrations. Ron Brown, who was a lobbyist and attorney for Haiti's "Baby Doc" Duvalier, is President Bill Clinton's Secretary of Commerce. Howard Paster, former head of H&K's Washington office, directed the confirmation process during the transition period and went on to become director of intergovernmental affairs for the White House. And after managing public relations for the Gulf War, H&K executive Lauri J. Fitz-Pegado became director of public liaison for the inauguration.

SSU Censored Researcher: Kristen Rutledge

COMMENTS: Johan Carlisle, a San Francisco-based investigative journalist, strongly believes that public relations firms and their ability to form public opinion have not received the coverage they deserve. "I don't think this subject, the incredible power of public relations companies to influence U.S. domestic and foreign policy, is dealt with at all in the mass media," Carlisle said.

"Since we supposedly live in a democracy, more information about how government policy is shaped and how public perceptions are manufactured would undoubtedly change the way the democratic process works. Public relations and lobbying, in particular, are two elements of our democracy that few citizens know much about. I asked an official at H&K why domestic lobbying and public relations are virtually unregulated. He said that would be a violation of free speech. I think the public has a right to know how these powerful companies affect our lives.

"The large transnational corporations that benefit from the militaristic foreign policy of the U.S. and from the widespread ignorance of Americans about what is really going on in this country and the world," are the primary beneficiaries of the limited coverage given this issue, according to Carlisle. He believes that public relations practitioners and lobbyists constitute the fifth branch of government—considering their influence and power.

Thousands of Cubans Losing Their Sight Because of Malnutrition

Sources:

PHILADELPHIA INQUIRER
Date: 4/16/93
Title: "Malnutrition in Cuba so severe, thousands are losing their sight"
Author: Lizette Alvarez

THE CUBA ADVOCATE
Date: May 1993
Title: "Dateline: Miami"
Authors: Jamie York and Emily Coffey

SAN FRANCISCO EXAMINER
Date: 11/4/93
Title: "Allies desert U.S. on Cuban
embargo"

SYNOPSIS: In mid-April, 1993, the Knight-Ridder News Service carried a lengthy article by journalist Lizette Alvarez that warned of a rare disease caused by malnutrition. The rare malnutritional ailment, called optic neuropathy, can lead to blindness.

Alvarez reported that after two years of severe food shortages, thousands of Cubans were going blind and that some 12,000 Cubans were treated for the ailment at hospitals and clinics in Havana during the last two months. On July 17th, the *Toronto Star* reported that some 45,000 Cubans had been affected by the epidemic of optical neuritis.

Cubans are losing their eyesight because of an almost total lack of meat, milk, cheese, and vegetables in their diet. A number of them also are suffering from beriberi, an illness related to Vitamin B1 deficiency that attacks muscles and nerves and can lead to paralysis.

Most Cubans can only afford the food they get from the government: one bread roll a day; ten ounces of beans a month; and six pounds of rice a month, for three people. Alvarez reported that when Cubans get hungry, they heat water and add sugar.

The article was an important one, well-researched and well-written, except for one critical oversight. The story did not mention one of the prime causes of malnutrition in Cuba—the U.S. economic blockade.

Jamie York and Emily Coffey, editors of *The Cuba Advocate*, in Boulder, Colorado, point out that the story accurately portrayed the scope of the crisis, but did not mention that the U.S. government was using food as a political weapon.

While the Cuban government confirms the epidemic, it says only a few thousand people have been affected and denies reports of widespread malnutrition. At the same time, it says excessive smoking and drinking—not just malnutrition— are to blame. U.S. doctors say smoking and drinking are not to blame— starvation is to blame. "It's an indication that these people are starving," said Matthew Kay, a neuro-ophthalmologist at Miami's Bascom Palmer Eye Institute.

A Havana doctor, who sees patients with neuropathy almost every day, said, "This is a big, big problem. Rice and beans just won't cut it. We are all petrified of going blind." Another Cuban doctor said that without the proper food and a steady supply of vitamins the crisis would become a plague.

The U.S. embargo, implemented in 1961, has already cost Cuba more than $37 billion in trade and investment; created fuel shortages that have slowed agricultural and industrial development; and now is causing tens of thousands of people to go blind. The United States stands nearly alone in world opinion on the Cuban embargo. On November 3, 1993, the United Nations General Assembly, in a non-binding but forceful resolution, repudiated the 33-year-old embargo and urged nations to ignore it. The vote in the General Assembly was 88-4, with 57 abstentions. The four nations voting against the resolution were the United States, Israel, Albania, and Paraguay.

Referring to the growing tragedy in Cuba, York and Coffey wondered, "How does the public learn about U.S. government policies if they are not mentioned by the media? What happened to the public's right to know?"

SSU Censored Researcher:
Kristen Rutledge

COMMENTS: Jamie York and Emily Coffey, co-editors of *The Cuba Advocate*, a monthly newsletter dedicated to providing "censored" news about Cuba, both feel that the mass media have failed to provide the U.S. public with an accurate, fair, and truthful account of life in Cuba and U.S.

policy on Cuba. "The Cuban Democracy Act of 1992 (The Torricelli Bill) is in effect preventing U.S. subsidiaries of foreign countries from around the world from trading with Cuba," Coffey said. "This turns the U.S. embargo into an economic blockade. Nothing is said in the media about the blockade preventing food and medicine from going to the Cuban people."

In response to who will benefit from better media coverage of the Cuban situation, Coffey said, "Everybody will. Most U.S. citizens do not realize that if we were free to travel to Cuba and trade with Cuba this would be good economics for both people. Cuba has 10 million people that would like to buy a lot of products from us."

York feels that the limited media "coverage of U.S. policy on Cuba benefits a handful of wealthy, influential Cuban-Americans who want the total capitulation of socialist Cuba to capitalism. This elite group has the most to gain by returning Havana to its former status as the gambling and prostitution playground of the Caribbean."

Both York and Coffey said there were a number of other stories that would contribute to public knowledge and understanding of U.S.-Cuba relations if they had not been censored by the media.

16 CENSORED

Tropical Rainforests— More Endangered Than Ever Before?

Sources:

Z MAGAZINE
Date: May 1993
Title: "Who is Destroying the Rainforests?"
Author: Susan Meeker-Lowry

GREEN MAGAZINE
Date: December 1992
Title: "The Drilling Fields"
Author: Damien Lewis

SYNOPSIS: The destruction of the world's rainforests has been one of the hottest topics in the past few years. Today, "Save the Rainforest" T-shirts, posters, calendars, and bags are seen everywhere; you'll find Rainforest Crisp Cereal and Rainforest Cashew Crunch Cookies in kitchen cupboards and Ben & Jerry's Rainforest Crunch Ice Cream in the freezer; it's truly a household word. Yet, in the face of this media blitz, in late September, 1993, an Associated Press wire story reported that satellite photos show the number of fires burning in Brazil's vast Amazon rain forests has increased by nearly 50 percent over the last year.

As author Susan Meeker-Lowry points out: "A major problem with our current understanding of the plight of rainforests and their inhabitants, like anything else that gets massive amounts of mainstream media attention, is the issue is oversimplified and presented in terms that fit our own experiences, rather than the experiences of the people actually affected. 'Solutions' such as debt-for-nature swaps, harvest projects, and eco-tourism often don't amount to more than putting a Band-Aid on a deeply infected wound."

Indeed, as industrialized nations become more concerned with protecting their own environment, oil companies are moving into deserts and rainforests in the Third World rather than accepting new environmental legislation. And, unfortunately, they're often welcome. In fact, Paul Horsman of Greenpeace points out that some countries have "drawn up new legislation to deregulate and de-legislate the oil sector, making oil exploration and production even more lucrative for foreign companies."

And who are the companies taking advantage of the Third World? In her article in Z *Magazine*, Meeker-Lowry names some 25 transnational corporations currently involved in various aspects of rainforest destruction.

Following are some of the U.S.-based spoilers:

- Georgia-Pacific: imported tropical hardwoods from Malaysia, the Philippines, and Indonesia;
- Alcoa: produced 1,722,000 metric tons of primary aluminum from South America, most of which came from rainforest areas;
- Amoco: exploring for oil in rainforests in the southeastern part of Colombia with Ecopetrol;
- Arco: contracted to develop nearly half a million acres of untouched rainforest for oil production in the Ecuadorian Amazon;
- Chevron: threatens forests with oil refinery at Lake Kutuba in the Southern Highlands of New Guinea;
- Exxon: exploring in Ecuador; exploring/producing in Colombia, Zaire, Indonesia, Malaysia;
- Maxus Energy: exploring/drilling Huaorani territory (Yasuni Park) in the Oriente;
- Mobil: exploring and drilling in the Oriente; drilling in the central rainforest in Santiago Basin, Peru;
- Occidental Petroleum: exploring for oil on both sides of the Rio Napo in Quichua territory in the Ecuadorian Oriente; ·
- Texaco: constructed the Trans-Ecuadorian Pipeline which spilled at least 16 million gallons of oil, mostly in the Oriente.

Meeker-Lowry also points out that the International Monetary Fund (IMF) and the World Bank play key roles in rainforest destruction.

SSU Censored Researcher: Laurie Turner

COMMENTS: Author Susan Meeker-Lowry said that despite the fact that the world's tropical rainforests have become a hot topic in the past few years, the mass media still do not tell us the extent of destruction that is continuing, and, more importantly, never give us the names of those responsible. Her story in Z *Magazine* did both.

Meeker-Lowry feels it is important for the public to know more about the ongoing destruction of the rainforests so that we understand the enormous impact we are having on the environment and indigenous peoples in the Third World.

Those who benefit from the limited coverage given the issue include timber, mining, and oil corporations as well as agribusiness and banking firms.

Meeker-Lowry says it's important to recognize specifically who is causing the problems and that we, as consumers, have to question the choices we make at the gas pump and elsewhere.

"Our major task lies in challenging not only the actual rainforest destroyers, but the underlying assumptions that give the destroyers license to destroy. These include belief in the necessity of unlimited economic growth, faith in the capitalist market, and the reduction of human activities and Earth's resources to purely economic terms and high-consumption lifestyles."

17 CENSORED

Clinton's Option 9 Plan: A Resounding Defeat for Ancient Forests

Sources:

LIES OF OUR TIMES
Date: November 1993
Title: "Ancient Forests Meet the Press"
Author: Jeffrey St. Clair

THE NATION
Date: 8/23/93
Title: "Munich in the Redwoods"
Author: Alexander Cockburn

SYNOPSIS: On July 1, in the wake of the forest summit held in Portland, Oregon on April 2, 1993, President Clinton announced his administration's plan for the ancient forests of the Pacific Northwest. The plan, known as Option 9, drew laudatory coverage from the mainstream media which heralded it as a victory for environmentalists. However, a close look at Option 9 reveals that it is a major defeat for environmentalists...and the ancient forests.

Immediately following the summit, a team of experts, headed by Forestry Service ecologist and ecosystems advocate Jack Ward Thomas, were given only two months by the Clinton administration to come up with a range of options for managing the Northwest forests in a way that would protect the spotted owl, the marbled murrelet, and salmon, "while also providing a steady flow to Northwest mills." The team met their June 2 deadline and presented the administration with eight options. All eight options called for significant reductions in timber sales. While Interior Secretary Bruce Babbitt earlier had promised loggers the administration would quickly release at least 2 billion board-feet of timber, most of the plans would have limited the cutting to 500 million board-feet annually.

This was simply unacceptable to the Clinton administration. Thomas was quickly replaced by Jerry Franklin of Washington University who put together Option 9 in less than three weeks.

The plan espouses the already discredited notion of a network of "riparian corridors" and old-growth reserves. A forest reserve is generally defined as an area where no logging is permitted. However, under Option 9, the system of reserves are considered to be neither inviolate nor permanent. Every reserve would be open to thinning operations and timber salvage sales.

Less than five percent of the original old growth forest still exists, located mainly in national forests and on public land. (The Mt. Hood National Forest in Oregon has been cut more heavily than the Brazilian rainforest). Nonetheless, under Option 9, "At least 40 percent of the remaining old-growth would be subject to clearcutting." And the remaining 60 percent isn't considered inviolate! These lands provide habitat for thousands of plant and animal species. Option 9 threatens over 100 of these species, which depend on the old growth forests, with eventual extinction.

According to Jeffrey St. Clair, editor of *ForestWatch* magazine, two million acres of Northwest forests are essentially wild roadless areas which are "vital repositories of biological diversity," critical to the survival of many species. Under Option 9, St. Clair said, these areas receive no special attention; "Clearcutting would continue even in the most ecologically sensitive roadless areas." Option 9 also proposes to exempt private landowners from the Endangered Species Act, allowing them to clearcut spotted owl and murrelet habitat.

Clinton's announcement of Option 9 came before the study itself was even released. St. Clair reported that the vast majority of news stories "were filed before reporters had actually seen the 1,800-page plan." Most of the stories, which the American public read, were based on a vague nine-page White House press release. Furthermore, the administration ordered its scientists to circumvent the Freedom of Information Act; and all background documents, relating to the development of Option 9 and detailing the extent of political pressure, were either shredded or sealed.

SSU Censored Researcher:
Sunil Sharma

COMMENTS: Jeffrey St. Clair, investigative author and editor of *ForestWatch* magazine, charged that President Clinton's new Option 9 forest plan "received lots of hype and initial exposure, but little analysis and almost no follow-up. The analysis that was published was either superficial, politically biased, and/or flat-out wrong."

St. Clair feels it was important for the public to know more about this issue: "The President's forest plan was the Clinton administration's first major policy decision on an environmental issue. The tactics of the administration on this issue revealed much about how they would treat other issues, like wetlands, public land grazing, the Endangered Species Act, and Clean Water Act."

According to St. Clair, the interests being served by the limited coverage given the Option 9 forest plan include the Clinton administration, labor, timber interests, and Japanese timber importers.

St. Clair said that *The Nation, High Country News*, and *Lies Of Our Times* continue to be the only publications to pursue in-depth political reporting and investigation into this issue. Other articles he has written on the subject have been rejected by the mainstream media.

Meanwhile, the Option 9 plan, so widely-touted by the mainstream media as the solution to the logging vs. environmentalist controversy in mid-1993 appeared to be unraveling by the end of the year.

On November 26, *USA Today* reported that the plan was "fraying at both ends." Environmentalists claim the plan breaks the law because it doesn't protect Northern spotted owls and 400 other species dependent on ancient forests. Timber and paper companies claim the plan is economically damaging, unscientific, and will result in dangerous wildfires in the region. And by December 11, the *Los Angeles Times* was reporting

that a new Clinton proposal to relax logging requirements on private lands in the Northwest had renewed the controversy over the spotted owl.

Ironically, as 1993 drew to a close, the Clinton administration turned to the person whose original eight proposals had been rejected. Jack Ward Thomas, the career Forest Service wildlife biologist from LaGrande, Oregon, was named the new chief of the U.S. Forest Service in an apparent effort to restore the reputation of the agency.

The Silent Slaughter in Bangladesh

Sources:

SURVIVAL INTERNATIONAL
Date: 4/5/93
Title: "Anniversary vigil to remember massacre of Bangladeshi hill tribes"
Author: Charlotte Sankey

THE GUARDIAN
Date: 5/8/92
Title: "Massacres in Bangladesh"
Author: Robin Hanbury-Tenison
Date: 5/24/92
Title: "Murder among the Hill People"
Author: Aditi Sharma

SYNOPSIS: One of the most horrifying acts of mass murder in recent years continues to go unreported in the U.S. and international press. On April 10, 1992, an estimated 1,200 tribal men, women, and children were massacred in Logang village, Bangladesh. All 1,200 victims were Jummas, the tribal peoples of the Chittagong Hill Tracts.

The massacre occurred after a group of boys from a village of Bengali settlers near Logang village attacked two Chittagong Hill Tract girls in an attempt to rape them. A boy was wounded when one of the girls defended herself with a knife. The other boys fled the scene and "reported the incident to their village." Within moments of the incident, a group of Bengalis, Bangladeshi soldiers, and paramilitary troops converged upon Logang village. Almost all of the tribal people were herded and locked into their homes and the houses were set ablaze. According to eyewitnesses, the bodies of the victims, some still alive, were then dumped into open pits.

The massacre of the predominantly Buddhist tribal people occurred a couple of days before the annual Chittagong Hill Tract festival in Biju. A number of lawyers, university professors, members of parliament, as well as a large number of friends and relatives of the tribal people happened to be in the Tract area. This group of people formed a commission to investigate the incident and to record evidence from the survivors. Had it not been for the fact that these people were in the area for the festival, the massacre would probably have gone totally unnoticed. The Chittagong Hill Tract area has been sealed off by the Bangladesh military for 15 years.

Despite the findings of the commission, the government only admitted that 13 people were killed, while the military conceded 140 deaths. Bangladesh, a country very dependent on foreign aid, did not want to draw attention to the tragedy.

According to human rights groups such as Survival International and Amnesty International, the April 10th Massacre, though unprecedented in scale, is not an isolated incident. Survival International reports that the Massacre "is part of the Bangladeshi government's attempt to wipe out the hill tribes altogether, who are mostly Buddhist." The organization also reported that for the last 20 years, "murder, rape, and torture are almost everyday events." The government offers the Buddhist hill tribes "the choice of conversion to Islam, death or exile."

Despite its abysmal human rights record, Bangladesh continues to receive Western aid. Twelve days after the Massacre, the World Bank, after consulting Western donor nations, approved a (US) $1.9 billion aid package to Bangladesh. In 1992, the U.S. provided Bangladesh with $136 million in grants via USAID and the Food for Peace program.

Charlotte Sankey, press officer for Survival International, charged, "It is appalling that the international media keep their eyes closed to the systematic destruction of the Jummas in the same way that it ignored the situation in East Timor—until a foreign journalist was killed among 180 other protesters."

SSU Censored Researcher: Sunil Sharma

COMMENTS: The press office of Survival International, in London, said that even now very few people know what is happening in Bangladesh and they need to be informed. "Doesn't the public have a right to know that 1,200 people were massacred?"

Survival International noted that it holds a vigil outside the Bangladesh High Commission in London every month and that the vigil will continue until the Bangladesh government stops its present policy toward tribal peoples.

19 CENSORED

Big Business Corrupts The Judicial System by "Buying a Clean Record"

Source:

MULTINATIONAL MONITOR
Date: July/August 1993
Title: "Justice for Sale"
Author: Holley Knaus

SYNOPSIS: While big corporations have, for years, pressured all areas of government to limit the corporate sector's level of responsibility for wrongdoing, they have developed a new practice that goes beyond simply stalling the legal process. Rather than denying the plaintiff an opportunity to be heard in court by costly long delays and pre-trial bluster, corporations are now using the dubious legal process of *vacatur*.

The *vacatur* process not only allows corporations to appear squeaky clean but more seriously undermines the fundamental issue of precedential law. Despite the significant impact that a *vacatur* ruling can have, the process seems remarkably simple. According to an editorial in *Multinational Monitor*,

"Justice for Sale," it is a little-publicized but growing phenomenon in corporate lawsuits.

Basically the *vacatur* process allows a corporation found guilty in a lower court action to make a settlement with the plaintiff so that the case will not be appealed to a higher court. Both plaintiff and defendant request that the presiding appeals judge "vacate" the decision and strike the previous finding from the record, ultimately eliminating the precedential value of the ruling.

A May 1992 settlement between U.S. Philips, a manufacturer of rotary electric shavers, and Windmere, a U.S. distributor for the Japanese firm Izumi, also a manufacturer of rotary shavers, illustrates how easy it is for powerful business groups to corrupt the judicial system. Locked in a battle over patent infringement and anti-trust violations, the court awarded Philips $6,500 in damages for the patent complaint. However, in a counter-suit charging anti-trust violations, a jury found in Windmere's favor and awarded Windmere $89 million on the antitrust claim. Faced with an appeal that might confirm Philips' wrongdoing, Philips struck a deal with Windmere.

The deal was for Philips to give Windmere an additional $57 million—on one condition: Windmere was required to join with Philips in requesting a federal appeals court to vacate the lower court jury's verdict. Philips' motivation was made clear in the agreement which said, "Windmere's anti-trust claim will be of no force and effect and shall have no precedential or other value."

Not satisfied that Philips was able to buy a clean record, Izumi filed suit in the Supreme Court raising the issue of whether a corporation can justifiably erase wrongdoing by simply paying off the plaintiff. Supporting Izumi's application for review of the decision to grant *vacatur*, the Washington, D.C.-based Trial Lawyers for Public Justice (TLPJ) has clearly outlined areas of real concern.

The *amicus curiae* filed by TLPJ notes that the granting of *vacatur* undermines the legal process, "It reduces respect for the judiciary by permitting a judicial decision to be bought and sold." The brief notes that the process favors wealthy corporate interests, particularly those that often land in court. "Certain types of litigation, including products liability, illegal toxic dumping cases, and employment discrimination claims, frequently pit an individual plaintiff with limited litigation experience...against an institutional defendant with repeated exposure to the litigation process. The defendants in these cases have both the reason and the resources to 'roll the dice' and then, if the gamble fails to pay off, to buy out unfavorable decisions. The plaintiffs do not."

SSU Censored Researcher:
Gerald Austin

COMMENTS: Holley Knaus, author of the *Multinational Monitor* editorial, said the issue of corporate manipulation of the judicial system does not receive the media exposure it deserves. "I learned about the subject from a very good article that ran in the *Legal Times*," Knaus said, "but I am unaware of any other coverage in the mainstream media.

"Part of the problem is that the large papers and the networks tend to cover 'events' rather than exposing and examining on-going institutional problems. And I suppose a challenge to a legal process (even before the Supreme Court) does not qualify as an event in the minds of the corporate media shapers."

Given that corporations are using the *vacatur* process to erase prior offenses and shape U.S. case law, Knaus feels that the "general public needs to know about a process that is undermining the public value of court decisions and rulings." She assumes that most of the public would agree that corporations have no place in shaping the law in any manner.

"Corporations are the only ones benefiting from the limited cov-

erage given this issue," Knaus said. "As with so many other issues, corporations are benefiting not from any active form of information suppression, but from mass media's failures to point out and analyze systemic problems."

Anti-Defamation League of B'nai B'rith—An Oxymoron?

Sources:

SAN FRANCISCO BAY
    GUARDIAN
Date: 4/14/93
Title: "Reports show ADL/SFPD spy net reach"
Author: Tim Redmond

Date: 9/29/93
Title: "ADL Deal Dies"
Author: Jane Hunter

LIES OF OUR TIMES
Date: July/August 1993
Title: "The ADL and Civil Liberties"
Author: Mitchell Kaidy

SAN FRANCISCO EXAMINER
Date: 10/7/93
Title: "Judge rules ADL need not open its files in civil suit"

Authors: Dennis J. Opatrny and Scott Winokur

Y'ACOV AHIMEIR
Date: 10/25/93
Interview at Sonoma State University

SYNOPSIS: The Anti-Defamation League of B'nai B'rith (ADL), established eight decades ago to combat anti-Semitism, has itself been charged with civil rights violations, involving domestic spying on a massive scale. With the help of a San Francisco police intelligence officer and at least one undercover operative, the ADL collected secret files on some 1,000 political organizations and 12,000 individuals, many in the San Francisco Bay Area.

The ADL-targeted groups allegedly were as diverse as Greenpeace, the Ku Klux Klan, the American-Arab Anti-Discrimination Committee, the Aryan Nation, the ACLU, the American Indian Movement, the American Nazi Party, the National Lawyers Guild, ACT-UP, the NAACP, the United Auto Workers, the African National Congress, and Project Censored.

Documents seized by the District Attorney's office in a raid on the San Francisco ADL office reportedly revealed that the ADL had run a systematic, long-term, private nationwide spy network with the help of Roy Edward Bullock, a San Francisco art dealer, and Tom Gerard, a one-time CIA agent in Latin America who had earlier worked as an intelligence officer for the San Francisco Police Department (SFPD).

The documents also suggested that Bullock and Gerard were working as paid informants not only for the Anti-Defamation League but also for the South African government—and that information was shared with South Africa as well as Israel.

While this extraordinary story received some major coverage in West Coast papers, including the *Los Angeles Times* and the *San Francisco Examiner*, it was basically ignored by the mainstream national press and, according to journalist Mitchell Kaidy, writing in *Lies Of Our Times* (LOOT), it received little scrutiny in *The New York Times*.

In fact, Kaidy wrote, "When *The New York Times* reported the issue on April 25, it ran an unsigned Sunday article innocuously headlined 'A Dealer in Art and, Some Say, a Dealer in Secret Police Data?' (p. 38). The article conspicuously failed to mention ADL's links to the State Department, CIA, and FBI, or to indicate the extensive range of the groups it targeted. Both Israel and South Africa allegedly benefited from the information ADL furnished, yet the *Times* downplayed 'one foreign government' while mentioning South Africa several times as a beneficiary."

Further, in a follow-up article in May, LOOT noted that *The New York Times* "inexplicably failed to exploit a local angle—that, according to authorities in San Francisco, where the scandal erupted, the underground operation was financed and directed by the ADL in New York for more than three decades. The *Times* ignored this, instead devoting its space to the justifications of ADL officials."

Ironically, the ADL spy-ring story also appeared to be ignored by the press in Israel. Y'acov Ahimeir, one of the first broadcasters with Israeli TV and former chief editor and anchorman of Israeli TV News, was unaware of the issue until he visited the United States in October 1993. Ahimeir, now a news talk show host with Israeli TV, told Project Censored he had not seen the issue reported in Israel.

SSU Censored Researcher:
Laurie Turner

COMMENTS: Several sources, from diverse publications, provided background for this nomination; following are some of their individual comments:

Tim Redmond, of the *San Francisco Bay Guardian*, felt that one aspect of the story that deserved more coverage was how the S.F. Police Department was involved in an extensive spy network reaching to South Africa and Central America and that the SFPD policies that allowed this to happen are still in place now. Redmond added that although he "broke this piece of the story, other *Bay Guardian* reporters, especially Jane Hunter, have also played a key role in keeping the story alive and deserve credit for their work. Martin Espinoza, who helped me research the story, also deserves credit." Redmond also acknowledged the role of the *Bay Guardian* as a whole in getting the story out.

Mitchell Kaidy, author of the article in *Lies Of Our Times*, said he was motivated to report the story because of the "deficiencies left by the mainstream media." Kaidy felt it was important for the public to know more about the story since it revealed how Americans, exercising their Constitutional right to dissent, became targets of covert-monitoring as well as infiltration." Noting that this is an on-going story with both national and international implications, Kaidy added, "Ironically, although several journalists and many newspaper letter writers were allegedly spied on, I know of no mainline newspapers, weeklies, wire services or journalism publications which have fully investigated the matter. And the only publications that evince continued interest are of limited circulation."

Dennis J. Opatrny and Scott Winokur covered the issue throughout the year for the *San Francisco Examiner*. Opatrny said he did not believe that the ongoing story had received sufficient exposure since it originally broke. Noting that while ABC did a piece early on and NBC did a newsmagazine piece later, "Only the *Washington Post*, 10 months after the story broke, finally did a main story with sidebars. The so-called Voice of the West, aka the San Francisco Comical, has been strangely silent for the most part, occasionally taking a nibble but never a bite of the story."

Opatrny, who also was speaking for Winokur, said the "general public would benefit with wider exposure of a domestic spying story by simply being made aware that there are groups, perhaps with good intentions, some with evil motives, watching, monitoring and spying on Americans exercising their constitutionally guaranteed civil rights and protected political rights. The Anti-Defamation League of the B'nai B'rith benefits from the limited coverage, as would any so-called fact-finding organization with a shining reputation for doing good that is suddenly under investigation for criminal activity. The ADL's stated purpose as a watchtower for anti-Semitism is admirable, but its tactics are questionable at best, perhaps illegal at worst."

Since all the authors agree that the story is not over yet, the mainstream media will have another chance to put it on the national agenda in 1994.

21 CENSORED

EPA Ignores Its Own Toxic Experience

Sources:

IN THESE TIMES
Date: 7/26/93
Title: "Deep Pile of Trouble"
Author: Aushra Abouzeid

PUBLIC CITIZEN HEALTH RESEARCH GROUP HEALTH LETTER
Date: March 1993
Title: "Carpet Chemicals May Pose Serious Health Risks"

SYNOPSIS: For a number of years, the carpet industry and the Environmental Protection Agency (EPA) have received complaints about health problems associated with new carpets. The health problems include nausea, headaches, and respiratory ailments. Despite tests performed by private laboratories *and the EPA itself*, which indicate a link between chemicals found in new carpeting and health problems, the EPA still sends out brochures that say carpeting poses no risks to the health of consumers. But the EPA notes that more research is needed.

It is difficult to understand the EPA's stonewalling, considering its own experience five years ago. According to the *Health Letter*, "In 1988, the agency installed 27,000 square yards of new carpeting in its own headquarters in Washington, DC. Shortly thereafter, the EPA's union received 1,000 complaints from the agency's own workers that the carpeting was damaging their health. To protect government employees, the EPA ripped out all of the new carpet. Since then... there have been 'no carpet-related complaints' from EPA workers."

Lab mice have been killed in tests which consisted simply of blowing air over the top of suspect carpet samples. This test has been completed by private labs, the Carpet & Rug Institute, and the EPA itself, all with the same results. If the mice didn't die within 24 hours, they suffered serious neurological disorders. Critics say that while more tests are needed to pinpoint the exact chemical(s) responsible, the EPA clearly has enough evidence to warn consumers and to enforce some form of regulation on the carpet industry. Nonetheless, the EPA continues to resist taking action and simply reiterates that more research is needed.

Representative Bernard Sanders (I-VT), has been pushing the EPA to take the necessary steps to finish the research and begin regulating. Senator Patrick Leahy (D-VT), also has been pushing the EPA for a response after numerous complaints from his constituents. In one case, a high school in Montpelier, Vermont, had new carpeting installed which created symptoms of nausea and eye and throat irritation. In response to a complaint by the school, the EPA sent "a voluminous pre-print copy of a manual on building air quality for building owners and facility managers."

And, of course, people from Vermont are not the only ones reporting toxic experiences with new carpeting. Across the country, so many have complained that 26 state attorneys general have petitioned the Consumer Product Safety Commission (CPSC) of the federal government to require warning labels on some carpets, and to set up a hotline to handle consumer complaints. However, the CPSC, like the EPA, does not feel there is enough evidence to require warning labels and doesn't feel that a hotline is needed either.

SSU Censored Researcher:
Tim Gordon

COMMENTS: Miles Harvey, managing editor of *In These Times* (ITT), responded to Project Censored's request on behalf of Aushra Abouzeid, author of "Deep Pile of Trouble," who was on assignment in Russia. Harvey said that, as far as he knew, there had been very little mass media coverage given to the dangers posed by carpets. In fact, he added, "The mainstream media still tend to treat people who complain about illnesses caused by their home or workplace environments as kooks or hypochondriacs."

In These Times received letters from its readers asking what prompted ITT to run a story about something as silly as carpets. "People seem to believe that toxic pollution only comes in leaky drums," Harvey said. "But the story shows that carpets can emit human carcinogens directly into a home. Consumers also need to know that the carpets bearing the 'Green Seal' for safety are not necessarily free of toxic chemicals. Our story points out that the Green Seal is an industry creation that falsely implies that a carpet will have no adverse effect on air quality."

Harvey noted that the carpet industry clearly benefits from the limited coverage given the issue and added, "the media also need to give the chemical industry much closer scrutiny. Chemical companies are big broadcast and print advertisers, but much of what they do—from producing dangerous and often unnecessary compounds, such as organochlorines, to mis-leading the public about the dangers of products—goes largely unreported. The media need to start looking at all aspects of the industrial process, from manufacture to disposal, in its environmental reporting."

In March 1993, the Public Citizen's Health Research Group *Health Letter* noted that the Carpet & Rug Institute had implemented a "green tag" labeling program to assure consumers that a carpet is safe to buy. It also reported that critics called the program "a smoke screen...a sham...a joke"...a program "based on false premises."

Interestingly enough, on December 1, 1993, David Moore, a staff writer for the *San Francisco Chronicle*, reported that "Under a new program launched by the carpet industry last month, most carpets manufactured after Jan. 1, 1994, will include a green information label indicating that samples of the carpet have been tested and have met criteria for limiting chemical emissions." Should consumers want to know more, the *Chronicle* story suggested they write the Carpet & Rug Institute. (The article read like a press release from the Institute.)

On the other hand, the *Health Letter* suggested that consumers with complaints should call the Consumer Product Safety Commission at 1/800/638-2772.

22 |CENSORED|

Stinger Missiles Sting Taxpayers Twice

Sources:

CHICAGO TRIBUNE
Date: 12/6/92
Title: "CIA stung in Afghan missile deal"
Author: Uli Schmetzer

SANTA ROSA (CA) PRESS DEMOCRAT NEWS SERVICES
Date: 7/24/93
Title: "U.S. outbid for Stingers"

SYNOPSIS: Now that the Cold War is over, the Central Intelligence Agency (CIA) is desperately trying to buy back hundreds of the surface-to-air Stinger missiles that it secretly gave Afghan guerrillas only a few years ago.

The Stinger missile, a shoulder-fired, heat-seeking missile, is small enough to fit in the trunk of a car but lethal enough to bring down an airliner. The missiles can travel at 1,200 m.p.h. and while they can shoot down an airliner at an altitude up to 15,000 feet, they are considered deadly accurate against aircraft in the landing or take-off mode.

Originally, the missiles were given to the guerrillas to help defeat the Soviet troops in Afghanistan. They were handed out to Afghanistan's anti-Soviet insurgents in August 1986 in a covert operation run by the CIA. Flown in on special CIA planes, the missiles were distributed among the guerrilla factions by Pakistan's Inter-Service Intelligence.

Investigative journalist Uli Schmetzer reported in December 1992 that the CIA, Pakistani Intelligence services, and Western military attachés have collaborated in Operation MIAS (Missing-In-Action Stingers) for more than two years trying to "pry the missiles from Afghan hands and stop them from being sold to terrorist and separatist groups."

While U.S. diplomats refused to comment, intelligence sources said the CIA's success rate in repatriating the missiles was not good. When Schmetzer wrote his piece last December, the CIA reportedly was offering as much as $70,000 for a missile with an original cost of $20,000.

In July 1993, the CIA requested $55 million to buy back the Stinger anti-aircraft missiles. This extraordinary sum, more than five times the last allocation for the covert Stinger buyback program, was needed because of the fierce competition for the prized missiles on the international black market, according to knowledgeable sources.

Officials reported that U.S. agents were being outbid for the missiles that now fetch upward of $100,000 a piece on the black market.

Somewhat ironically, the best barrier against the Stingers falling into the wrong hands seems to be the reported "childlike attachment" local commanders have to them. They are status symbols and military toys of choice; commanders lose prestige when they sell them for money, said Abdul Haq, commander of a once-powerful guerrilla faction in Afghanistan.

Nonetheless, Haq reported that 24 Stingers already had fallen into the hands of Iran from pro-Iranian mujahedeen factions.

One European military attaché reported that every Western intelligence service is trying to help the Americans retrieve the missiles "because all our governments are dead scared one of those things is going to end up in the wrong hands."

SSU Censored Researcher:
Paul Chambers

COMMENTS: By November 21, 1993, the Stinger scandal had started to receive more coverage as the Associated Press reported that "more than 50,000 of the 4-foot-plus missiles have been produced for the U.S. armed forces and 16 other governments."

While the article noted that the missiles are kept under tight security, it confirmed that "hundreds of other Stingers, shipped by the CIA to anti-Communist rebels in Afghanistan and Angola, are believed to be feeding a multimillion-dollar black market." It noted that the going market for Stingers in the Pakistani arms markets is now more than $200,000, substantially more than the CIA reportedly had been offering.

It also said that the Stingers are now believed to be deployed in at least five of the world's small wars, including Somalia, and may have brought down aircraft in each.

Uli Schmetzer, journalist with the *Chicago Tribune* and author of the original Stinger source story, was on assignment in China and unavailable to respond to our query.

23 CENSORED

The Biggest Drug Bust of All

Sources:

USA TODAY
Date: 10/11/93
Title: "Studies find drug program not effective"
Author: Dennis Cauchon

PREVENTION FILE

Date: Fall 1993

Title: "Schools and Prevention: What's the Right Mix?"

Author: University of California at San Diego Extension

SYNOPSIS: In 1983, Daryl Gates, then Los Angeles police chief, created DARE—Drug Abuse Resistance Education—to fight drug abuse in American schools. The program and its catchy slogan—"DARE To Keep Kids Off Drugs"—exploded nationally, and internationally, after the Bush administration gave it heavy federal subsidies.

Today DARE is the nation's leading drug education program, reaching five million fifth-graders in 60 percent of school districts. It's in all 50 states and several foreign countries, including Australia, Mexico, Norway, Sweden, and Canada. It's on bumper stickers, T-shirts, KFC boxes; its national ambassador is Arsenio Hall and junkbond king Michael Milken is doing his community service for securities fraud at a DARE program; it's a favorite of dozens of members of Congress and an always popular subject of the news media. Taxpayers, police, and businesses give it $700 million a year to operate.

It's a drug-fighting miracle... except for one thing—it just doesn't work. And DARE's biggest supporter, law enforcement, has known that for at least six years. Since 1987, studies conducted at more than 100 schools in the U.S. and Canada have produced the same results: "[There were] no statistically significant differences between experimental groups and control groups in the percentage of new users of...cigarettes, smokeless tobacco, alcohol, marijuana." A Canadian government study found that "DARE had no significant effect on the students' use of any of the substances measured." The study tested for substances including tobacco, beer, soda, marijuana, acid, Valium, wine, aspirin, uppers, downers, heroin, crack, cocaine, liquor, candy, glue, and PCP.

Gilbert Botvin, of the Institute for Prevention at Cornell University Medical Center, flatly stated, "It's well-established that DARE doesn't work." A national conference on schools and drug prevention, held at UC-San Diego, in March 1993, concluded: "A review of a number of DARE evaluations has found that the program had little or no effect on the use of drugs by students." An analysis of eight validated studies found that DARE had a substantial effect on knowledge about drugs, a modest effect on social skills, and a more limited effect on self-esteem and children's attitudes toward law enforcement. But, the analysis concluded,

DARE's affect on students' actual drug-use was "limited to essentially nonexistent."

William Hansen, of the Wake Forest University Medical School in Winston Salem, NC, helped design the original DARE program in 1983. Hansen told the group, "I think the program should be entirely scrapped and redeveloped anew." The conference also found: "Publishing and marketing anti-drug curriculum materials have become big business, and some of the best-selling programs have turned out to have the least impressive results when their outcomes are given an objective evaluation."

Nonetheless, DARE continues to have high-level support; on September 9—National DARE Day (by congressional decree)—DARE officials and students met with dozens of Congress members, Attorney General Janet Reno, and First Lady Hillary Rodham Clinton.

Given the consistent negative results of all the studies, it is time for a major reappraisal of the DARE program and a possible redirection of the hundreds of millions of dollars being spent on it.

SSU Censored Researcher:
Katie Maloney

COMMENTS: Not surprisingly, Dennis Cauchon's article on DARE generated some heated denials that the program was failing. Gilbert

Botvin said he was surprised to see himself quoted in the *USA Today* story since he had not done any research or written any reports on DARE. However, Cauchon told Project Censored that his story continues to hold up. "It was well-documented," Cauchon said, "and all the data were taken from reliable studies."

However, Cauchon went on to say that there was another story he felt was very important and even more neglected. It has two parts:

"1) The U.S. is now implementing a policy of mass imprisonment, although it is never described this way. Historically, the U.S. incarceration rate has been about one per 300 adults. But since 1980, the number of prisoners has swelled, because of the drug war, from 500,000 to 1.4 million, pushing the incarceration rate to nearly one per 100 adults. This macro issue of how much of society ought we to imprison is *never* discussed.

"2) The drug war and changes in the criminal justice system (over the last 13 years) have reversed fundamental and longstanding rights and procedures that protected people against government power. The result has been an increase in the application of police power against the powerless, especially minorities, the poor, etc. The truth is in the details. The particulars of the war on drugs and the "get tough" on crime effort are seldom written about in newspapers. (Actually, many major metros do excellent stuff; it's just *The New York Times* and *Washington Post* that never do anything.)...Police have been given a broad license to exercise power in the last 10 years, a massive amount of new funds, the right to seize property and keep it for police use, etc., and all these issues are playing out on the street every day. Yet they are never covered."

Setting the Fox to Guard the Chickens in the 90s

Source:

THIS WORLD, SAN FRANCISCO CHRONICLE
(reprinted from *The Recorder*, 8/11/93)
Date: 9/19/93
Title: "Fishy Deals"
Author: Todd Woody

SYNOPSIS: If California is a national trendsetter, as is often said, the rest of the nation had better become aware of the latest environmental trend underway there.

With Governor Pete Wilson's strong support, the California Department of Fish and Game has decided that it can best protect endangered wildlife by turning them over to commercial interests. This privatization of the Department's traditional watchdog role has essentially defanged it.

In brief, California has adopted a new environmental policy where it has turned over the responsibility for protecting endangered species to private corporations and developer-friendly local governments.

One example involves ARCO, the oil company that owns or leases about 500,000 acres stretching from Santa Barbara to the Central Valley. As environmental reporter Todd Woody points out, "Not only is the land a prime oil and gas production area, it is home to more than two dozen rare and endangered species."

Environmental laws normally require a company to obtain permits each time it plans to disturb a protected plant or animal. But under the new program, that is no longer necessary. The solution devised by ARCO and the state agency calls for the company to dedicate 6,000 acres of its land as a preserve to compensate for any habitat lost through oil and gas operations.

But then, in an unprecedented move, the Department of Fish and Game made ARCO a game warden, transferring day-to-day responsibility for protecting any imperiled wildlife to the company. According to the agreement, ARCO can be removed as manager of the preserve only for gross negligence.

Further, ARCO can sell "mitigation credits" to other companies that want to use the preserve to replace habitat they've destroyed elsewhere and, in fact, has already sold some 700 acres worth of credits to three energy companies.

Some department lawyers and biologists have attacked the agreement. One Fish and Game staff attorney wrote that he had "substantial problems" with ARCO's proposal to manage the preserve itself, noting that Fish and Game could not legally delegate that responsibility to others when it could perform such duties itself.

Outraged environmentalists criticized Fish and Game for permitting ARCO to continue existing oil and gas operations on the preserve and to lease land to other companies. According to the agreement, "The department acknowledged that oil spills and leaks might result in the death—called 'take'—of the very wildlife the preserve was meant to protect."

Another case involved the endangered species laws protecting the imperiled Swainson's hawk. While developers usually must acquire land to replace habitat they destroy, and endow a trust fund for its upkeep, Fish and Game eliminated that requirement for the Dana Corp. It allowed the company to build its plant on the hawk's home in exchange for a one-time, no-strings-attached payment of $46,299. State officials acknowledge that no new habitat has been dedicated nor is there a deadline to do so. Environmentalists called this deal "cash for critters."

SSU Censored Researcher:
Tim Gordon

COMMENTS: Todd Woody is an environmental reporter for *The Recorder*, a daily legal newspaper based in San Francisco. Woody said that "Mainly because of Interior Secretary Bruce Babbitt's embrace of the concept, *The New York Times* and other major media have covered the broad strokes of Governor Pete Wilson's biodiversity approach to saving species while permitting development. Although the *Los Angeles Times* has done more than other major media, scant attention has been paid to the individual deals brokered under this scheme and the subsequent winners and losers.

"For instance, when the state took the unprecedented step of turning over primary responsibility for protecting species on a Central California wildlife preserve to an oil company, only the local media ran stories. And few, if any, mentioned the fact that ARCO Corp. not only would act as game warden but would be allowed to continue drilling for oil and gas on the preserve.

"Similarly, while a few outlets noted the agreement that allowed a truck manufacturer to build a factory on the habitat of an imperiled hawk—focusing on the jobs created—none reported the 'cash for critters' component of the deal or the fact that the state was allowing the hawk's home to be destroyed without a deadline for acquiring replacement habitat.

"And the political machinations in the California Fish and Game Department have received little coverage by the networks or papers."

Woody feels that the public needs to know what is happening so that it can better judge whether these deals truly will help preserve the fragile ecosystems while allowing economic development. And he warns of the national implications of this effort. "Given the fact that Babbitt has hailed this approach as a national model and has applied it elsewhere, it's crucial that the public know the behind-the-scenes politics of this concept—at least as practiced in California."

According to Woody, one of the people benefiting from the limited coverage of this issue is Pete Wilson. "As the (California) election year approaches, Pete Wilson

has been able to portray himself as a 'green governor' who has helped solve some of the more intractable environmental problems facing California. While his approach is indeed innovative, Wilson also has been able to reward some of his top campaign contributors and supporters—including Southern California developers, agribusiness, and oil companies. These interests in turn can also assume the mantle of environmental sensitivity without disclosing the economic and political benefits they reap."

25 | CENSORED

EPA Fiddles While Illegal Incinerator Pollutes Ohio

Sources:

THE NATION
Date: 9/27/93
Title: "E.P.A. Fiddles While W.T.I. Burns"
Author: Liane Clorfene-Casten

SYNOPSIS: On the banks of the Ohio River, near the town of East Liverpool, Ohio, there sits a hazardous waste incinerator—one of the largest of its kind in the country. It illegally burns unidentified wastes in violation of countless Environmental Protection Agency (EPA) regulations, in spite of campaign promises by Bill Clinton and Al Gore to block its operation. The incinerator also operates against the advice of the Ohio Department of Natural Resources because it is located within a few hundred feet of private homes, in an area with flood hazards and air inversions that prevent pollutants from escaping.

The $160 million incinerator operates in defiance of opposition from scientists, environmentalists, government experts and local activists. Additionally, it has failed to pass three trial burns which have indicated that it releases dioxins at two to five times the legal levels. Why, one might reasonably ask, is it there?

Senator Howard Metzenbaum (D-OH) is convinced it is there because of deals made between EPA officials and the company that runs it—Waste Technologies Industries (WTI). Writing in *The Nation*, investigative journalist Liane Clorfene-Casten provides evidence that the incinerator's "charmed regulatory life" is a product of political favoritism, lax and even illegal regulatory activity, and highly questionable courtroom proceedings.

Example: Financier Jackson Stephens, chairman of Stephens Inc., one of the nation's largest investment banking companies, based in Little Rock, Arkansas, founded WTI in 1980. In 1988, he gave $100,000 to the Republican Party and hosted an inaugural bash for President George Bush. Four years later he raised $100,000 for Bill Clinton and extended a $3.5 million line of credit to his campaign through one of his banks.

Example: A secret memo written by EPA attorney Nancy-Ellen Zusman lists a "schedule of items to be accomplished" in order to get the incinerator started. It includes a timetable for bringing the illegal incinerator on line and modifications to a flawed 1983 permit. After reading the memo, Senator Metzenbaum protested loudly in a communiqué to then-EPA Administrator William Reilly: "The memo makes clear the position of the U.S.E.P.A. all along is to give W.T.I. the go-ahead.... I don't believe I have ever seen such irresponsibility on the part of government officials."

Example: Ohio Valley residents went to court to block the incinerator. A Federal District Court, in spite of its own findings that "the operation of the W.T.I. facility... clearly may cause imminent and substantial endangerment to health and the environment," nevertheless permitted WTI to conduct an eight-day trial burn, noting the cost of delay to WTI outweighed the risk of harm to the community.

All this prompted EPA official Hugh Kaufman, a longtime critic of the project, to comment, "The W.T.I. case is a symptom of a national problem. The E.P.A. process for regulating waste disposal is riddled with deceit at best, and fraud at worst." Kaufman's voice is a lonely one in Washington. Neither the President nor the environmentally-concerned Vice President seem inclined to make any moves regarding WTI. Meanwhile, the incinerator continues to spew toxins from its stacks, heedless of the protests of Ohio Valley residents and curiously ignored by the major media.

**SSU Censored Researcher:
Jesse Boggs**

COMMENTS: Liane Clorfene-Casten, author of *The Nation* article, reported that while several media sources dealt with the story before she did, it was mostly in bits and pieces. "However," she added, "Network TV failed to cover anything and most of the major daily newspapers refused to cover it at all after my publication (in *The Nation*)—despite the fact my piece was comprehensive and data was available for anyone to continue investigating, especially since the story is on-going, a constant drama."

Clorfene-Casten feels there is much for the public to learn from greater exposure of the WTI issue since it "is a powerful lesson in environmental corruption....The national public has a right to know the EPA, and our national leaders, are corruptible. Human life is fodder for the power seekers. It's a fundamental civil liberties issue."

Clorfene-Casten feels that the primary beneficiary of the limited coverage given this subject is the "incineration industry whose hunger to build more and more burning machines (which at this

THIS MODERN WORLD by TOM TOMORROW

CONSIDERING THAT IN 1980, THE TOP TAX RATE WAS 70%, CLINTON'S TAX HIKES ARE RELATIVELY MODEST... STILL, SOME PANIC-STRICKEN CONSERVATIVES SEEM TO BELIEVE A *SOCIALIST TAKEOVER* OF THE *UNITED STATES* HAS BEGUN...

WHY--HE WANTS TO *REDISTRIBUTE* THE *WEALTH!*

THE NEXT THING YOU KNOW, HE'LL BE FORCING US ALL TO SING THE "*INTERNATIONALE*"!

THE MEDICAL INDUSTRY CONSIDERS CLINTON A WILD-EYED *RADICAL* FOR PROPOSING THAT GOVERNMENT SHOULD SOMEHOW INTERVENE TO GUARANTEE AFFORDABLE HEALTH CARE FOR *EVERYONE*...

I TELL YOU-- IT'S *UNAMERICAN!*

point are totally unnecessary), is only matched by the EPA's perverted enthusiastic support for this flawed and dangerous technology.

"The polluting industry is *not* reined in by the EPA but fined. As a result, thousands of people living in incinerator communities across the country are at high risk for cancer, birth defects, impaired childhood development, infertility and other reproductive effects, suppression of the immune system, neurological disease or impairment, hormonal alterations and toxicity to the lungs, heart, kidneys, liver and skin—for long-term health effects.

"The food chain is profoundly affected as well. Documents tell us the EPA technocrats know this but will not act. And since the mainstream media has already bought into the lie that 'dioxin is not as dangerous as we once thought it was,' the mainstream press won't discuss the hazards of a dioxin-spewing machine without admitting what they are not prepared to admit; in smaller doses than once believed, dioxin is *very* toxic, is carcinogenic, and is capable of serious hormonal damage.

"In general, media has a tendency to cover up for all our presidents—from Kennedy's sexual exploits to Bush's connection to Iran-contra and more, and Clinton's criminal consent to burn thousands of barrels of Agent Orange in Jacksonville, Arkansas. (It's an on-going dioxin producing machine.) Either we have some warped idea that we need to protect the 'morality' of the presidency, despite the evidence of dishonesty, payoffs and compromises, or the corruption is so pervasive, everyone connected gets protected.

"The American people are mostly shielded from the truth of how the compelling, intoxicant of power translates into dreadful,

unethical and life-threatening tradeoffs. The law doesn't count. The Justice Department will *not* prosecute certain environmental criminals. People pay the price. WTI protesters are given little more than bureaucratic runarounds in Washington. They go from the Justice Department to the FBI with their petitions, and nothing ever happens.

"I'd love to see this story told on network news, but reality tells me to forget it. WTI burns merrily along. On 12/10/93 WTI malfunctioned, pouring forth unknown, fugitive emissions: 'black clouds of smoke hovered over the smokestack.' Then, WTI took its sweet time in alerting the EPA. The local health officials were appalled by WTI silence. Since that time, Ohio EPA understood WTI might fail another trial burn, so on 12/17/93, in an effort to avoid a possible failure, the Ohio Agency told them not to conduct it. Ohio EPA knew there were sufficient problems and didn't want them to risk it."

In response to a letter by EPA's Bob Sussman (*The Nation* 12/6/93) criticizing Clorfene-Casten's article for being "fraught with error," she responded "Well, since the EPA itself admitted it violated the law, and since the attorney general of Ohio stated clearly the same in 1993, and since EPA whistleblower Hugh Kaufman officially petitioned Janet Reno for a criminal investigation, specifically citing Val Adamkus of Region V and Sussman, I'm not concerned. The drama continues as does the poison."

"We live and learn,
but not the wiser grow."
—John Pomfret

CHAPTER 4

Censored Déjà Vu

Once cited as an early warning system for society's problems, Project Censored annually sounds the alarm on emerging social, environmental, economic, and other issues. The original concept was that by bringing early attention to these problems, we would be better able to resolve them before they get out of control. Unfortunately, too often the warnings issued by America's alternative press go unheeded.

On the plus side, however, each year we do find issues that were first cited years ago and have now finally attracted the attention of the national news media and been put on the national news agenda.

One of the most encouraging signs of the first year of the Clinton Presidency is the total number of "censored déjà vu" stories. There are more than twice the number of important "déjà vu" stories in the *1994 Censored Yearbook* than there were in the 1993 edition.

Interestingly, many of them deal with stories of fraud, deceit, and malfeasance that should have been widely publicized during the Reagan/Bush administrations while they were occurring. *Censored* aficionados will recall a number of such stories, including the war on drugs, Ed Meese's FEMA debacle, the Black Budget, EPA's disinformation program, Nicaragua's World Court claim, and, of course, the expected answer to that ever-popular question—Where was George?

We would attribute the sudden spotlight being cast on media omissions about the sins of the Reagan/Bush administrations to the appearance, if not the reality, of a more open administration under Clinton. The good news is that Clinton apparently will not assume the Reagan mantle of "America's Chief Censor" (the #6 *Censored* story of 1982); the bad news is the number of "censored" and déjà vu stories already attributed to the Clinton presidency.

Getting right to the heart of one of the major cover-ups of the Reagan/Bush era, one of the classic déjà vu stories of 1993 dealt with what really happened in El Salvador more than a decade earlier.

THE TRUTH ABOUT EL SALVADOR

On March 15, 1993, the mainstream media in the United States finally reported what the alternative press had been publishing for more than a decade—that the government of El Salvador was responsible for horrible atrocities during its 12-year civil war while the Reagan and Bush administrations knowingly supported and funded it.

The Commission on the Truth of El Salvador, appointed by the United Nations to investigate human rights abuses, identified the criminals responsible for the assassination of Archbishop Oscar Arnulfo Romero at mass in 1980; the abduction and murder of three American nuns and a lay American church worker in 1980; the massacre of as many as 1,000 villagers in 1981; and the murder of six Jesuit priests, their housekeeper and her daughter in 1989.

The horrible atrocities which took the lives of an estimated 75,000 people, mostly Salvadoran civilians, including many women and children, were supported with more than $6 billion in economic and military aid, including $1 billion in covert aid, furnished by the Reagan and Bush administrations.

While the tragedy was unfolding in El Salvador, the mainstream press in the United States, with few exceptions, looked the other way. Two notable exceptions were Ray Bonner, of *The New York Times*, and Alma Guillermoprieto, of the *Washington Post*, both of whom paid the price for trying to tell the truth. Bonner was forced to leave the *Times* while Guillermoprieto said she lost credibility among her editors and others after being accused of communist sympathies, as reported by Mike Hoyt, associate editor of the *Columbia Journalism Review* (Jan/Feb 1993).

The two journalists' reports on the 1981 El Mozote massacre were attacked by the Reagan administration, questioned by their own editors, criticized by the mainstream media including the *Wall Street Journal* and *Time* magazine, and pilloried by Reed Irvine's *Accuracy in Media Report*.

Meanwhile the alternative press, as documented by Project Censored, was keeping its readers informed as to what was really happening in El Salvador starting with the #1 *Censored* story of 1980—"Distorted Reports of the El Salvador Crisis."

Questions raised in our 1980 synopsis of the El Salvador crisis included: Why should a purported defense of democracy take the form of financial and military aid to a repressive regime? Why did 80 percent of El Salvador's population oppose the so-called "reform" government? What possible goodwill did the United States hope to generate in Latin America with an unpopular foreign policy in El Salvador? And, most importantly, why did the U.S. media parrot governmental policy rather than seriously question our involvement in El Salvador?

Some publications and organizations tried to warn us about El Salvador during that period and deserve recognition for their efforts. They include *The Nation, Inquiry, Christianity and Crisis, Pacifica Radio, Pacific News Service, Mother Jones, FoodFirst Action Alert, Covert Action Information Bulletin, Columbia Journalism Review, The Progressive,* Marin Interfaith Task Force on Central America, San Francisco's KRON-TV Target 4 Unit, *San Francisco Bay Guardian,* Christic Institute Special Reports, *In These Times,* and *EXTRA!*.

Incredibly, despite these long-delayed revelations, the cover-up continues. Shortly after the United Nation's Truth Commission report of the atrocities in El Salvador, the S.O.A. (School of the Americas) Watch, a watchdog group in Columbus, Georgia, revealed an equally disturbing report concerning U.S. complicity in those and many other atrocities.

The S.O.A. Watch obtained a complete list of Salvadoran, Guatemalan, Bolivian, Colombian, and Peruvian graduates of the School of the Americas from the National Security Archives in Washington, DC, and compared the Truth Commission findings with the list of Salvadoran graduates of the School of the Americas.

What the S.O.A. Watch found was truly disturbing. Father Roy Bourgeois and Vicky A. Imerman, of the S.O.A. Watch, said, "Initially expecting to find a dozen or more graduates among the officers cited in the report, we were surprised—and outraged —to find that the majority of human rights abuses documented in the report were directly attributable to graduates of the U.S. Army School of the Americas." Forty-five of the 46 S.O.A. graduates were implicated in deplorable human rights abuses.

The S.O.A. Watch also reported that the graduates who received the most training at the Army school were implicated in the most serious offenses. It also noted that hundreds of Latin American and Caribbean soldiers were *still being trained* at the U.S. Army School of the Americas at Fort Benning, Georgia, at taxpayers' expense.

The #6 *Censored* story of 1981, "Training Terrorists in Florida," reported how the federal government permitted earlier guerrilla training camps for Latin American and Caribbean exiles and soldiers to operate openly in Florida. According to the Pacifica National News Service, whose investigation was ignored by the major news media at the time, the training camps were in violation of the U.S. Neutrality Act.

U.S. complicity in the atrocities in El Salvador were further supported by an Associated Press report (7/16/93) which confirmed that State Department officials, including Secretary of State Alexander M. Haig Jr., had lied about events in El Salvador. In his March 1981 testimony, Haig lied about the murders of four American churchwomen in December 1980.

Sen. Patrick Leahy, (D-VT), said that "...the lies, half-truths, and evasions that we came to expect from the State Department during that period...contributed to the torture and murder of thousands of innocent people."

Altogether, many of the 75,000 people killed during the tragic civil war in El Salvador were civilians suspected of leftist sympathies who were slain by death squads linked to the military. On July 2, 1993, The Associated Press reported that President Alfredo Cristiani replaced four of the 106 people that the U.N. special commission had recommended be purged.

The smoking gun evidence of U.S. complicity with the El Salvador death squads was finally published by *The New York Times* on November 9. Intelligence reports revealed that the Reagan and Bush administrations knew about the assassinations by right-wing leaders in El Salvador in the 1980s but continued to work with them nonetheless. On December 14, *The New York Times* reported that recently declassified State Department documents provided the first evidence to link U.S. support to Salvadoran death squad activities in the 1990s.

And finally, for those who might still have some lingering doubts, *The New Yorker* reported "The Truth of El Mozote," by Mark Danner, on December 6. It was the cover story and it ran 74 pages.

Despite all this, no lessons seem to have been learned. In its December issue, *The Progressive* revealed that Bill Clinton has sent some 450 U.S. soldiers to El Salvador to participate in joint operations with the Salvadoran armed force as part of the largest-ever U.S. military deployment to the country.

Meanwhile, there are reports that Salvadorans are still suffering at the hands of a regime aided and abetted by the United States. On December 6, Van Gosse, director of the Center for Democracy in the Americas, reported that "From January to October of this year, U.N. human rights monitors reported an average of 135 violations a month—60 percent of them attributed to the government. And since late October, the death squads have been reborn—eight members of the opposition party of the former guerrilla movement have been ambushed and six killed."

OTHER DÉJÀ VU STORIES OF 1993

EARLY COVERUP OF SAVINGS AND LOAN SCANDAL—*Censored* stories #1 and #3 in 1990 and #4 in 1991 revealed various efforts to cover-up the costly savings and loan scandal. On January 16, 1993, David Skidmore of the Associated Press reported that former Federal Reserve Chairman Paul Volker admitted he could have provided a stronger warning to the public but was worried about panicking depositors. Volker made his statement before the National Commission on Financial Institution Reform, Recovery and Enforcement, which was created in 1989, but, oddly enough, didn't hold its first public hearing until *after* the 1992 presidential election.

RETURN OF ELECTROSHOCK—On February 3, 1993, the CBS-TV Evening News with Dan Rather reported that electroshock therapy, once totally discredited as a psychiatric therapy system, is quietly coming back. "Electroshock: The 'New, Improved' Psychiatric Therapy," the #24 *Censored* story of 1990, reported how hospitals were secretly bringing back highly lucrative electroshock treatments.

FEMA FINALLY FINGERED—A six-month investigation by Cox newspapers, carried by the Associated Press on 2/22/93, reported how the Federal Emergency Management Agency (FEMA) failed to provide needed aid during natural disasters because it had spent most of its money on top-secret military programs during the past decade. This was the subject of the #9 *Censored* story of 1984 which revealed how Edwin Meese, Ronald Reagan's attorney general, redirected FEMA to combat domestic terrorism. Another prescient nomination was the #11 *Censored* story of 1989 which was titled "FEMA: The 'Emergency Management' Agency That Failed."

FEDERAL SEIZURE LAWS REVISED—The #18 *Censored* story of 1991 revealed how the federal seizure laws, cited by many as unconstitutional, were making crime pay. On February 25, 1993, the *Chicago Tribune* reported that the Supreme Court ruled that government agents can no longer automatically seize all property they *think* is linked to illegal drug sales; they can still seize such property, but not until it has been proven that drug profits were involved in the purchase. On May 17, 1993, the Scripps Howard News Service reported the first major reversal in government policy when a federal judge ordered the Drug Enforcement Agency to return $9,000 it had taken from an innocent person two years earlier. On June 28, 1993, the Supreme Court set new limits on the government's power to seize property, ruling that the Constitution forbids prosecutors to seek forfeitures that go far beyond a reasonable punishment. On December 13, 1993, the Supreme Court ruled that prosecutors must notify drug suspects before seizing property. Finally, as a result of a series of Supreme Court rulings against the government, the Justice Department said it was considering a major overhaul of forfeiture law.

JACK IN THE BOX AND THE USDA—The outbreak of bacterial food poisoning that killed three children and sickened more than 500 other people brought quick action from the U.S. Department of Agriculture (USDA) which announced it would hire 160 new meat and poultry inspectors in a massive campaign to reduce harmful microorganisms (3/17/93). By May 28, 1993, the Associated Press was able to report that surprise inspections by the USDA of 90 beef slaughterhouses found that more than half of them had flaws that could cause bacterial contaminated meat. On August 8, the *Minneapolis Star Tribune* published an extraordinary exposé of the meat industry titled "Warning: The Beef Gamble." It consisted of ten articles and sidebar features and was based on a two-month investigation into the meat industry. Ironically, the wire services reported (11/20/93) that the results of the government's surprise inspections of *turkey* plants would not be announced until mid-December, long after the Thanksgiving turkey-buying period. The #10 *Censored* story of 1989 revealed that under the Reagan administration, the USDA cut its inspection staff, lowered health standards, and cracked down on employees who tried to warn the public about contaminated food.

THE FLUORIDATION CONTROVERSY—An article on "bad science" in *Newsweek* (3/22/93) featured fluoridation as an example of scientific research that proved to be wrong. The potential dangers of fluoridation, a controversial issue since fluoride was added to public drinking water in the 1940s to prevent tooth decay, was the #22 *Censored* story of 1991, "Fluoridation Risks Raised By New Public Health Report." It reported that while a research paper published in 1966 concluded that drinking fluoridated water reduces the risk of skeletal fractures, better studies in the 1980s failed to find such a link and that several studies suggest fluoridated water may actually increase fractures. Nonetheless, on August 18, 1993, *USA Today* cited a report by the National Research Council that said fluoride poses no health risk at the levels allowed in drinking water.

RETURN OF THE CAR BOOK?—Under pressure from the Consumers Union, the National Highway Transportation Administration (NHTA) has once again started to publish booklets that rate cars based on their repair cost histories. The #20 *Censored* story of 1981 revealed how the Reagan administration knuckled under to the auto industry and, in what may have been its first overt example of censorship, forced the NHTA to stop publishing *The Car Book*, which did a similar but more comprehensive evaluation of car safety. *The Car Book*, now a privately-published bestseller, was available in bookstores across the country for $11.

EAST TIMOR FINALLY GETS ITS DAY IN COURT—The April 1993 issue of the TAPOL Bulletin No. 116, published by the Indonesia Human Rights Campaign, reported how Indonesia suffered a major defeat at the United Nations Commission on Human Rights when the East Timor resolution, proposed and supported by the European Community under the leadership of Denmark, was adopted by 23 votes to 12 with 15 abstentions. In a major reversal of its past policy, the United States supported the resolution. On August 17, 1993, wire services reported that Indonesia agreed to withdraw all of its combat forces from East Timor, replacing them with troops engaged only in development projects. "The Tragedy in East Timor," was the #7 *Censored* story of 1979 and #3 of 1985.

POISONED WATER CONTINUES TO FLOW—After thousands of Milwaukee residents reported diarrhea, cramps, and vomiting from contaminated water, the Natural Resources Defense Council, an environmental watchdog group, released an Environmental Protection Agency report that revealed there are now some 90 U.S. cities at risk from the same drinking water parasite, as reported by the Associated Press, April 15, 1993. On

September 27, 1993, the Natural Resources Defense Council released the results of one of the most comprehensive drinking water studies ever undertaken; it revealed that more than 120 million people may be needlessly exposed to unhealthy drinking water. On December 8, the EPA advised people who live and work in the District of Columbia to boil all drinking water because of possible contamination (*Washington Post*). Four days later, the EPA declared the water safe to drink. The White House, which has its own water filtration system, was not affected by the advisory. "Poisoned Water" was the #10 *Censored* story of 1980 and "Our Water is Being Poisoned" was the #5 *Censored* story of 1981.

THE WAR ON DRUGS WAS A MYTH—The #4 *Censored* story of 1989 revealed that the "government's war on drugs is more hype than reality." In May, 1993, Richard Held, the FBI's chief agent in San Francisco, retired after 25 years with the bureau and confirmed the 1989 story. "The war on drugs was an example of rhetorical excess coming out of Washington," Held said. "There's not been any war on drugs. That's the worst kind of manipulating appearances...to give the public the impression something is being done."

HIGH VOLTAGE POWER LINES & CANCER—Reuters reported on May 1, 1993, that the San Diego Gas and Electric Company won a landmark trial when the jury rejected claims that electric power lines contributed to a five-year-old girl's cancer. The suit was the first to go to trial over the issue. Nonetheless, on November 11, Reuters reported an analysis of three studies (conducted in Denmark, Finland, and Sweden) that revealed that children living close to high voltage power lines may be doubling their risk of contracting leukemia. Meanwhile, Paul Brodeur, longtime critic of high voltage power lines, published a well-documented book warning of the hazards in *The Great Power-Line Cover-up: How the Utilities and the Government Are Trying to Hide the Cancer Hazards Posed by Electromagnetic Fields*, in mid-1993. "High Voltage: Hazards Over Our Heads" was one of the top 25 *Censored* stories of 1978.

ADVERTISING PRESSURE ON A FREE PRESS—The #9 *Censored* story of 1992 cited a report by The Center for the Study of Commercialism that confirmed the subtle yet pervasive influence of advertisers on the content of the news. On May 15, 1993, *Editor & Publisher* reported a study from the Ethics Committee of the American

Society of Newspaper Editors that revealed that newspapers do face more advertiser pressure than they report. While 90% of the advertising executives at 93 of the country's 100 largest daily newspapers admitted to ad cancellations by advertisers upset with news content, only 10% of them told their readers about it.

MILITARY TOXIC WASTES POISON AMERICA—On May 16, 1993, the Associated Press reported that radioactive or chemical wastes at more than 11,000 sites—at more than 900 Department of Defense and Department of Energy facilities throughout the United States—will cost some 250 billion taxpayer dollars and take more than 30 years to clean up. This does not include the health effects on workers at the polluted facilities and on people living nearby. The #2 *Censored* story of 1985 warned that the military annually generates more than half a million tons of hazardous waste, radioactive wastes, chemical solvents, and leaking nerve gas rockets, and that the military is not subject to EPA regulations that monitor industrial waste procedures.

NEWSPAPER MONOPOLY FEARS IGNORED—On May 31, wire services reported that *The New York Times* was going to buy the *Boston Globe*, one of the last big independently owned newspapers in the United States. The #12 *Censored* story of 1979, titled "All The News That Makes a Profit," warned of the dangers of an unpublicized trend toward the increasing monopolization among newspapers.

TAXPAYERS GET STUCK WITH POLLUTERS CLEAN-UP BILL— On June 21, 1993, the Associated Press reported that the Environmental Protection Agency had written off $270 million it was supposed to charge polluters for the clean-up of the nation's worst Superfund toxic waste sites and was expected to write off hundreds of millions more. As an explanation, the EPA said that many polluters disappear, or are unable to pay, or that the EPA doesn't have the resources or evidence to file lawsuits. A better explanation might be found in the #22 *Censored* story of 1989— "The Profitable Revolving Door at the EPA." This story revealed the cozy revolving employment door between the EPA and the companies prospering from contracts to clean up hazardous dumps. It seems that former EPA professionals are now employed by the booming waste disposal industry which, in turn, is supported by corporate donors, including many of the firms responsible for the original pollution.

THE DOD DID LIE ABOUT THE SOVIET MILITARY BUILD-UP— The top *Censored* story of 1984 revealed that estimates of a Soviet military build-up were highly inflated, i.e. lies. On June 28, 1993, *The New York Times* revealed that eight secret reports in a three-year probe by the General Accounting Office confirmed that the Pentagon had overestimated the strength of Soviet air defenses, exaggerated the Soviet nuclear threat, and lied about the need, cost, and performance of U.S. weapons.

EPA LIES OF 1988 STILL POLLUTE THE NEWS—The #2 *Censored* story of 1988 revealed how the EPA's disinformation campaign about improvement in environmental pollution levels was given credibility in the media. Even while medical waste was washing up on East Coast beaches, *The New York Times'* environmental reporter published a reassuring story noting that nearly 90 percent of the nation's publicly-owned sewer systems met their pollution-control requirements. However, just five summers later, the Associated Press (7/1/93) reported that beach-goers still risk disease from sewage and other contaminants on many of the nation's shores. One of the major causes of high bacteria levels in beach water is inadequate and overloaded sewage treatment plants. An EPA official agreed that better beach protection is needed.

ORGANIC VERSUS CHEMICAL FARMING—The #2 *Censored* story of 1978 revealed that successful multi-million dollar organic farms, in Switzerland and the U.S., have proven there is an economically feasible alternative to farming with potentially dangerous agricultural chemical pesticides. Now, just 15 years later, the federal government has given the concept its seal of approval. In a joint announcement made in June 1993, the Department of Agriculture, the Food and Drug Administration, and the EPA, have promised to provide help to farmers who want to find an alternative to chemicals. A USA *Today* article (7/8/93) reported that after half a century of reliance on chemicals, many farmers are cutting back, trying non-toxic alternatives, some cutting out all chemicals...going organic. According to the article, farming is about to undergo its biggest change since World War II.

PENTAGON'S SECRET BLACK BUDGET TAKES A HIT—The nation's intelligence budget, also known as the "Black Budget" as cited in the #7 *Censored* story of 1990, apparently will no longer be a sacrosanct official state secret. On July 17, 1993, *The New York Times* reported that the Senate intelligence committee had cut $1.3 billion from the budget and Senator Dennis DeConcini, (D-AZ), chair of the committee, said the budget would now be subject to public debate on the floor of the Senate.

JUSTICE DEPARTMENT TRIES TO CLOSE BOOK ON CASO-LARO—*Editor & Publisher* reported on July 17, 1993, that the Department of Justice (DOJ) investigation into the mysterious death of free-lance reporter Dan Casolaro concluded that 1) Casolaro committed suicide; 2) the DOJ did not conspire with former UPI owner Earl W. Brian and others to steal software known as PROMIS from a company called Inslaw; and 3) the DOJ did not improperly influence Inslaw bankruptcy proceedings. The #11 *Censored* story of 1991, based on articles in the *Village Voice, San Francisco Bay Guardian,* and *In These Times,* suggested

that Casolaro was murdered for his investigation into what he called the "Octopus," a web of intrigue involving the S&L debacle, the October Surprise, Iran-contra, the contra-connected Wackenhut Corp., and BCCI, as well as the Inslaw software theft. Critics of the DOJ's conclusions question the validity of the investigation since DOJ's investigation was done in secret with no contact or interviews with confidants or associates of Casolaro.

EASY ACCESS TO MEDICAL FILES FINALLY DISCOVERED— On July 27, 1993, the "Cover Story" on page one of *USA Today* revealed the threat to privacy from easy access to the medical records of millions of Americans. The #15 *Censored* story of 1978 revealed that the Medical Information Bureau (MIB), a little known firm that collected and spread intimate information about the private lives of American citizens, had files on 15 million Americans at the time and was adding about 400,000 new names a year. Today the largest provider of consumer database information is Equifax, a billion-dollar corporation based in Atlanta, which has files on over 160 million individuals, including personal medical histories. The *USA Today* article, which devoted 48 column inches to the exposé (and an additional 18 column inches to an editorial calling for a congressional law to protect personal privacy), failed to mention either MIB or Equifax.

VIETNAM VETERANS FINALLY VINDICATED ON AGENT ORANGE—After more than two decades of fighting for justice, Vietnam veterans won recognition that Agent Orange, a toxic chemical many of them were exposed to, can cause cancer and other health problems, as reported by Knight-Ridder Newspapers (7/28/93). Agent Orange was a regular *Censored* nomination through the years; in 1981, the #19 *Censored* story revealed how veterans suffering from Agent Orange illnesses were denied access to the judicial system; in 1984, the #15 story reported how women Vietnam veterans had been excluded from a $73 million epidemiological study of Agent Orange conducted by the U.S. Centers for Disease Control.

CONTROVERSIAL BST DAIRY HORMONE GETS AMA SUPPORT—On August 9, 1993, the *San Francisco Examiner* reported that it had obtained a videotape produced by the American Medical Association that supports BST, the controversial bovine growth hormone that reportedly boosts milk production by up to 25 percent. The video argues that the drug could ease world hunger. It must have been an effective video since the Food and Drug Administration approved BST for use on November 5. But the video did not mention previous efforts by dairymen to maintain high milk prices despite millions of starving children throughout the world. In mid-March 1967, America's "concerned" dairymen poured milk down sewer drains to make a point about milk prices; the #22 Censored story of 1985 revealed that more than a million of America's dairy cows were slaughtered in an ill-conceived, secretive plan to reduce milk production to maintain prices. Now they say they want to boost milk production in order to ease world hunger by making milk the first food the government would allow to be produced with genetic engineering.

NATIVE AMERICAN TRIBES TARGETS OF GENOCIDE —The Associated Press reported (8/12/93) that American Indian tribes who are considering government proposals for storing nuclear waste on their lands are targets of genocide and unfair politics. The #10 Censored story of 1982 revealed how toxic waste firms were targeting Indian reservations; the #16 Censored story of 1992 reported that corporate waste brokers and the U.S. federal government believed that Native American lands were the solution to America's toxic/nuclear waste problem.

PBS: THE PETROLEUM BROADCASTING SYSTEM—On August 24, 1993, the Associated Press reported that an analysis of programs on the Public Broadcasting System (PBS) by Fairness & Accuracy In Reporting (FAIR), a media watchdog group, revealed that PBS was not too liberal, as often charged by conservatives, but rather too mainstream. The #8 Censored story of 1979 charged that PBS was the handmaiden of major oil companies that served as key underwriters, while the #25 Censored story of 1980 reported that PBS had gone commercial.

SMOKING DEATHS IN U.S. DROP—On August 27, 1993, the Washington Post cited a report by the Centers for Disease Control and Prevention that reported a decrease in the number of Americans dying from cigarette smoking from 434,000 in 1988 to 419,000 in 1990—the first such decline since the agency began keeping records in 1985. While the hazards of cigarette smoking were known as early as 1939 (see Chronology), the tobacco industry and the media were still downplaying the dangers as recently as the 1980s. Nonetheless, while heart disease and cancer may be listed as the nation's leading killers, government researchers announced that the biggest underlying cause of death in the U.S. is tobacco use (*Los Angeles Times*, 11/10/93). *Censored* stories included #8 in 1980—"Tobacco Companies Censor the Truth About Cigarettes and Cancer;" #20 in 1984—"Cigarette Advertising and *The New York Times*: An Ethical Issue That's Unfit to Print;" #21 in 1985—"Tobacco Industry Appeals to Children and the Third World."

YASSER ARAFAT OUTLASTS THE NEW YORK TIMES—On Monday, September 13, 1993, Yasser Arafat, the chairman of the PLO, and Yitzhak Rabin, the prime minister of Israel, made international headlines as they shook hands sealing the first agreement between Jews and Palestinians to end their historic conflict. The #12 *Censored* story of 1984 revealed how America's most influential newspaper had earlier misinformed the American public about Arafat. Warren Hoge, the foreign editor of *The New York Times*, stated in a personal letter to a reader, dated May 29, 1984, "When and if Mr. Arafat calls for mutual recognition and negotiations with Israel, you will read about it prominently displayed on the front page of *The New York Times*." Not quite the truth. Incredibly, Hoge's statement was made a month after *The London Observer* (4/29/84) published an interview by Patrick Seale with Yasser Arafat which said, in part, "Yasser Arafat, chairman of the PLO, called last week for direct talks with Israel, under the umbrella of the United Nations, to secure 'a just peace in which there is no victor and no vanquished.'" Not only did that story *not* make the *Times'* front page, it was conspicuously absent from *any* of the *Times'* pages, and from the pages of the *Washington Post*, for that matter.

USN&WR DISCOVERS HAZARDS OF MULTINATIONAL CORPORATIONS—*U.S. News & World Report* guilelessly asks "Are multinational firms violating America's national interest?" in an article titled "Meet the new economic bogymen" (10/18/93). The question was authoritatively and conclusively answered in one of the top 25 *Censored* stories of 1976, titled "The Impact of Multinational Corporations on the U.S. Unemployment Rate."

NIGHTMARE ON THE MEXICAN BORDER—The lead story in *USA Today* on October 27, 1993, asked "What's killing the people of Nogales, Arizona?" and went on to document the growing incidence of cancer in this community on the Mexican border. The answer could have been found in the #12 *Censored* story of 1988 titled "U.S./Mexican Plants Turn the Border into a Toxic Wasteland." Yet it wasn't until five years later that authorities started to take some positive steps. On December 8, *USA Today* reported that authorities said "It's a problem that we are aware of now." Arizona Governor Fife Symington traveled to Nogales and 1) ordered a probe into reports of myeloma, lupus, and leukemia; 2) promised to support better funding of a cancer registry to track deaths and spot anomalies; and 3) created a task force that includes Nogales residents and Mexican officials.

NEW TEST FOR CHLAMYDIA RECOMMENDED—Medical experts announced a new, easier, cheaper, and more accurate method of testing men for chlamydia to help control one of the most common sexually transmitted diseases. The announcement, which appeared in the *Journal of the America Medical Association*, was reported by Reuters (11/3/93). "Chlamydia: The Most Widespread Venereal Disease Leads to Sterility" was one of the top 25 *Censored* stories of 1984.

NICARAGUA'S WORLD COURT CLAIM AGAINST U.S. QUIETLY DROPPED—The #9 *Censored* story of 1988 revealed that the World Court had found the United States guilty of violating international law by interfering in the affairs of a sovereign nation—specifically by mining Nicaragua's harbors and illegally funding the contras. The United States ignored the ruling, saying that the Court had neither the "jurisdiction or competence" to rule on the case. On November 8, C. Miranda Silva, a researcher at New York *Newsday*, reported that shortly after Nicaraguan president Violeta de Chamorro was elected in 1990 with generous campaign funding from the Bush administration, she withdrew Nicaragua's World Court claim against the United States (New York *Newsday* "Viewpoints," 11/8/93).

IT APPEARS THAT GEORGE BUSH IS A FELON—In the #5 *Censored* story of 1992 concerning Iraqgate, investigative author Stephen Pizzo asked "Is Bush a Felon?" In covering Iraqgate developments in 1993, *USA Today* reporter Sam Vincent Meddis suggests the answer is "yes" (*USA Today*, 11/8/93). Citing Alan Friedman's new book, *Spider's Web: The Secret History of How the White House Illegally Armed Iraq*, Meddis reports how the U.S. government directed covert weapons transfers to Iraq, starting with the Reagan administration in 1982 and continuing into the Bush administration, which ignored CIA information concerning secret loans funneled to Baghdad from the Atlanta branch of an Italian bank, Banca Nazionale del Lavor (BNL).

NATIONAL GEOGRAPHIC DISCOVERS WATER CRISIS—On November 10, 1993, a *National Geographic* special on PBS-TV warned that a scarcity of water was a little-known but growing global problem. "Our Water is Running Out and What's Left is Being Poisoned" was the #5 *Censored* story of 1981, as reported by *The Progressive* (7/81) and the *National Wildlife Federation* (4/81).

WORLD PACT TO STOP OCEAN NUKE DUMPING—On November 12, 1993, the Associated Press reported that the United States and 36 other nations finally agreed to stop dumping nuclear waste at sea. Four nuclear powers—Britain, France, Russia, and China—abstained from the agreement. The #3 *Censored* story of 1981 revealed that the U.S. government's program to monitor some 50 radioactive dump sites on both coasts, including prime fishing areas, was a sham. At the time, experts suggested that U.S. fisheries could be radioactive time bombs with peak release of radioactivity from the dumps expected during the 1980s.

WHAT TO DO WITH 50 TONS OF PLUTONIUM—The #6 *Censored* story of 1976 warned about missing plutonium; now the problem is what to do with 50 tons of deadly plutonium from nuclear weapons abandoned by the end of the Cold War. Keay Davidson, science writer for the *San Francisco Examiner*, reported (11/18/93) that the plutonium is stored in 16 bunkers surrounded by armed guards with M-60 machine guns near Amarillo, Texas. One of the plutonium-disposal schemes discussed by experts wouldn't eliminate the last scrap of plutonium until 2275 A.D. Meanwhile, on December 9, 1993, the Associated Press reported that tons of highly radioactive reactor fuel are being stored precariously, sometimes in rusting containers, and an unknown quantity of reactor fuel was buried but could not be located.

CIA SMUGGLES TON OF COCAINE INTO U.S.—When the CIA learned that "60 Minutes" was going to expose the agency on Sunday, November 21, 1993, for smuggling a ton of nearly pure cocaine into the United States in 1990, it immediately issued a statement (11/19/93) saying it was an accident. While the cocaine wound up being sold on the street in the United States, the CIA called it a "most regrettable incident." The #7 *Censored* story of 1986, by investigative author Michael Emery, told about a secret team of official and retired U.S. military and CIA officials that trafficked in drugs, assassinated political enemies, stole from the U.S. government, armed terrorists, and subverted the will of Congress and the public with hundreds of millions of drug dollars at their disposal. At that time, authorities denied it.

FIRST MAJOR GUN CONTROL LAW SINCE 1968—One of the top 25 *Censored* stories of 1980 was titled "Gun Wars: Americans Held Hostage by the National Rifle Association." On November 30, President Bill Clinton signed the Brady Bill into law—a sweeping handgun control law designed to keep weapons out of the hands of criminals. Commenting on why it was so difficult to get this law passed, James Brady, former press secretary to President Ronald Reagan, said: "There were three letters of the alphabet: NRA." (*Los Angeles Times*, 11/25/93). That, and, we would add, the mainstream media's failure to put it on the national agenda for many years.

PROSTATE CANCER LINKED TO NUCLEAR WORKERS—The first definitive link between workers in the nuclear industry exposed to certain radioactive substances and an increased risk of prostate cancer was cited in the *British Medical Journal* (11/27/93) as reported by the *London Independent*. The occupational hazards of nuclear power were cited in the #6 *Censored* story of 1976, "Inadequate Nuclear Reactor Safeguards," and in the #1 *Censored* story of 1978, "The Dangers of Nuclear Power."

IRAN-CONTRA SCANDAL: FINALLY ON THE AGENDA— "Contragate: The Untold Story" was the #7 *Censored* story of 1986. When independent counsel Lawrence Walsh's final report on the Iran-contra scandal was revealed on December 5, 1993, (Associated Press), it finally received the mainstream media coverage it deserved years earlier. Two of the major findings of the lengthy investigation confirmed what the nation's alternative press had been reporting for years: 1) former President Ronald Reagan "set the stage" for the scandal's illegal activities; and 2) George Bush lied when he vociferously proclaimed he was "out of the loop" and an innocent victim of over-zealous aides. Peter Dale Scott had accurately reported George Bush's role in the Iran arms deal through the *Pacific News Service* on December 21, 1987.

THE NUCLEAR WAR THE U.S. FOUGHT AGAINST ITSELF—On July 2, 1980, the *Pacific News Service*, carried an article titled, "Underground Tests Every Three Weeks," by investigative author Norman Solomon. Solomon tried to tell the American people about the 235 nuclear bombs that had been detonated in the hidden 17-year nuclear war the U.S. had fought against itself. He revealed that an atomic weapon was detonated underground nearly every three and one-half weeks at the U.S. nuclear test site in Nevada. But the mainstream media weren't interested. (It was the #3 *Censored* story of 1980.) Suddenly, on December 8, 1993, the Associated Press "revealed" that the U.S. government had concealed more than 200 nuclear weapon tests since the 1940s and conducted some 800 radiation tests on humans. Energy Secretary Hazel O'Leary said she was "appalled, shocked and deeply saddened" by the news. Ms. O'Leary wouldn't have been so surprised if she had followed the alternative press, which had been covering that issue through the years.

IT'S BUSINESS AS USUAL AT THE WHITE HOUSE—Presidential candidate Bill Clinton promised to stop the profitable revolving door exchange between government and lobbyists; indeed, he launched his presidency with the "most rigid ethics standards" ever imposed on government officials. (The dangers of revolving door politics was a *Censored* story of 1989.) But just a year later, two of Clinton's most senior White House aides left to take charge of lobbying enterprises at salaries of $500,000 (*The New York Times*, 12/8/93). The Clinton escape clause: his new rules prohibited lobbying...not the *supervision* of lobbying. Welcome back to business as usual at the White House...and a return to the ethics of the Reagan/Bush administrations.

Buried by the media, old problems that could have been resolved years ago resurface time and time again. George Pomfret's warning of some three centuries ago remains relevant—it is not enough to live and learn if we do "not the wiser grow."

"When a dog bites a man,
that is not news,
because it happens so often.
But if a man bites a dog,
it's news."
—John B. Bogart

CHAPTER 5

The Junk Food News Stories of 1993

More than a century ago, John B. Bogart, an editor with the *New York Sun*, offered a definition of news that has not only endured but, indeed, seems to have become more deeply entrenched in recent years.

His definition—it's news when a man bites a dog—implies the need for a sensationalistic aspect for an event to become news. It's an ingredient that now appears to be endemic in the press.

On November 3, 1993, the Santa Rosa (CA) *Press Democrat*, a *New York Times* newspaper, headlined an item with the century old cliché—"Man bites dog." The story, not even a local one, was datelined San Diego. It described how "a man accused of biting a police dog to elude capture was found innocent of interfering with the dog."

A few weeks earlier, on October 10, the *San Francisco Examiner*, a Hearst newspaper, dedicated one of three editorials to an item titled "Truth in dogs." The editorial lamented the death of Spuds MacKenzie, a pedigreed English bull terrier with one black eye, who had gained national media attention as a spokesdog for Budweiser beer.

It would seem that while the media have assumed unparalleled power in our society, they have squandered it on matters of little import. (We'll refrain from saying they have gone to the dogs.) This is best seen in our annual selection of the Junk Food News (JFN) stories.

If any single subject dominated the Junk Food News genre of 1993, it would have to be sex.

The mainstream media's yearlong descent into a sexual abyss of Junk Food News was launched in January when New York *Newsday* published a special section titled "The Meaning of Amy," a thoughtful overview of the Amy Fisher-Joey Buttafuoco story. A group of social historians, writers, religious leaders, and celebrities discussed the sociological implications of the duo's activities.

In March, *NewsInc*, a monthly trade journal which examines and reports on the press, published its own serious analysis of the *Newsday* section about Amy and Joey.

By November, when the trial ended with Buttafuoco given the maximum six months in jail for statutory rape, the Amy & Joey story had produced three network made-for-TV movies, a best seller titled "My Story" by Amy, a music video, and untold hours of filler for talk shows and tabloid TV pseudo-news programs.

Throughout the year, the orgy of sex news continued unabated with reams of copy and hours of time devoted to Heidi Fleiss, the Hollywood Madam; the allegations of child molestation aimed at Michael Jackson; the reported sexual harassment by Senator Bob Packwood (R-OR); the sexual molestation attributed to a Roman Catholic Cardinal; not to men-

THIS MODERN WORLD by TOM TOMORROW

...AND SO, AS YOU'VE JUST SEEN, THE *HERO DOG* WAS ABLE TO RESCUE *ALL* THE ORPHANS FROM THE BURNING BUILDING!

GOSH, WANDA--IF YOU ASK ME, DRAMATIC FOOTAGE LIKE *THAT* IS WHAT THE NEWS BUSINESS IS ALL *ABOUT!*

IN OTHER NEWS TONIGHT...

ACTION McNEWS

--REGULATORS TODAY ANNOUNCED THAT THE NATION'S BANKING SYSTEM IS ON THE VERGE OF A TOTAL *COLLAPSE!* OUR ECONOMY PROBABLY WON'T RECOVER FROM THIS CATASTROPHE FOR A *CENTURY!* UNFORTUNATELY, NO MATTER HOW *VITALLY IMPORTANT* THIS STORY MAY BE TO *EVERY AMERICAN*--

ACTION McNEWS

tion Woody Allen's intra-family relations or the always newsworthy sexual gyrations of Madonna.

The sex-saturated news year finally reached its nadir with the story of John Wayne Bobbitt and his knife-wielding wife, Lorena. Apparently unable to control itself, the normally super-serious weekly, *The Nation*, weighed in with its own three-page analysis titled "Phallus Interruptus." It even managed to produce a quote from Karl Marx—"In one word, you reproach us with intending to do away with your property. Precisely so; that is just what we intend."

But there were other Junk Food News stories to be reported as well. And, hard as it is to believe, considering all the time and space given to sex, celebrities, dinosaurs, and body parts, the media managed to hype a presidential haircut into a major JFN story.

President Bill Clinton reportedly had a $200 haircut on board Air Force One that held up traffic at Los Angeles International Airport on May 18. The media feeding frenzy that followed compelled Michael Deaver, once chief media adviser to President Ronald Reagan, to pompously prognosticate: "The hair thing is going to be with him forever....not only did he hold up traffic at LAX, but he gets a $200 haircut."

Well not quite, Mr. Deaver. About a month later, an enterprising journalist at *Newsday* reported that the stories of planes circling while the president had his hair coifed were wrong. Using Federal Aviation Administration documents, obtained through the Freedom of Information Act, the *Newsday* report found no significant delays of regularly scheduled passenger flights, no circling planes, no traffic jams on the runways. It

--THE ONLY ACCOMPANYING *VISUALS* WE HAVE ARE OF THIS *DULL SENATE HEARING!* AND SINCE WE DON'T *DARE* RISK BORING YOU VIEWERS, WE'RE GOING TO GLOSS OVER THIS REPORT AND MOVE RAPIDLY ALONG--

--TO THE RESULTS OF THE *MISS SKIMPY BIKINI CONTEST!* THAT SHOULD KEEP US IN THE RATINGS, EH, WANDA?

YOU BET, BIFF! ESPECIALLY SINCE WE'VE GOT AN *EXCLUSIVE, IN-DEPTH INTERVIEW* WITH *MISS SKIMPY BIKINI* HER-*SELF!* BUT FIRST, THESE *IMPORTANT MESSAGES*...

ACTION McNEWS

doesn't seem that the "hair thing" is going to be with President Clinton forever. But we'll just leave it to Deaver to apologize to Bill.

Normally, it is difficult to cite stories that don't get the coverage they deserve because they were bumped by some specific Junk Food News story; however, this year, with the help of USA *Today's* columnist Barbara Reynolds, we can cite one.

In her October 15, 1993 column, Reynolds described a special event where 35 distinguished women were inducted into the Women's Hall of Fame at Seneca Falls, New York. You probably weren't aware of this since the event had to compete with Michael Jordan's retirement for coverage. As Reynolds reported, despite the significance of the event, the newly honored inductees to the Women's Hall of Fame went under-reported. Reynolds added, "As the media showered the well-deserving superstar Michael Jordan with megacoverage, they overlooked an entire room of superstars."

On a less than somber note, it appears that we have lost one of our perennial JFN superstars. Last June, 1993, the *Weekly World News* (WWN) announced that Elvis Presley died from diabetes not far from Graceland, his former home. Readers not familiar with this source, should know that WWN was the original source to "reveal" that Elvis was alive in 1988; others thought he had died in 1977. We suspect the media will be able to fill the time and space no longer required for Elvis sightings.

We also may have lost another perennial JFN nominee. Princess Diana, noting that the media are "hard to bear," announced in December that she was scaling her public appearances back.

Nonetheless, 1993 was truly a vintage year for Junk Food News. There were so many unimportant, trivial matters for the mass media to cover that some of the perennial JFN Hall of Fame subjects, including Donald Trump, Roseanne Arnold, the Kennedy Family, as well as the always popular British Royal Family, didn't even make the top ten list.

The typical Junk Food News diet consists of sensationalized, personalized, and homogenized inconsequential trivia, that is often served in the following basic varieties:

NAME-BRAND NEWS: latest rumors of the John Kennedy-Darryl Hannah wedding, scandals of the British Royal family, Madonna's sexcapades, the David Letterman/Jay Leno/Arsenio Hall/Chevy Chase battle for insomniacs, Roseanne and Tom Arnold's virtual ménage-a-trois.

SEX NEWS: Senator Bob Packwood's diary, John Wayne Bobbitt's severed penis, Michael Jackson's alleged interest in young boys, the Hollywood Madam's "black book," Joey and his Long Island Lolita.

YO-YO NEWS: The stock market is up or down, the unemployment rate is up or down, the inflation rate is up or down, the crime rate is up or down, the interest rate is up or down, and gold, silver and pork bellies are up or down.

CRAZED NEWS: The latest diet craze, fashion craze, computer craze, dance craze, sports craze, drug craze, video game craze, and, of course, the always newsworthy latest crazed killer.

PLAY-IT-AGAIN NEWS: The fire across town (nighttime fires are particularly popular on television news), the routine freeway pileup, a local drug bust in the never-ending war on drugs, the downtown bank robbery, and, of course, another Elvis sighting.

SEASONAL NEWS: The drought in the Southwest, tornadoes in the Midwest, floods in the Northeast, hurricanes in the Southeast, fires in the West, and the always dependable bi-annual Political News Season when the candidates pledge to solve unemployment, reduce the deficit, lower prices, rid the streets of crime, defend us from foreign invaders, and promise not to raise taxes.

Our annual Junk Food News effort evolved from criticism by news editors and directors that the real issue isn't censorship —but rather a difference of opinion as to what information is important to publish or broadcast. Editors point out that there is a finite amount of time and space for news delivery—about 23 minutes for a half-hour network television evening news program —and that it's their responsibility to determine which stories are most critical for the public to know.

This appeared to be a legitimate criticism, so I decided to review the stories that editors and news directors consider to be most important and worthy enough to fill their valuable news time and space. In the course of this research project, I haven't found an abundance of hard-hitting investigative journalism. Quite the contrary. Indeed, what has become evident is the journalistic phenomenon I call Junk Food News, which, in essence, represents the flip side of the "Best Censored Stories."

The problem is not the lack of time and space for news, but the quality of the news selected to fill that limited time and space. We're suffering from news inflation—there seems to be more of it than ever before—and it isn't worth as much as it used to be.

News should be nutritious for society. We need more steak and less sizzle from the press. The news should warn us about those things that make our society ill, whether economically, politically, or physically. And there *is* a significant amount of such news out there, as Project Censored has revealed each year since 1976.

But the media continue to ignore many important issues while titillating the public with Junk Food News. At the end of each year, I survey members of the national Organization of News Ombudsmen to solicit their selections for the most over-reported, least deserving news stories of the year.

Some of the top-ranked Junk Food News stories of the past:

1984 Clara Peller's "Where's the beef?"
1985 Coca Cola's new old classic Cherry Coke
1986 Clint Eastwood's campaign for mayor of Carmel
1987 The tribulations of Jim and Tammy Faye
1988 The trapped whales of Alaska
1989 Zsa Zsa Gabor's cop-slapping trial
1990 The marital woes of Donald and Ivana Trump
1991 The William Kennedy Smith rape trial
1992 Dan Quayle's misspelling of potato

Following are the top ten Junk Food News stories of 1993 as cited by the news ombudsmen. As you read them, compare how much you heard about them last year with how much you heard about the top ten *Censored* stories cited in Chapter 3.

1. AMY FISHER/JOEY BUTTAFUOCO
2. WOODY ALLEN/MIA FARROW
3. BILL CLINTON'S $200 HAIRCUT
4. MADONNA
5. JOHN WAYNE BOBBITT'S SEVERED PENIS
6. THE MICHAEL JACKSON ALLEGATIONS
7. BURT & LONI'S DIVORCE
8. LATE NIGHT TALK SHOW ARMAGEDDON
9. HEIDI FLEISS—THE HOLLYWOOD MADAM
10. JURASSIC PARK DINOSAURITIS

Rounding out the top 25 JFN nominations of 1993 were Hillary's Changing Hairstyles, Roseanne & Tom Arnold, Cheers—The Final Episode, Ross Perot, Baby Jessica II, Beavis & Butt-head, Barney (another spinoff of #10 above), Michael Jordan's Retirement, Socks: The First Cat, Sharon Stone's Basic Instinct, The British Royal Family, Bill Clinton Likes Junk Food (the other kind), Travelgate, Bill Clinton's Long-lost Relatives, and John & Leeza & Regis & Kathie Lee.

Nominations not making the top 25 list but deserving of mention included: Julia Roberts & Lyle Lovett, Harley Davidson's 90th Birthday, John Kennedy & Darryl Hannah, The 90210 Graduating Class, Ted Danson's Blackface, Joe Montana's Move to Kansas City, The Death of Spuds MacKenzie, Super Bowl XXVII, Senator Bob Packwood, and 20 Naked Pentecostals Packed in a Pontiac (an alliterative Associated Press story that burned up the wires on August 21).

Following are explanations suggested by some of the news ombudsmen who participated in the selection of the top 1993 Junk Food News Subjects as to why the media tend to sensationalize such stories as those cited above:

"Because the public tends to enjoy the adverse side of people rather than positive aspects."—Paul Bartley, *The Bradenton Herald*, Bradenton, Florida.

"1. Newspapers' efforts to compete with (alas, by mimicking) popular media; 2. Some people *are* interested in these stories—and editors are some of those people."—Charles Bond, *The Palm Beach Post*, West Palm Beach, Florida.

"Because newspapers can't be as boring as I want them to be."—Joann Byrd, *The Washington Post*, Washington, D.C.

"Sleaze gets editors interested during a dull and dreary day but readers love to sink their teeth into sex and slime. Each twist of the story is more alien to the average person's lifetime experience than we, who are sequestered in the newsroom, can imagine."—Ina B. Chadwick, *Gannett Suburban Newspapers*, White Plains, New York.

"Because we're getting too damned lazy and because we underestimate the intelligence of our readers and listeners."—Charlotte W. Craig, *Detroit Free Press*, Detroit, Michigan.

"Television tends to sensationalize more than print media. Newspapers simply try to meet a perceived demand created by TV."—Roger J. Edge, *The Chronicle-Herald*, Halifax, Nova Scotia, Canada.

"Sensationalism may come with repetition as stories progress through the various media. Initially, though, the stories provide some lighten-up material for readers concerned about the economy, health care, crime and other heavy subjects. That is not, I think, a bad thing. Besides, folks need something to talk about at cocktail parties and during game halftimes..."—Jerry Finch, *The Richmond Times-Dispatch*, Richmond, Virginia.

"In trying not to be dull, we overdo it."—Larry Fiquette, *St. Louis Post-Dispatch*, St. Louis, Missouri.

"Editors too frequently are out of touch with readers and choose stories based on their perceptions of what they *think* readers want. I am also concerned that many are unduly influenced by TV talk shows and 'newsy' segment shows, which are more entertainment than journalism/reporting."—Lynne Enders Glaser, *The Fresno Bee*, Fresno, California.

"Easy targets. Not too much thinking involved. Usually flash and trash. This is not serious journalism. Media were irresponsible about Clinton's $200 haircut. It didn't happen as reported. The media didn't bother to check it out—except for one reporter at *Newsday*."—Gina Lubrano, *The San Diego Union-Tribune*, San Diego, California.

"No single reason. In the case of John Wayne Bobbitt, I'm convinced that a major factor was that radio and TV people got to say 'penis' over the air and get away with it, and the print media followed suit. 'Beavis and Butt-head' gave journalists the opportunity to be amateur psychologists. As for Michael Jordan's retirement, we wouldn't give him that much ink if he had collapsed and died."—Henry McNulty, *The Hartford Courant*, Hartford, Connecticut.

"They are the easiest to cover, require almost no background, whet and satisfy the public appetite for gossip, and create a taste for more of the same." Jean Otto, *Rocky Mountain News*, Denver, Colorado.

THIS MODERN WORLD by TOM TOMORROW

IT'S TIME FOR THE *LOCAL NEWS*...

GOOD EVENING! SEVERAL HOURS AGO, A POLITICAL RALLY WAS HELD IN OUR CITY AND FOR MORE ON THE STORY, LET'S GO NOW TO *BIFF WILLIAMS*, WHO'S STANDING BY LIVE! BIFF?

THANKS, WANDA! I'M STANDING HERE ON THE STREET WHERE THE RALLY WAS HELD EARLIER TONIGHT! AS YOU CAN SEE, EVERYONE HAS LONG SINCE GONE HOME! THERE'S ABSOLUTELY *NOTHING* HAPPENING HERE NOW! THERE'S NO REASON FOR ME TO *BE* HERE, WANDA, EXCEPT TO MAKE USE OF OUR STATION'S GIMMICKY *MOBILE-CAM NEWS VAN!*

"Because they know it feeds an appetite of readers. And, I fear, they feed an appetite of our own. They represent 'lazy' journalism—they take little thought."—Phil Record, *Fort Worth Star-Telegram*, Fort Worth, Texas.

"They are easy reading, and they are usually basically unimportant. Who cares if Socks is adjusting well to his new digs? Amy Fisher—just another case of adultery and sex gone awry. These things don't really matter to our everyday lives, but they serve a purpose: they titillate and entertain us. And because these events happen to real people—or, in the case of Socks, real animals—it's better than watching a fictitious comedy on video, or a TV sitcom."—Frank Ritter, *The Tennessean*, Nashville, Tennessee.

"Most are legitimate stories that are done to death because (a) they have elements of sensationalism and/or sex; (b) the staffed story keeps getting reported because others on the scene keep reporting it and no one wants to be first to drop that bone; inconclusive reporting perpetuates them."—Emerson Stone, The RTNDA Magazine "The Communicator," Greenwich, Connecticut.

"Editors run such stories ad nauseam because they know they appeal to most readers. Most relate to pop culture and pop icons—including the Clinton's. They are an accurate (if disturbing) reflection of what is important in the lives of many North Americans.—Jim Stott, *The Calgary Herald*, Calgary, Alberta, Canada.

Joe Sheibley, reader representative for *The News-Sentinel*, in Fort Wayne, Indiana, offered several explanations why the news media tend to sensationalize some news stories:

"Sex, crime, scandal, violence, gossip and real life adventures are today's top selling junk food news! One only has to look at the growing list

of 1) news magazine shows and what percentage of their stories deal with sex, crime, violence, scandal, etc.; 2) eyewitness and home video programs; 3) real, 'as it happens' police shows; 4) talk shows and what percentage of their subjects deal with sex, crime, violence, scandal, etc.

"In addition, lawyers, public relations experts and the so-called 'spin-doctors' have become much more adept at manipulating the national media. What other possible reasons could there have been for so much national media attention to Amy Fisher, Burt & Loni and Woody & Mia? The Amy Fisher (who?) story just happened to occur in one of the media capitals of the world. And Burt & Loni and Woody & Mia are not much different from a lot of ordinary people. That's showbiz, folks!

"Today, unfortunately, people seem to want to be 'entertained' more than informed. There are plenty of readers and viewers hooked on that kind of 'entertainment.' If their newspaper doesn't provide it, they'll switch to a newspaper that does, or if one TV channel doesn't provide it, they'll switch to a channel that does.

"The trick for a newspaper is to satisfy the appetites of all of its readers without stuffing them too full of 'junk food.'"

Whether it is because Junk Food News is easier and cheaper to produce, or because of the influence of pseudo-news programs like "A Current Affair," or an effort to boost ratings and circulation, or merely a diversion from the gritty side of life, or perhaps because of all of them, we suspect that JFN will always be with us.

But this doesn't mean we shouldn't try to reduce the gargantuan size servings of Junk Food News so we don't, as Joe Sheibley warns, stuff our readers and viewers too full of it, not leaving room for what should be the nutritious main course.

There still may be time for us to get off the Junk Food News diet before we become hopelessly addicted to it. But to do this, we all have to participate.

The corporate media owners should start to earn their unique First Amendment privileges. Editors should rethink their news judgment. Journalists should persevere in going after the hard stories. Journalism professors should emphasize ethics and critical analysis and turn out more muckrakers and fewer buckrakers. The judicial system should defend the freedom-of-the-press provision of the First Amendment with far more vigor. And the public should show the media it is more concerned with the high crimes and misdemeanors of its political and corporate leaders than it is with dinosaurs, sluts, and adulterers.

The effort will be well worth it. America today is not the nation it once was—nor is it the nation it could be. We need a free and aggressive press more now than ever before, a press that will stand up to those who would control it and assume once again the independence it once celebrated.

Indeed, the effort is not merely worth it; it is critical. Few have said it better than Joseph Pulitzer, who warned, "We are a democracy, and there is only one way to get a democracy on its feet...and that is by keeping the public informed about what is going on."

Pulitzer did not have Amy Fisher in mind when he said that.

"Those who cannot
remember the past
are condemned to repeat it."
—George Santayana

APPENDIX A

An Eclectic Chronology of Censorship From 605 B.C. To 1994

The following eclectic chronology culls information and events from a variety of sources, both traditional and nontraditional. It also reflects the alternative definition of censorship offered in Chapter 1 ("Project Censored: Raking Muck, Raising Hell"), one that is less restricted than traditional definitions.

Normally, a chronology plots a series of *events*, dating from the earliest to the most recent. However, this eclectic chronology of censorship departs from the traditional date-based listing of events to include comments and insights and even a poem, as well as events. I hope it provides you with insights not readily apparent in more traditional formats.

A thorough reading of this chronology should make it clear that censorship is not merely an occasional social aberration, but rather a threat that has been with us from the earliest recorded times. As A. Holmes said, "If history without *chronology* is dark and confused, *chronology* without history is dry and insipid." At the very least, I hope you find this neither dry nor insipid.

A thorough reading also should persuade you that censorship historically has been a tool of a powerful elite which attempts to control society through the manipulation of thought, speech, and all other forms of expression. There are, to my knowledge, very few examples, if any, where the poor or powerless are able to use censorship as a tool to influence decisions affecting themselves, let alone a wealthy and powerful elite.

In addition, this chronology should provide you with insights into how we as a society have supported rules, regulations, leaders and institutions that have fostered censorship.

Finally, I hope the following persuades you that freedom of expression is never permanently secured; it must be fought for and won each day. Project Censored is but one of many combatants who have fought against censorship. While the battle is never-ending, it is truly worthy.

A CENSORED CHRONOLOGY

605 B.C. Perhaps the earliest recorded case of censorship occurred when Jehoiakim, the king of Judah, burned Jeremiah's book of prophecies. This prescient event, found in the *Bible* (Jeremiah 36, 1-32), may also be the earliest example of self-censorship since Jeremiah had written the book at Jehoiakim's bidding.

500 B.C. While we revere the Greeks for their respect for freedom of speech, censorship was not unknown. In the fifth century B.C., poets, philosophers, musicians, authors, and others were subject to bans, persecution, and exile.

443 B.C. Most dictionaries trace censorship back to ancient Rome when two magistrates, called "censors," were appointed to conduct an annual census to register citizens and to assess their property for taxation and contract purposes. The censors also were authorized to censure and penalize moral offenders thought to be guilty of vice and immorality by removing their voting rights and tribe membership. This form of censorship was discontinued in 22 B.C. when emperors took over the censorial powers.

399 B.C. The ultimate form of censorship is death, and Socrates—one of the first philosophers to express a rational defense of freedom of speech— became an early victim of it. After he was tried and convicted of impiety and of corrupting youth, Socrates was put to death. Ironically, his best-known pupil, Plato, outlined the first comprehensive system of censorship, particularly of the arts. In *The Republic*, Book II, Plato warned against allowing children to hear any casual tales by casual persons and called for the establishment of a censorship system for writers of fiction.

221 B.C. About two centuries after the appointment of censors in Rome, the Chinese launched their own office of censorship under the Ch'in dynasty (221-206 B.C.) Originally designed to critique the emperor's performance, the office of censor soon was used by the emperor to investigate and punish official corruption. The institution eventually became a huge bureaucracy that effectively ended with the overthrow of the Ch'ing dynasty in 1911.

213 B.C. One of China's most famous monarchs, Tsin Chi Hwangti, built the Great Wall of China (214-204 B.C.) He also exercised a most impressive act of censorship in 213 B.C. by ordering all books in China destroyed, except those concerning science, medicine, and agriculture. In addition, he executed 500 scholars and banished thousands of others.

48 B.C. The famous and great Alexandrian Library was burned on orders from Julius Caesar and some 700,000 rolls of manuscripts were lost forever. An effort was made to rebuild it, and this later library, known as the "Daughter Library," was destroyed in A.D. 389 by an edict of the Emperor Theodosius.

A.D. 58 In Acts 19:19 of the Bible, the apostle Paul praised converts who burned books (worth 50,000 pieces of silver) in the purifying fires of orthodoxy, providing modern-day Christian censors with scriptural authorization for their book burning.

A.D. 95 Following-up on Paul's advice, the Apostolic Constitutions, written by St. Clement of Rome, warned Christians that the Scriptures provided everything a true believer needed to read.

A.D. 499 Under Pope Gelasius, the concept of the Papal Index, a list of books unsuitable for Roman Catholics, first appeared. It was formalized in 1564 and still exists to this day.

1215 On June 15, King John of England, under pressure from English barons, sealed the Magna Carta at Runnymede, guaranteeing certain civil and political liberties to the English people.

1231 The Inquisition, an open season for censors, was launched by the Roman Catholic Church as a formal way of discovering heresy and punishing heretics. Thousands of scriptures were inspected, reviewed, and often destroyed by the Inquisitors—self-described defenders of the Truth of the Sacred Text—from 1231 to 1596. For almost four centuries, book burners also were empowered to burn authors at the stake.

1450 Johann Gutenberg invented the printing press, with its movable type, thereby providing the technological breakthrough for the intellectual revolution of the Renaissance and its challenge to the institution of censorship. It also threatened the tight control secular and religious leaders exercised over the production and distribution of information.

1501 In an effort to protect the Church of Rome against heresy, Pope Alexander VI issued an edict banning the printing of books. Not unlike their colleagues in the Roman Catholic Church, leaders of the Protestant Reformation (including John Knox, Martin Luther, and John Calvin) persecuted heretics and papists. In England, Henry VIII burned copies of William Tyndale's *New Testament* and had Thomas More beheaded for refusing to acknowledge the king's power over religion. In 1529, Henry VIII issued an official list of banned books, some 30 years before the widely known Roman Catholic Index was institutionalized. By 1586, prior restraint was running rampant in England where all books had to be read and approved by the Archbishop of Canterbury or the Bishop of London prior to publication.

1512 Nicolaus Copernicus published "Commentarious," his hypothesis on the revolutions of the heavenly bodies. It stated that the earth was not the center of the universe but revolved around the sun. The theory, which contradicted the geocentric theory favored by the Catholic church, was condemned and placed on the Papal Index in 1616.

1517 Protesting papal censorship, the sale of indulgences, and other papal expedients, Martin Luther, an ordained priest, posted his 95 theses on the door of the Palast Church in Wittenberg, laying the foundations for the German Reformation and the Lutheran Church. Luther later was one of the prohibited authors cited in an abortive earlier version (1559) of the *Index of Prohibited Books* formally authorized and published by the Roman Catholic Church in 1564.

1541 Concerned about nude figures in Michelangelo's fresco, "The Last Judgment," in the Sistine Chapel, Pope Paul IV ordered artists to paint over the more provocative parts to protect the innocent. During a major four-year restoration that was completed in 1993, the Vatican authorities decided not to remove the draperies or "breeches" painted on to the Sistine nudes 452 years earlier. Gianluigi Colalucci, head of the Vatican Museum's restoration project, explained, "The decision we took is of a historic nature, not an aesthetic one; we have chosen to respect the acts of the Council of Trent." It now appears the world will never again see the fresco exactly as Michelangelo painted it.

1564 After abortive attempts dating back more than a thousand years, the papacy successfully issued the formal *Index Librorum Prohibitorum* (Index of Prohibited Books) as authorized by the Council of Trent. Approximately 500 pages in length, it listed books and authors condemned by the Roman Catholic Church. While it survived until 1774 in France and 1834 in

Spain, the Index (as it is known colloquially) remains in force for Roman Catholics up to present day. It is the longest running, and possibly most effective, example of censorship in world history.

1633 Galileo Galilei was forced by the Inquisition to renounce and reject *Dialago*, published in 1632, which supported the theories of Copernicus concerning the revolutions of the planet. *Dialago* was added to the infamous Index where it remained until 1822.

1643 The British Parliament reintroduced the Licensing Act, ending a brief respite from censorship which occurred in 1640 with the abolishment of the Court of Star Chamber. It was this renewal of book licensing which instigated John Milton's eloquent plea for free speech a year later.

1644 *Areopagitica; a Speech of Mr. John Milton For the Liberty of Unlicenc'd Printing, To the Parlament of England,* published in 1644, is considered to be the English-speaking world's first and most powerful statement urging freedom of expression. Some of its better known excerpts include:

> *Who kills a man kills a reasonable creature, God's image; but he who destroys a good book, kills reason itself....Give me the liberty to know, to utter, and to argue freely according to conscience, above all liberties....Though all the winds of doctrine were let loose to play upon the earth, so Truth be in the field, we do injuriously, by licensing and prohibiting to misdoubt her strength. Let her and Falsehood grapple; whoever knew Truth put to the worse in a free and open encounter?*

While Milton's eloquent statement is rightfully credited with being the genesis of press freedom in America, his treatise actually dealt with the right to license, or prior restraint, not with post-publication censorship. The latter finally was addressed by the First Amendment to the Constitution of the United States in 1791.

1690 A small, three-page newspaper, measuring just six by nine-and-one-half inches, titled "Numb. 1, PUBLICK OCCURRENCES Both FOREIGN and DOMESTICK, Boston, Thursday Sept. 25th, 1690," is generally agreed to be the first newspaper published in America. There was no "Numb. 2" because the governor and council issued a statement four days after its publication declaring their "high resentment and Disallowance of said Pamphlet, and order that the same be Suppressed and called in; strictly forbidding any person or persons for the future to Set forth any thing in Print without License first obtained." They found that the editor, Benjamin Harris, had printed "Reflections of a very high nature: As also sundry doubtful and uncertain Reports." While this was an inauspicious beginning for a free press in the New World, there remain many reflections of a very high nature (Iran-contra, Iraqgate, BCCI, etc.) that continue to be subject to censorship today.

1695 Because of increasing resistance, partially generated by Milton's *Areopagitica*, the Licensing Act in England was not renewed in 1695, a date which has come to signify the establishment of freedom of the press in England. However, this did not mark the end of censorship in that country. Prior censorship, through licensing, was replaced with punitive (or post-publication) censorship, a form that, though preferable to prior censorship, is still found in most societies to this day. This is not to say that prior censorship is no longer attempted: consider the case of *The Progressive* magazine, the target of the first case of press prior restraint in America (*U.S. v. Progressive*, 1979). Again, in 1988, the Supreme Court's *Hazelwood* decision gave school administrators prior restraint control over student newspapers.

1735 The John Peter Zenger case provided a classic example of an attempt at punitive, or post-publication, censorship in America; but it established that truth was a defense against charges of libel. Zenger was arrested and charged with seditious libel for criticizing New York Governor William Cosby in his *New York Weekly Journal*. At the age of 80, Andrew Hamilton, one of the leading attorneys in the colonies, took on the case pro bono, considering the issue to be critical to the future of liberty. Putting Milton's *Areopagitica* at the core of the defense, Hamilton won the case with the presumption that truth could not be libel. The case is often referred to as the birth of freedom of the press in America.

1765 The British Stamp Act of 1765 taxed all printed materials circulated in the colonies; the Taunted Acts of 1766 placed duties on American imports of glass, lead, paint, tea, and paper. Together these documents outraged colonial journalists and encouraged press protests until all duties, except those on tea, were removed in 1770. The famed Boston Tea Party (planned at the home of an editor of the *Boston Gazette*) followed in 1773. Then, in rapid succession, the British reacted with the Intolerable Acts of 1774, the First Continental Congress met that same year, and the first shot of the War of Independence was fired in 1775.

1776 In Philadelphia, on July 4, the Declaration of Independence was signed by representatives from the thirteen states of America. It opened with these words: "When in the Course of human events it becomes necessary for one people to dissolve the political bonds which have connected them with another...;" and it continued, "We hold these truths to be self-evident, that all men are created equal, that they are endowed by their Creator with certain unalienable Rights, that among these are Life, Liberty and the pursuit of Happiness..." These eloquent words, with their emphasis on liberty and equality, paved the way for a free society granting free speech and a free press.

1787 The Constitution of the United States was drafted in 1787, ratified in 1788, and went into effect on the first Wednesday of March 1789, thereby formally establishing the United States of America.

1789 The French Revolution of 1789 specifically enshrined the freedoms of "speech, thought, and expression" in Clause 11 of its Declaration of the Rights of Man.

1791 On December 15, the first ten amendments, known collectively as the Bill of Rights, were added to the Constitution. These provisions established a formal contractual agreement between the government and its citizens, encompassing specific concerns not addressed in the Constitution. Foremost among these is Article I, dealing with the freedoms of religion, speech, the press, and the right of petition: "Congress shall make no law respecting an establishment of religion, or prohibiting the free exercise thereof; or abridging the freedom of speech, or of the press; or the right of the people peaceably to assemble, and to petition the Government for a redress of grievances." What might be most remarkable about this most extraordinary document is not what it says but what it does not say. There are no restrictions, contingencies, exclusions, or other provisos dealing with heresy, blasphemy, pornography, obscenity, defamation, national security, sedition, public morals, racism, sexism, libel, slander, political correctness, or a host of other social concerns that have threatened to dilute the strength of the First Amendment for more than 200 years.

1798 The ink was barely dry on the Bill of Rights when Congress enacted the Alien and Sedition Acts of 1798. The legislation would punish anyone who spoke, wrote, or published "any false scandalous and malicious (speech) against the government of the United States" or used speech that would bring the President or Congress "into contempt or disrepute." Although the acts expired in 1801, it wasn't until 1964 that the Supreme Court declared them "inconsistent with the First Amendment."

1802 The English Society for the Suppression of Vice was launched in England, paving the way for similar groups in the United States later in the 19th century.

1818 Dr. Thomas Bowdler, an early British version of Jerry Falwell, was an unsuccessful physician consumed with cleansing the language of any indelicate words or phrases. Specifically, he wanted to eliminate from Shakespeare "whatever is unfit to be read aloud by a gentleman in the company of ladies." In 1818, in London, he published his "Family Shakespeare" which was also widely distributed in the United States. The expurgated version of Shakespeare led to the term "bowdlerized," referring to this form of censorship.

1841 Ralph Waldo Emerson published his famed essay, "Self-Reliance." In this tribute to free expression, he wrote "The virtue in most request is conformity. Self-reliance is its aversion....Whoso would be a man must be a nonconformist....A foolish consistency is the hobgoblin of little minds, adored by little statesmen and philosophers and divines."

1842 At the age of 24, Karl Marx began his career as a working journalist with an essay titled "Remarks on the Latest Prussian Censorship Instruction." Censored by German authorities, it was published a year later by a German-exile press in Switzerland. Marx went on to decry censorship for protecting the interests of the elite and perpetuating the domination of the powerless by the powerful. Ironically, communist societies subsequently used censorship to protect the interest of the elite and to dominate the powerless. Marx himself went on to become one of the most censored authors of modern times, particularly, of course, in capitalist societies.

1842 While Marx was being censored in Germany, the U.S. Congress passed the Tariff Law of 1842, prohibiting "all indecent and obscene prints, paintings, lithographs, engravings, and transparencies" from being imported. In 1857, the law was expanded to include images, figures, and photographs, in order to prevent the importation of Greek statues of "questionable" taste into the U.S.

1856 French novelist Gustave Flaubert was charged with immorality and lasciviousness for publishing *Madame Bovary*. When Flaubert was acquitted, the book, that otherwise might have reached a small audience, became an instant bestseller. The first American edition was published in 1896.

1857 In England, the Obscene Publications Act of 1857 led to an early definition of obscenity. It was also known as the Campbell Act, named for its proponent, the Lord Chief Justice. To assure passage of his bill, Campbell defined an obscene work as one written for the single purpose of corrupting the morals of youth and designed to shock the sense of decency in any well-regulated mind.

1859 In his famous essay "On Liberty," John Stuart Mill, who believed every man is competent to choose what he will read or hear, recorded his thesis on the expression of thought: "Who can compute what the world loses in the multitude of promising intellects combined with timid characters, who dare not follow out any bold, vigorous, independent train of thought, lest it should land them in something which would admit of being considered irreligious or immoral?...No one can be a great thinker who does not recognize that as a thinker it is his first duty to follow his intellect to whatever conclusions it may lead.... There is always hope when people are forced to listen to both sides. It is when they attend only one that errors harden into prejudices and truth itself ceases to have the effect of truth, by being exaggerated into falsehood."

1861 During the Civil War, the U.S. War Department warned journalists against providing any military information that would aid the enemy. The order was generally disregarded, though, leading to casualties. However, more responsible correspondents and editors proved able to report on the war while still concealing information of value to the enemy. In the North, the greatest censorship came from angry mobs who attempted to destroy newspapers with which they disagreed.

1861 William Makepeace Thackeray, founder and editor of *The Cornhill Magazine*, rejected Elizabeth Barrett Browning's poem, "Lord Walter's Wife," as one of many poems and stories he thought to be indecent or indelicate.

1873 The New England Watch and Ward Society and the New York Society for the Suppression of Vice were founded for the purpose of pressuring publishers, editors, and news agents into rejecting controversial writers.

1873 Anthony Comstock was America's answer to England's Thomas Bowdler. Comstock, a religious fanatic whose motto was "Morals, Not Art or Literature," joined with the YMCA to found the New York Society for the Suppression of Vice. As head of this organization, he was given a monopoly by New York to eliminate vice in the state. He also succeeded in getting Congress to pass what was known as The Comstock Act of 1873 which consolidated various statutes and regulations dealing with "obscene, lewd, and lascivious" publications and specifically barred birth-control material from the mail.

Comstock was extraordinarily successful in "fighting vice." In 1874, he reported that in a two-year period, his society had seized 130,000 pounds of bound books along with 60,300 "articles made of rubber for immoral purposes." When he retired in 1915, he estimated that he had destroyed over 160 tons of obscene literature.

One of his great successes was the suppression of Paul Chabas' "September Morn," a romantic painting of a young nude girl bathing on the shore of a lake. The censored painting led to a controversy over the distinction between "nude" and "naked" that persisted for nearly 120 years. Finally, in 1992, Anne-Imelda Radice, acting head of the National Endowment for the Arts in the United States, announced her personal ability to differentiate between "nude" and "naked."

1885 The board of trustees of the Concord Public Library censored a book which "deals with a series of adventures of a very low grade of morality; it is couched in the language of a rough dialect, and all through its pages there is a systematic use of bad grammar....The book is flippant and irreverent....It is trash of the veriest sort." Mark Twain, the author of this dangerous book, *The Adventures of Huckleberry Finn*, responded by saying, "That will sell 25,000 copies for us, sure."

1896 A simple kiss in a play, "The Widow Jones," when seen magnified to a larger than life scale on a screen in the May Irwin-John C. Rice film "Kiss," resulted in the first known attempt at film censorship.

1900 The turn of the century marked the Golden Age of Muckraking—a brief glowing uncensored moment in history when journalists exposed the ills of society, publishers gave them the soapbox, people reacted with indignation, and politicians responded with corrective legislation. The first two decades of the 20th century were distinguished by the clamorous, sometimes sensationalized, efforts of investigative writers like Rheta Child Doss, Finley Peter Dunne, Frank Norris, Upton Sinclair, Lincoln Steffens, and Ida Tarbell. Their investigative style of journalism intrigued readers, exposed the widespread corporate and political corruption of times, and paved the way for many of the social reforms that followed. While President Theodore Roosevelt applied the term "muckrakers" to journalists in a pejorative manner, today it is considered a mark of distinction among some reporters and authors such as Jessica Mitford. Unfortunately, except for the contributions of a few notable journalists, like Drew Pearson, George Seldes, and I.F. Stone, contemporary America has not enjoyed a comparable period of socially aware, concerned, and effective journalism.

1909 Appearing before the Select Committee of both Houses of Parliament which was considering censoring stage plays in 1909, George Bernard Shaw opened his testimony by citing his qualifications as a witness: "I am by profession a playwright...I am not an ordinary playwright in general practice. I am a specialist in immoral and heretical plays. My reputation has been gained by my persistent struggle to force the public to reconsider its morals.... I object to censorship not merely because the existing form of it grievously injures and hinders me individually, but on public grounds." The statement, titled "The Necessity of Immoral Plays," was rejected by the Committee. Shaw subsequently published it as part of the preface to *The Shewing-Up of Blanco Posnet*. Shaw also pointed out, in *The Rejected Statement*, Part I, that "Assassination is the extreme form of censorship."

1911 From 1911 to 1926, the Hearst media empire used its various propaganda techniques to persuade the U.S. to declare war against Mexico. The public would have had a better understanding of Hearst's clamorous propaganda if it had known that his real motivation was to protect his family's land-holding of some 2500 square miles in Mexico against possible expropriation.

Apparently impressed by Hearst's endeavors, Colonel Robert Rutherford McCormick, owner of the *Chicago Tribune*, sent reporter George Seldes to Mexico in 1927 to cover the "coming war" with the United States. Seldes never did find a "war," but he did write a series of ten columns on the situation in Mexico. The first five echoed the official State Department line, supporting American business interests; the second five reported the other side of the issue which Seldes had observed or verified himself. Despite promises to publish all ten columns, the *Tribune* ran only the first five; disgusted with this obvious act of censorship, Seldes quit the *Tribune*.

1912 The first radio-licensing law was passed by Congress and signed by William Howard Taft. It authorized the Secretary of Commerce and Labor to assign wavelengths, time limits, and broadcast licenses. The only control at the time was a loose form of self-censorship by the stations whose taboos included lewd jokes and any discussion of birth control. H.V. Kaltenborn, who lectured on current events over WEAF in New York became one of the first broadcasters to become embroiled in a controversy over the content of a radio talk. Kaltenborn had criticized Secretary of State Charles Evans Hughes regarding the way he had dealt with the Russians.

This led to a request from Washington, through the American Telephone and Telegraph Company, which leased the telephone lines to WEAF, that Kaltenborn be taken off the air. Recognizing the threat to its own best interests, WEAF acquiesced, and Kaltenborn left the station. AT&T saw nothing wrong with its actions; in fact, it acknowledged that it had "constant and complete" cooperation with governmental agencies and had indulged in censorship to maintain this cooperative relationship. The government's first attempt at electronic censorship was a resounding success.

Undaunted by the threat of censorship, radio expanded rapidly; by 1927 there were 733 stations and considerable interference on the broadcast bands. The near-chaotic situation ended with the passage of the Federal

Radio Act of 1927, establishing the Federal Radio Commission (FRC). The Federal Communications Commission (FCC) was later established with passage of the Federal Communications Act of 1934.

1914 *The Woman Rebel,* a feminist newspaper edited by Margaret Sanger, advocated the practice of birth control. After five issues, it was stopped by the U.S. Post Office, which had the authority to censor the press at the time.

1917 The National Civil Liberties Bureau was founded and renamed the American Civil Liberties Union (ACLU) in 1920. The organization was created to deal with civil liberties problems arising out of World War I, including the Espionage and Sedition Acts, conscientious objectors, and political prisoners. It gained national recognition in the mid-1920s by defending the accused individuals in the Scopes trial, the Sweet case, and the Sacco-Vanzetti case. In 1988, it attracted national attention when presidential candidate George Bush resorted to red-baiting by referring derisively to "card-carrying members" of the ACLU.

1917 World War I kept Congress busy churning out legislation designed to prevent any conceivable sign or sound of disloyalty from occurring. First, the Espionage Act of June 15 provided heavy fines and imprisonment for anyone encouraging disloyalty or obstructing recruitment; in practice, it made it easier to jail Wobblies, communist sympathizers, and radicals. Next, on October 6, came the Trading-with-the-Enemy Act, which called for the censorship of all messages sent abroad and required domestic media containing articles in a foreign language to file sworn translations with local postmasters.

1918 Following on the heels of the two paranoia-induced decrees cited above came the Sedition Act of May 16. This made it unlawful to "utter, print, write, or publish any disloyal, profane, scurrilous, or abusive language about the form of the government of the United States, of the Constitution of the United States, or the uniform of the Army or Navy of the United States." As if this were not sufficient, President Woodrow Wilson authorized the formation of the Committee on Public Information (CPI), a propaganda machine headed up by George Creel, a journalist.

Now, for the first time, the brute forces of official censorship were buttressed by the slick techniques of propaganda, self-censorship, and disinformation, in what Creel called "a fight for the mind of mankind." And it worked. While the press eventually rejected CPI's manipulative efforts, most newspapers reportedly published all 6,000 press releases sent out by the CPI News Division.

In late November, *The Nation* magazine warned of the apparent control of the press not merely by the government and its legislation but also by the patriotic desire of the press itself to support the government in its efforts. This cheerleading function of the press was most recently observed during the Gulf War in 1991.

1918 Lenin reintroduced censorship in the Soviet Union as a temporary emergency measure to protect the incipient Bolshevik regime against hostile propaganda, demonstrating how censorship is often rationalized as necessary for self-protection.

1918 The biggest censored story of World War I started on November 11, Armistice Day, when journalist George Seldes and three colleagues broke the Armistice regulations and drove into Germany to see what was happening.

Through luck and bravado, they managed to get an interview with Field Marshal Hindenburg. When Seldes asked him what ended the war, Hindenburg replied it was the American infantry attack in the Argonne that won the war. Without it, Germany would have held out much longer. As a form of punishment for breaking regulations, Seldes' story of Hindenburg's confession was suppressed by military censors, with the support of other U.S. journalists angry because they had been scooped.

The historic interview was never published, except by Seldes, who believed it could have altered the course of history. Hitler built Nazism on what Seldes called a total lie, i.e. that Germany did not lose the war on the battlefield but rather because of the Dolchstoss, or stab-in-the-back "by civilians," "by the Socialists," "by the Communists," and "by the Jews." Had the world known of Hindenburg's confession, Hitler might not have so easily manipulated German citizens into supporting his cause. We'll never know what might have been because of a military censor.

1918 While there were many victims of the repressive censorship laws of World War I, Eugene V. Debs was one of the most famous. Founder of the Social Democratic Party in the United States and five-time presidential candidate (between 1900 and 1920), Debs was tried for espionage for opposing the war effort. His citizenship was revoked and he was sentenced to ten years in prison While in jail in 1920, he ran for president as the Socialist candidate and received nearly a million votes. President Harding commuted his sentence on Christmas Day 1921.

1919 In a Supreme Court ruling in the espionage case *Schenck v. United States*, Justice Oliver Wendell Holmes, delivering the unanimous opinion of the Court, supported the ruling with the now-famed example of censorship warranted by a clear and present danger—"The most stringent protection of free speech would not protect a man in falsely shouting fire in a theatre and causing a panic."

1920   Walter Lippmann, an outstanding journalist, author, and ethicist of the time, issued an early warning about latter day journalists and media moguls in his essay, "Journalism and the Higher Law"—"Just as the most poisonous form of disorder is the mob incited from high places, the most immoral act the immorality of a government, so the most destructive form of untruth is sophistry and propaganda by those whose profession it is to report the news. The news columns are common carriers. When those who control them arrogate to themselves the right to determine by their own consciences what shall be reported and for what purpose, democracy is unworkable. Public opinion is blockaded."

1922   The Motion Picture Producers and Distributors of America (MPPDA) was formed as a self-censoring response to outside critics. The MPPDA, chaired by Will Hays, former Postmaster General and Chairman of the Republican National Committee, paved the way for the creation of a formal motion picture code in 1930.

1924   In *Literature and Revolution*, Leon Trotsky established the role of art in a revolutionary society as a service to the revolutionary state with artists allowed to create in relative freedom but, of course, always under "watchful revolutionary censorship."

1925   John T. Scopes, a young high school teacher, was convicted of violating Tennessee's law that prohibited the teaching of biological evolution (Darwin's theory). In one of the most famous courtroom confrontations in American history, famed liberal attorney Clarence Darrow defended Scopes while William Jennings Bryan assisted the state with the prosecution. Scopes later was released on a technicality by the Tennessee State Supreme Court.

1927   The seeds for repressive censorship measures in Germany were sown when the Reichstag passed a morality law to protect young people from indecent prints and pictures. In the guise of maintaining morality among the youth, the law was used by the police to enter private homes, to supervise dancing in homes, and to protect children from parents. By the time the National Socialists came to power in 1933 with the appointment of Adolph Hitler as Chancellor, modern art was banned and leaders of the Expressionist movement were exiled.

1929   Boston earned its "Banned in Boston" epithet in late 1929 when a wave of censorship swept through the city resulting in what was called a "memorable wholesale book holocaust." Among the 68 books by prominent authors banned during that period were *What I Believe* by Bertrand Russell, *Oil* by Upton Sinclair, *An American Tragedy* by Theodore Dreiser,

Elmer Gantry by Sinclair Lewis, *The Sun Also Rises* by Ernest Hemingway, and *Antic Hay* by Aldous Huxley.

1930 The Motion Picture Producers and Distributors of America (MPPDA) adopted its first Motion Picture Production Code (also known as the Hays Code after the head of the MPPDA). At first, adhering to it was strictly voluntary. Then, in 1933, in response to the National Legion of Decency—founded by the Catholic Church, which had started to review movies—the MPPDA established a stronger code and began to review all scripts. Acceptable films were given a Hays Office seal of approval.

In 1968, again in reaction to outside efforts at censorship, the Motion Picture Association of America (MPPDA became MPAA in 1948) developed a formal, but still voluntary, rating system of four categories: G for general audiences; PG for parental guidance suggested; R for restricted (children under 17 must be accompanied by a parent or guardian); and X (no one under 17 admitted). In 1984, the MPAA added a fifth category: PG-13 (parental guidance suggested for children under 13). In 1990, the X rating was revised to NC-17 (no children under 17 admitted). The X rating had become so popular among promoters of hard-core pornography, it was no longer suited for general use by the theaters.

Finally, in mid-1992, the MPAA revamped its ratings once again, this time to include explanations as to why films are given ratings other than G. For example, the MPAA gave the film "Christopher Columbus—The Discovery" a PG-13 rating, noting that it included "some action violence" and "nudity."

Since its inception in 1930, the MPAA has claimed that the ratings code is not designed to censor a film but rather to warn parents about the content of a film.

1933 James Joyce's celebrated novel *Ulysses* broke the historic barrier of customs censorship when the New York Federal District Court and the Circuit Court of Appeals ruled that it was not obscene within the meaning of federal statutes. Judge John Woolsey, of the District Court, said, "although it contains...many words usually considered dirty, I have not found anything that I consider to be dirt for dirt's sake."

1934 The Federal Communications Act established the Federal Communications Commission (FCC) to succeed the earlier Federal Radio Commission, granting it the right to renew a license as long as the broadcaster operated in the "public interest, convenience, and necessity." It was explicitly stated that the FCC would not have the authority of censor; however, it did have the authority to withhold a license from a broadcaster not operating in the "public interest." Thus, while the FCC could not prohibit liquor advertising, it could emphasize that a station that did advertise liquor, which children could hear, would have to prove that it was acting in the public interest to do so when its license came up for renewal. Not surprisingly, stations have not accepted liquor advertising since. The ban on cigarette advertising is also voluntary.

Although the FCC was not allowed to practice censorship, it wasn't long before advertisers discovered that they were not subject to the same restrictions. Cream of Wheat, which sponsored best-selling author Alexander Woollcott on CBS, received some complaints from listeners that Woollcott had made derogatory remarks about Adolph Hitler. When the author refused the advertiser's request to refrain from such remarks, his series was canceled.

1937 Automobile safety, essentially, has been a censored subject since the 1930s. Auto manufacturers haven't liked to acknowledge that driving can be hazardous to your health. Yet, in January 1937, Dr. Clair Straith, a plastic surgeon who specialized in treating facial injuries from auto accidents, published an article in the *American Medical Association Journal* warning of the dangers and suggesting ways the industry could make cars safer. Nonetheless, Detroit ignored the warnings and continued to stress power and speed.

Nearly three decades later, Ralph Nader, in *Unsafe At Any Speed*, wrote, "It is more than coincidental that radio, television, newspapers and magazines have so long ignored the role of vehicle design in producing...collisions." Not one out of 700 newspapers accepted the offer to run a serialization of his book. In September 1993, Health and Human Services Secretary Donna E. Shalala attributed a decrease in deaths from motor vehicle accidents to an increased use of safety belts and other safety devices and added, "We're now seeing how effective injury control programs and highway design can be."

1938 Information concerning the hazards of cigarette smoking was available as early as 1938 but was ignored, or censored, or played down by the media to such an extent that, even two decades later, only 44 percent of the public thought smoking was a cause of lung cancer. Today, more than a half century after the hazards of smoking were first known, tobacco manufacturers continue to deny such health hazards. Moreover, in the face of a declining market share among people who now understand the dangers, the tobacco industry targets more vulnerable audiences, including young people and residents of the Third World. In August, 1993, the Centers for Disease Control and Prevention announced that smoking related deaths in the United States dropped substantially for the first time since the CDC began gathering the data in 1985.

1938 The infamous House Un-American Activities Committee (HUAC) was founded under the chairmanship of Congressman Martin Dies, Jr. (D-TX) to "expose communist infiltration" in the Congress of Industrial Organizations (CIO) and in FDR's New Deal administration. This powerful congressional body was particularly successful in using the principle of guilt by association.

1938 *Fortune* magazine sent a copy of an editorial about hunger in America to six New York City daily newspapers; it warned of the dangers to a democracy when a third of its citizens were starving. The *New York Post* featured the editorial on its front page and noted that four of the six dailies, including *The New York Times*, completely ignored the story.

The issue continued to attract media attention even three years later when Senator Robert M. La Follette addressed the Senate saying that 45 million people were below the safety line in nutrition; in addition, "Twenty million families must live on not more than eight or nine cents per person per meal. About 14 percent of all American families must live on an average of five cents per person per meal." Again, *The New York Times*, which proudly claims that it prints "all the news that's fit to print," failed to report a word of this the next day.

1939 Communist dictator Joseph Stalin redefined the role of the artist in Russia to require active participation in the political guidance of the country. To accomplish this, Russian artists were expected to practice self-censorship in the interest of the state; those who didn't cooperate often vanished suddenly.

1940 On May 20, 1940, George Seldes—America's Emeritus Journalist and the most censored journalist in history—published Volume I, Number 1, of *In Fact*, a biweekly newsletter for "the millions who want a free press." The premiere issue exposed a secret meeting of 18 prominent American leaders who decided to "do their utmost to abrogate existing neutrality legislation," reprimanded the press for its failure to reveal how a major soap manufacturer had been caught "fooling the American people through fake advertising," and warned readers about Father Coughlin and his anti-Semitic hate campaign. George Seldes, hailed as the grandfather of the alternative press and the creator of modern investigative journalism, celebrated his 103rd birthday in September 1993. He also is a former Project Censored judge.

1940 Morris Ernst, one of the nation's leading crusaders against censorship, compiled and categorized a comprehensive list of works censored in the United States. The list included some of the world's greatest classics, including works by Homer, Shakespeare, Whitman, and Darwin.

1940 The American Library Association (ALA) established the Committee on Intellectual Freedom, one of the nation's leading advocates of the First

Amendment and free speech. Part of the committee's responsibility is to guard, protect, defend, and extend intellectual freedom.

1940 "The Outlaw," a sexy western starring a sultry Jane Russell in a push-up bra designed by Howard Hughes, was denied the film industry's "seal of approval" because, as one judge put it, Jane Russell's breasts "hung over the picture like a thunderstorm spread out over a landscape." While the film is now available in the 95 and 103 minute versions, no one appears to have a copy of the original uncensored 117-minute version.

1941 The Manhattan Project, the research effort that led to the atomic bomb, was launched in total secrecy. Within a few years, more than a half-million people across the U.S. were involved in one of the most secretive scientific projects in history. The successful information-control practices employed by the Manhattan Project paved the way for the news management, manipulation, and obfuscation which has since characterized the nation's nuclear research, in peacetime as well as wartime.

1941 An extraordinary two-year U.S. Senate investigation of the concentration of economic power in the U.S. concluded that the National Association of Manufacturers (representing large corporations) and the United States Chamber of Commerce were receiving favored treatment from the press. Although similar charges often have been made since then, America's corporate elite and the press continue to deny that such favored treatment exists.

1941 World War II censorship was initiated when President Franklin Delano Roosevelt created the U.S. Office of Censorship with Byron Price, former executive news editor of The Associated Press, as director. Price had the authority to censor all international communications, including mail, cable, and radio. At its peak, the postal section of his office had more than 10,000 employees. Nonetheless, there was little public outrage over censorship during WWII, the result of Price's successful efforts to encourage editors and publishers to practice "voluntary cooperation" with the censorship program.

That effort, along with the Office of War Information (OWI), a propaganda organization headed up by Elmer Davis, formerly with CBS News and *The New York Times*, co-opted the traditional negative reaction to information control. The fact that American citizens were more united behind the nation during WWII than WWI also aided the censorship effort. The Office of Censorship closed on August 15, 1945, a few hours after the surrender of Japan. Shortly after the end of the war, the OWI was succeeded by the United States Information Service, under the auspices of the State Department.

1947 "A Free and Responsible Press," a comprehensive and critical report on the status of the media, was issued by the Commission on Freedom of the Press, headed by Dr. Robert M. Hutchins, Chancellor of the University of Chicago. The study, funded by a $200,000 grant from Henry Luce, owner of *Time* and *Life*, found free speech to be in grave danger—not so much from the government as from those who controlled access to the media. The report warned, "One of the most effective ways of improving the press is blocked by the press itself. By a kind of unwritten law the press ignores the errors and misrepresentation, the lies and scandals, of which its members are guilty." Not surprisingly, the landmark report was given a lukewarm reception by the press. Commenting on the press coverage of the Commission's report, Hutchins said, "Some treated it unfairly, some used untruthful headlines, and some just plain lied about it."

1947 The Dead Sea Scrolls, dating from approximately 22 B.C. to A.D. 100, were discovered in Wadi Qumran. They were almost immediately subjected to censorship by controlled access, which continued until 1991 when biblical scholars forced official researchers to share the information.

1947 Charlie Chaplin's "Monsieur Verdoux," a satirical film criticizing munitions makers and military leaders and espousing a more humanistic morality, drew protests and pickets by veterans and religious groups. The outcry resulted in the film being withdrawn from distribution. Chaplin, one of the world's greatest filmmakers, whose impersonation of "the little tramp" created laughter everywhere it was shown, left the U.S. for a self-imposed exile in Switzerland.

1947 Prompted by allegations that the government was infiltrated by communist spies, President Harry S Truman issued an executive order establishing a loyalty-security program for government employees. The program paved the way for one of the nation's most repressive political periods, from 1949 to 1953, which came to be known as the McCarthy era, named after Senator Joseph McCarthy (R-Wisconsin). McCarthy, who incessantly charged that "card-carrying communists" had infiltrated our government from top to bottom, was one of the most feared and controversial men in U.S. Senate history. He was eventually censured by the U.S. Senate on a vote of 67-22 and died a discredited disgrace in 1957.

1948 The Library Bill of Rights was adopted by the American Library Association to resist "all abridgment of the free access to ideas and full freedom of expression." With the First and Fourteenth Amendments to the Constitution as its foundation, the Bill took an unequivocal stand on the freedom to read and supported democracy in full measure, stating, "There should be the fullest practicable provision of material presenting all points of view concerning the problems and issues of our times, international, national, and local." America's librarians are the nation's first line of defense in the ongoing battle against censorship.

1948 Alfred Kinsey published *Sexual Behavior in the Human Male*, first of the "Kinsey Reports," which influenced public attitudes toward sex, helped promote sexual freedom and expression, and, at the same time provided a major target for censors. The second report, *Sexual Behavior in the Human Female*, was published in 1953.

1948 The Universal Declaration of Human Rights was adopted by the General Assembly of the United Nations as "Article XIX." It holds that freedom of expression is not the property of any political system or ideology but is, rather, a universal human right, now defined and guaranteed in international law. Article 19 also became the name of an international human rights organization founded in England in 1986.

1949 Apparently seeing a threat of communism in certain murals on the walls of public buildings, Richard Nixon, then a Republican Congressman from California, wrote, "I believe a committee should make a thorough investigation of this type of art in government buildings with the view of obtaining removal of all that is found to be inconsistent with American ideals and principles." Nixon went on to even greater efforts at censorship as his career progressed.

1952 The Television Code, adopted by the National Association of Broadcasters, spoke eloquently about commercial television's responsibility to augment the "educational and cultural influence of schools, institutions of higher learning, the home, the church, museums, foundations, and other institutions devoted to education and culture." It also addressed the medium's specific responsibilities toward children and the community. The Code has been subject to a number of interpretations and revisions since. Potential dangers of censorship by the networks, affiliates, advertisers, and the government have yet to be addressed.

1953 On January 17, 1953, I.F. Stone published the first issue of *I.F. Stone's Weekly* in Washington, DC. Following in the footsteps of George Seldes, whom he cited as a mentor, Stone used his extraordinary investigative skills to criticize the U.S. government and its policies. The *Weekly* was an early and clamorous opponent to U.S. involvement in the Vietnam War. Stone's wit and wisdom attracted more than 70,000 subscribers by the time the final issue was published in December 1971.

1953 President Dwight D. Eisenhower, often maligned for his military background, warned of censorship during a talk at Dartmouth College: "Don't join the book burners. Don't think you are going to conceal faults by concealing evidence that they ever existed. Don't be afraid to go into your library and read every book as long as it does not offend your own ideas of decency. That should be the only censorship." In June, 1953, in a letter to the American Library Association Convention, President Eisenhower wrote: "As it is an ancient truth that freedom cannot be legislated into existence, so it is no less obvious that freedom cannot be censored into existence."

1954 The evening of March 9, 1954, has been called television's finest hour. It was the night that Edward R. Murrow, on his weekly program "See It Now," permitted Senator Joseph R. McCarthy to destroy himself in front of millions of viewers. Murrow concluded his program saying, "The actions of the junior senator from Wisconsin have caused alarm and dismay amongst our allies abroad and given considerable comfort to our enemies. And whose fault is that? Not really his; for he didn't create this situation of fear, he merely exploited it and rather successfully. Cassius was right. 'The fault, dear Brutus, is not in our stars but in ourselves.'"

Referring to the years the press had permitted McCarthy to decimate Americans' civil rights, Murrow later said, "The timidity of television in dealing with this man when he was spreading fear throughout the land is not something to which this art of communication can ever point with pride. Nor should it be allowed to forget it." McCarthy was surely not the first demagogue to intimidate the press; nor will he be the last.

1957 The Supreme Court made its first significant effort to define obscenity. Until now it had worked with what was known as the Hicklin rule, a carry-over description of obscenity from British law, which ruled that obscenity had a tendency to deprave and corrupt those whose minds were open to such immoral influences (such as children) and into whose hands it might fall. In 1957, the Supreme Court replaced this extraordinarily strict interpretation of obscenity with what came to be known as the Roth-Memoirs Test. This ruling established three tests, or standards, for ruling a work obscene: 1) The dominant theme of the material, taken as a whole, appeals to an average person's prurient interest in sex; 2) the material is patently offensive because it affronts contemporary community standards, assuming a single national standard, relating to sexual matters; and 3) the material is utterly without redeeming social value. This test for obscenity, while less restrictive than Hicklin, permitted a wide range of legal maneuvering and remained in effect until 1973.

1958 In defending the absolutist theory of the First Amendment, which holds that "no law" means *no law*, William O. Douglas, Supreme Court Justice, wrote: "The First Amendment does not say that there is freedom of expression provided the talk is not 'dangerous.' It does not say that there is freedom of expression provided the utterance has no tendency to subvert. It does not put free speech and freedom of the press in the category of housing, sanitation, hours of work, factory conditions, and the like, and make it subject to regulation for the public good. Nor does it permit legislative restraint of freedom of expression so long as the regulation does not offend due process. All notions of regulation or restraint by government are absent from the First Amendment. For it says in words that are unambiguous, 'Congress shall make no law...abridging the freedom of speech, or of the press.'"

1959 D.H. Lawrence's novel, *Lady Chatterly's Lover*, first published in Italy in 1928, was banned by the Federal Post Office Department when published in New York in 1959. The New York Postmaster withheld some 200,000 copies of a circular announcing the new Grove Press edition of the book. The Federal Courts subsequently ruled that the book was not hard-core pornography and dismissed the banning restriction. *Lady Chatterly's Lover* and James Joyce's *Ulysses* are among the most important contemporary censorship cases. Both books, by noted literary artists, were subjected to obscenity charges; both were tried, appealed, and approved in federal courts; and both remain controversial to this day.

1959 Clarifying the distinction between freedom and pornography in a capitalist system versus a communist system, Soviet premier Nikita Khrushchev said, "This is a dance (the Can-Can) in which girls pull up their skirts.... This is what you call freedom—freedom for the girls to show their backsides. To us it's pornography. The culture of people who want pornography. It's capitalism that makes the girls that way.... There should be a law prohibiting the girls from showing their backsides, a moral law."

1960 A classic example of the misguided foolishness of news media self-censorship was provided by the events surrounding the Bay of Pigs disaster. In November, 1960, editors of *The Nation* magazine tried to interest major news media in an article charging that the U.S. was preparing to invade Cuba, but no one took the story. While reports of the impending invasion were widely known throughout Central America, the American press followed the lead of *The New York Times* which dismissed the reports as "shrill...anti-American propaganda." Following the tragic, ill-fated invasion, President John F. Kennedy, who had persuaded the *Times* to withhold the story, acknowledged that had the press fulfilled its traditional watchdog role and reported the pending invasion, it would have saved the nation from a disastrous decision and the subsequent national disgrace; he told *The New York Times:* "If you had printed more about the operation, you could have saved us from a colossal mistake."

1960 *The New York Times vs Sullivan*—a landmark case in libel law, introduced the concept of malice in journalism. On March 29, 1960, *The New York Times* published a full-page ad signed by some 64 people who charged that thousands of black Southern students engaging in nonviolent protests had been deprived of their constitutional rights. The ad specifically cited an event that occurred in Montgomery, Alabama. L.B. Sullivan, the commissioner of public affairs in Montgomery at the time, filed a libel suit against the New York Times Company and others. In finding for the *Times*, Supreme Court Justice William J. Brennan Jr., said: "We are required in this case to determine for the first time the extent to which the constitutional protections for speech and press limit a State's power to award damages in a libel action brought by a public official against critics of his official conduct." In doing so in this case, the court ruled that it would be more difficult, under law, for a public official to win a libel suit than it is for a private citizen. The ruling now requires that the public official must prove that the statement was made with "actual malice"—that is, with knowledge that it was false, or with reckless disregard as to whether it was false. The 1981 movie, "Absence of Malice," starring Sally Field and Paul Newman, popularized this court decision regarding libel.

1963 Whatever the truth may be behind the assassination of President John F. Kennedy, the news media cannot justify their early and uncritical endorsement of the Warren Commission Report. Their initial attempts to silence the critics of the official version smacked of raw censorship. When a leading scholar offered to write an analysis of the commission's operations, *The New York Times* rejected the offer, saying, "The case is closed." Mark Lane's book on the same subject, *Rush To Judgment*, was not rushed to print. Lane could not find a publisher for 15 months and it was only published after the media decided the issue was acceptable for coverage as a "controversy."

Lane's second book, *A Citizen's Dissent*, published in early 1968, records how his pleas for a national examination of the evidence was rejected by *Look*, *Life*, the *Saturday Evening Post* and others. When UPI was offered advanced proof sheets, they replied they "would not touch it." This book provides what may be the most exhaustive and documented study ever undertaken of the mass media's use of hidden bias on one issue. Not surprisingly, three years after publication, Lane reported that he hadn't been able to discover "one newspaper story in the mass media noting that the book had been published." Lane said that several media representatives told him: "We will bury that book with silence." And they did.

Incredibly, the media's conspiracy-like efforts to attack anything critical of the original Warren Commission Report's interpretation of the assassination was still in evidence in 1991. The press, in what appeared to be a well-orchestrated campaign, left no stone unturned in its criticism of film producer Oliver Stone and his movie, "JFK," which did not support the commission's findings. The effort was so exceptional, Stone had to hire one of the nation's leading public relations firms, Hill & Knowlton, to counteract the attacks and defend himself.

Indicative of the extent of censorship surrounding the Kennedy assassination was the way Abraham Zapruder's eight-millimeter film of the assassination was handled. This extraordinary bit of footage, which recorded the actual assassination, raised serious questions about the Warren Commission's version of the event. The film, originally purchased by Time Inc. and later sold back to Zapruder, was not shown on national television until 1975, when it was aired on Tom Snyder's late-night "Tomorrow" show.

1966 In passing the Freedom of Information Act (FOIA), Congress established the American public's "right to know." It was signed into law by President Lyndon Johnson and went into effect on July 4, 1967. Unfortunately, years of information control and manipulation, as well as disdain for the FOIA by the Reagan/Bush administrations, encouraged federal agencies to find ways to circumvent it. Today, it's extremely time-consuming and expensive for the public—as well as the press—to use it.

1966 At 10 a.m., on February 10, the U.S. Senate Foreign Relations Committee began hearings on the Vietnam war with the testimony of Ambassador George F. Kennan. Over the objections of Fred W. Friendly, president of CBS News, the network aired a fifth CBS rerun of "I Love Lucy" instead of the hearings. Because of that decision, Friendly quit CBS and subsequently wrote *Due to Circumstances Beyond Our Control...*to tell what happened. The book begins with a quotation: "What the American people don't know can kill them." And it did. More than 58,000 Americans died in Vietnam, and many tens of thousands of returned Vietnam veterans have died from war-related problems since.

1968 Dr. Paul Ehrlich's book *The Population Bomb* created a stir with its prediction that mass famines would plague the world within 20 years. Ehrlich warned that to avoid the tragedy of overpopulation, birth rates must be curbed. In 1971, media critic Robert Cirino, referring to Ehrlich's book, was equally prescient with his warning that "Experts have been making urgent pleas for controlling population and pollution for the last twenty-five years. But did the news media alert us in time?" Ehrlich's prediction has been tragically fulfilled with the African famines of the 1980s and 1990s, yet his warning continues to go unheeded. The earth's population is now growing at a rate of more than 100 million people a year, and few people, including the press, seem to be aware that this is indeed a problem.

1968 The Columbia University Center for Mass Communications in New York offered all three networks a documentary using U.S. Army footage which depicted the horrifying effects of the atomic bomb on individual Japanese victims. The Army had suppressed the film since 1945 and only released it at the insistence of the Japanese government. The film was described by Columbia University Professor Sumner J. Glimcher as "perhaps the best argument for people to live in peace." All three networks rejected the offer to run the documentary, telling the University they just weren't interested; nor did they use the Army's film, which also was available to them, to produce a documentary of their own.

1968 On March 16, some 570 South Vietnamese civilians were slaughtered in Mylai by the U.S. military. Although the massacre was reported over the radio in South Vietnam and in French publications, neither the U.S. press nor that of any other country challenged the official Pentagon version that 128 "Reds" had been killed. Ronald Ridenhour, a former soldier, spent six months investigating the tragedy and talking to witnesses before trying to interest federal officials and the media in the story. He contacted the President, Secretary of State, Secretary of Defense, numerous congressmen, *Life, Look, Newsweek, Harper's*, major newspapers, two wire services, and at least one of the networks. Neither the politicians nor the media was interested.

By September, 1969, nearly 18 months after the tragedy, David Leonard, a reporter for the *Columbus Enquirer,* followed up on a lead about Lt. William Calley Jr., and published a front-page story about him. The media ignored it, and the story died. In October, Seymour Hersh, then a freelance writer in Washington, DC, investigated the report and tried to sell his version to several publications, including *Life* and *Look*. Again they were not interested. He finally sold the story to the Dispatch News Service, which released it on November 13; at last, the media put the issue on the national agenda.

1968 On September 24, "60 Minutes" was launched on the CBS television network. The weekly hour-long program became known for its hard-hitting investigative reports and went on to become the most popular show in the history of television. The "father" of television news magazines celebrated its 25th anniversary in 1993.

1968 The critical need for mass media coverage of social problems, and the potential impact such coverage can have, was made clear when CBS-TV News broadcast a documentary, titled "Hunger in America." The documentary stirred a public debate, made hunger a national issue overnight, and had a lasting impact. The U.S. Department of Agriculture expanded its food program to more counties, increased its monthly surplus of food going to the poor, and called for an expansion of the food stamp program.

1968 "The Final Report: President's Task Force on Communications Policy," published December 7, was highly critical of the nation's commercial television system. It strongly recommended creating a television communications system that would ensure a diversity of ideas and tastes, so that all minorities and majorities could be represented on television. President Johnson refused to make the report public before he left office, and the new president, Richard Nixon, delayed its release for another four months, until May 1969. Neither Johnson nor Nixon should have been worried; when the media finally did get the report, they essentially suppressed the potentially explosive information. The *Los Angeles Times* "covered" the report in a two-inch article on Page 2 under the daily news roundup; *The New York Times* reported it under a small headline in the middle of Page 95.

1969 "The Smothers Brothers Comedy Hour," a weekly entertainment program, was canceled by CBS for failing to cooperate with the network's program-previewing policies. According to the brothers, the program was often censored by CBS, with up to 75 percent of a program being edited out before being aired. In one classic case of broadcasting censorship, as cited by Robert Cirino in his book *Power to Persuade*, CBS asked Pete Seeger, the famed folk singer who was blacklisted by broadcasters for 17 years, to drop the following verse from one of his songs on the Smothers Brothers program. It referred to the position in which the U.S. found itself in Vietnam in 1967:

> *But every time I read the papers*
> *That old feeling comes on;*
> *We're waist deep in the Big Muddy*
> *And the big fool says to push on.* ©

When Seeger refused to drop the verse, CBS censored the entire song, prompting Seeger to say, "It is wrong for anyone to censor what I consider my most important statement to date.... I think the public should know that the airwaves are censored for ideas as well as for sex."

1969 In a letter to *The New York Times*, Charles Tower, chairman of the National Association of Broadcasters Television Board, proposed an interesting new definition of censorship. Tower criticized *The Times* for attacking CBS-TV for "censoring" social commentary on the Smothers Brothers show (see above). He suggested, "There is a world of difference between the deletion of program material by Government command and the deletion by a private party (such as a broadcaster).... Deletion by

Government command is censorship.... Deletion of material by private parties...is not censorship." While Tower's definition was spurious as well as self-serving, there are probably some who would support his thesis, even now.

1969 In August, the outrageous but historic three-day Woodstock Music and Art Fair in New York State paved the way for future rock festivals by showing it was possible to overcome censorship rules and regulations set-up by local authorities to prevent such festivals.

1969 On November 13, during a speech in Des Moines, Iowa, Vice President Spiro Agnew launched a series of scurrilous and unsubstantiated attacks on the nation's media, accusing them of favoring liberals. His stand was applauded by the vast majority of media owners who shared Agnew's opinion. These accusations are still used today to support the pervasive myth of "the liberal American media."

1970 Agnew continued his verbal assault, attacking the underground press, rock music, books, and movies for luring American youth into a drug culture. He told his audience, "You need a Congress that will see to it that the wave of permissiveness, the wave of pornography, and the wave of moral pollution never become the wave of the future in our country." In a speech in Las Vegas he specifically criticized radio stations for playing songs that contain "drug culture propaganda." On March 5, 1971, the FCC issued a notice to broadcasters, holding them responsible for airing songs that would "promote or glorify the use of illegal drugs" and made it abundantly clear that any station ignoring this notice could lose its license.

1970 On May 4, four students protesting the Cambodian incursion during the Vietnam War were killed by the National Guard on the Kent State University campus in Ohio.

1970 *How To Talk Back To Your Television Set*, a strident criticism of television by Nicholas Johnson, a former member of the FCC, cites a series of CBS-TV documentaries that were "shelved, turned down, or killed," including "a 'hard-hitting' documentary on homosexuals gutted before showing by the management....an 'in-depth investigation' of Saigon corruption, also tabled.... film footage of North Vietnam rejected for broadcast.... an hour production on [the] black middle class, dumped...a project on 'Police Brutality,' turned into 'an industrial promo film for sponsor IBM'...a probe of the military industrial complex, ultimately devoted to 'the nomenclature of military rockets.'" Johnson also noted that CBS had pending for several years a project on "Congressional ethics"; he wondered whether we'd ever see it. The relevancy of the subjects of those censored documentaries to today's social problems is self-evident.

1970 The President's Commission on Obscenity and Pornography failed to find evidence linking obscene materials to criminal behavior, a conclusion that led both President Richard M. Nixon and the U.S. Senate to reject the report. The lesson was not lost on President Ronald Reagan, who later appointed Attorney General Edwin Meese to direct his own Commission on Pornography in 1985.

1971 Robert Cirino, a secondary school teacher in San Fernando, California, published an extraordinary book *Don't Blame the People: How the news media use bias, distortion and censorship to manipulate public opinion.* After being rejected by mainstream publishers, Cirino published the book himself. Following its success as a college textbook, it was picked up and published by Random House in 1972. Cirino's closing paragraph sums up the role of the press in America and suggests a solution:

> The effort to improve the quality of life in America has to be first the fight to save America from the distorted view of reality presented by the communication industry. It is a fight to restore the average man's participation in government by really letting him decide important questions. It is the average man, the man who doesn't have large corporate interests to protect, that is the strength of a democracy. His reasoning ability and sense of justice enacted into decisions and policies constitute the type of government envisioned by those who wrote America's Declaration of Independence. There has never been a better idea of governing a nation. Our major mistakes have not been the result of democracy, *but of the erosion of democracy made possible by mass media's manipulation of public opinion.* This erosion could only be stopped in the unlikely event that the Courts, the Congress and the American people were to demand that all political viewpoints have equal control over access to a mass communication system that is not for sale to anyone.

1971 On June 13, *The New York Times* started to print the Pentagon Papers, part of a top-secret 47-volume government study of decision-making on Vietnam. Two days later, *The Times* was barred from continuing the series. In pleading its right to publish the papers before the Supreme Court, *The Times*, in effect, appeared to abandon the First Amendment in proposing the establishment of guidelines for prior restraint. Supreme Court Justice William O. Douglas warned *The Times*: "The First Amendment provides that Congress shall make no laws abridging the freedom of the press. Do you read that to mean that Congress can make some laws abridging freedom of the press?" It was, added Justice Douglas, "a very strange argument for *The Times* to be making." On June 30, the Supreme Court, by a 6-3 vote, told *The Times* it could go ahead and print the rest of the material.

1971 In December, I.F. Stone, marking the end of a special era in journalism, published the last issue of *I.F. Stone's Weekly*. In his essay, "Notes On Closing, But Not In Farewell," Stone wrote: "To give a little comfort to the oppressed, to write the truth exactly as I saw it, to make no compromises other than those of quality imposed by my own inadequacies, to be free to follow no master other than my own compulsions, to live up to my idealized image of what a true newspaper man should be and still be able to make a living for my family—what more could a man ask?"

1971 "The Selling of the Pentagon," a hard-hitting CBS documentary, told the American people how much money the Pentagon was spending to buy a favorable public image for itself. Congress, particularly Rep. F. Edward Hebert, chair of the House Armed Services Committee, and members of the Nixon administration were outraged. When CBS-TV rebroadcast the show about a month later, it had to add 15 minutes of rebuttal from Hebert (who called it "un-American"), Vice President Spiro Agnew (who called it a "vicious broadside against the nation's defense establishment"), and Secretary of Defense Melvin Laird (often caricatured with a missile head). The House Committee on Interstate and Foreign Commerce unsuccessfully attempted to subpoena the film, and a committee vote to request a contempt citation against CBS had to be voted down.

1972 The break-in of the Democratic National Committee offices in the Watergate complex by the Republican CREEP (Committee to Re-elect the President) in June sparked one of the biggest political cover-ups in modern history. And the press, to its lasting shame, was an unwitting, if not willing, partner in the cover-up. The break-in, by CREEP employees known as the "plumbers," was described as a "two-bit burglary" not worthy of press attention. It didn't manage to get on the national news agenda until after November, when Richard Nixon was re-elected with a landslide vote. Carl Bernstein and Bob Woodward, both with the *Washington Post*, eventually made it a national story. Bernstein noted that out of some 2,000 full-time reporters for major news organizations, just 14 were assigned to the story on a full-time basis, even six months after the break-in. When Walter Cronkite tried to do an extraordinary two-part series on Watergate on the "CBS-TV Evening News," *before* the election, a phone call from the Nixon White House to Bill Paley, chair of CBS, resulted in Cronkite's scheduled program being reduced. The power of a President to directly intervene and censor the nation's leading broadcast news organization was revealed. Ironically, 21 years after the Watergate break-in, when the government released three additional hours of the tapes to the public, Nixon was heard plotting to deflect the blame for the break-in and calculating that Watergate was "a Washington son-of-a-bitching story" most Americans would shrug off.

1972 The Supreme Court ruled that dancing, even topless dancing, was a type of expression entitled to protection under the First Amendment. This judicial ruling encouraged the growth of topless, and eventually bottomless, dancing in bars throughout America.

1972 The Supreme Court ruled that the Central Intelligence Agency could preview its employees' speeches and publications to protect against any disclosure of classified information. In 1980, this ruling was expanded to include pre-publication review of all materials, including unclassified information. This decision was based on a case involving a former CIA agent who published a book criticizing U.S. actions during the Vietnam War. The book contained no classified information.

1972 The first issue of the *Index On Censorship* was published, acknowledging that "the need for such a magazine would become clear in the next few years"—and it has. The *Index*, an international advocate of free expression, focuses on the censorship, banning, and exile of writers and journalists throughout the world.

1973 Beginning with the case of *Miller v. California*, the Supreme Court refined the Roth-Memoirs 1957 definition of obscenity, replacing national standards with local community standards. What is known as the Miller Test for obscenity is used today by American courts to determine whether a work is, by law, obscene. Written material is legally obscene under the following three conditions: 1) An average person, applying contemporary local community standards, finds that the work, taken as a whole, appeals to prurient interest; 2) The work depicts, in a patently offensive way, sexual conduct specifically defined by applicable state law; and 3) The material lacks serious literary, artistic, political, or scientific value.

1973 "Sticks and Bones"—a dramatic, filmed version of an award-winning stage drama about the homecoming of a blind Vietnam veteran and his callous reception—was scheduled to be shown on CBS on March 9. Just four days before air date, CBS executives postponed the program, saying it would be "unnecessarily abrasive to the feelings of millions of Americans whose lives or attention were dominated at the time by the returning POWs and other veterans." Joseph Papp, producer of the film, called the postponement "a cowardly cop-out, a rotten affront to freedom of speech." When the drama was finally shown five months later, only 91 affiliate stations carried it (less than half of the 184 that normally would carry the network's programs). Many advertisers canceled their commercials.

1975 Ruling on the constitutionality of a Tennessee ban on the rock musical "Hair," the U.S. Supreme Court decided that live theater had legal protection against prior restraint, as was the case with books, movies, and other forms of expression.

1976 Project Censored, the national media research project focusing on news media censorship, was founded by Carl Jensen, Ph.D., at Sonoma State University, Rohnert Park, California. The top ten *Censored* stories of 1976 were:

1. Jimmy Carter and the Trilateral Commission
2. Corporate Control of DNA
3. Selling Banned Pesticides and Drugs to Third World Countries
4. The Oil Price Conspiracy
5. The Mobil Oil/Rhodesian Connection
6. Missing Plutonium and Inadequate Nuclear Reactor Safeguards
7. Workers Die for American Industry
8. Kissinger, the CIA, and SALT
9. Worthless or Harmful Non-prescription Drugs
10. The Natural Gas "Shortage"

1976 On June 2nd, Don Bolles, investigative reporter for the *Arizona Republic* was permanently "censored" when his car exploded in the parking lot of the Hotel Chardon in Phoenix. Bolles was investigating a lead dealing with massive land frauds, political payoffs, the underworld, and corporate crime. Following the assassination, nearly 100 journalists, organized as the Investigative Reporters and Editors Inc. (IRE), produced a 23-installment series on crime and corruption in Arizona. John Harvey Adamson, who admitted to planting the dynamite under Bolles' car, testified that Bolles was killed as a favor to Kemper Marley, one of Arizona's richest and most powerful figures and a target of Bolles exposés. Ironically, in 1993, the University of Arizona named one of its buildings after Kemper Marley following a $6 million contribution to the university. Marley died in 1990 at 83.

1977 The FCC outlawed a monologue, "Seven Words You Can't Say On Radio" by comedian George Carlin, from being broadcast on radio or television. While the words still have shock value in print, they're surely not strangers on television, particularly on cable. The seven words that assured Carlin of lasting First Amendment fame were "shit," "piss," "fuck," "cunt," "cocksucker," "motherfucker," and "tits."

1977 When the ACLU defended the rights of the Nazi party to demonstrate in Skokie, near Chicago, 15 to 20 percent of ACLU members dropped their membership in protest. While the Illinois Appellate Court gave the Nazis permission to demonstrate but not to wear the swastika, the Illinois Supreme Court subsequently ruled that the Nazis had a right to display the swastika.

1977 The problem of decommissioning nuclear power plants—one of Project Censored's top ten Censored stories of 1977—wasn't discovered until some of the original plants and reactors had to be shut down. In two cases, the costs for dismantling the plant ran almost as high as the original construction costs. Decommissioning nuclear power plants remains an unresolved issue in 1994.

1978 The specter of sterility was raised when researchers discovered that the average sperm count among American men had dropped substantially since a landmark study done less than 30 years earlier. The research revealed that the probable causes were industrial and agricultural chemicals similar to the DBCP pesticide (which, earlier, had led to male sterility at a chemical plant), and that the trend may represent a potential sterility threat to the entire male population. The threat, one of the top ten Censored stories of the year, wasn't dramatic enough to attract the attention of the mass media at the time. However, in mid-September, 1992, a new study made front-page news when a growing number of scientists concluded that changes in sexuality, including reduced fertility, may have occurred in humans exposed to chemical pollution.

1979 The longest period of government censorship by prior restraint of a publication in U.S. history began March 9. A Federal District Court in Wisconsin imposed a temporary restraining order on *The Progressive*, a Wisconsin-based monthly magazine, censoring publication of the article, "The H-Bomb Secret: How We Got It, Why We're Telling It." The government claimed that the description of how a hydrogen bomb was designed would help foreign countries produce H-bombs more swiftly. But the government finally acknowledged the meaning of the First Amendment on September 17, when it ruled the magazine could publish the article.

1979 To find cheap labor and to escape U.S. health and safety regulations, increasing numbers of major American corporations set up branches or contracted jobs under "sweatshop" conditions in Third World countries. This story—one of the top ten *Censored* stories of 1979—attracted national attention during the 1992 presidential election year, as unemployment plagued workers in the U.S., and health problems and environmental pollution plagued workers in Third World countries.

1980 The top Censored story of 1980, "Distorted Reports of the El Salvador Crisis," launched more than a decade of top ten Censored stories dealing with underreported or biased reports of U.S. intervention in Central America.

1981 The American people were told that the over-regulation of business and the "declining moral fiber of the American worker" had caused the worst economic crisis since the depression. But Maurice Zeitlin, a UCLA economic sociologist, testifying before the California Senate Committee on Industrial Relations, charged that we no longer had a competitive economy, and that monopoly, militarism, and multinationalization were at the root of our economic crisis. His testimony, cited as the top *Censored* story of 1981, also suggested that we could expect more of the same until the root causes are examined and changed.

1982 President Reagan established an oppressive system of security classification with his Executive Order 12356. It reversed a trend toward openness on the part of previous administrations by eliminating what was known as the balancing test. Now it was no longer necessary to weigh the public's need to know against the need for classification. In addition, the Executive Order reduced the threshold standard for classification. That same year, Project Censored cited Reagan as "America's Chief Censor" for his efforts to reduce the amount of information available to the public about the operation of the government, the economy, the environment, and public health, and for his attempts to weaken the Freedom of Information Act.

1982 *The Media Monopoly*, by Ben Bagdikian, was published, revealing that just 50 corporations control half or more of the media in America.

1983 National Security Decision Directive 84 (NSDD 84), issued by the Reagan Administration in March, required all government personnel with access to classified materials to sign a lifetime secrecy pledge.

1984 Fulfilling the Orwellian expectations of the year, President Reagan implemented NSDD 84—the largest censoring apparatus ever known in the United States. For the first time in history, millions of federal employees were required to submit their speeches, articles, and books for prepublication review by their superiors for the rest of their lives. Under pressure from Congress, the administration suspended the pre-publication review provision in September 1984, but a 1986 General Accounting Office report on its impact concluded that the suspension had little effect, and that pre-publication review was alive and well in America.

1984 On September 14, CBS reporter Mike Wallace appeared on the "Phil Donahue Show" and predicted that one of the segments he was working on for

"60 Minutes" could possibly change the course of the presidential election. The story focused on one of Ronald Reagan's closest friends, Nevada Senator Paul Laxalt, who was high on Reagan's list of potential Supreme Court nominees. Journalists investigating Laxalt found he had accepted political contributions from supporters linked to organized crime, received highly questionable loans, tried to limit FBI investigations into Nevada gaming operations and owned a Carson City casino that engaged in illegal skimming operations. After being contacted by Laxalt and his attorney, CBS decided not to run the story. And although the story didn't have a chance to change the course of the 1984 election, as predicted by Wallace, Ronald Reagan never nominated Laxalt to the Supreme Court.

1985 President Ronald Reagan appointed Attorney General Edwin Meese to head his Commission on Pornography. The members, reportedly hand-picked for their support of censorship, spent considerable time investigating erotic films, books, and magazines protected by the First Amendment. Based on the testimony of the Rev. Donald Wildmon, executive director of the National Federation of Decency, the commission sent a letter to 26 major corporations, including K-mart, Southland (7-Eleven stores), and Stop N Go Stores, that accused them of selling and distributing pornography by selling publications such as *Playboy* and *Penthouse*. A U.S. District Court subsequently ruled that the commission had threatened the First Amendment rights of magazine publishers and distributors and ordered the letter withdrawn.

1985 The drive for profits, coupled with the apparent collapse of the FCC, led to a frenzy of media mergers and paved the way for an international information monopoly. Consumer advocate Ralph Nader warned of the increased threat of censorship resulting from conglomerate self-interest: "Self-censorship is alive and well in the U.S. media."

1986 The American Library Association (ALA) charged the Reagan administration with efforts to eliminate, restrict, and privatize government documents; with launching an official new "disinformation" program that permitted the government to release deliberately false, incomplete and misleading information; and with developing a new category of "sensitive information," restricting public access to a wide range of previously unclassified data. While the ALA charges were accurate and well documented, they were ignored by the major news media.

1986 FAIR, Fairness & Accuracy In Reporting, an anti-censorship organization based in New York, was formed to shake up the establishment-dominated media. It draws attention to important news stories that have been neglected and defends working journalists when they are muzzled.

1986 Article 19, an international human rights organization named after Article XIX of the Universal Declaration of Human Rights (see 1948), was founded in London to document and fight censorship on an international basis. The UN declaration holds that "Everyone has a right to freedom of opinion and expression; this right includes freedom to hold opinions without interference and to seek, receive and impart information and ideas through any media regardless of frontiers."

1986 The Final Report of Attorney General Edwin Meese's Commission on Pornography was released. As expected, it simply ignored the First Amendment. But what can you expect from Edwin Meese, the subject of a 1984 *Censored* story that charged him with directing a secret operation involving a variety of illegal and unconstitutional activities while a California state official in the late '60s and early '70s. The effort was aimed at subverting the anti-war movement in California.

1987 The continuing centralization of media ownership raised critical questions about the public's access to a diversity of opinion as Ben Bagdikian updated his 1982 book, *The Media Monopoly*. He found that just 26 corporations now controlled the majority of America's media enterprise. Bagdikian also predicted that by the 1990s, a half dozen giant firms would control most of the world's media.

1988 In what many consider to be an unconstitutional ruling, the Supreme Court's *Hazelwood* decision provided renewed support for censorship through the use of prior restraint. In essence, the court gave high school administrators the power to censor student publications in advance. The ruling reversed a long-time trend of First Amendment support for freedom of expression issues on high school campuses. Oddly enough, this violation of the First Amendment has been ignored by the major news media. Despite widespread on-going student protest, it is still unchallenged in 1994.

1988 Top *Censored* story of this election year revealed how the major mass media ignored, overlooked, or undercovered at least ten critical stories reported in America's alternative press that raised serious questions about the Republican candidate, George Bush. The stories dated from his reported role as a CIA "asset" in 1963 to his Presidential campaign's connection with a network of anti-Semites with Nazi and fascist affiliations in 1988.

1988 Author Salman Rushdie's novel, *The Satanic Verses*, was attacked by Muslims for sacrilege and blasphemy. In 1989, the late Ayatollah Khomeini issued a "fatwa," or death sentence, on Rushdie who went into hiding. In 1991, Hitoshi Igarashi, the Japanese translator of Rushdie's book, was stabbed to death. Also in 1991, Ettore Capriolo, who translated the book into Italian, was injured in a knifing at his home in Milan. In October 1993, William Nygaard, the Norwegian publisher whose firm published a translation of the book, was shot and serious wounded outside his home in Oslo. In November, 1993, Muslim groups denounced President Clinton for meeting with Rushdie.

1989 Fulfilling his 1987 predictions about world media conglomerates, Ben Bagdikian revealed in a well-documented article in *The Nation* that five global media lords already dominated the fight for hundreds of millions of minds throughout the world. Further, these media monopolies conceded that they may control most of the world's important newspapers, magazines, books, broadcast stations, movies, recordings, and video cassettes by the turn of the century. The Big Five of 1989:

Time Warner Inc., the world's largest media corporation

German-based Bertelsmann AG, owned by Reinhard Mohn

Rupert Murdoch's News Corporation Ltd., of Australia

Hatchette SA, of France, the world's largest producer of magazines

U.S.-based Capital Cities/ABC Inc.

1990 In April, for the first time in history, an American museum and its director faced criminal charges for pandering obscenity. Their crime was a display of erotic photographs by Robert Mapplethorpe. The director, Dennis Barrie, and the Contemporary Arts Center in Cincinnati were both acquitted of pandering in October. Cincinnati earned its name "Censornati."

1990 The flawed coverage of events leading up to the Persian Gulf crisis was the top *Censored* story of the year. Traditional press skepticism of government/military activities was the first casualty in the days immediately following Iraq's invasion of Kuwait as the U.S. media became cheerleaders for the Bush Administration.

1991 For the second year in a row, the top *Censored* story of the year focused on the Gulf War. It revealed how the networks rejected uncensored videotape footage of the heavy Iraqi civilian damage, the result of American-led bombing campaigns. Instead, the networks continued to publicize the Pentagon-approved, high-tech, smart-bomb, antiseptic, non-threatening version of the war. The second overlooked story of the year revealed a number of specific Gulf War issues that didn't receive the coverage they deserved; while the #6 story provided photographic evidence that challenged President Bush's original explanation for our rapid deployment in the Gulf.

1991 On May 24, the Supreme Court, in a ruling as unconstitutional as its earlier *Hazelwood* decision, upheld a Reagan administration interpretation of
Title X, the Public Health Services Act, that prohibited abortion counseling at federally funded family planning clinics. The 1987 interpretation
suggested that Title X "required physicians and counselors to withhold
information about abortion even from patients who were at medical risk
from continuation of the pregnancy." The Court ruled that the word
"abortion" cannot be uttered in any of America's 4,500 federally supported
clinics that provide aid and counseling to millions of poor women. In
essence, the United States Supreme Court ruled that First Amendment
free speech rights are a function of federal funding. The abortion "gag
rule" was repealed by President Clinton in January 1993.

1991 The introduction to the *Article 19 Yearbook* of 1991 (see 1986) provides
some sobering statistics about censorship on an international scale. In 62
of the 77 countries surveyed for the report, people were detained for peace-
fully expressing their opinions. In 27 of the countries, people, including
journalists, were reportedly tortured, killed, or otherwise maltreated on
account of their opinions.

1991 In the introduction to Volume IV of *The Right To Know*, published in 1992
by the DataCenter, in Oakland, California, Zoia Horn, a long-time cham-
pion of intellectual freedom and the public's right to know, made the following comments about how we "celebrated" the 200th anniversary of the
Bill of Rights in 1991. "The 200th anniversary of the Bill of Rights, should
have been the occasion for a reaffirmation of democratic principles.
Unfortunately, it fizzled into just another public relations campaign profiting Philip Morris, Inc., the sponsor of a widely viewed exhibit. Many
people polled during the Persian Gulf war saw no contradiction between
the censorship and manipulation of the media by the Pentagon, and the
Bill of Rights. Indeed, previous polls have revealed that people on the
street, asked to read the Bill of Rights, thought it was a communist document, and thus rejected parts of it. Ignorance of our basic democratic
tenets requires a serious, massive, educational campaign at all age levels,
through all mediums of communication."

1992 The Department of Defense and a group of self-selected media executives
agreed on nine out of ten ground rules for press coverage of America's next
military engagement. The contested and unresolved issue concerned prior
restraint on the part of the military. The policy, which apparently "supple-
ments" the First Amendment, evolved from the pool concept of censorship
developed by the Reagan administration for the Grenada War, subsequently refined by the Bush administration for the Panama War, and
finally given a full-scale test during the Gulf War—where it failed.

1992 The Center for the Study of Commercialism (CSC) invited 200 media out-lets to a press conference to be held on March 11 in Washington, DC. The purpose was to reveal how advertisers, one of the nation's most powerful media voices, influence, corrupt, and censor a free press. Not a single radio or television station or network sent a reporter and only two newspapers, the *Washington Post* and the *Washington Times*, bothered to attend. The *Post* didn't run a story on the press conference while the *Times* (also known as the Capitol's Moonie Paper since it is owned by Sun Yung Moon) ran one but didn't name the advertisers cited in the CSC study. The well-doc-umented study, which has been seen by few Americans, was titled "Dictating Content: How Advertising Pressure Can Corrupt A Free Press."

1992 In the June introduction to "Less Access To Less Information By and About the U.S. Government: XVIII," the American Library Association, Washington Office, reflected on how the Reagan/Bush administrations have significantly limited access to public documents and statistics and warned that it might get worse, given the increasing commercialization of what was once public information. It noted that since 1982, one of every four of the government's 16,000 publications has been eliminated. For the future it warned "...the growing tendency of federal agencies to utilize computer and telecommunications technologies for data collection, storage, retrieval, and dissemination. This trend has resulted in the increased emergence of contractual arrangements with commercial firms to disseminate information collected at taxpayer expense, higher user charges for government information, and the proliferation of government information available in electronic form only."

1993 In his latest update on the increasing monopolization of the media, the Fourth Edition of *The Media Monopoly*, Ben Bagdikian reported that fewer than 20 corporations now own and control the majority of the media in America.

1993 Franklyn S. Haiman, John Evans Professor Emeritus of Communication Studies at Northwestern University and leading First Amendment scholar, systematically challenges the criminalization of purely expressive behavior, sometimes referred to as speech act theory, because it is felt to be offen-sive, provocative, or even dangerous. In his book *"Speech Acts" and the First Amendment*, Haiman persuasively argues that controlling speech is neither constitutional nor effective as a means of preventing antisocial conduct.

1993 Reminiscent of an attempt to censor a film titled "Kiss," nearly a century ago (see 1896), the director of a children's theater in Dallas ordered a kiss elimi-nated from a wedding scene after a businessman complained because the actor was black and the actress was white. The actor went ahead and kissed his "bride" in the production of "Ramona Quimby," anyway, and, after a flood of complaints, the director reinstated the kiss in the performance.

1993 An ABC-TV movie about a Marine held hostage during the Vietnam war was itself held hostage for more than two years. "The Last P.O.W.: The Bobby Garwood Story" was finally broadcast on June 28, about two and a half years after its originally scheduled air date. ABC reportedly felt "it was inappropriate to air it" in early 1991 during the Gulf War since it raised questions about patriotism. The rationale sounds much the same as that given for the CBS censorship of "Sticks and Bones" in 1973.

1993 Robert Maynard, 56, a high school dropout who rose to become the first African-American owner-publisher of a major metropolitan daily newspaper, died of cancer. Before buying the *Oakland Tribune*, Maynard was a pioneering black journalist and founder of the Institute for Journalism Education in Oakland, which has trained more than 600 minority journalists to be reporters, editors and managers. Maynard also had served as a judge for Project Censored.

1993 The Uniform Defamation Act, a complex and widely criticized approach to reforming libel law across the country, was replaced with a version more acceptable to the media. The Uniform Correction or Clarification of Defamation Act of 1993 allows for the publication of a correction or clarification to mitigate damages, or even to settle a claim completely, and it sets up the framework and timetable for the process.

1993 One of the most important libel trials in modern media history continued through 1993 with mixed results. Psychoanalyst Jeffrey Masson had sued journalist Janet Malcolm for libel by misquoting him in a 1983 *New Yorker* magazine article. The first round ended in June when a jury found that five quotes attributed to Masson had been fabricated or distorted and that Malcolm was aware that two of them were libelous. The second round ended in September when a U.S. District Judge dismissed Masson's suit against the *New Yorker* but granted a new libel trial to Malcolm. The outcome of the third and final round should be available for next year's chronology.

1993 In September, the Pontifical Council for Social Communications, of the Roman Catholic Church, based in Vatican City, announced that it was going to take a long, very official look at truth and ethics in advertising. While advertising industry officials claim they are not concerned, others recall the impact of the National Legion of Decency, founded by the Catholic Church in 1933, on the film industry.

1993 IRE (Investigative Reporters & Editors) announced one of its most ambitious projects ever with the development of a computerized bulletin board service that would provide a comprehensive news and information library available to journalists throughout the world.

1993 The top *Censored* story of the year focused on the failure of the mass media to widely report that the United States had become one of the most dangerous places in the world for young people. A study by the United Nations Children's Fund revealed that nine out of ten young people murdered in industrialized countries are slain in the U.S.

THE WRITER AND THE ASTERISK

A writer owned an Asterisk,
And kept it in his den,
Where he wrote tales (which had large sales)
Of frail and erring men;
And always, when he reached the point
Where carping censors lurk,
He called upon the Asterisk
To do his dirty work.

Stoddard King (1889-1933)

BIBLIOGRAPHY TO CHRONOLOGY

American Library Association, Washington Office. "Less Access To Less Information By and About the U.S. Government: XVIII." Washington, DC.: American Library Association, June 1992.

Attorney General. "Commission on Pornography Final Report, July 1980, Vol. I & II." Washington, DC: U.S. Department of Justice, 1980.

Bagdikian, Ben H. *The Information Machines: Their Impact on Men and the Media.* New York: Harper & Row, 1971.

Bagdikian, Ben H. *The Effete Conspiracy and Other Crimes By the Press.* New York: Harper & Row, 1972.

Bagdikian, Ben H. *The Media Monopoly.* Boston: Beacon Press, 1983, 1992.

Bartow, Edith Merwin. *News and These United States.* New York: Funk & Wagnalls Company, 1955.

Black, Jay, and Jennings Bryant. *Introduction to Mass Communication, Third Edition.* Dubuque, Iowa: Wm. C. Brown Publishers, 1992.

Boyle, Kevin, ed. *Article 19: Information, Freedom and Censorship.* New York: Times Books, 1988.

Busha, Charles H., ed. *An Intellectual Freedom Primer.* Littleton, Colorado: Libraries Unlimited, Inc., 1977.

Cirino, Robert. *Don't Blame the People.* Los Angeles: Diversity Press, 1971. (Later published by Random House, 1972.)

Cirino, Robert. *Power To Persuade: Mass Media and the News.* New York: Bantam Books, 1974.

Curry, Richard O., ed. *Freedom at Risk: Secrecy, Censorship, and Repression in the 1980s.* Philadelphia: Temple University Press, 1988.

D'Souza, Frances, Editorial Team Director. *Article 19: Information Freedom and Censorship.* Chicago: American Library Association, 1991.

DeGrazia, Edward. *Censorship Landmarks.* New York: R.R. Bowker Co., 1969.

Downs, Robert B., ed. "The First Freedom." Chicago: American Library Association, 1960.

Emery, Edwin. *The Press and America: An Interpretative History of the Mass Media, Third Edition.* Englewood Cliffs, New Jersey: Prentice-Hall, Inc., 1972.

Ernst, Morris L. and Alexander Lindey. *The Censor Marches On.* New York: Da Capo Press, 1971.

Friendly, Fred. *Due To Circumstance Beyond Our Control...* New York: Vintage Books, 1967.

Goetz, Philip W. *The New Encyclopædia Britannica.* Chicago: Encyclopædia Britannica, Inc., 1991.

Haiman, Franklyn S. *"Speech Acts" and the First Amendment.* Carbondale: Southern Illinois University Press, 1993.

Hentoff, Nat. *The First Freedom: The Tumultuous History of Free Speech in America.* New York: Delacorte Press, 1980.

Hoffman, Frank. *Intellectual Freedom and Censorship: An Annotated Bibliography.* Metuchen, New Jersey: Scarecrow Press, 1989.

Horn, Zoia, Nancy Gruber, and Bill Berkowitz, eds. *The Right To Know, Volume 4.* Oakland, California: Data Center, 1992.

Hoyt, Olga G. and Edwin P. *Freedom of the News Media.* New York: The Seabury Press, 1973.

Jansen, Sue Curry. *Censorship: The Knot That Binds Power and Knowledge.* New York: Oxford University Press, 1988.

Jenkinson, Clay. "From Milton to Media: Information Flow in a Free Society." Media&Values. Spring 1992.

Johnson, Nicholas. *How To Talk Back To Your Television Set.* New York: Bantam Books, 1970.

Kendrick, Alexander. *Prime Time: The Life of Edward R. Murrow.* Boston: Little, Brown and Company, 1969.

Kent, Allen and Harold Lancour, eds. *Encyclopedia of Library and Information Science, Volume 4.* New York: Marcel Dekker, 1970.

Knight, Arthur. *The Liveliest Art: A Panoramic History of the Movies.* New York: New American Library, 1957.

Lee, Martin A. and Norman Solomon. *Unreliable Sources: A Guide to Detecting Bias in News Media.* New York: Lyle Stuart, 1990.

Lippmann, Walter. *Liberty and the News.* New York: Harcourt, Brace and Howe, 1920.

Liston, Robert A. *The Right To Know: Censorship in America.* New York: Franklin Watts, Inc., 1973.

McCormick, John and Mairi MacInnes, eds. *Versions of Censorship.* Garden City, New York: Anchor Books, 1962.

McKeon, Richard, Robert K. Merton, and Walter Gellhorn. *The Freedom to Read: Perspective and Program.* New York: R. R. Bowker Company, 1957.

Minor, Dale. *The Information War.* New York: Hawthorn Books, Inc., 1970.

Mott, Frank Luther. *American Journalism: A History of Newspapers in the United States through 260 Years: 1690 to 1950.* New York: The Macmillan Company, 1950.

The New York Public Library. *Censorship: 500 Years of Conflict*. New York: Oxford University Press, 1984.

Parenti, Michael. *Inventing Reality: The Politics of the Mass Media*. New York: St. Martin's Press, 1986.

Pember, Don R. *Mass Media Law, Fifth Edition*. Dubuque, Iowa: Wm. C. Brown Publishers, 1990.

Powledge, Fred. *The Engineering of Restraint: The Nixon Administration and the Press*. Washington, DC: Public Affairs Press, 1971.

Project Censored. The 10 Best Censored Stories: 1976-1993. Rohnert Park, CA: Censored Publications, 1976-1993.

Rivers, William L., and Wilbur Schramm. *Responsibility in Mass Communication: Revised Edition*. New York: Harper & Row, 1969.

Seldes, George. *Lords of the Press*. New York: Julian Messner, Inc., 1938.

Seldes, George. *Witness to a Century: Encounters With the Noted, the Notorious, and the Three SOBs*. New York: Ballantine Books, 1987.

Sills, David L. ed. *International Encyclopedia of the Social Sciences, Volume 2*. New York: The Macmillan Company & The Free Press, 1968.

Stephens, Mitchell. *A History of News From the Drum to the Satellite*. New York: Viking, 1988.

Stone, I.F. "Notes On Closing, But Not In Farewell." I.F. Stone's Bi-Weekly, December 1971.

Tebbel, John. *The Media in America*. New York: Thomas Y. Crowell Company, 1974.

Theiner, George. *They Shoot Writers, Don't They?* London: Faber and Faber, 1984.

Wallraff, Günter. *Wallraff: The Undesirable Journalist*. London: Pluto Press Limited, 1978.

Widmer, Kingsley, and Eleanor. *Literary Censorship: Principles, Cases, Problems*. Belmont, California: Wadsworth Publishing Company, 1961.

The CENSORED! Resource Guide

One of Project Censored's long-standing goals is to improve the lines of communication between the public and the media that serve the public. Just knowing where to direct concerns, compliments, ideas or even offers to help is a question many people have when trying to reach either the alternative or establishment media.

With this in mind, Project Censored assembled a simple, easy-to-use and dependable resource guide for anyone who wants to contact the media to follow-up on these stories or to get actively involved in doing something about an issue or the media.

Following is a collection of names, addresses, phone and fax numbers, when available, to a variety of organizations, individuals, and electronic and print media outlets that might prove useful.

Although this information was current as of late 1993, you may want to double-check to ensure the names, addresses, etc., are still accurate. If you are aware of any changes and/or corrections to the list, please send them to Censored Resource Guide, Sonoma State University, Rohnert Park, CA 94928.

We plan to update the list in the 1995 edition of CENSORED! If you have any additions that should be included, please send them to the same address.

TABLE OF CONTENTS—CENSORED RESOURCE GUIDE

ALTERNATIVE BROADCAST MEDIA PRODUCERS & ORGANIZATIONS

8MM NEWS COLLECTIVE
c/o Squeaky Wheel
372 Connecticut Street
Buffalo, NY 14213
Tel: 716/884-7172

ALTERNATIVE RADIO
2129 Mapleton
Boulder, CO 80304
Tel: 303/444-8788
Fax: 303/546-0592

ALTERNATIVE NEWS
Box 7297
Austin, TX 78713
Tel: 512/477-5148
Fax: 512/471-4806

AMERICA'S DEFENSE MONITOR
1500 Massachusetts Ave., NW
Washington, DC 20005
Tel: 202/862-0700
Fax: 202/862-0708

BLACK PLANET PRODUCTIONS/
NOT CHANNEL ZERO
P.O. Box 435, Cooper Station
New York, NY 10003-0435
Tel: 212/886-3701
Fax: 212/420-8223

CALIFORNIA NEWSREEL
149 9th Street, Suite 420
San Francisco, CA 94103
Tel: 415/621-6196

COMMON GROUND
Stanley Foundation
216 Sycamore Street, Suite 500
Muscatine, IA 52761
Tel: 319/264-1500

DIVA-TV
c/o ACT-UP
135 W. 29th Street, #10
New York, NY 10001
Tel: 212/564-2437

EARTH COMMUNICATIONS
(Radio For Peace International)
Box 10869
Eugene, OR 97440
Tel: 503/283-8958
Fax: 503/289-5056

EL SALVADOR MEDIA PROJECT
335 W. 38th Street, 5th Fl.
New York, NY 10018
Tel: 212/714-9118
Fax: 212/594-6417

EMPOWERMENT PROJECT
3403 Highway 54 West
Chapel Hill, NC 27516
Tel: 919/967-1963
Fax: 919/967-1863

ENVIROVIDEOS
P.O. Box 629000
El Dorado Hills, CA 95762
Tel: 1/800/227-8955

GLOBALVISION
1600 Broadway
New York, NY 10019
Tel: 212/246-0202

LABOR BEAT
37 S. Ashland Avenue
Chicago, IL 60607
Tel: 312/226-3330

MEDIA DEMOCRACY PROJECT
c/o Made in USA Productions
330 W. 42nd Street, Suite 1905
New York, NY 10036
Tel: 212/695-3090
Fax: 212/695-3086

MEDIA NETWORK/
ALTERNATIVE MEDIA
INFORMATION CENTER
39 W. 14th Street, #403
New York, NY 10011
Tel: 212/929-2663
Fax: 212/929-2732

NATIONAL ASIAN AMERICAN
TELECOMMUNICATIONS
ASSOCIATION
346 9th Street, 2nd Fl.
San Francisco, CA 94103
Tel: 415/863-0814
Fax: 415/863-7428

NATIONAL FEDERATION
OF COMMUNITY BROADCASTERS
666 11th Street NW, Suite 805
Washington, DC 20001
Tel: 202/393-2355

PACIFICA NETWORK NEWS
702 H Street NW, Suite 3
Washington, DC 20001
Tel: 202/783-1620
Fax: 202/393-1841

PACIFICA RADIO ARCHIVE
3729 Cahuenga Blvd., West
North Hollywood, CA 91604
Tel: 818/506-1077
Fax: 818/985-8802

PAPER TIGER TV/DEEP DISH
339 Lafayette Street
New York, NY 10012
Tel: 212/420-9045

P.O.V. (Points Of View)
330 W. 19th Street, 11th Fl.
New York, NY 10019
Tel: 212/397-0970

SECOND OPINION
Erwin Knoll (Host)
c/o The Progressive
409 E. Main Street
Madison, WI 53703
Tel: 608/257-4626
Fax: 608/257-3373

UNDERCURRENTS
130 W. 25th Street
New York, NY 10001
Tel: 212/691-7370

VIDEO DATABANK
37 S. Wabash
Chicago, IL 60603
Tel: 312/899-5172
Fax: 312/263-0141

THE VIDEO PROJECT:
FILMS AND VIDEOS FOR A SAFE
AND SUSTAINABLE WORLD
5332 College Avenue, Suite 101
Oakland, CA 94618
Tel: 510/655-9050
or: 1/800-4-PLANET
Fax: 510/655-9115

ALTERNATIVE & ELECTRONIC NEWS SERVICES

ALTERNET—Alternative News Network
2025 Eye Street NW, Suite 1124
Washington, DC 20006
Tel: 202/887-0022
Fax: 202/887-0024
CompuServe ID: 71362,27

CALIFORNIA ALTERNATIVE
NEWS BUREAU
2210 21st Street
Sacramento, CA 95616
Tel: 916/737-1234
Fax: 916/737-1437

INSIGHT FEATURES
Networking for Democracy
3411 Diversey, Suite 1
Chicago, IL 60647
Tel: 312/384-8827
Fax: 312/384-3904

INTERNET
(See Library and Reference Sources)

INTERPRESS SERVICE
Global Information Network
777 United Nations Plaza
New York, NY 10017
Tel: 212/286-0123
Fax: 212/818-9249

LATIN AMERICA DATA BASE
Latin American Institute
University of New Mexico
801 Yale Blvd., NE
Albuquerque, NM 87131-1016
Tel: 800/472-0888
or 505/277-6839
Fax: 505/277-5989

NEW LIBERATION NEWS SERVICE
P.O. Box 41
MIT Branch
Cambridge, MA 02139
Tel: 617/492-8316

NEWS INTERNATIONAL
PRESS SERVICE
6161 El Cajon Blvd., #4
San Diego, CA 92115
Tel: 619/696-9531

PACIFIC NEWS SERVICE
450 Mission Street, Rm. 506
San Francisco, CA 94105
Tel: 415/243-4364

PEACENET; ECONET; CONFLICNET
INSTITUTE FOR GLOBAL
COMMUNICATIONS
18 DeBoom Street
San Francisco, CA 94107
Tel: 415/442-0220
Fax: 415/546-1794

PEOPLE'S NEWS AGENCY
7627 16th Street NW
P.O. Box 56466
Washington, DC 20040
Tel: 202/829-2278
Fax: 202/829-0462
E-mail Internet: prout wdc @ igc.apc.org

ALTERNATIVE PERIODICALS & PUBLICATIONS

ACROSS THE LINE
Seeds of Peace
P.O. Box 12154
Oakland, CA 94604
Tel: 510/420-1799

ACTION FOR CULTURAL SURVIVAL
Cultural Survival, Inc.
215 First Street
Cambridge, MA 02142
Tel: 617/621-3818
Fax: 617/621-3814

THE ADVOCATE
6922 Hollywood Blvd., 10th Fl.
Los Angeles, CA 90028
Tel: 213/871-1225
Fax: 213/467-6805

AFRICA NEWS
P.O. Box 3851
Durham, NC 27702
Tel: 919/286-0747
Fax: 919/286-2614

AGAINST THE CURRENT
Center for Changes
7012 Michigan Avenue
Detroit, MI 48210
Tel: 313/841-0161
Fax: 313/841-8884

AKWESASNE NOTES
Mohawk Nation
P.O. Box 196
Rooseveltown, NY 13683-0196
Tel: 518/358-9531
Fax: 613/575-2935

ALERT: Focus on Central America
CISPES
P.O. Box 12156
Washington, DC 20005
Tel: 202/265-0890
Fax: 202/265-7843

ALTERNATIVE PRESS REVIEW
C.A.L. Press
P.O. Box 1446
Columbia, MO 65205-1446

ALTERNATIVES
Lynne Rienner Publishers
1800 30th Street, Suite 314
Boulder, CO 80301-1032
Tel: 303/444-6684
Fax: 303/444-0824

AMICUS JOURNAL
40 W. 20th Street
New York, NY 10011
Tel: 212/727-2700
Fax: 212/727-1773

BLACK SCHOLAR
P.O. Box 2869
Oakland, CA 94609
Tel: 510/547-6633
Fax: 510/547-6679

CITY PAPER
Baltimore's Free Weekly
812 Park Avenue
Baltimore, MD 21201
Tel: 410/523-2300
Fax: 410/523-2222

COMMON CAUSE
2030 M Street NW
Washington, DC 20036
Tel: 202/833-1200
Fax: 202/659-3716

CONNECT
The Center for Media and Values
1962 South Shenandoah Street
Los Angeles, CA 90034
Tel: 310/559-2944
Fax: 310/559-9396

COVERT ACTION QUARTERLY
1500 Massachusetts Ave. NW, #732
Washington, DC 20005
Tel: 202/331-9763
Fax: 202/862-0708

CUBA ADVOCATE
1750 30th Street, #152
Boulder, CO 80301

THE DAILY CITIZEN
P.O. Box 57365
Washington, DC 20037
Tel: 202/429-6929
Fax: 202/659-1145

DEADLINE
Center for War, Peace
and the News Media
New York University
10 Washington Place, 4th Fl.
New York, NY 10003
Tel: 212/998-7960
Fax: 212/995-4143

DEFENSE MONITOR
1500 Massachusetts Ave. NW
Washington, DC 20005
Tel: 202/862-0700
Fax: 202/862-0708

DENVER WESTWORD
P.O. Box 5970
Denver, CO 80217
Tel: 303/296-7744

DISSENT
521 Fifth Avenue
New York, NY 10017
Tel: 212/595-3084

DOLLARS AND SENSE
1 Summer Street
Somerville, MA 02143
Tel: 617/628-8411
Fax: 617/628-2025

E: THE ENVIRONMENTAL
MAGAZINE
P.O. Box 5098
Westport, CT 06881
Tel: 203/854-5559
Fax: 203/866-0602

EARTH ISLAND JOURNAL
300 Broadway, Suite 28
San Francisco, CA 94133-3312
Tel: 415/788-3666
Fax: 415/788-7324

ENVIRONMENTAL ACTION
6930 Carroll Avenue, Suite 600
Takoma Park, MD 20912
Tel: 301/891-1106
Fax: 301/891-2218

ENVIRONMENTAL IMPACT
REPORTER
P.O. Box 1834
Sebastopol, CA 95473
Tel: 707/823-8744

EXTRA!
Fairness and Accuracy in Reporting
130 W. 25th Street
New York, NY 10001
Tel: 212/633-6700
Fax: 212/727-7668

GENDER & MASS MEDIA
Stockholm University—JMK
P.O. Box 27861
S-115 93
Stockholm, Sweden

GLOBAL EXCHANGES
2017 Mission Street, Rm. 303
San Francisco, CA 94110
Tel: 415/255-7296

GREEN MAGAZINE
P.O. Box 381
Mill Harbour
London E14 9TW
England

HEALTH LETTER
2000 P Street NW
Washington, DC 20036

HIGH COUNTRY NEWS
P.O. Box 1090
Paonia, CO 81428
Tel: 303/527-4898

THE HUMAN QUEST
Churchman Co., Inc.
1074 23rd Avenue N.
St. Petersburg, FL 33704-3228
Tel: 813/894-0097

HURACAN
P.O. Box 7591
Minneapolis, MN 55407

IN CONTEXT
P.O. Box 11470
Bainbridge Island, WA 98110
Tel: 206/842-0216
Fax: 206/842-5208

THE INDEPENDENT
540 Mendocino Avenue
Santa Rosa, CA 95401
Tel: 707/527-1200
Fax: 707/527-1288

INDEX ON CENSORSHIP
485 Fifth Avenue
New York, NY 10017
Tel: 212/972-8400
Fax: 212/972-0905

IN THESE TIMES
2040 N. Milwaukee Avenue, 2nd Fl.
Chicago, IL 60647-4002
Tel: 312/772-0100
Fax: 312/772-4180

IRE JOURNAL
INVESTIGATIVE REPORTERS
& EDITORS
100 Neff Hall
University of Missouri
School of Journalism
Columbia, MO 65211
Tel: 314/882-2042
Fax: 314/882-5431

ISSUES IN SCIENCE &
TECHNOLOGY
National Academy of Sciences
2101 Constitution Avenue, NW
Washington, DC 20418
Tel: 202/334-3305
Fax: 202/334-1290

LATIN AMERICAN PERSPECTIVES
2455 Teller Road
Newbury Park, CA 91320
Tel: 805/499-0721
Fax: 805/499-0871

LEFT BUSINESS OBSERVER
250 W. 85th Street
New York, NY 10024-3217
Tel: 212/874-4020

LIES OF OUR TIMES
Institute for Media Analysis
145 W. 4th Street
New York, NY 10012
Tel: 212/254-1061
Fax: 212/254-9598

MEDIACULTURE REVIEW
2025 Eye Street, NW, #1118
Washington, DC 20009
Tel: 202/887-0022
Fax: 202/887-0024

THE METRO TIMES
743 Beaubien, Suite 301
Detroit, MI 48226
Tel: 313/961-4060
Fax: 313/961-6598

MOTHER JONES
731 Market Street, Suite 600
San Francisco, CA 94103
Tel: 415/665-6637
Fax: 415/665-6696

MS. MAGAZINE
230 Park Avenue
New York, NY 10169
Tel: 212/551-9595

MUCKRAKER
Center for Investigative Reporting
568 Howard Street, 5th Fl.
San Francisco, CA 94105-3007
Tel: 415/543-1200
Fax: 415/543-8311

MULTINATIONAL MONITOR
P.O. Box 19045
Washington, DC 20036
Tel: 202/387-8034
Fax: 202/234-5176

THE NATION
72 Fifth Avenue
New York, NY 10011
Tel: 212/242-8400
Fax: 212/463-9712

NATIONAL CATHOLIC REPORTER
P.O. Box 419281
Kansas City, MO 64141
Tel: 816/531-0538
Fax: 816/531-7466

NATIONAL REVIEW
150 E. 35th Street
New York, NY 10016
Tel: 212/679-7330
Fax: 212/696-0309

THE NEW REPUBLIC
1220 19th Street NW
Washington, DC 20036
Tel: 202/331-7494
Fax: 202/331-0275

NEWSLETTER ON
INTELLECTUAL FREEDOM
American Library Association
50 E. Huron Street
Chicago, IL 60611
Tel: 312/280-4223
Fax: 312/440-9374

NORTHERN SUN NEWS
P.O. Box 581487
Minneapolis, MN 55458-1487
Tel: 612/729-8543

PACIFIC SUN
P.O. Box 5553
Mill Valley, CA 94942
Tel: 415/383-4500
Fax: 415/383-4159

PBI/USA REPORT
Peace Brigades Int'l/USA
P.O Box 381233
Cambridge, MA 02238

PEACE REVIEW:
The International
Quarterly of World Peace
1800 30th Street, Suite 314
Boulder, CO 80301-1032
Tel: 303/444-6684
Fax: 303/444-0824

POVERTY, INC.
P.O. Box 4691
Roanoke, VA 24015
Tel: 703/989-4127

THE PROGRESSIVE
409 E. Main Street
Madison, WI 53703
Tel: 608/257-4626
Fax: 608/257-3373

PROPAGANDA REVIEW
Media Alliance
Fort Mason, Bldg. D, 2nd Fl.
San Francisco, CA 94123
Tel: 415/441-2557

PUBLIC CITIZEN
2000 P Street NW, Suite 610
Washington, DC 20036
Tel: 202/833-3000

THE RECORDER
625 Polk Street
San Francisco, CA 94102

ROLLING STONE
1290 Ave. of the Americas, 2nd Fl.
New York, NY 10104
Tel: 212/484-1616
Fax: 212/767-8203

THE SAN FRANCISCO BAY
GUARDIAN
520 Hampshire
San Francisco, CA 94110
Tel: 415/255-3100
Fax: 415/255-8762

SANTA ROSA SUN
1275 Fourth Street, #608
Santa Rosa, CA 95404
Tel: 707/544-3448
Fax: 707/544-4756

SECRECY & GOVERNMENT
BULLETIN
Federation of American Scientists
307 Massachusetts Avenue NE
Washington, DC 20002
Tel: 202/675-1012

SF WEEKLY
425 Brannan Street
San Francisco, CA 94107
Tel: 415/541-0700
Fax: 415/777-1839

SOJOURNERS
2401 15th Street, NW
Washington, DC 20009
Tel: 202/328-8842
Fax: 202/328-8757

SOUTHERN EXPOSURE
P.O. Box 531
Durham, NC 27702
Tel: 919/419-8311
Fax: 919/419-8315

THE SPOTLIGHT
300 Independence Avenue SE
Washington, DC 20003
Tel: 202/544-1794

STRATEGIES
Strategies for Media Literacy
1095 Market Street, Suite 617
San Francisco, CA 94103
Tel: 415/621-2911

TEXAS OBSERVER
307 West 7th Street
Austin, TX 78701-2917
Tel: 512/477-0746

TIKKUN
251 W. 100th Street, 5th Fl.
New York, NY 10025
Tel: 212/864-4110
Fax: 212/864-4137

U. THE NATIONAL COLLEGE
MAGAZINE
1800 Century Park East #820
Los Angeles, CA 90067
Tel: 310/551-1381
Fax: 310/551-1659

UNCLASSIFIED
Association of National Security Alumni
2001 S Street NW, Suite 740
Washington, DC 20009
Tel: 202/483-9325

URGENT ACTION BULLETIN
Survival International
310 Edgeware Road
London W2 1DY
England
Tel: 071/723-5535
Fax: 071/723-4059

UTNE READER
1624 Harmon Place, Suite 330
Minneapolis, MN 55403
Tel: 612/338-5040

VILLAGE VOICE
36 Cooper Square
New York, NY 10003
Tel: 212/475-3300
Fax: 212/475-8944

WAR AND PEACE DIGEST
War and Peace Foundation
32 Union Square East
New York, NY 10003-3295
Tel: 212/777-6626
Fax: 212/995-9652

THE WASHINGTON SPECTATOR
London Terrace Station
P.O. Box 20065
New York, NY 10011

WHOLE EARTH REVIEW
27 Gate Five Road
Sausalito, CA 94965
Tel: 415/332-1716
Fax: 415/332-3110

WILLAMETTE WEEK
Portland's Newsweekly
2 NW Second Avenue
Portland, OR 97209
Tel: 503/243-2122
Fax: 503/243-1115

WORLD PRESS REVIEW
200 Madison Avenue, Suite 2104
New York NY 10016
Tel: 212/889-5155
Fax: 212/889-5634

WORLD WATCH
Worldwatch Institute
1776 Massachusetts Avenue NW
Washington, DC 20036
Tel: 202/452-1999
Fax: 202/296-7365

Z MAGAZINE
116 Botolph Street
Boston, MA 02115
Tel: 617/787-4531
Fax: 508/457-0626

FREE PRESS/RIGHT-TO-KNOW PUBLICATIONS & ORGANIZATIONS

ALTERNATIVE PRESS CENTER
P.O. Box 33109
Baltimore, MD 21218
Tel: 410/243-2471
Fax: 410/235-5325

AMERICAN LIBRARY ASSOCIATION
INTELLECTUAL FREEDOM
COMMITTEE
50 E. Huron Street
Chicago, IL 60611
Tel: 312/280-4223
or 800/545-2433
Fax: 312/440-9374

ARTICLE 19: INTERNATIONAL
CENTRE AGAINST CENSORSHIP
90 Borough High Street
London SE1 1LL
England
Tel: 071/403-4822
Fax: 071/403-1943

ASSOCIATION OF
ALTERNATIVE NEWSWEEKLIES
c/o The New Times
1201 East Jefferson, Suite A-260
Phoenix, AZ 85034
Tel: 602/229-8487
Fax: 602/253-5871

BILL OF RIGHTS JOURNAL
175 Fifth Avenue, Rm. 814
New York, NY 10010
Tel: 212/673-2040
Fax: 212/460-8359

CALIFORNIA FIRST AMENDMENT
COALITION
926 J Street, Suite 1406
Sacramento, CA 95814-2708
Tel: 916/447-2322
Fax: 916/447-2328

CALIFORNIANS AGAINST
CENSORSHIP TOGETHER (ACT)
1800 Market Street, Suite 1000
San Francisco, CA 94103
Tel: 510/548-3695

CIVIL LIBERTIES
American Civil Liberties Union
132 W. 43rd Street
New York, NY 10036
Tel: 212/547-4440
Fax: 212/547-7363

COALITION vs PBS CENSORSHIP
P.O. Box 291555
Hollywood, CA 90029
Tel: 310/288-6693

COMMITTEE TO PROTECT
JOURNALISTS
330 Seventh Ave., 12th Fl.
New York, NY 10001
Tel: 212/465-1004
Fax: 212/465-9568

DATA CENTER
Right-to-Know Project
464 19th Street
Oakland, CA 94612
Tel: 510/835-4692
Fax: 510/835-3017

FEMINISTS FOR FREE EXPRESSION
2525 Times Square Station
New York, NY 10108
Tel: 212/713-5446

FIRST AMENDMENT CENTER
Society of Professional Journalists
1050 Connecticut Avenue NW
Suite 1206
Washington, DC 20036
Tel: 202/628-1411

FIRST AMENDMENT CONGRESS
1445 Market Street, Suite 320
Denver, CO 80202
Tel: 303/820-5688
Fax: 303/534-8774

FREEDOM FORUM
First Amendment Center
1222 16th Avenue South
Nashville, TN 37212
Tel: 615/321-9588

FREEDOM FORUM
Media Studies Center
Columbia University
2950 Broadway
New York, NY 10027-7004
Tel: 212/678-6600
Fax: 212/678-6663

FREEDOM OF EXPRESSION
FOUNDATION
5220 S. Marina Pacifica
Long Beach, CA 90803
Tel: 310/985-4301
Fax: 310/985-2369

FREEDOM OF INFORMATION
CENTER
20 Walter Williams Hall
University of Missouri at Columbia
Columbia, MO 65211
Tel: 314/882-4856
Fax: 314/882-9002

FREEDOM OF INFORMATION
CLEARINGHOUSE
P.O. Box 19367
Washington, DC 20036
Tel: 202/833-3000

FREE PRESS ASSOCIATION
P.O. Box 15548
Columbus, OH 43215
Tel: 614/291-1441

FUND FOR FREE EXPRESSION
485 Fifth Avenue
New York, NY 10017
Tel: 212/972-8400
Fax: 212/972-0905

THE GAP MEDIA PROJECT
1415 Birch Street
Yellow Springs, OH 45387
Tel: 513/767-2224
Fax: 513/767-1888

THE GIRAFFE PROJECT
P.O. Box 759
Langley, WA 98260
Tel: 206/221-7989

HEAL
Hanford Education Action League
1720 North Ash Street
Spokane, WA 99205
Tel: 509/326-3370

INFACT
256 Hanover Street
Boston, MA 02113
Tel: 617/742-4583

INTER AMERICAN PRESS
ASSOCIATION
2911 NW 39th Street
Miami, FL 33142
Tel: 305/634-2365
Fax: 305/635-2272

THE INVESTIGATIVE
REPORTING FUND
P.O. Box 7554
Asheville, NC 28802
Tel: 704/259-9179
Fax: 704/251-1311

LEONARD PELTIER DEFENSE
COMMITTEE
P.O. Box 583
Lawrence, KS 66044
Tel: 913/842-5774

LEONARD PELTIER FREEDOM
CAMPAIGN
c/o International Action Center
39 West 14th Street, Room 206
New York, NY 10011
Tel: 212/633-6646
Fax: 212/633-2889

MEDIA COALITION/AMERICANS
FOR CONSTITUTIONAL FREEDOM
1221 Avenue of the Americas, 24th Fl.
New York, NY 10020
Tel: 212/768-6770
Fax: 212/391-1247

MEDIA/ED
The Media Education Foundation
26 Center Street
Northhampton, MA 01060
Tel: 413/586-4170
Fax: 413/586-8398

MEIKLEJOHN CIVIL LIBERTIES
INSTITUTE
P.O. Box 673
Berkeley, CA 94701
Tel: 510/848-0599
Fax: 510/848-6008

NATIONAL COALITION
AGAINST CENSORSHIP
275 7th Avenue, 20th Fl.
New York, NY 10001
Tel: 212/807-6222
Fax: 212/807-6245

NATIONAL COMMITTEE AGAINST
REPRESSIVE LEGISLATION
3321 12th Street NE
Washington, DC 20017
Tel: 202/529-4225

PEOPLE FOR THE AMERICAN WAY
2000 M Street NW, Suite 400
Washington, DC 20036
Tel: 202/467-4999
Fax: 202/293-2672

REPORTERS' COMMITTEE
FOR FREEDOM OF THE PRESS
1735 Eye Street NW, Suite 504
Washington, DC 20006
Tel: 202/466-6312

STUDENT PRESS LAW CENTER
1735 Eye Street NW, Suite 504
Washington, DC 20006
Tel: 202/466-5242
Fax: 202/466-6326

THE THOMAS JEFFERSON CENTER
FOR THE PROTECTION OF FREE
EXPRESSION
400 Peter Jefferson Place
Charlottesville, VA 22901
Tel: 804/295-4784

WORLD PRESS FREEDOM
COMMITTEE
c/o The Newspaper Center
11600 Sunrise Valley Drive
Reston, VA 22091
Tel: 703/648-1000
Fax: 703/620-4557

WOMEN'S INSTITUTE
FOR FREEDOM OF THE PRESS
3306 Ross Place NW
Washington, DC 20008
Tel: 202/966-7783

JOURNALISM/MEDIA ANALYSIS PUBLICATIONS & ORGANIZATIONS

ACCURACY IN MEDIA
AIM
1275 K Street NW, Suite 1150
Washington, DC 20005
Tel: 202/371-6710
Fax: 202/371-9054

ADBUSTERS: A Magazine of
Media and Environmental Strategies
The Media Foundation
1243 W. Seventh Avenue
Vancouver, British Columbia
Canada V6H 1B7
Tel: 604/736-9401
Fax: 604/737-6021

AMERICAN JOURNALISM REVIEW
8701 Adelphi Road
Adelphi, MD 20783
Tel: 301/431-4771
Fax: 301/431-0097

AMERICAN SOCIETY OF
JOURNALISTS AND AUTHORS
1501 Broadway, Suite 302
New York, NY 10036
Tel: 212/997-0947
Fax: 212/768-7414

AMERICAN SOCIETY OF
NEWSPAPER EDITORS
P.O. Box 4090
Reston, VA 22090-1700
Tel: 703/648-1144
Fax: 703/620-4557

ASIAN AMERICAN
JOURNALISTS ASSOCIATION
1765 Sutter Street, Rm. 1000
San Francisco, CA 94115
Tel: 415/346-2051
Fax: 415/931-4671

THE ASPEN INSTITUTE
Communications and Society Program
1755 Massachusetts Avenue NW
Suite 501
Washington, DC 20036
Tel: 202/736-5818
Fax: 202/986-1913

ASSOCIATION OF AMERICAN
PUBLISHERS
220 E. 23rd Street
New York, NY 10010
Tel: 212/689-8920
Fax: 212/696-0131

ASSOCIATION OF HOUSE
DEMOCRATIC PRESS ASSISTANTS
House of Representatives
2459 Rayburn Bldg.
Washington, DC 20515
Tel: 202/225-1554
Fax: 202/225-4951

BAY AREA CENSORED
Media Alliance
Fort Mason Center, Bldg. D, 2nd Fl.
San Francisco, CA 94123
Tel: 415/441-2557

BLACK PRESS INSTITUTE
2711 E. 75th Place
Chicago, IL 60649
Tel: 312/375-8200
Fax: 312/375-8262

BLACK WOMEN IN PUBLISHING
P.O Box 6275
FDR Station
New York, NY 10150
Tel: 212/772-5951

CENTER FOR INVESTIGATIVE
REPORTING
568 Howard Street, 5th Fl.
San Francisco, CA 94105-3007
Tel: 415/543-1200
Fax: 415/543-8311

CENTER FOR MEDIA AND PUBLIC
AFFAIRS
2101 L Street NW, Suite 300
Washington, DC 20037
Tel: 202/223-2942
Fax: 202/872-4014

CENTER FOR MEDIA AND VALUES
1962 South Shenandoah
Los Angeles, CA 90034
Tel: 310/559-2944
Fax: 310/559-9396

CENTER FOR MEDIA EDUCATION
P.O Box 33039
Washington, DC 20033
Tel: 301/270-3938
Fax: 301/270-2376

CENTER FOR THE STUDY
OF COMMERCIALISM
1875 Connecticut Avenue NW
Suite 300
Washington, DC 20009-5728
Tel: 202/797-7080
Fax: 202/265-4954

CENTER FOR WAR,
PEACE AND THE NEWS MEDIA
New York University
10 Washington Place, 4th Fl.
New York, NY 10003
Tel: 212/998-7960
Fax: 212/995-4143

CHRISTIC INSTITUTE
8773 Venice Boulevard
Los Angeles, CA 90034
Tel: 310/287-1556
Fax: 310/287-1559

CITIZENS FOR MEDIA LITERACY
38 1/2 Battery Park Avenue, Suite G
Asheville, NC 28801
Tel: 704/255-0182
Fax: 704/254-2286

COLUMBIA JOURNALISM REVIEW
700 Journalism Building
Columbia University
New York, NY 10027
Tel: 212/854-1881
Fax: 212/854-8580

COMMUNICATIONS CONSORTIUM
1333 H Street NW, 11th Fl.
Washington, DC 20005
Tel: 202/682-1270
Fax: 202/682-2154

CULTURAL ENVIRONMENT
MOVEMENT
P.O. Box 31847
Philadelphia, PA 19104

DOWNS MEDIA EDUCATION
CENTER
P.O. Box 1170
Stockbridge, MA 01262
Tel: 413/298-0262
Fax: 413/298-4434

EDITOR AND PUBLISHER
11 W. 19th Street
New York, NY 10011
Tel: 212/675-4380
Fax: 212/929-1259

ESSENTIAL INFORMATION
P.O. Box 19405
Washington, DC 20036
Tel: 202/387-8030
Fax: 202/234-5176

FAIRNESS AND ACCURACY
IN REPORTING
130 W. 25th Street
New York, NY 10001
Tel: 212/633-6700
Fax: 212/727-7668

FUND FOR INVESTIGATIVE
JOURNALISM
1755 Massachusetts Avenue NW
Washington, DC 20036
Tel: 202/462-1844

GAY AND LESBIAN PRESS
ASSOCIATION
P.O. Box 8185
Universal City, CA 91608
Tel: 818/902-1476

GLAAD
Gay and Lesbian Alliance
Against Defamation
150 W. 26th Street, Suite 503
New York, NY 10001
Tel: 212/807-1700
Fax: 212/807-1806

THE INDEPENDENT
Association of Independent
Video and Film (AIVF)
625 Broadway, 9th Fl.
New York, NY 10012
Tel: 212/473-3400
Fax: 212/677-8732

INSTITUTE FOR
ALTERNATIVE JOURNALISM
2025 Eye Street, NW, Suite 1124
Washington, DC 20006
Tel: 202/887-0022
Fax: 202/887-0024
CompuServe: 71362, 27

INVESTIGATIVE JOURNALISM
PROJECT
Fund for Constitutional Government
122 Maryland Avenue NE, Suite 300
Washington, DC 20002
Tel: 202/546-3732
Fax: 202/543-3156

INVESTIGATIVE REPORTERS
& EDITORS
100 Neff Hall
University of Missouri
School of Journalism
Columbia, MO 65211
Tel: 314/882-2042
Fax: 314/882-5431

JOURNALISM QUARTERLY
George Washington University
Journalism Program
Washington, DC 20052
Tel: 202/994-6226

INSTITUTE FOR MEDIA ANALYSIS
145 W. 4th Street
New York, NY 10012
Tel: 212/254-1061
Fax: 212/254-9598

MEDIA ACCESS PROJECT
2000 M Street NW, Suite 400
Washington, DC 20036
Tel: 202/232-4300
Fax: 202/223-5302

MEDIA ALLIANCE
Fort Mason Center, Bldg. D, 2nd Fl.
San Francisco, CA 94123
Tel: 415/441-2557
Fax: 415/441-4067

THE MEDIA INSTITUTE
1000 Potomac Street NW, Suite 204
Washington, DC 20007
Tel: 202/298-7512
Fax: 202/337-7092

MEDIA WATCH
P.O. Box 618
Santa Cruz, CA 95061-0618
Tel: 408/423-6355
Fax: 408/423-6355

NATIONAL ALLIANCE OF
THIRD WORLD JOURNALISTS
1325 G Street NW
Washington, DC 20005
Tel: 202/737-6225
Fax: 202/737-6824

NATIONAL ASSOCIATION OF
BLACK JOURNALISTS
P.O. Box 17212
Washington, DC 20041
Tel: 703/648-1270
Fax: 703/476-6245

NATIONAL ASSOCIATION OF
HISPANIC JOURNALISTS
National Press Bldg., Suite 1193
Washington, DC 20045
Tel: 202/662-7145
Fax: 202/662-7144

NATIONAL CONFERENCE OF
EDITORIAL WRITERS
6223 Executive Boulevard
Rockville, MD 20852
Tel: 301/984-3015

NATIONAL NEWSPAPER
ASSOCIATION
1627 K Street NW, Suite 400
Washington, DC 20006
Tel: 202/466-7200
Fax: 202/331-1403

NATIONAL WRITERS UNION
873 Broadway, Rm. 203
New York, NY 10003
Tel: 212/254-0279

NEWSPAPER ASSOCIATION
OF AMERICA
11600 Sunrise Valley Drive
Reston, VA 22091
Tel: 703/648-1000
Fax: 703/620-4557

NEWSPAPER GUILD
8611 Second Avenue
Silver Spring, MD 20910
Tel: 301/585-2990

NEWSPAPER RESEARCH JOURNAL
Scripps Hall School of Journalism
Ohio University
Athens, OH 45701
Tel: 614/593-2590
Fax: 614/593-2592

ORGANIZATION OF
NEWS OMBUDSMEN
c/o Art Nauman
Sacramento Bee
P.O. Box 15779
Sacramento, CA 95852
Tel: 916/442-8050

PROJECT CENSORED
Communications Studies
Sonoma State University
1801 E. Cotati Avenue
Rohnert Park, CA 94928-3609
Tel: 707/664-2500
Fax: 707/664-0597

PROJECT CENSORED CANADA
Department of Communication
Simon Fraser University
Burnaby, BC V5A 1S6
Canada
Tel: 604/291-3687
Fax: 604/291-4024

PUBLIC MEDIA CENTER
446 Green Street
San Francisco, CA 94133
Tel: 415/434-1403
Fax: 415/986-6779

THE QUILL
Society of Professional Journalists
16 S. Jackson
Greencastle, IN 46135
Tel: 317/653-3333
Fax: 317/653-4631

ST. LOUIS JOURNALISM REVIEW
8380 Olive Boulevard
St. Louis, MO 63132
Tel: 314/991-1699
Fax: 314/997-1898

SOUTHWEST ALTERNATE MEDIA
PROJECT
1519 West Main
Houston, TX 77006
Tel: 713/522-8592
Fax: 713/522-0953

STRATEGIES FOR MEDIA LITERACY
1095 Market Street, Suite 617
San Francisco, CA 94103
Tel: 415/621-2911
Fax: 415/255-9392

TIMES MIRROR CENTER
FOR THE PEOPLE & THE PRESS
1875 Eye Street NW, Suite 1110
Washington, DC 20006
Tel: 202/293-3126

TYNDALL REPORT
135 Rivington Street
New York, NY 10002
Tel: 212/674-8913
Fax: 212/979-7304

WOMEN IN COMMUNICATIONS
2101 Wilson Boulevard, Suite 415
Arlington, VA 22201
Tel: 703/528-4200
Fax: 703/528-4205

LIBRARY & REFERENCE SOURCES

THE ACTIVIST'S ALMANAC:
The Concerned Citizen's Guide
to the Leading Advocacy Organizations
in America
By David Walls, 1993
Simon & Schuster Fireside Books
New York

ALTERNATIVE PRESS INDEX
Alternative Press Center, Inc.
P.O. Box 33109
Baltimore, MD 21218
Tel: 410/243-2471
Fax: 410/235-5325

CONNECTING TO THE INTERNET
O'Reilly & Associates, 1993
103 Morris Street, Suite A
Sebastopol, CA 95472
Tel: 707/829-0515

DIRECTORY OF ELECTRONIC
JOURNALS, NEWSLETTERS AND
ACADEMIC DISCUSSION LISTS
by Kovacs and Strangelove
Association of Scientific
and Academic Publishing
1527 New Hampshire Avenue NW
Washington, DC 20036

ECOLINKING: EVERYONE'S GUIDE
TO ONLINE INFORMATION
by Don Rittner, 1992
Peachpit Press, Berkeley, CA

ENCYCLOPEDIA OF ASSOCIATIONS
1993 ed., 4 vols.
Gale Research Inc., Detroit and London

ERIC
Clearinghouse on Information Resources
Syracuse University
School of Education/Information Studies
030 Huntingdon Hall
Syracuse, NY 13244-2340
Tel: 315/443-3640

FROM RADICAL TO
EXTREME RIGHT
A bibliography of current periodicals
of protests, controversy, advocacy and
dissent
by Gail Skidmore and Theodore Jurgen
Spahn, 1987, 3rd ed.
Scarecrow Press, Inc.
Metuchen, NJ, and London

GALE DIRECTORY OF PUBLICA-
TIONS AND BROADCAST MEDIA
1992 ed., 3 vols, plus supplement
Gale Research Inc., Detroit and London

THE INTERNATIONAL DIRECTORY
OF LITTLE MAGAZINES AND
SMALL PRESSES
Len Fulton, ed., 26th ed., 1990/91
Dustbooks
P.O. Box 100
Paradise, CA 95967

THE LEFT INDEX: A QUARTERLY
INDEX TO PERIODICALS OF THE
LEFT
Reference and Research Services
Santa Cruz, CA

MACROCOSM USA: POSSIBILITIES
FOR A NEW PROGRESSIVE ERA
Sandi Brockway, ed., 1992
Macrocosm USA, Inc.
P.O. Box 185
Cambria, CA 93428-8030
Tel: 805/927-8030
BBS (MacroNet): 805/927-1987

FORBES MEDIA GUIDE
1400 Route 206 N
P.O. Box 89
Bedminster, NJ 07921
Tel: 908/781-2078
Fax: 908/781-5635

NATIONAL FORUM ON
INFORMATION LITERACY
c/o American Library Association
50 East Huron Street
Chicago, IL 60611

PROGRESSIVE PERIODICALS
DIRECTORY
by Craig T. Canan
2nd ed., 1989
Progressive Education
P.O. Box 120574
Nashville, TN 37212

ULRICH'S INTERNATIONAL
PERIODICALS DIRECTORY
1992/93, 3 vols.
R.R. Bowker, New Providence, NJ

THE WHOLE INTERNET
O'Reilly & Associates, 1992
103 Morris Street, Suite A
Sebastopol, CA 95472
Tel: 707/829-0515

THE WORKING PRESS OF THE
NATION, 1991 ed.
National Research Bureau
225 W. Wacker Drive, Suite 2275
Chicago, IL 60606-1229
Tel: 312/346-9097

NATIONAL BROADCAST AND CABLE MEDIA

48 HOURS
CBS News
524 W. 57th Street
New York, NY 10019
Tel: 212/975-4848

60 MINUTES
CBS News
524 W. 57th Street
New York, NY 10019
Tel: 212/975-2006

20/20
ABC News
147 Columbus Avenue
New York, NY 10023
Tel: 212/456-2020
Fax: 212/456-2969

AMERICAN PUBLIC RADIO
100 North Sixth Street, Suite 900 A
Minneapolis, MN 55403
Tel: 612/338-5000
Fax: 612/330-9222

ABC WORLD NEWS TONIGHT
47 W. 66th Street
New York, NY 10023
Tel: 212/456-4040

ASSOCIATED PRESS RADIO
NETWORK
1825 K Street NW, Suite 710
Washington, DC 20006
Tel: 202/955-7200

CBS EVENING NEWS
524 W. 57th Street
New York, NY 10019
Tel: 212/975-3693

CBS THIS MORNING
524 W. 57th Street
New York, NY 10019
Tel: 212/975-2824

CHRISTIAN BROADCASTING
NETWORK
700 CBN Center
Virginia Beach, VA 23463-0001
Tel: 804/523-7111

CONUS COMMUNICATIONS
3415 University Avenue
Minneapolis, MN 55414
Tel: 612/642-4646

CNN
One CNN Center
Box 105366
Atlanta, GA 30348
Tel: 404/827-1500

CNN
Washington Bureau
820 First Street NE
Washington, DC 20002
Tel: 202/898-7900

C-SPAN
400 N. Capitol Street NW, Suite 650
Washington, DC 20001
Tel: 202/737-3220
Fax: 202/737-3323

CROSSFIRE
CNN
820 First Street NE
Washington, DC 20002
Tel: 202/8989-7951

THE CRUSADERS
1011-F West Alameda Avenue
Burbank, CA 91506
Tel: 818/556-2155
Fax: 818/556-2111

DATELINE
NBC News
30 Rockefeller Plaza/510
New York, NY 10112
Tel: 212/664-6170

DAY ONE
ABC News
147 Columbus Avenue, 8th Fl.
New York NY 10023
Tel: 212/456-6100

PHIL DONAHUE SHOW
30 Rockefeller Plaza
New York, NY 10019
Tel: 212/975-2006

ESPN
ESPN Plaza
Bristol, CT 06010
Tel: 203/585-2000

EYE TO EYE
CBS News
555 W. 57th Street
New York, NY 10019
Tel: 212/975-2000

FACE THE NATION
CBS News
2020 M Street NW
Washington, DC 20036
Tel: 202/457-4481

FRONT PAGE
FOX
10301 West Pico Blvd., 2nd Floor
Los Angeles, CA 90064
Tel: 310/284-3600

THE GERALDO RIVERA SHOW
555 West 57th Street
New York, NY 10019
Tel: 212/265-8520

GOOD MORNING AMERICA
ABC News
147 Columbus Avenue
New York, NY 10023
Tel: 212/456-5900
Fax: 212/456-7290

HOME BOX OFFICE
1100 Avenue of the Americas
New York, NY 10036
Tel: 212/512-1329

INVESTIGATIVE REPORTS
Arts & Entertainment Network
235 E. 45th Street
New York, NY 10017
Tel: 212/661-4500

LARRY KING SHOW (RADIO)
Mutual Broadcasting
1755 S. Jefferson Davis Highway
Arlington, VA 22202
Tel: 703/413-8475
Fax: 703/413-8442

LARRY KING LIVE TV
CNN
820 First Street NE
Washington, DC 20002
Tel: 212/898-7900

MACNEIL/LEHRER NEWSHOUR
New York Office:
WNET-TV
356 W. 58th Street
New York, NY 10019
Tel: 212/560-3113

MACNEIL/LEHRER NEWSHOUR
Washington Office:
Arlington, VA 22206
Tel: 703/998-2870

MEET THE PRESS
NBC News
4001 Nebraska Avenue NW
Washington, DC 20016
Tel: 202/885-4200
Fax: 202/362-2009

MORNING EDITION:
ALL THINGS CONSIDERED
National Public Radio
2025 M Street NW
Washington, DC 20036
Tel: 202/822-2000
Fax: 202/822-2329

BILL MOYERS
Public Affairs Television
356 W. 58th Street
New York, NY 10019
Tel: 212/560-6960

MTV NEWS
1515 Broadway, 24th Fl.
New York, NY 10036
Tel: 212/258-8000

NATIONAL PUBLIC RADIO
2025 M Street NW
Washington, DC 20036
Tel: 202/822-2000
Fax: 202/822-2329

NBC NIGHTLY NEWS
30 Rockefeller Plaza
New York, NY 10112
Tel: 212/664-4971

NIGHTLINE (New York)
ABC News
47 W. 66th Street
New York, NY 10023
Tel: 212/456-7777

NIGHTLINE (Washington DC)
ABC News
1717 DeSales Street NW
Washington, DC 20036
Tel: 202/887-7360

NOW
NBC News
30 Rockefeller Plaza
New York, NY 10112
Tel: 212/664-7501

PBS
1320 Braddock Place
Alexandria, VA 22314-1698
Tel: 703/739-5000
Fax: 703/739-0775
PBS Comment Line: 1/800/356-2626

PRIMETIME LIVE
ABC News
147 Columbus Avenue
New York, NY 10023
Tel: 212/456-1600

RADIO FREE EUROPE/
RADIO LIBERTY
1201 Connecticut Avenue NW
Suite 1100
Washington, DC 20036
Tel: 202/457-6900
Fax: 202/457-6997

RELIABLE SOURCES
CNN
820 First Street NE
Washington, DC 20002
Tel: 202/898-7900

RUSH LIMBAUGH
WABC Radio
2 Penn Plaza, 17th Fl.
New York, NY 10121
Tel: 212/613-3800
Fax: 212/563-9166

STREET STORIES
CBS News
555 W. 57th Street
New York, NY 10019
Tel: 212/975-8282

THIS WEEK WITH DAVID BRINKLEY
ABC News
1717 DeSales Street NW
Washington, DC 20036
Tel: 202/887-7777

TODAY SHOW
NBC News
30 Rockefeller Plaza
New York, NY 10112
Tel: 212/664-4249

TURNER BROADCASTING SYSTEM
1 CNN Center
Atlanta, GA 30348-5366
Tel: 404/827-1792

OPRAH WINFREY
Harpo Productions
P.O. Box 9909715
Chicago, IL 60690
Tel: 312/633-1000

NATIONAL COLUMNISTS

RUSSELL BAKER
The New York Times
229 W. 43rd Street
New York, NY 10036

DAVID BRODER
The Washington Post
1150 15th Street NW
Washington, DC 20071

ALEXANDER COCKBURN
The Nation
72 Fifth Avenue
New York, NY 10011
Tel: 212/242-8400
Fax: 212/463-9712

ROBERT NOVAK
Chicago Sun Times
401 N. Wabash Avenue
Chicago, IL 60611
Tel: 312/321-3000
Fax: 312/321-3084

ELLEN GOODMAN
The Boston Globe
P.O. Box 2378
Boston, MA 02107
Tel: 617/929-2000

NAT HENTOFF
The Village Voice
36 Cooper Square
New York, NY 10003
Tel: 212/475-3300
Fax: 212/475-8944

MOLLY IVINS
Fort Worth Star-Telegram
P.O. Box 1870
Fort Worth, TX 76101
Tel: 817/390-7400
Fax: 817/390-7520

JAMES KILPATRICK
Universal Press Syndicate
4900 Main Street, 9th Fl.
Kansas, MO 64112
Tel: 800/255-6734
or   816/932-6600

MORTON KONDRACKE
ROLL CALL
900 Second Street NE
Washington, DC 20002
Tel: 202/289-4900
Fax: 202/289-5337

MAX LERNER
New York Post
210 South Street
New York, NY 10002
Tel: 212/815-8000
Fax: 212/732-4241

MARY MCGRORY
The Washington Post
1150 15th Street NW
Washington, DC 20071
Tel: 202/334-6000

CLARENCE PAGE
Chicago Tribune
435 N. Michigan Avenue
Chicago, IL 60611
Tel: 312/222-3232

TOM PETERS
555 Hamilton Avenue
Palo Alto, CA 94031

ANNA QUINDLEN
New York Times
229 W. 43rd Street
New York, NY 10036
Tel: 212/556-1234

A.M. ROSENTHAL
New York Times
229 W. 43rd Street
New York, NY 10036
Tel: 212/556-1234

MIKE ROYKO
Chicago Tribune
435 N. Michigan Avenue
Chicago, IL 60611
Tel: 312/222-3232

WILLIAM SAFIRE
New York Times
229 W. 43rd Street
New York, NY 10036
Tel: 212/556-1234

GEORGE WILL
Newsweek
444 Madison Avenue
New York, NY 10022
Tel: 212/350-4000

NATIONAL PUBLICATIONS & NEWS SERVICES

ASSOCIATED PRESS
National Desk
50 Rockefeller Plaza
New York, NY 10020
Tel: 212/621-1600

BRITISH MEDICAL JOURNAL
B.M.A. House
Tavistock Square
London WC1H 9JR
England
Tel: 071/387-4499

CHICAGO TRIBUNE
435 N. Michigan Avenue
Chicago, IL 60611
Tel: 312/222-3232

CHRISTIAN SCIENCE MONITOR
One Norway Street
Boston, MA 02115
Tel: 617/450-2000

FORTUNE
Time Warner, Inc.
Time & Life Building
Rockefeller Center
New York, NY 10020
Tel: 212/586-1212

HARPER'S MAGAZINE
666 Broadway
New York, NY 10012-2317
Tel: 212/614-6500
Fax: 212/228-5889

KNIGHT-RIDDER NEWS SERVICE
790 National Press Building
Washington, DC 20045
Tel: 202/383-6080

LOS ANGELES TIMES
Times-Mirror Square
Los Angeles, CA 90053
Tel: 800/528-4637

MCCLATCHY NEWS SERVICE
P.O. Box 15779
Sacramento, CA 95852
Tel: 916/321-1895

NEWSWEEK
444 Madison Avenue
New York, NY 10022
Tel: 212/350-4000

NEW YORK NEWSDAY
235 Pinelawn Road
Melville, NY 11747
Tel: 516/843-2470

NEW YORK TIMES
229 W. 43rd Street
New York, NY 10036
Tel: 212/556-1234

NEW YORK TIMES
Washington Bureau
1627 Eye Street NW, 7th Fl.
Washington, DC 20006
Tel: 202/862-0300

REUTERS INFORMATION SERVICES
1700 Broadway
New York, NY 10019
Tel: 212/603-3300
Fax: 212/603-3446

SAN FRANCISCO CHRONICLE
901 Mission Street
San Francisco, CA 94103
Tel: 415/777-1111
Fax: 415/512-8196

SAN FRANCISCO EXAMINER
110 Fifth Street
San Francisco, CA 94103
Tel: 415/777-2424
Fax: 415/512-1264

SCRIPPS/HOWARD NEWS SERVICE
1090 Vermont Avenue NW, Suite 1000
Washington, DC 20005
Tel: 202/408-1484

TIME MAGAZINE
Time Warner, Inc.
Time & Life Building
Rockefeller Center
New York, NY 10020-1393
Tel: 212/522-1212

TRIBUNE MEDIA SERVICES
64 E. Concord Street
Orlando, FL 32801
Tel: 800/332-3068 or
     407/420-6200

UNITED PRESS INTERNATIONAL
1400 Eye Street NW
Washington, DC 20005
Tel: 202/898-8000

U.S. NEWS & WORLD REPORT
2400 N Street NW
Washington, DC 20037
Tel: 202/955-2000
Fax: 202/955-2049

USA TODAY
1000 Wilson Boulevard
Arlington, VA 22229
Tel: 703/276-3400

WALL STREET JOURNAL
200 Liberty Street
New York, NY 10281
Tel: 212/416-2000

WASHINGTON POST
1150 15th Street NW
Washington, DC 20071
Tel: 202/334-6000

APPENDIX C

The 1994 Alternative Writer's Market

If you are a journalist writing yet another exposé on Donald Trump's sex life, you should have no problem getting your story published in one of the nation's many periodicals.

If, however, you are a journalist writing an exposé of the cozy relationship between *The New York Times* and the nuclear power industry, you probably will be hard-pressed to find a ready market for your work.

The traditional and authoritative resource for writers is the *Writer's Market: Where & How To Sell What You Write*, published annually by Writer's Digest Books. However, while the *Writer's Market* is a must for all freelance writers, it falls somewhat short when it comes to fulfilling the needs of alternative writers.

For example, a natural market for a well-researched piece on how *The New York Times* has played a remarkably supportive role for nuclear power would be *Lies Of Our Times*, or LOOT, as it's commonly known. The "Times" in *Lies Of Our Times*, is, of course, *The New York Times*, and LOOT has published innumerable articles about the cozy relationship between *The New York Times* and the nuclear power industry.

However, LOOT is not found in the *Writer's Market*, at least not in the 1994 edition of the *Writer's Market*. But LOOT *is* found in the "1994 Alternative Writer's Market."

Throughout its 18-year history, Project Censored has received numerous queries from journalists and authors seeking publishers for exposés that challenge the conventional wisdom of the establishment press.

It is this ongoing succession of queries that led to the development of the following guide.

Since this is the first edition of the "Alternative Writer's Market" (AWM), it has a limited number of entries; nonetheless, it includes some of the most promising markets for alternative writers.

If you know of any additional listings that should be included in the 1995 AWM, please write the "Alternative Writer's Market," Project Censored, Sonoma State University, Rohnert Park, CA 94928, for a listing application.

Also, if you are aware of any changes and/or corrections for the current list, please send them to the same address.

AMERICAN JOURNALISM REVIEW
8701 Adelphi Road
Adelphi, MD 20783
Tel: 301/431-4771 Fax: 301/431-0097
Editor: Rem Rieder

The American Journalism Review, formerly the Washington Journalism Review, is published ten times a year. About 80 percent of its articles are provided by freelance writers. It is interested in articles, analysis, book reviews, interviews, exposés, of upwards of 2,000 words; short pieces of 500-700 words.

Rates: Features—20 cents a word; short features—$100.

Queries with published clips required; response time three-to-four weeks.

Tips: "Read the magazine before submitting queries; know what we've done, what we do, what we're looking for. We're always looking for good ideas, especially investigations of media coverage."—Associate Editor Chip Rowe

CALIFORNIA ALTERNATIVE NEWS BUREAU
2210 21st Street
Sacramento, CA 95616
Tel: 916/737-1234 Fax: 916/737-1437
Editor: Tom Johnson

The California Alternative News Bureau is a monthly news service which includes 15 California alternative papers among its subscribers. About 50 percent of its articles are provided by freelance writers. It is interested in hard news, features, and profiles of statewide California interest. Articles range from 500 to 2,000 words.

Rates: $100 to $400 depending on quality and work involved.

Queries with published clips required; response time normally within a week.

Tips: "Take a story the mainstream papers have missed or downplayed, and, with lively writing tell Californians about it. No polemics, editorials. If you want your audience outraged, reflect it in your writing, not your lead."—Editor Tom Johnson

CITY PAPER
Baltimore's Free Weekly
812 Park Avenue
Baltimore, MD 21201
Tel: 410/523-2300 Fax: 410/523-2222
Managing Editor: Jim Duffy

The City Paper is a weekly newspaper distributed free in the Baltimore area. About 50 percent of its articles are provided by freelance writers. It is interested in articles, profiles, book reviews, interviews, essays, exposés, all of which should have a strong Baltimore connection.
Rates: $25 to $400 depending on length.
Queries with published clips required; response time normally two weeks; send SASE for Writer's Guidelines.
Tips: We are particularly interested in the issues, people, and character of Baltimore City."—Managing Editor Jim Duffy

CULTURAL DEMOCRACY
P.O. Box 7591
Minneapolis, MN 55407
Fax: 612/721-2160

Cultural Democracy is a quarterly publication of the Alliance for Cultural Democracy, a 17-year-old national network of community and neighborhood based cultural workers.
Rates: None.
Queries not required; response time is two weeks to two months; send SASE for Writer's Guidelines.
Tips: "We are looking for writings that express the interconnection between cultural rights, community, arts, and ecology and ongoing, or historical, examples of projects or programs reflecting these concerns."

DETROIT METRO TIMES
743 Beaubien, Suite 301
Detroit, MI 48226
Tel: 313/961-4060

The Detroit Metro Times is a weekly newspaper; about 70 percent of its material is provided by freelance writers. It is interested in articles, profiles, reviews, opinion pieces of 600 to 3,500 words on cutting edge culture and progressive political and social change. It is not interested in consumer news or mainstream religion, medicine, or sports.
Rates: None cited.
Queries with published clips required; response time two weeks.
Tips: "We are interested in feminism, progressive politics, analysis of U.S. government and corporate abuse, environmentalism, race relations, danger of the right-wing, media monopoly and manipulation, etc."—Jim Dulzo

DOLLARS AND SENSE
1 Summer Street
Somerville, MA 02143
Tel: 617/628-8411 Fax: 617/628-2025
Editors: Betsy Reed and Marc Breslow

Dollars and Sense is a bimonthly magazine that focuses on economic issues and perspectives not normally found in Forbes Magazine or the Wall Street

Journal. About 20 percent of its articles are provided by freelance writers. It will consider full-length features, interviews, and book reviews (200-600 words each) for publication.

Rates: Regrets that it cannot compensate authors at this time.

Queries required; response time is a month; send SASE for Writer's Guidelines.

Tips: "Articles on progressive economics and political economy will be of interest."—Editor Betsy Reed

EARTH ISLAND JOURNAL
300 Broadway, #28
San Francisco, CA 94133-3312
Tel: 415/788-3666 Fax: 415/788-7324
Editor: Gar Smith

Earth Island Review is an environmentally-oriented quarterly magazine. Only about 5 percent of its articles are provided by freelance writers. However, half-page (500 words) and full page (1,000 words) stories are most likely to win consideration; feature-length reports (1,500-3,000 words) occasionally result from outside writers.

Rates: Year's free subscription in exchange.

Queries required; response time normally ten days to three months; send SASE for Writer's Guidelines.

Tips: "Our beat: 'Local News From Around the World.' First-person reports on under-reported environmental stories from abroad—particularly with a U.S. hook. Is some U.S. corporation causing harm overseas? Are there solutions from abroad that we can apply in the U.S.?"—Editor Gar Smith

ENVIRONMENTAL ACTION MAGAZINE
6930 Carroll Avenue, Suite 600
Takoma Park, MD 20912
Tel: 301/891-1100 Fax: 301/891-2218
Editors: Barbara Ruben and David Lapp

Environmental Action Magazine (EA) is a quarterly magazine that primarily explores the human environment. About 10 percent of its articles are provided by freelance writers. While it is mainly interested in book reviews and essays by established experts/leaders in particular fields, it does publish a few investigative pieces.

Rates: up to $150 but most authors are unpaid.

Queries with published clips and resume required; response time four to eight weeks.

Tips: "We stopped taking most freelance work in 1992 due to budget cuts and reduced frequency of the magazine. EA focuses primarily on the human environment (as opposed to wilderness issues) and on issues relating to the environmental movement itself. "—Editor Barbara Ruben

EXTRA!
130 W. 25th Street
New York, NY 10001
Tel: 212/633-6700 Fax: 212/727-7668
Editor: Jim Naureckas

EXTRA! is a bimonthly news media review journal published by Fairness and Accuracy In Reporting, a national media watchdog organization. It is

interested in well-documented articles related to issues of media bias.
Rates: Ten cents a word.
Queries not required; send SASE for Writer's Guidelines.
Tips: "Stories should focus more on the media than on the information not reported by the media. We look at media coverage of specific issues relating to government control of the media, corporate interference, racial and gender bias, etc."—Editor Jim Naureckas

THE HUMAN QUEST
1074 23rd Avenue N.
St. Petersburg, FL 33704-3228
Tel: 813/894-0097
Editor: Edna Ruth Johnson

The Human Quest is a bimonthly national magazine that is "in the mail on the 25th of the month." 100 percent of its material is provided by freelance writers. Emphasis of *The Human Quest* is world peace; its religious conviction is spiritual humanism. It welcomes thoughtful articles ranging from 150 to 500 to 1,000 words in length.
Rates: None.
Queries not required; response time normally within a week; in lieu of formal guidelines, editor will "happily furnish a copy of the publication" on request.
Tips: "*The Human Quest* is an independent journal of religious humanism, under the sponsorship of The Churchman Associates, Inc. It is edited in the conviction that religious journalism must provide a platform for the free exchange of ideas and opin-

ions; that religion is consonant with the most advanced revelations in every department of knowledge; that we are in a fraternal world community; and that the moral and spiritual evolution of man is only at the beginning."
—Editor Edna Ruth Johnson

THE INDEPENDENT FILM & VIDEO MONTHLY
625 Broadway, 9th Floor
New York, NY 10012
Tel: 212/473-3400Fax: 212/677-8732
Editor: Patricia Thomson

The Independent Film & Video Monthly is a national magazine with about 90 percent of its articles provided by freelance writers. It is interested news articles, 500-800 words; profiles of film/video makers, distributors, festival directors, 700-1,000 words; business, legal, technical articles, 700-1,200 words; features 1,500-3,000 words.
Rates: news articles, $50; profiles, $100; features, 10 cents a word.
Queries with published clips required; response time from two weeks to two months.
Tips: "Interested in film/video-related articles that are not *too* theoretical or *too* mainstream. Recent features include 'The Money Game: Foundation Insiders Explain the Rules,' and 'Made in Japan: Current Trends in Japanese Independent Filmmaking.'"—Michele Shapiro.

INDEX ON CENSORSHIP
32 Queen Victoria Street
London, England EC4N 4SS
Tel: 071-329-6434 Fax: 071-329-6461
Editor: Ursula Owen

The Index on Censorship is an international bimonthly review and analysis of censorship issues. It is interested in articles, profiles, book reviews, interviews, opinion pieces, essays, exposés, etc. Also interested in factual news on censorship and freedom of expression issues and analytic articles on these issues. Articles range from 800 to 4,000 words.

Rates: £60 per 1,000 words for original pieces

Queries not required.

Tips: Special interests include "all areas concerned with freedom of expression and censorship, world-wide (including Britain)."—Editor Ursula Owen.

IN THESE TIMES
2040 N. Milwaukee
Chicago, IL 60647
Tel: 312/772-0100 Fax: 312/772-4180
Editor: James Weinstein; Managing Editor: Miles Harvey

In These Times (ITT) is a biweekly news and views magazine. About 50 percent of its articles are provided by freelance writers. It is interested in articles, profiles, book reviews, interviews, opinion pieces, essays, and exposés.

Rates: none cited.

Queries with published clips required; response time normally two to three weeks; send SASE for Writer's Guidelines.

Tips: "Writers should be familiar with the magazine before sending submissions. A huge percentage of our rejections are pieces that are submitted by writers who obviously haven't read ITT."—Managing Editor Miles Harvey

LIES OF OUR TIMES (LOOT)
145 West 4th Street
New York, NY 10012
Tel: 212/254-1061 Fax: 212/254-9598
Senior Editor: Edward S. Herman

Lies Of Our Times publishes ten issues a year and about 85 percent of its articles are provided by freelance writers. It is interested in articles, interviews, and exposés. Articles range from 1,000 to 2,000 words.

Rates: $75.

Queries required; response time about a month; send SASE for Writer's Guidelines.

Tips: "LOOT is interested in articles that critique the mainstream media's coverage of current issues—both national and international. Attention to how issues are framed, what sources are used, what information is omitted, what hidden premises shape reporting—are all of interest."—Nancy Watt Rosenfeld

MEDIAFILE
Fort Mason, Bldg. D
San Francisco, CA 94123
Tel: 415/441-2557 Fax: 415/441-4067
Editor: Larry Smith

Media/File is a bimonthly newspaper published by the Media Alliance, an organization of more than 2,000 San Francisco Bay Area media professionals. About 80 percent of its articles are provided by freelance writers. It is interested in articles and analyses relating to the media, with a specific interest in the San Francisco/Bay Area; book reviews on books about media; profiles of interesting media workers; and investigative media exposés encouraged.

Rates: depends on experience; frequently trade.

Queries not required but helpful along with published clips; response time normally in two weeks; send SASE for Writer's Guidelines

Tips: "Media, First Amendment, censorship issues are our bag."—Editor Larry Smith

MOTHER JONES
731 Market Street, Suite 600
San Francisco, CA 94105
Tel: 415/558-8881Fax: 415/863-5136
Editor: Jeffrey Klein; Managing Editor: Katharine Fong

Mother Jones is a bimonthly magazine known for its investigative journalism and exposés, and its coverage of social issues, public affairs, and popular culture. Most of its articles are written by freelancers. It is interested in hard-hitting investigative reports exposing government, corporate, scientific, institutional cover-ups, etc.; thoughtful articles that challenge the conventional wisdom on national issues; and people-oriented stories on issues such as the environment, labor, the media, health care, consumer protection, and cultural trends. "Outfront" stories run 250-500 words; short features run 1,200-3,000 words, and longer features run 3,000-5,000 words.

Rates: 80 cents per word for commissioned stories.

Queries with published clips required; send SASE for Writer's Guidelines; please do not query by phone or fax.

Tips: "Keep in mind that our lead time is three months and submissions should not be so time-bound that they will appear dated. We are not a news magazine."

Ms.
230 Park Avenue
New York, NY 10169
Tel: 212/551-9595

Ms. is a bimonthly magazine that focuses primarily on women's issues and news. About 80 percent of its articles are provided by freelance writers. It is interested in articles, profiles, book reviews, opinion pieces, essays, and exposés. Article lengths—most departments, 1,200 words; features, 3,000-4,000 words; U.S. news, 1,000-2,000 words.

Rates: between 70 cents and $1 per word, approximately.

Queries with published clips required; address queries to Manuscripts Editor; response time about 12 weeks; send SASE for Writer's Guidelines.

MULTINATIONAL MONITOR
P.O. Box 19405
Washington, DC 20036
Tel: 202/387-8030 Fax: 202/234-5176
Editor: Robert Weissman

The Multinational Monitor is a monthly magazine that focuses on the activities and escapades of multinational corporations. About 50 percent of its articles are provided by freelance writers. It is interested in articles, profiles, book reviews, interviews, opinion pieces, essays, exposés, features and news items relating to multinational corporate issues. No fiction.
Rates: Ten cents a word.
Queries required; send SASE for Writer's Guidelines.
Tips: "Issues include all topics related to the activities of multinational corporations and their impact on labor and environment, especially in the Third World."—A. Freeman

THE NATION
72 Fifth Avenue
New York, NY 10011
Tel: 212/242-8400 Fax: 212/463-9712
Editor-in-Chief: Victor Navasky

The Nation is a weekly magazine (biweekly through the summer) dedicated to reporting on issues dealing with labor, national politics, business, consumer affairs, environmental politics, civil liberties, and foreign affairs. About 75 percent of its articles are provided by freelance writers. It is interested in articles, book reviews, opinion pieces, essays, and exposés.
Rates: $75 per Nation page

Queries with published clips required; normal response time is four weeks; send SASE for Writer's Guidelines.
Tips: "Leftist politics."—Dennis Selby

NATIONAL CATHOLIC REPORTER
P.O. Box 419281
Kansas City, MO 64141
Tel: 816/531-0538 Fax: 816/531-7466
Editor: Tom Fox

The National Catholic Reporter is published weekly from September through May with the exception of Thanksgiving week and the first week in January. It publishes articles, profiles, book reviews, interviews, opinion pieces, essays, exposés, features and news items. About 50 percent of its articles are provided by freelance writers. Average length is from 750 to 1,500 words.
Rates: Fifteen cents a word.
Queries required.

NEWSLETTER ON INTELLECTUAL FREEDOM
50 E. Huron Street
Chicago, IL 60611
Tel: 312/280-4223 Fax: 312/440-9374
Editor: Judith F. Krug

The Newsletter On Intellectual Freedom is a bimonthly magazine published by the American Library Association (ALA). Book reviews are published in every issue of the NEWSLETTER. Interested reviewers should contact the ALA Office for Intellectual Freedom for guidelines. Articles focusing on intellectual freedom, freedom of the press, censorship, and the First Amendment will be considered for publication.

Rates: pro bono.

Queries required; send SASE for Writer's Guidelines.

Tips: "Authors should contact the Office for Intellectual freedom for information and guidelines."—Editor Judith Krug

THE PROGRESSIVE
409 E. Main Street
Madison, WI 53703
Tel: 608/257-4626 Fax: 608/257-3373
Editor: Erwin Knoll

The Progressive is a politically-oriented monthly magazine. About 30 percent of its articles are provided by freelance writers. It is interested in features, 2,500 words; activist profiles, 750 words; Q&A, 2,500 words; book reviews, 300-1,500 words; and exposés, 2,500-3,500 words.

Rates: Features, $250; book reviews, $100; interviews, $250; exposés, $250; and activist profiles, $100.

Queries preferred with published clips; normal response time is ten days; send SASE for Writer's Guidelines.

PUBLIC CITIZEN MAGAZINE
2000 P Street NW
Washington, DC 20036
Tel: 202/833-3000 Fax: 202/659-9279
Editor: Peter Nye

Public Citizen Magazine is published six times a year and focuses on national policy issues and their impact on the public. About 15 percent of its articles are provided by freelance writers. It is interested in book reviews, 400 words (two reviews per magazine page); features up to 4,500 words; profiles of extraordinary individuals who work for improving their local community up to three pages.

Rates: negotiable, $400 tops; buys one-time rights only.

Queries required; normal response time is two weeks.

Tips: "Our articles deal with national policy involving accountability of corporations and the government. It's best to read our magazine and be familiar with how our stories are published, their slant. We also rely heavily on facts, quotes, specific information."
—Editor Peter Nye

ST. LOUIS JOURNALISM REVIEW
8380 Olive Boulevard
St. Louis, MO 63132
Tel: 314/991-1699 Fax: 314/997-1898
Editor: Charles L. Klotzer

The St. Louis Journalism Review is a regionally based but nationally oriented journalism review magazine published monthly except for combined issues in July/August and December/January. About 80 percent of its articles are provided by freelance writers. It is interested in articles, profiles, interviews, opinion pieces, essays, and exposés dealing with the news media.

Rates: $20 to $100.

Queries not required; normal response time is three to four weeks.

Tips: "While the St. Louis region is of primary interest, national and international pieces dealing with media criticism are considered."—Editor Charles L. Klotzer

SOJOURNERS
2401 15th Street NW
Washington, DC 20009
Tel: 202/328-8842 Fax: 202/328-8757
Editor: Jim Wallis

Sojourners is published monthly (10 times a year) and about 25 percent of its articles are provided by freelance writers. It is interested in features on issues of faith, politics, and culture (1,800-3,200 words); book, film, and music reviews (600-1,000 words).

Rates: features, $100-$200; reviews, $40.

Queries not required; submit published clips; normal response time is six to eight weeks; send SASE for Writer's Guidelines.

SOUTHERN EXPOSURE
P.O. Box 531
Durham, NC 27702
Tel: 919/419-8311
Editor: Eric Bates

Southern Exposure is a quarterly magazine that focuses on Southern politics and culture. About 50 percent of its articles are provided by freelance writers. It is interested in investigative journalism, essays, profiles, book reviews, oral histories, and features on Southern politics and culture.

Rates: $50-$250

Queries not required; submit published clips; normal response time is four to six weeks; send SASE for Writer's Guidelines.

TIKKUN Magazine
251 W. 100th Street, 5th Floor
New York, NY 10025
Tel: 212/864-4110 Fax: 212/864-4137
Editor & Publisher: Michael Lerner

Tikkun is a bimonthly magazine that focuses on political and cultural issues. It is interested in articles, profiles, book reviews, interviews, opinion pieces, essays, exposés, features and news items; all types of material of varying lengths.

Rates: varies.

Queries not required; normal response time is four months.

Tips: "Political/cultural critiques—magazine has a liberal/progressive slant but does publish all sorts of viewpoints. A non-profit magazine."

UTNE READER
1624 Harmon Place
Minneapolis, MN 55403
Tel: 612/338-5040
Managing Editor: Lynette Lamb

The UTNE Reader is an eclectic bimonthly magazine that has earned the reputation of being the *Reader's Digest* of the alternative media. About 20 percent of its articles are provided by freelance writers. It is interested in short essays, articles, and opinion pieces.

Rates: $100-$500.

Queries not required; submit published clips; normal response time is two to three months; send SASE for Writer's Guidelines.

Tips: "We use unsolicited material most often in our 'Gleanings' section. Most of our other freelance articles are assigned. The majority of UTNE Reader articles are reprinted from other publications."—Managing Editor Lynette Lamb

WASHINGTON SPECTATOR
541 E. 12th Street
New York, NY 10009
Tel: 212/995-8527 Fax: 212/979-2055
Editor: Ben Franklin;
Publisher: Phillip Frazer

The Washington Spectator is a small, but influential, political watchdog newsletter published 22 times a year. About 10 percent of its articles are provided by freelance writers. It is primarily interested in articles and exposés.

Rates: varies: 50 cents a word and up.

Queries with published clips required; normal response time is one week.

Tips: "Write a very brief (one page maximum) note as a first proposal."
—Publisher Phillip Frazer

WILLAMETTE WEEK
2 NW 2nd Avenue
Portland, OR 97209
Tel: 503/243-2122 Fax: 503/243-1115
Editor: Mark Zusman

Willamette Week is an alternative weekly newspaper published and distributed in the Portland, Oregon, area. About 50 percent of its articles are provided by freelance writers. It is interested in articles (if regional in perspective), interviews, book reviews, music reviews, profiles—again with a regional focus.

Rates: ten cents a word.

Queries with published clips required; normal response time is about three weeks; send SASE for Writer's Guidelines.

WRITER'S GUIDELINES
P.O. Box 608
Pittsburg, MO 65724
Fax: 417/993-5544
Publisher & Editor: Susan Salaki

Writer's Guidelines is a bimonthly magazine designed to help writers get published. About 99 percent of its articles are provided by freelance writers. It is interested in articles, book reviews, interviews, opinion pieces, and essays that will help writers.

Rates: depends on quality of material.

Queries not required; normal response time is two weeks; send SASE for Writer's Guidelines.

Tips: "Use a friendly relaxed style in your material but not chummy. Our objective is to help writers get published. If your article or essay contains information that will make that happen, we want to see it. We look for material the other writer publications usually overlook."—Editor Susan Salaki

Top 10 CENSORED! Reprints

1

The U.S. Is Killing Its Young

"U.N. SAYS U.S. DANGEROUS FOR CHILDREN," By Gayle Reaves; *Dallas Morning News*, 9/25/93

The United States is one of the most dangerous places to live for young people, according to a United Nations report released this week. And while many other places are getting better, the United States is getting worse.

A report from the United Nations Children's Fund called "The Progress of Nations" said that nine out of 10 young people slain in industrialized countries are slain in the United States.

The United States' homicide rate for young people ages 15 to 24 is five times that of its nearest competitor, Canada.

The U.S. poverty rate for children is more than double that of any other major industrialized nation, UNICEF researchers said. In the last 20 years, while other industrialized nations were bringing children out of poverty, only the United States and Britain slipped backward.

The report ranks countries around the globe not by their wealth or political power but by the well-being of their peoples, especially children.

Although the news about U.S. conditions was grim, said Peter Adamson, the report's editor, the last 30 years have seen huge advances for people in developing countries. Real income has more than doubled. Child death rates have been halved. Life expectancy has increased by about a third, and malnutrition rates have dropped by about the same percentage.

And in just one generation, researchers said, approximately half the married women in the developing world have begun using contraceptives to plan thier families.

In most developing nations, average family size is falling at a speed unprecedented in history. Apparently it would drop faster if women were making all the decisions, the researchers said.

World population projections for 2025 would fall by about 1 billion people if all women could choose how many children to have, the report said. Population growth rates in developing countries would drop by 30 percent.

BIRTH CONTROL LACKING

An estimated 120 million women in developing countries don't want more children, the report said, but are not using—and in many cases have no access to—effective birth control.

Birth rates are greatly affected by the ability of living children to survive, according to UNICEF. For that reason, researchers said, saving children's lives will not worsen population pressures but decrease them.

"When child death rates are high, parents often insure against an anticipated loss by having more children," the report said.

Only in countries where the death rates of young children have begun to drop do large numbers of women begin to use contraceptives, researchers found.

The document embodies UNICEF's case for giving chidren the first call on the world's resources.

"The day will come," reads the preface, "when the progress of nations will be judged not by their military or economic strength, nor by the splendor of their capital cities and public buildings, but by the well-being of their peoples."

REPORT TO BE UPDATED

The report had its beginnings in a World Summit for Children in 1990. It will be updated annually, as countries measure their progress toward goals set for 2000.

Mr. Adamson, in his summary of the report, urged developed countries not to lose hope in the possibility of solving the world's basic-needs problems.

Despite the relatively small proportion of public money spent worldwide on such concerns, he said, "the majority of people in the developing world have progressed to the point at which their minimum needs are being met."

He pointed to the spectacular rise in immunization rates as a reason for continued efforts.

Ten years ago, Mr. Adamson wrote, fewer than 20 percent of babies around the world were being immunized against major preventable diseases. But by 1990, most developing countries had reached the target of 80 percent, set by UNICEF and the World Health Organization.

That meant, he said, that the right vaccines, at the right time and right temperature, had been delivered to more than 100 million babies four or five times a year.

If the countries could accomplish that, he suggested, they could accomplish many more things for children and families. The question, he said, is not so much wealth as it is political will.

U.S. SINGLED OUT

The report shows the United States to be a particularly pointed example of wealth failing to promote welfare.

The economic woes that have affected the United States in recent years have affected much of the rest of the world, too, the UNICEF report said. But in other countries, taxes and other government policies helped ease the situation. In the United States, it says, that did not happen.

"Children have been hurt by big-picture economic changes that seem to have happened all over the world," said Arloc Sherman, research analyst with the Children's Defense Fund. "But what really distinguishes the United States from all these countries is that we started off with less generous benefits, and as we went through the 1980s...other nations got more generous and we got even less generous."

The UNICEF report puts into a global perspective many problems affecting young people in the United States—and in the Dallas area in particular.

Violence has reached such proportions that the national Centers for Disease Control and Prevention recently issued a report on violence as an epidemic in this country.

SLAYINGS STAGGERING

"If you look at homicide rates for young males, it's staggering," said Dr. Patrick Kachur, an epidemic intelligence officer for the CDC's National Center for Injury Prevention and Control. For men of color, he said, the rate "probably rivals if not exceeds that of South Africa."

In Dallas, "violence is a daily thing our patients have to deal with," said Dr. Laurie Dekat, who oversees three West Dallas health clinics within the Parkland Memorial Hospital system.

In a survey of 10-year-olds participating in a program at one clinic, she said, "over 50 percent had seen a gun brandished or someone actually shot. We know some of our own kids, just for protection, have to carry weapons."

The rate of violence has increased dramatically in the 5 1/2 years she has worked at the clinics, Dr. Dekat said.

Mr. Sherman, of the Children's Defense Fund, said other recent studies show that, among industrialized nations, as income distribution becomes more unequal, "their death rates become worse."

The UNICEF-promulgated goals for children have been accepted by most nations and shaped into national action plans.

The United States has drawn up an action plan. But, unlike every other industrialized nation, the United States has not signed nor ratified the Convention on the Rights of the Child, a set of principals adopted by the U.N. General Assembly in 1989.

"I think it (the United States' failure to ratify the principles) is a sign and part of something larger—that we haven't yet committed ourselves to saying that children are our future and deserve to be taken care of," Mr. Sherman said. "We haven't done that on a whole range of policies."

2 CENSORED

Why Are We Really In Somalia?

"THE OIL FACTOR IN SOMALIA," by Mark Fineman;
Los Angeles Times, 1/18/93

MOGADISHU, Somalia—Far beneath the surface of the tragic drama of Somalia, four major U.S. oil companies are quietly sitting on a prospective fortune in exclusive concessions to explore and exploit tens of millions of acres of the Somali countryside.

That land, in the opinion of geologists and industry sources, could yield significant amounts of oil and natural gas if the U.S.-led military mission can restore peace to the impoverished East African nation.

According to documents obtained by The Times, nearly two-thirds of Somalia was allocated to the American oil giants Conoco, Amoco, Chevron and Phillips in the final years before Somalia's pro-U.S. President Siad Barre was overthrown and the nation plunged into chaos in January, 1991. Industry sources said the companies holding the rights to the most promising concessions are hoping that the Bush Administration's decision to send U.S. troops to safeguard aid shipments to Somalia will also help protect their multimillion-dollar investments there.

Officially, the Administration and the State Department insist that the U.S. military mission in Somalia is strictly humanitarian. Oil industry spokesmen dismissed as "absurd" and "nonsense" allegations by aid experts, veteran East Africa analysts and several prominent Somalis that President Bush, a former Texas oilman, was moved to act in Somalia, at least in part, by the U.S. corporate oil stake.

But corporate and scientific documents disclosed that the American companies are well positioned to pursue Somalia's most promising potential oil reserves the moment the nation is pacified. And the State Department and U.S. military officials acknowledge that one of those oil companies has done more than simply sit back and hope for peace.

Conoco Inc., the only major multinational corporation to maintain a functioning office in Mogadishu throughout the past two years of nationwide anarchy, has been directly involved in the U.S. government's role in the U.N.-sponsored humanitarian military effort.

Conoco, whose tireless exploration efforts in north-central Somalia reportedly had yielded the most encouraging prospects just before Siad Barre's fall, permitted its Mogadishu corporate compound to be transformed into a *de facto* American embassy a few days before the U.S Marines landed in the capital, with Bush's special envoy using it as his temporary headquarters. In addition, the president of the company's subsidiary in Somalia won high official praise for serving as the government's volunteer "facilitator" during the months before and during the U.S. intervention.

Describing the arrangement as a "business relationship," an official spokesman for the Houston-based parent corporation of Conoco Somalia Ltd. said the U.S. government was paying rental for its use of the compound, and he insisted that Conoco was proud of resident general manager Raymond Marchand's contribution to the U.S.-led humanitarian effort.

John Geybauer, spokesman for Conoco Oil in Houston, said the company was acting as "a good corporate citizen and neighbor" in granting the U.S. government's request to be allowed to rent the compound. The U.S. Embassy and most other buildings and residential compounds here in the capital were rendered unusable by vandalism and fierce artillery duels during the clan wars that have consumed Somalia and starved its people.

In its in-house magazine last month, Conoco reprinted excerpts from a letter of commendation for Marchand written by U.S. Marine Brig. Gen. Frank Libutti, who has been acting as military aid to U.S. envoy Robert B. Oakley. In the letter, Libutti praised the oil official for his role in the initial operation to land Marines on Mogadishu's beaches in December, and the general concluded, "Without Raymond's courageous contributions and selfless service, the operation would have failed."

But the close relationship between Conoco and the U.S. intervention force has left many Somalis and foreign development experts deeply troubled by the blurry line between the U.S. government and the large oil company, leading many to liken the Somalia operation to a miniature version of Operation Desert Storm, the U.S.-led military effort in January, 1991, to drive Iraq from Kuwait and, more broadly, safeguard the world's largest oil reserves.

"They sent all the wrong signals when Oakley moved into the Conoco compound," said one expert on Somalia who worked with one of the four major companies as they intensified their exploration efforts in the country in the late 1980s.

"It's left everyone thinking the big question here isn't famine relief but oil—whether the oil concessions granted under Siad Barre will be transferred if and when peace is restored," the expert said. "It's potentially worth billions of dollars, and believe me, that's what the whole game is starting to look like."

Although most oil experts outside Somalia laugh at the suggestion that the nation ever could rank among the world's major oil producers—and most maintain that the international aid mission is intended simply to feed Somalia's starving masses—no one doubts that there is oil in Somalia. The only question: How much?

"It's there. There's no doubt there's oil there," said Thomas E. O'Connor, the principal petroleum engineer for the World Bank, who headed an in-depth, three-year study of oil prospects in the Gulf of Aden off Somalia's northern coast.

"You don't know until you study a lot further just how much is there," O'Connor said. "But it has commercial potential. It's got high potential... once the Somalis get their act together."

O'Connor, a professional geologist, based his conclusion on the findings of some of the world's top petroleum geologists. In a 1991 World Bank-coordinated study, intended to encourage private investment in the petroleum potential of eight African nations, the geologists put Somalia and Sudan at the top of the list of prospective commercial oil producers.

Presenting their results during a three-day conference in London in September, 1991, two of those geologists, an American and an Egyptian, reported that an analysis of nine exploratory wells drilled in Somalia indicated that the region is "situated within the oil window, and thus [is] highly prospective for gas and oil." A report by a third geologist, Z. R. Beydoun, said offshore sites possess "the geological parameters conducive to the generation, expulsion and trapping of significant amounts of oil and gas."

Beydoun, who now works for Marathon Oil in London, cautioned in a recent interview that on the basis of his findings alone, "you cannot say there definitely is oil," but he added: "The different ingredients for generation of oil are there. The question is whether oil generated there has been trapped or whether it dispersed or evaporated."

Beginning in 1986, Conoco, along with Amoco, Chevron, Phillips and, briefly, Shell all sought and obtained exploration licenses for northern Somalia from Siad Barre's government. Somalia was soon carved up into concessional blocs, with Conoco, Amoco and Chevron winning the right to explore and exploit the most promising ones.

The companies' interest in Somalia clearly predated the World Bank study. It was grounded in the findings of another, highly successful exploration effort by the Texas-based Hunt Oil Corp. across the Gulf of Aden in the Arabian Peninsula nation of Yemen, where geologists disclosed in the mid-1980s that the estimated 1 billion barrels of Yemeni oil reserves were part of a great underground rift, or valley, that arced into and across northern Somalia.

Hunt's Yemeni operation, which is now yielding nearly 200,000 barrels of oil a day, and its implications for the entire region were not lost on then-Vice President George Bush.

In fact, Bush witnessed it firsthand in April, 1986, when he officially dedicated Hunt's new $18-million refinery near the ancient Yemeni town of Marib. In remarks during the event, Bush emphasized the critical value of supporting U.S. corporate efforts to develop and safeguard potential oil reserves in the region.

In his speech, Bush stressed "the growing strategic importance to the West of developing crude oil sources in the region away from the Strait of Hormuz," according to a report three weeks later in the authoritative Middle East Economic Survey.

Bush's reference was to the geographical choke point that controls access to the Persian Gulf and its vast oil reserves. It came at the end of a 10-day Middle East tour in which the vice president drew fire for appearing to advocate higher oil and gasoline prices.

"Throughout the course of his 17,000-mile trip, Bush suggested continued low [oil] prices would jeopardize a domestic oil industry 'vital to the national security interests of the United States,' which was interpreted at home and abroad as a sign the one-time oil driller from Texas was coming to the aid of his former associates," United Press International reported from Washington the day after Bush dedicated Hunt's Yemen refinery.

No such criticism accompanied Bush's decision late last year to send more than 20,000 U.S. troops to Somalia, widely applauded as a bold and costly step to save an estimated 2 million Somalis from starvation by opening up relief supply lines and pacifying the famine-struck nation.

But since the U S. intervention began, neither the Bush Administration nor any of the oil companies that had been active in Somalia up until the civil war broke out in early 1991 have commented publicly on Somalia's potential for oil and natural gas production. Even in private, veteran oil company exploration experts played down any possible connection between the Administration's move into Somalia and the corporate concessions at stake.

"In the oil world, Somalia is a fringe exploration area," said one Conoco executive who asked not to be named. "They've overexaggerated it," he said of the geologists' optimism about the prospective oil reserves there. And as for Washington's motives in Somalia, he brushed aside criticisms that have been voiced quietly in Mogadishu, saying, "With America, there is a genuine humanitarian streak in us...that many other countries and cultures cannot understand."

But the same source added that Conoco's decision to maintain its headquarters in the Somali capital even after it pulled out the last of its major equipment in the spring of 1992 was certainly not a humanitarian one. And he confirmed that the company, which has explored Somalia in three major phases beginning in 1952, had achieved "very good oil shows"— industry terminology for an exploration phase that often precedes a major discovery—just before the war broke out.

"We had these very good shows," he said. "We were pleased. That's why Conoco stayed on....The people in Houston are convinced there's oil there."

Indeed, the same Conoco World article that praised Conoco's general manager in Somalia for his role in the humanitarian effort quoted Marchand as saying, "We stayed because of Somalia's potential for the company and to protect our assets."

Marchand, a French citizen who came to Somalia from Chad after a civil war forced Conoco to suspend operations there, explained the role played by his firm in helping set up the U.S.-led pacification mission in Mogadishu.

"When the State Department asked Conoco management for assistance, I was glad to use the company's influence in Somalia for the success of this mission," he said in the magazine article. "I just treated it like a company operation—like moving a big rig. I did it for this operation because the [U.S.] officials weren't familiar with the environment."

Marchand and his company were clearly familiar with the anarchy into which Somalia has descended over the past two years—a nation with no functioning government, no utilities and few roads, a place ruled loosely by regional warlords.

Of the four U.S. companies holding the Siad Barre-era oil concessions, Conoco is believed to be the only one that negotiated what spokesman Geybauer called " a standstill agreement" with an interim government set up by one of Mogadishu's two principal warlords, Ali Mahdi Mohamed. Industry sources said the other U.S. companies with contracts in Somalia cited *"force majeure"* (superior power), a legal term asserting that they were forced by the war to abandon their exploration efforts and would return as soon as peace is restored.

"It's going to be very interesting to see whether these agreements are still good," said Mohamed Jirdeh, a prominent Somali businessman in Mogadishu who is familiar with the oil-concession agreements. "Whatever Siad did, all those records and contracts, all disappeared after he fled.... And this period has brought with it a deep change of our society.

"Our country is now very weak, and, of course, the American oil companies are very strong. This has to be handled very diplomatically, and I think the American government must move out of the oil business, or at least make clear that there is a definite line separating the two, if they want to maintain a long-term relationship here."

Fineman, Times Bureau chief in Nicosia, Cyprus, was recently in Somalia. Copyright, 1993, Los Angeles Times. Reprinted by permission.

"SOMOILIA," by Rory Cox; *Propaganda Review,* Number 10, Page 42

Could the preponderance of images of starving Somalis all over the major media outlets during the end of 1992 and the first half of 1993 have been just a more refined and cynical method of selling yet another war for oil? The US/UN military involvement in Somalia began in mid-November, yet it wasn't until January 19, Bush's last day in office, that the *LA Times'* Mark Fineman came out with an article that revealed the oil connection in Somalia. According to the piece, nearly two-thirds of the land in Somalia was allocated to Conoco, Amoco, Chevron, and Phillips in the years before President Mohamed Siad Barre was overthrown in 1991.

While State Department and oil industry spokesmen dismiss as "absurd" and "nonsense" allegations that oil was even in part a motivating factor behind Operation Restore Hope, the oil industry's role in Somalia paints a different picture. If peace is restored to Somalia, geologists see a potential bonanza of untapped oil resources. According to a 1991 World Bank-coordinated study, geologists put Somalia and Sudan at the top of the list of perspective oil resources.

Conoco is the only major multinational corporation which has maintained an office in Mogadishu throughout the past two years. In what Conoco is describing as a "business relationship," the Conoco office is now serving as a de facto US Embassy. Some may see this as a blurred line separating Conoco and the State Department; Conoco sees it as being a "good corporate citizen and neighbor." Further blurring that line, the president of the Conoco Somalia office, according to the *Times*, "won high official praise for serving as the government's volunteer 'facilitator' during the months before and during the US intervention."

This petroleum dimension to Operation Restore Hope points to a rather cynical scenario. Certainly there is nothing new about famine in Africa, and while any country as well-fed as ours should feel compelled to offer aid, using military force as a means to feed the hungry seems uncharacteristically ambitious.

During the build-up phase of Operation Desert Shield, the threat to US oil supply was initially given as a rationale by Bush. That trial balloon sank fast in the public opinion polls, however, and was quickly forgotten as stories of Iraqi atrocities in Kuwait began to surface. Nevertheless, "No blood for oil" was the rally cry amongst the opposition.

Could this be why the State Department hasn't even mentioned the oil prospects of Somalia? Or why Fineman's story isn't on the front page of the *LA Times* or any other US paper? In the beginning days of Operation Restore Hope, opposition, even on the left, was minimal, as it's hard to oppose the idea of feeding the hungry. Would that have been different had the oil connection been made earlier?

3 CENSORED

The Sandia Report on Education: A Perfect Lesson In Censorship

PERSPECTIVES ON EDUCATION IN AMERICA
By Robert M. Huelskamp;
Phi Delta Kappan, May 1993

Whenever feasible, the Sandia researchers looked at the data over time to put the performance of the U.S. education system in proper perspective. Mr. Huelskamp summarizes the surprising findings.

When the governors and President George Bush set forth national education goals in the wake of the September 1989 education summit in Charlottesville, Virginia, we at Sandia National Laboratories took note. We also listened to a challenge from the then-secretary of energy, Adm. James Watkins, who charged the national laboratories to become more involved in education.

Because Sandia conducts scientific research for the U.S. government, we have a keen interest in the education system that develops future scientists, engineers, and mathematicians. Therefore, we initiated several new programs. Much of our past effort was directed toward education at the postsecondary level, but a significant portion of the new emphasis is directed toward elementary and secondary education.

In support of these new efforts, we in the New Initiatives Department of Sandia's Strategic Studies Center were asked to conduct a wide-ranging analysis of local, state, and national education systems to determine where Sandia could make its most effective contribution. The study that Charles Carson, Thomas Woodall, and I conducted produced some interesting results. It greatly changed our initial perceptions in several areas and reinforced our perceptions in others. Overall, it sought to provide an objective, "outsider's" look at the status of education in the U.S.

Whenever feasible, we looked at the data over time to put the performance of the current system in proper perspective. To our surprise, on nearly every measure we found steady or slightly improving trends. Does this mean that we are adamant defenders of the status quo, as has been suggested? The answer is no—for three reasons. First, it is not clear to us that all the measures analyzed by us and others are appropriate barometers of performance for the education system. Thus the trend data on some of these measures, positive or negative, may be irrelevant. Second, even if a particular measure is appropriate, steady or slightly improving performance may not be adequate to meet future societal requirements in an increasingly competitive world. Finally, on some appropriate measures, the performance of the U.S. education system is clearly deficient.

As our work unfolded in the spring of 1991, we subjected a draft to peer review with the U.S. Department of Education, the National Science Foundation, and other researchers (most notably Gerald Bracey). Within weeks we found ourselves swept up in the national debate on the status of education. The draft report has been the subject of congressional testimony, editorials in the media, an audit by the General Accounting Office, and additional peer reviews. To date we have received nearly 1,000 requests for the final report and have been cited by authors in several publications, including the *Kappan*. The attention we have received seems to validate one of our five key findings—the need to upgrade the quality of data regarding education. The following is a brief summary of our major findings. The full report will be published in the May/June issue of the *Journal of Educational Research*.

DROPOUT AND RETENTION RATES

America's on-time high school graduation rate has remained steady for more than 20 years, hovering somewhere between 75% and 80%. However, some students require more than four years to complete high school, and many dropouts avail themselves of opportunities to reenter the system (night school, the General Education Development testing program, and so on), resulting in an overall high school completion rate for young adults of better than 85%. This rate, which is still improving, is among the best in the world.

However, gross national data can mask underlying problems. For example, the most significant dropout problems are evident among minority youths and students in urban schools. Nearly 80% of white students complete high school on time, and roughly 88% do so by age 25. Only 70% of black students and 50% of Hispanic students graduate on time. By age 25, roughly 82% of blacks have completed high school, but only 60% of Hispanics have done so. Finally, dropout reports indicate that urban students, regardless of race, drop out at very high rates.

Our report shows that recent immigration of undereducated adults who are beyond high school age is significantly inflating dropout figures for the overall Hispanic population. Further analysis of this phenomenon is essential to a proper understanding of the educational needs of this growing segment of our population.

STANDARDIZED TESTS

We evaluated student performance on both the National Assessment of Educational Progress (NAEP) and the Scholastic Aptitude Test (SAT). We found that performance has been steady or improving on the NEAP, with the greatest gains in basic skills. Furthermore, these gains have not been at the expense of advanced skills.

We also discovered that the much-publicized "decline" in average SAT scores misrepresents the true story about student SAT performance. Although it is true that the average SAT score has declined since the 1960s, the reason for the decline is *not* decreasing student performance. We found that the decline arises from the fact that more students in the bottom half of the class are taking the SAT today than in years past. Since 1971 the median test-taker has dropped from the 79th percentile in class rank to the 73rd percentile. Because more Americans are aspiring to achieve a college education today than ever before, the national average SAT score is lowered by the larger numbers of students in lower quartiles who take the test.

When we break down the data as we did for dropouts, we find that minority youths continue to lag behind their white peers on standardized tests (even though every minority ethnic group taking the test is performing better today than 15 years ago). For example, in spite of a 50-point improvement over the past decade in their average SAT score, black students still average nearly 200 points lower than whites. Similarly, the scores of Hispanic and Native American students trail the scores of whites by more than 100 points.

HIGHER EDUCATION

Nearly 60% of today's young people pursue postsecondary studies at accredited institutions, and two-thirds of those students enroll in four-year institutions. Eventually, one-fourth of today's young people will obtain at least a bachelor's degree. These rates are the highest in the world.

The changing population on today's college campuses is significant as well. The number of women enrolled in college has been increasing for 30 years, while male enrollment has remained steady. Female enrollment surpassed male enrollment in the mid-1970s. College populations are also aging as more people enroll in postsecondary studies later in life. Moreover, four out of five college students nationwide are commuters, and more than 25% hold full-time jobs while in school.

As part of the Department of Energy laboratory complex, Sandia is particularly interested in the attainment of technical degrees. We found that roughly 200,000 U.S. students earn bachelor's degrees in the natural sciences and engineering each year—up significantly from 20 years ago but representing a fairly steady rate of 4% to 5% of U.S. youths. Meanwhile, the U.S. grants a large number of advanced technical degrees to non-U.S. citizens. Each year, nearly 50% of doctorates in engineering and 25% of doctorates in science are awarded to non-U.S. citizens. However, more than half of these degree recipients remain in the U.S. It is important to note that, despite improvements in the past two decades, female and minority students continue to lag far behind their white male peers in the attainment of technical degrees.

SPENDING FOR EDUCATION

In investigating expenditures for education, we learned that, during the past 15 years, spending on K-12 education rose roughly 30% per pupil in constant dollars. However, disaggregating the available data showed that little of this increase went to "regular" education. Much of the increase went to "special" education and fixed costs such as insurance and retirement funds. Compared to 16 other industrialized nations, we found that U.S. spending for "regular" education is about average, when adjusted for purchasing power parity, though how it stacks up against any specific country is heavily dependent on the method of accounting used.

INTERNATIONAL COMPARISONS

We found little credible data regarding international comparisons. The most complete data are found in the reports of the International Assessment of Educational Progress (IAEP). The results of the IAEP and other international studies indicate that average U.S. student performance in both math and science continues to be low compared to that of other participating nations. However, we discovered that many factors influence these rankings. Quite often the major differences in education systems across countries greatly weaken the value of such single-point comparisons. In addition, reporting only the average performance of a large and heterogeneous population provides little insight into the quality of educational services provided to various subpopulations (urban students, various ethnic groups, and so on).

Other international indicators of the performance of education systems reflect well on the U.S. Only Belgium and Finland exceed the U.S. in the percentage of 17-year-olds enrolled in school. The U.S. continues to lead the world in the percentage of young people who earn bachelor's degrees and in the percentage of degrees obtained by women and minorites. This is true for both technical and nontechnical degrees.

Our research on the technical work forces of various nations also reflected well on the U.S. education system.

Although the U.S. lags behind other countries in certain specialties (e.g., industrial engineering), the overall technical degree attainment by the work force is unparalleled in the world.

STATUS OF EDUCATORS

Direct quantitative measures of the status of teachers are very difficult to obtain. Indirect measures (e.g., interviews, opinion polls, and so on) indicate that the status of educators in the U.S. is low both within and outside the profession. From our interviews of nearly 400 educators, low self-esteem emerged as a common theme. We believe that the low opinion educators hold of themselves and the poor public perception of teachers are based on misinterpretations of simplistic data, such as average SAT scores and international comparisons. This unfortunate cycle of low self-esteem, followed by unfounded criticism from the public, raises the specter of a downward spiral in future educational quality.

SKILLS OF THE WORK FORCE

Of late, much debate in education has focused on the system's inability to produce students with adequate "skills" for the work force. According to many, this deficiency is a primary cause for a decline in U.S. international economic competitiveness.

However, our review of the limited research on the education and training practices of business found that very few companies offer training that is intended to compensate for inadequate academic preparation of new employees. Rather, the training focuses on such social "skills" as punctuality and personal appearance. Much of the negative data circulating in our home state of New Mexico is anecdotal, and we suspect that the same is true on the national level. Nationally, nearly 90% of business training dollars go to college-educated employees (e.g., managers, professional salespeople) and to skilled laborers. Business dedicates very few of its training dollars to academic remediation. Moreover, much of the current "basic skills" training that does take place is directed at older workers and immigrants—not at recent graduates. Finally, our major economic competitors, Japan and Germany, far outspend the U.S. in workplace training—in spite of the fact that many view the education systems in these countries as superior to our own.

CHANGING DEMOGRAPHICS

Perhaps more than any other factor, the changing demographic makeup of the student body will have a profound effect on future education requirements. Immigration was higher in the 1980s than in any other decade in this century except the first, and projections for the 1990s are even higher. Coupled with low native-born birth rates, this phenomenon is creating significant changes in the demographic makeup of today's classroom. It is estimated that as many as five million children of immigrants will be entering the K-12 education system in the 1990s. More than 150 languages are represented in schools nationwide, and figures nearing this number occur in single large districts.

The American family structure is changing, and teachers are encountering more children from single-parent homes and from homes in which both parents work. These demographic changes are real, persistent, and accelerating. They will drive changes in the schools, especially since we continue to accept the challenge to educate all of our young people. According to many educators we interviewed, society is asking the schools to be engineers of social change by becoming increasingly involved in meeting students' nonacademic needs.

NATIONAL EDUCATION GOALS

With respect to leadership in educational improvement, we found that the call for education reform is truly widespread and includes many new voices. However, we believe that some suggested initiatives to achieve the national goals for education for the year 2000 may be in conflict. The implementation of a number of programs without proper coordination or a clear understanding of desired outcomes could result in little or no gain.

American society has not clearly articulated the changes required to meet its future foals. In fact, we assert that forming a consensus on required changes may be the greatest challenge facing education today. However, the concept of a national consensus is itself debatable. The U.S. education system was built on the foundation of a combination of local control, state influence, and federal interest. The existence of more than 15,000 independent school districts attests to this concept.

SUMMARY OF THE ISSUES

We believe that our research points to several issues that will pose the greatest challenges to the U.S. education system in the 1990s. First, the nation must clarify and agree on the changes that are needed and must find strong leadership for the improvement efforts. Our schools must improve the performance of disadvantaged minority and urban students and adjust to immigration and other demographic changes. The status in our society of elementary and secondary educators must be heightened. Finally, in order to make the soundest decisions possible about all these issues, we need to upgrade the quality of the available data regarding education.

ROBERT M. HUELSKAMP is a senior member of the technical staff of the Strategic Studies Center, Sandia National Laboratories, Albuquerque, N.M. This article is adapted from his testimony before the Subcommittee on Elementary, Secondary, and Vocational Education of the Committee on Education and Labor, U.S. House of Representatives, 18 July 1991. The research reported here, performed at Sandia National Laboratories, was supported by the U.S. Department of Energy (Contract DE-AC04-76DP00789).

4 CENSORED

The Real Welfare Cheats: America's Corporations

PUBLIC ASSETS, PRIVATE PROFITS: THE U.S. CORPORATE WELFARE ROLLS;
Multinational Monitor,
January/February 1993

Introduction to the following series
of five articles:
"Public Assets, Private Profits,"
by Chris Lewis
"Bankruptcy Bailouts,"
by Laurence H. Kallen
"Gold-Plated Giveaways,"
by Jonathan Dushoff
"The Price of Power,"
by David Lapp
"Last Stand," by Randal O'Toole

The 1992 U.S. presidential campaign was marked by a new round of welfare bashing. Borrowing an issue from Reagan's first presidential run, when candidates traded anecdotes of Cadillac-driving foodstamp beneficiaries, suggested ways to foil welfare cheats and demanded the up-from-the-bootstraps revival of individual federal aid recipients, Clinton called for welfare reform and emphasized workfare in his platform.

Missing from the attacks on welfare was any mention of the largest recipients of taxpayer largesse: U.S. corpora-

tions. None of the three presidential candidates proposed providing big companies with a system of workfare to force companies receiving taxpayer support to pull their own weight. No clever reforms, such as limiting corporate stints on the welfare rolls to two years, were suggested.

When it comes to saving the floundering banking or nuclear industries or buttressing the pharmaceutical industry, politicians do not employ the rhetoric of bootstrap capitalism. Instead, these industries are encouraged to take liberal advantage of the business subsidies, bailouts, inflated contracts and other "aids to dependent corporations" available from Washington.

The largest government subsidies to big business are found in the tax code. In the 1950s and 1960s, corporate income tax supplied 25 percent of all federal government revenues. On average, during the 1950s, corporations paid about $.67 for every dollar in taxes paid by citizens. By the 1970s, corporations were paying $.31 for each public dollar; in the 1980s, companies put in about $.21 for each public dollar. In 1991, only 7 percent of government revenue came from corporations.

The Economic Recovery Tax Act of 1981, Ronald Reagan's gift to the CEOs who promoted his election, created the largest business tax reduction in history and virtually eliminated corporate taxes, and provided a new system of write-offs for business investments. The theory behind this legislation was that corporations would take the cash they saved from taxes and invest in new machines and factories, which would result in higher productivity and new jobs. In fact, the 44 companies surveyed in 1989 by Citizens for Tax Justice paid no taxes at all (despite $53.6 billion in profits), reduced their capital spending and cut their number of employees. The extra money was spent on higher dividends, pay hikes to CEOs averaging 54 percent and corporate mergers.

The Louisiana Coalition for Tax Justice, in its study of the state's 10-Year Industrial Property Tax Exemption during the years 1980-1989, found that tax exemptions have cost Louisiana taxpayers and local governments an estimated $2.5 billion, 90 percent of which went to the 50 largest corporations in Louisiana. Nine Fortune 500 corporations took home more than half of the tax benefits. Almost three-fourths of all industrial property tax exemption contracts were granted for projects for which no new permanent employees were hired. While the state granted the taxpayer subsidies for the supposed creation of new jobs, overall employment in industries that received the most subsidies declined by 8,000 jobs, or 13 percent.

Tax breaks are only one of the many magnanimous subsidies to corporations. U.S. taxpayers finance:

■ At least $97 billion worth of subsidies over the last four decades to the nuclear industry. Taxpayers foot the bill for costs relating to R&D, regulation, construction and uranium enrichment programs, and pay for costs associated with insuring the nuclear industry, environmental damage and state government appropriations to the industry.

■ $76 billion worth of research and development at federal agencies, national laboratories, non-profit universities and research centers; the fruits of much of this research, however, pass straight into corporate hands. Despite taxpayer defrayment of the discovery and development of the AIDS-fighting drug AZT, for example, the government has relinquished control of the drug to Burroughs Wellcome and receives no royalties from its sales. While people with AIDS pay in excess of $4,000 per year for this drug, Burroughs Wellcome, in each of the last two years, has reaped over $300 million in worldwide AZT sales.

■ The management of 192 million acres of publicly owned forests by the U.S. Forest Service, which will squander over a billion dollars each year on providing the timber industry with below-cost timber sales.

■ Corporate mining of valuable minerals from over 300 million acres of federal land under the 1872 Mining Act, which allows companies to mine without paying a cent in royalties, or to purchase public land for $5 an acre or less, providing a multi-billion dollar windfall for U.S. and foreign corporations.

■ The S&L bailout—to the tune of between $300 and $500 billion.

■ The flight of U.S. jobs and capital to low-wage havens in Central America and the Caribbean. To make investments in offshore free trade zones attractive, U.S. AID officials have orchestrated a foreign investment incentives package for companies moving South that includes 100 percent exemption from corporate income tax; 100 percent exemption from all import and export duties; and 100 percent exemption on all dividend and equity taxes.

The terms of the welfare debate shift when these hundreds of billions of dollars worth of corporate subsidies are compared to subsidies to citizens, such as the mere $14.3 billion allocated for Aid to Families with Dependent Children; $17.3 billion allocated for foodstamps; or $53.3 billion allocated for Medicaid in 1991.

As the Clinton administration establishes its priorities, it should balance the tremendous costs of corporate welfare against meager federal allotments to social welfare and direct its efforts against the real drain to the federal treasury: the corporate welfare cheats.

5 CENSORED

The Hidden Tragedy of Chernobyl Has Worldwide Implications

"CHERNOBYL—THE HIDDEN TRAGEDY," by Jay M. Gould; *The Nation*, 3/15/93

A heartbreaking report on the hidden dimensions of the 1986 Chernobyl disaster, written by the Ukrainian nuclear physicist chosen to "liquidate the consequences" of the accident, was published last year in Germany. The book, *Chernobyl: Insight From the Inside* (Springer-Verlag, Berlin/New York), may never be published in Ukraine or

Russia, and the author, Vladimir Chernousenko, now dying of radiation poisoning along with thousands of others involved in the emergency cleanup, was dismissed from his post at the Ukrainian Academy of Science for telling the truth about the accident's catastrophic effect on Soviet society.

Chernousenko's treatment was reminiscent of that accorded to the Soviet Union's greatest scientist, Andrei Sakharov, who was also punished for revealing the lethal effects on the immune system of ingesting food or water containing man-made nuclear fission products.

In his 1990 *Memoirs* Sakharov writes that he came to the conclusion that the nuclear bomb was primarily a biological weapon. After the success of his 1955 H-bomb test, he worried more and more about the biological effects of nuclear tests....The long-term biological consequences (particularly atmospheric testing, in which radioactive fallout is dispersed throughout the hemisphere) can be predicted and the total number of casualties calculated with some accuracy.

Considering only such fission products as radioactive carbon, strontium and cesium, he calculated that genetic damage, plus the immediate and delayed damage to immune systems, would accelerate the deaths of between 500,000 and 1 million people worldwide for every fifty megatons of nuclear explosive power. An important consideration was what he termed "nonthreshhold effects," by which he meant that every radioactive particle released had a statistical probability of doing damage to either the DNA of a cell or to the immune system, by low-level internal radiation from ingesting such particles. He also predicted that radiation would accelerate the mutation of microorganisms, leading to the inference that persons with damaged immune systems would in time succumb more easily to these new strains of infectious diseases.

Chernousenko's revelations about the health effects of the Chernobyl accident validate Sakharov's ominous predictions. He begins by demolishing many Chernobyl myths propagated by the Soviet authorities and eagerly accepted by the international nuclear establishment. The accident, he says, was not the result of operator error but was caused by major flaws of design present in fifteen other Soviet reactors that are still in operation. In contrast to the widely accepted belief that only thirty-one people died from exposure to radiation in the effort to contain the emissions, Chernousenko asserts that between 7,000 and 10,000 volunteers were killed.

But his most serious charge is that the accident released the lethal contents of 80 percent of the reactor core rather than the 3 percent figure announced to the world. Chernousenko estimates that the radioactivity released was equivalent to more than one curie for every person on earth, i.e., more than 1 trillion picocuries per capita, to use the unit in which radioactivity concentrations in milk and water are customarily measured. The radiation released was roughly equivalent to the explosion of 1,000 Hiroshima bombs.

Chernousenko offers the first set of figures available on the great wave of morbidity that swept through the Soviet population after Chernobyl. The fallout was concentrated mainly in the three Soviet republics of Belarus (formerly Byelorussia), Ukraine and Russia, where the bulk of the emissions settled on more than 100,000 square kilometers. But the reluctance of the Soviet authorities to recognize the true extent of the contamination of farmland resulted in the shipment of contaminated food and grain to all the former Soviet republics, thus spreading radiation illness.

Public health surveys in which Chernousenko participated revealed that in Belarus, which was hardest hit, there is hardly a child who is not suffering from some immune deficiency disease, either cardiovascular, lymphoid or oncological; most of these children are unable to attend a full day in school. A 1989 public health survey indicated that in the three biggest provinces of Ukraine every second adult was ill. In Ukraine and Belarus, the incidence of immune deficiency diseases has doubled or tripled since 1985 and is now spreading to all other areas that have been consuming radioactive food. Confirmation of this finding came in a letter endorsed by World Health Organization officials that was published in the September 3, 1992, issue of *Nature*. The letter revealed that the incidence of thyroid cancer cases among children in Belarus rose from two in 1986 to fifty-five in 1991. Similar extraordinary increases in children's thyroid cancer were reported in Gdansk, Poland, using the same World Health Organization criteria.

Chernousenko suggests that Chernobyl's massive secondary insult to human immune systems literally sickened Soviet society. Effects of the Chernobyl accident were even apparent in the small but statistically significant excess mortality in the United States in May 1986 that was noted by myself and Dr. Ernest Sternglass and published by the American Chemical Society in January 1989. Our findings have never been challenged. Similar observations on excess infant mortality immediately after the arrival of Chernobyl radiation in southern Germany were made by Professor Jens Scheer of the University of Bremen and published in the November 4, 1989, *Lancet*.

Sakharov's thesis received other confirmations in a report by a Canadian pediatrician, Dr. R.K. Whyte, published in the February 8, 1992, *British Medical Journal*, attributing some 320,000 excess neonatal deaths (babies dying within the first month) since 1950 in the United States and Britain to fallout from nuclear bomb testing. Low birthweight is the largest single cause of neonatal mortality, and a review of data on the percentage of live births in New York State of babies weighing less than 5.5 pounds reveals a rise from about 6 percent in 1945 to a peak of 8 percent in 1966, when the buildup of strontium-90 in the bones of New York adults reached an all-time high. When the United States first transferred bomb testing from the Pacific to the Nevada Test Site in 1951, the per-centage of low birthweight infants in Nevada that year rose by 70 percent!

It now seems clear that the atmospheric bomb tests caused sufficient harm to developing hormonal and immune systems to justify Sakharov's fear of future immune deficiency epidemics. Radiation physicists Sternglass and Scheer point out that the AIDS epidemic first emerged during the early 1980s in the high rainfall areas of Africa that twenty years earlier registered the highest levels in the world of strontium-90 in human bone after receiving heavy fallout from the atmospheric bomb tests. They conclude that fallout is a factor in the impairment of immune response that can show up when young adults encounter the newly mutated strains of sexually transmitted viruses.

In the 1980s, concomitant with the continued routine and accidental emissions from military and civilian reactors, mortality rates were on the rise in some major nuclear nations, reversing the declines registered in the 1970s. Data on civilian reactor emissions of radioactive iodine and strontium, published each year by the Brookhaven National Laboratory, indicate that from 1970 to 1987 some 370 trillion picocuries of these deadly fission products were released into the atmosphere, enough to expose Americans to a cumulated total of 1.6 million picocuries per capita. While the nuclear establishment will claim that not enough of these dangerous fission products would be ingested by any one individual to produce adverse health effects, Sternglass and I calculated that there is a significant degree of correlation between the varying degrees of geographic exposure to such fission products and mortality from cancer and other immune deficiency diseases.

Another example relates to the anomalous recent increases in the mortality rates of young people. According to the United Nations Annual Demographic Yearbooks, in the United States, Britain and France mortality rates for the most productive component of the labor force—those between the ages of 25 and 44—have been increasing since 1983 for the first time since World War II. This surprising trend for American males was acknowledged by the Atlanta Centers for Disease Control in an article by J.W. Buehler et al. in the September 1990 *American Journal of Public Health*. The increase was attributed to AIDS, although the article admitted that in states with high AIDS mortality rates there are "associated" abnormal increases in septicemia (blood poisoning), pneumonia, tuberculosis, diseases of the central nervous system, heart and blood disorders, and "other immune defects."

People in this age group were born between 1945 and 1965, and were therefore most heavily exposed *in utero* to the low-level bomb-test radiation. In an aging population, in which deaths of old people make up an increasing share of total deaths, the proportion of deaths among younger age groups should decline over time. In the United States this percentage had declined fairly steadily, from 11.3 in 1940 to 5.4 in 1983, but it then abruptly rose to 6.6 in 1989, according to data from the National Center for Health Statistics.

The corresponding percentage in France, according to the United Nations Demographic Yearbook, rose from 4.26 in 1983 to 4.71 in 1987, and in Britain from 2.42 in 1983 to 2.61 in 1988. No comparable data were available from the former Soviet Union.

In the United States, we can assume that in addition to the surviving number of baby boomers born with low birthweight, there may be an equivalent number whose radiation-induced damage took other forms, so that a significant number of baby boomers, perhaps one-third, now make up a disproportionate segment of the swelling ranks of those who are mentally ill, permanently unemployed, homeless, in prison, on drugs or ill with AIDS and other immune deficiency diseases, such as chronic fatigue, toxic shock, tuberculosis, etc. The removal from the U.S. labor force of such a large part of the most productive age group may be one of the most neglected factors in explaining why our productivity is lagging so far behind that of the Japanese and Germans, whose baby-boom generations display no mortality deterioration since 1983.

Immune deficiency problems of the kind anticipated by Sakharov can also be seen in the epidemic rise, since 1950, of cancer and septicemia mortality among the aged. Mortality from septicemia, the quintessential immune deficiency disease of old people, was extremely rare in 1950. Since then it has risen fifteenfold.

The biochemical link between low-level internal radiation and immune deficiency anticipated by Sakharov was discovered in 1971 by Abram Petkau, a biophysicist working for the Canadian Atomic Energy Commission. That year he performed an unplanned experiment on an animal membrane that completely overturned conventional ideas on the biological damage produced by extremely low levels of radiation. In the March 1972 issue of *Health Physics*, under the innocuous title "Effect of Na-22 on a Phospholipid Membrane," he described how he found that cells that had withstood radiation doses as large as tens of thousands of rads without breaking ruptured at less than one rad when subjected to low-intensity, protracted radiation from mildly radioactive sodium salts.

Petkau and his followers have theorized that ingested radionuclides promote the formation of oxygen free-radicals, which, in a chain reaction, can quickly destroy the membranes of cells, such as those of the immune system. At higher intensities of radiation, the free-radical concentrations increase and quench each other. As a result, per unit of radiation absorbed in tissue, the process is perversely more efficient at lower rather than higher doses or intensities. The has been confirmed by recent findings of Dr. Alice Stewart, the world-renowned British epidemiologist, that low-level radiation raised the cancer risk for workers at the Hanford, Washington, nuclear weapons plant *more rapidly than high doses.*

Thus the so-called Petkau Effect explains why man-made fission products introduced into a pristine biosphere in the earliest years of the nuclear age did so much damage that remained unrecognized at the time. The Petkau Effect also explains what happened to the many millions of people in the former Soviet Union forced to ingest food and water contaminated by Chernobyl fallout; most of the damage is done by the initial exposure, when the dose response rises most rapidly.

Chernousenko suggests that in the case of Chernobyl, for every death there were a large number of premature illnesses. Such widespread illness could not be concealed despite all efforts by Soviet authorities to do so, and it contributed to the consequent despair that helped unravel the social fabric of Soviet society after the accident. It may help explain the mystery of why the Soviet Union collapsed so quickly after 1986, with a suddenness that completely upset the geopolitical balance Chernousenko's book should prepare us for the nuclear horrors that will come with another such catastrophe, but if we really wish to heed the warnings of both Sakharov and Chernousenko, we must put an end to all forms of nuclear emissions released into the environment.

Jay M. Gould, a member of the E.P.A.'s Science Advisory Board during the Carter Administration, is co-author of Deadly Deceit: Low-Level Radiation, High-Level Cover-Up *(Four Walls Eight Windows)*

6 CENSORED

U.S. Army Quietly Resumes Biowarfare Testing After Ten-Year Hiatus

"ARMY RESUMES BIOLOGICAL-AGENT TESTS AT DUGWAY AFTER 10-YEAR CESSATION,"
by Jim Woolf;
Salt Lake Tribune, 1/27/93

The Army this week resumed its most dangerous type of testing with disease-causing agents at western Utah's Dugway Proving Ground, ending a 10-year hiatus.

Researchers at the isolated Baker Laboratory injected weakened or killed strains of two deadly organisms into the air in a test chamber to see whether they could be detected by a machine designed to warn American troops of an attack with biological-warfare agents. The military does not have such a machine.

Mixing biological agents with air—a process called "aerosolization"—is risky because a tiny leak in the test equipment could allow the organisms to escape.

Army experts claim their elaborate safety precautions will prevent such a leak, but critics contend a serious accident is possible.

State officials and independent scientists were briefed on this test during a public meeting April 1, 1992. They raised no objections.

Such testing was routine at Dugway until early 1983 when the army concluded its equipment was too old to ensure safety. The Baker Laboratory has been renovated since then, allowing testing to resume.

Dugway officials have announced plans to conduct several biological-defense tests involving the aerosolization of disease-causing organisms and natural toxins. The tests were supposed to have started last year, but unexpected problems delayed testing until this week.

Melynda J. Petrie, spokeswoman for Dugway, said scientists have started tests of a Chemical Biological Mass Spectrometer (CBMS). This hand-held device is designed to sound an alarm when it detects the presence of either biological- or chemical-warfare agents.

The tests will determine whether the device can detect two dangerous micro-organisms: Coxiella burnetii, the bacteria that causes Q fever; and Yersinia pestis, the bacteria that causes bubonic plague.

Ms. Petrie said the Q fever bacteria is killed prior to testing to reduce the chance of an accident. That is done by heating it for an hour in an autoclave. The plague bacteria is from a weakened strain used to vaccinate humans.

The CBMS detector cannot tell the difference between the organisms being tested and their more dangerous cousins, said Ms. Petrie.

She said some of the tests will mix the disease-causing organism with such things as diesel fumes and the smoke from burning plants to see whether the device is overwhelmed by chemicals that might be found on the battlefield.

"BIOWARFARE IS BACK,"
by Jon Christensen;
High Country News, 8/9/93

The Army has resumed tests with disease-causing bacteria and viruses at the Dugway Proving Ground in western Utah after a 10-year hiatus. Researchers are spraying deadly, infectious micro-organisms into an isolated chamber to test a "chemical biological mass spectrometer." The device warns soldiers of biological and chemical warfare agents in the air or on the battlefield. The tests involve bacteria that cause bubonic plague and Q fever, reports the *Salt Lake Tribune.* Such "aerosol" testing was routine until 1983, when the Army concluded that its containment equipment was too old to ensure safety. The biowarfare lab has been renovated since then, and when Utah state officials were briefed on the testing plans last year, they raised no objections. The Army also announced plans to test the equipment's ability to test five other biological agents in water, including the poison that causes botulism, the bacteria that causes anthrax and a virus that causes encephalitis.

7

The Ecological Disaster That Challenges The Exxon Valdez: Selenium Runoff in Western States

"THE KILLING FIELDS,"
by Robert H. Boyle;
Sports Illustrated, 3/22/93

It's hard to believe, but the ecological disasters caused by the oil spills from the *Exxon Valdez,* in Prince William Sound, Alaska, in 1989 and the *Braer,* off Scotland's Shetland Islands, in 1993 seem to pale when compared with the chronic environmental nightmare being wrought by selenium-contaminated drainwater flowing from irrigated lands in California and 13 other Western states. Selenium is an element essential for growth in humans and animals. In high concentrations it is more poisonous than arsenic. With the government's blessing, and even its connivance, it is pouring into rivers, lakes, wetlands and wildlife refuges and is ringing up a tragic toll: Tens of thousands—some say hundreds of thousands—of birds have died or have been born dead or with grotesque deformities.

The calamity has not attracted the attention it demands, not even in California, though several reporters have written about it. "It amazes me that not a single environmental group has done anything to stop the killing," says Lloyd Carter, a reporter who left UPI's Fresno bureau in 1990 to attend law school.

"Selenium is a very politically sensitive issue because it challenges powerful economic interests in this part of the country," says Russell Clemings of *The Fresno Bee*. Adds Tom Harris, who recently retired from *The Sacramento Bee*, "The government wouldn't allow a metal-plating shop in a city to contaminate wildlife, so why does it let industrial farms discharge drainwater with equally noxious and potent compounds into our waterways? There is political leverage and strength in the agricultural industry that has been able to put off aggressive pollution enforcement."

Although selenium runoff is also a problem in Arizona, Colorado, Idaho, Kansas, Montana, Nebraska, Nevada, New Mexico, Oregon, South Dakota, Utah, Washington and Wyoming, no state has been hit as hard as California, where agricultural interests wield clout out of all proportion to their importance to the state economy. Farming consumes at least 80% of all water in California, but cash receipts for all crops came to less than 3% of the state's gross product—$17.5 billion out of $700 billion—in 1989, the most recent year for which statistics are available. Beyond that, one third of the state's water is devoted to growing alfalfa hay, cotton, pasturage and rice, crops that require huge amounts of water—a particularly valuable resource in California, where many of the most intensely farmed regions are semiarid. As Marc Reisner, author of *Cadillac Desert; The American West and Its Disappearing Water*, points out, "It takes 48,000 pounds of water to grow one pound of cow in the San Joaquin Valley."

To indulge the agricultural interests, California has been transformed into one of the biggest plumbing works on earth. Rivers have been dammed and their flows diverted into a maze of aqueducts, canals and tunnels: salmon runs have been ended; tides have been reversed; water has even been made to flow uphill.

The cost of all this in lost wildlife habitat has been staggering: At the time of the Gold Rush, California had five million acres of wetlands, mostly in the huge Central Valley, which runs 500 miles down the middle of the state; now there are 300,000 acres of wetlands. Just one refuge, Kesterson, has a firm supply of water, and that's because, as we shall see, it was poisoned in the 1980s.

During the 19th century an estimated 60 million waterfowl on the Pacific Flyway—ducks, geese and swans—stopped to feed or to spend the winter in the Central Valley. By the late 1970s the number had decreased to six million. Now it's 2.5 million.

Because of the diversion of water to irrigate toxic fields (that is, fields that naturally contain high levels of selenium and other potentially poisonous elements), birds have been killed or horribly deformed. The western and southern sides of the San Joaquin Valley, which itself is the lower part of the Central Valley, alone produce half a trillion gallons of drainwater a year. In addition to selenium, this drainwater contains arsenic, boron, uranium, chromium, molybdenum and sodium sulfates. And some of the water—no one knows how much—is routinely discharged into the California Aqueduct, which carries drinking water to 15 million people living in Los Angeles and other parts of Southern California.

Like the savings-and-loan bailout, the drainwater mess will someday cost taxpayers a bundle. The government may have to buy up land and mount an enormous cleanup. But some sites probably can never be made completely safe again for birds. Take, for instance, the Salton Sea, which covers 380 square miles in the Imperial Valley, near the Mexican border. The water level of the sea, which was accidentally created by a flood almost 90 years ago, is maintained by piping in drainwater and raw sewage. Last winter 150,000 eared grebes died at the Salton Sea. Infectious disease was ruled out as the cause. The grebes contained a level of selenium three times greater than that found in birds in 1989, and selenium poisoning is seen as a contributing factor in the massive kill.

For the last three years eared grebes nesting in the Tulare Basin, the site of the Kern and the Pixley national wildlife refuges, at the southern end of the San Joaquin Valley, have suffered complete reproductive failure. Some grebes nest on nearby evaporation ponds, which are man-made waste-water-collection sites. In a near-desert environment an evaporation pond acts as a magnet for wildlife, and what appears to be a welcoming oasis is, in fact, a death trap. Other birds that have suffered deformities or reproductive failure include mallard, northern pintail, gadwalls, redheads, American avocets, black-necked stilt and killdeers. The term *ponds* for these sites is a misnomer—*lakes* would be more accurate. There is enough selenium in many grebe eggs found on the evaporation ponds that border the Kern refuge to kill the embryos outright; other contaminants, such as sodium sulfates, are also suspected of killing embryos.

Though the mission of the U.S. Interior Department's Fish and Wildlife Service is "to conserve, protect, and enhance the nation's fish and wildlife and their habitats for the continuing benefit of the people," Fish and Wildlife officials have downplayed the importance of the drainwater problem and also have attempted to muzzle and punish their own scientists who have been working on the issue. "It's political science, not biological science, that rules at Interior," says Felix Smith, a 60-year-old biologist who in 1990 retired from the Fish and Wildlife Service after his warnings about the hazards of selenium in drainwater were ignored.

Though selenium is an essential element for growth, as little as 2.3 parts per billion of selenium in water is enough to make plants and invertebrates deadly to the water-fowl that eat them. Deposited by volcanic action in western North America millions of years ago, selenium is readily absorbed by certain plants, notably locoweed. The first known case of selenium poisoning occurred in 1857, when cavalry horses in the Nebraska Territory died after eating naturally contaminated pasturage. Cattle in many areas west of the Mississippi suffered from what ranchers called "alkali disease," which resulted in loss of hooves and hair, listlessness, liver lesions and death. But the cause of the disease remained a mystery until 1933,when W.O. Robinson, a U.S. Department of Agriculture chemist, identified it as selenium.

About 200,000 square miles of land west of the Mississippi have naturally high levels of selenium, less than 12 inches of rainfall a year and a shallow water table. It is dangerous to irrigate land like this because fields must be drained to prevent crop roots from drowning, and the drainwater, laced with selenium and other toxins leached from the soil, is bound to end up causing difficulties somewhere else.

In 1941 U.S. Department of Agriculture scientists warned that the desertlike west side of the San Joaquin Valley contained high levels of selenium, and in '49 David Love, the grand old man of Rocky Mountain geology, wrote to the chief of the U.S. Geological Survey proposing a program to identify high-selenium lands: "If this program is properly effected it will save...millions of dollars, by preventing livestock deaths and human debility, preventing the raising of poison crops, eliminating poisoned pastures and preventing unwise investments in land and livestock." According to Love, the federal government, under pressure from real estate interests, rejected his proposal because it would depress the value of land with high selenium levels.

In the 1960s, at a cost to U.S. taxpayers of about $1.4 billion, the Interior Department's Bureau of Reclamation and California's Department of Water Resources built a system to bring irrigation water to the west side of the San Joaquin Valley. To carry off drainwater the Bureau of Reclamation in 1968 began constructing a canal, the San Luis Drain, from Westlands to the Sacramento-San Joaquin Delta. For lack of funds, the project only got as far as the old Kesterson Ranch, a tract of land near Gustine that contained 1,280 acres of gouged-out ponds. In '70 the Fish and Wildlife Service also assumed management of that land, now called the Kesterson National Wildlife Refuge, and all went well until '78, when Westlands drainwater began flowing into the ponds. Gary Zahm, who was appointed refuge manger in '80, was struck by the absence of fish there— except for mosquito fish, a very hardy species. He reported this to his superiors, though his findings were not made public. In '82 Zahm got Michael Saiki, a Fish and Wildlife Service fishery biologist, to analyze the mosquito fish, and they turned out to have the highest levels of selenium ever found in any fish anywhere.

In 1980 Harry M. Ohlendorf, a wildlife research biologist who had been deputy director of Fish and Wildlife's Patuxent Wildlife Research Center, in Laurel, Md., became leader of the center's Pacific Coast field station in Davis, Calif. In 1983 he and

Smith began studying nesting birds at Kesterson. They found a high incidence of dead adults, dead embryos, deformed embryos and deformed young coots, ducks, eared grebes, black-necked stilt and killdeers. The birds had missing eyes, brains bulging through the tops of their skulls, misshapen wings and legs (or no wings and legs at all), and twisted bills.

Ohlendorf and Smith briefed the Fish and Wildlife Service's regional office in Portland, Ore., on these findings. After no action was taken, Smith wrote to the sevice's regional director, warning about possible violations at Kesterson of the Migratory Bird Treaty Act, which prohibits the taking of birds except by regulated hunting. When Smith mentioned migratory birds in the draft of a larger memo on soil issues, Joe Blum, the regional deputy director, told Smith to delete those references, saying that the subject was "totally out of context—does not lend anything but a red flag to the people."

In 1984 virtually no nesting birds were seen at Kesterson. Instead, 16,000 adult birds died from selenium poisoning. In 1985 Blum attributed their deaths to "avian cholera." At the same time, ranchers whose lands bordered the refuge complained of headaches and upset stomachs and that their livestock were dying. One rancher, Jim Claus, alerted 60 Minutes, and in March 1985 the program reported on the horrors of Kesterson. Five days later Interior Department officials, calling Kesterson "an anomaly," ordered the refuge closed because of violations of the Migratory Bird Treaty Act. Fish and Wildlife personnel ran around the refuge firing shotgun blanks to frighten away birds. Later, automatic cannons firing every 30 seconds took over until Interior finally plugged the drain and filled in the ponds with earth, at a cost of $31 million.

Meanwhile, Harold O'Connor, a biologist who was then associate director for environment of Fish and Wildlife and is now director of the Patuxent research center, warned Smith and his colleagues not to talk to environmental groups. O'Connor also cautioned them against holding memberships in professional organizations. O'Connor does not deny that Smith was gagged but says that it is the service's policy to have only one spopkesman on controversial issues.

Despite Ohlendorf's years of outstanding research, Patuxent informed him that his prospects for promotion weren't good, and in 1990 he resigned to work for a consulting firm. Four months later, after spending the last five of his 34 years in the service working in a windowless office, Smith retired.

Joseph Skorupa, an avian ecologist who had been Ohlendorf's assistant, continued Ohlendorf's work. In 1987, when Skorupa began doing work on the drainwater in the Tulare Basin, operations of evaporation ponds in the area allowed him to visit the sites to do research. But when he began finding dead and deformed bird embryos, some of the pond operators began limiting his access and, he says, tried to get his research funding ended. So far Skorupa has not been able to get unrestricted entry to many of the ponds; the Interior Department has taken the stance that its personnel do not have the right of access to private property even in the face of reported violations of federal law. In addition, Skorupa says, his superiors at Patuxent began harrassing him, citing him for unauthorized use of letterhead and publishing articles that had not been cleared by his superiors. David L. Trauger, a biologist who is Patuxent's deputy director, says of Skorupa, "He was publishing his research in the newspapers instead of scientific journals, and we were very concerned about that."

Skorupa replies, "The press has never had access to any of my research data that was not officially approved for public release. What this charge is really about is that I do not follow the service's entrenched practice of dodging questions from the press on issues of public concern. When the press, representing the American public—my wage payers—asks for a scientifically based perspective on an issue, I try to fulfill my public-trust responsibilities by giving honest responses. If that's publishing in the press, I'm guilty."

Says Trauger, "Joe's job was to address the science and leave the policy-making to others."

The money for Skorupa's research in the Tulare Basin comes from the California Department of Water Resources. In 1991 Doug Buffington, an ecologist who is director of the Fish and Wildlife Service's Region 8, the designation given to Patuxent and all the service's other research centers and their field stations, declared that there would be no more federal funding for drainwater studies. Buffington says

that he aggressively sought to obtain funding through the regular budget process or through a congressional appropriation but had been unsuccessful. Yet only a few months earlier a 26-member independent Blue Ribbon Panel (the term used by the Fish and Wildlife Service) of scientists and administrators who were invited to review Patuxent's operations had concluded in a scathing report in 1991, "Where there is clear direction from upper management, such as the decision to discontinue drainwater work, this direction appears to be motivated by politics rather than by science or merit...competent staff have been caught between their professional interpretations and the conservation of the agency, which reflects the federal [Bush] administration's view. The [panel] especially commends the staff at the California field station for its work on drainwater...These individuals paid a personal price for upholding good science in the face of heavy political, bureaucratic and social pressures."

Trauger blames Skorupa, whom he calls "one of our dissidents," for the assessment, even though it was Trauger himself who selected the members of the review panel. The report, says Trauger, "is old news. All our service managers and researchers have an open exchange of information and discussion of issues."

Says Carter, now a third-year student at the San Joaquin College of Law, "Anyone in Interior who dares speak the truth about what is really happening will be swiftly punished or driven from government service. The people in charge have abdicated their responsibilities to protect wildlife in favor of careerism, big agribusiness and political expediency.

"The morally corrupt politics of the Patuxent National Wildlife Research Center are disgusting beyond belief. These people...are political hacks with little if any concern for the disappearance of the Pacific Flyway. The U.S. Geological Survey, an Interior agency, has also kept its head in the sand over the extent of implications of selenium poisoning in the West. I can't wait to finish law school so I can fight this battle in court."

Adds Smith, "I don't know what the Clinton-Gore folks are going to do about the drainwater disaster—the Reagan-Bush people did nothing—but somewherer along the line, law enforcement is going to have to do the job, not just for wildlife but for humans as well."

America's Deadly Doctors

"DEADLY DOCTORS,"
by Sue Browder;
Woman's Day, 10/12/93

When Avis and Mark Bennett moved to Dover, New Hampshire, they were delighted to find the town had its own neurosurgeon. Their daughter Heather, 3, had been born with a cyst on her brain and required regular medical care. Dr. Stephen Dell said that a tube that ran from Heather's brain to her stomach needed to be lengthened, and assured Avis he'd done the procedure many times. Afterward, when the little girl vomited, cried, and complained of headaches (all common signs of tube blockage), Dr. Dell insisted she was suffering normal side effects from the anesthetic.

Only after Heather died and the Bennetts sued for malpractice did they learn that Dr. Dell had lied about his experience and his credentials. Dr. Dell has settled eight malpractice suits in New Hampshire for a total of $2.2 million and his license is under investigation in four states: New Hampshire, Vermont New York and Massachusetts. His license was recently suspended in Massachusetts, but he's still licensed and free to practice in California.

Dr. Dell is not the only dangerous doctor still practicing. In another case, Mary Miller, 33, completely trusted her gynecologist, Steven I. Weber, M.D. "He seemed so warm and concerned," she said. On January 6, 1992, Dr. Weber removed a growth on Mary's cervix, took tissue from her endometrium and ordered a biopsy. Ten days later, he called her into his office for some "blood work." The next day, he called her in again to remove some "remaining tissue" to prevent infection. The following day Mary began bleeding heavily and wound up in a hospital emergency room, where she learned the awful truth: Dr. Weber had accidentally damaged her fetus while taking the issue and had secretly given her an abortion.

Mary hadn't even known she was pregnant. "I'd struggled with infertility for six years and had four operations," she says. "When I heard what he'd done, I felt like I'd been kicked the teeth. I cried and cried."

Dr. Weber saw no need to get Mary Miller's consent, he said, because the fetus had already been destroyed and he didn't consider removal of remaining tissue to be an abortion. He defended his decision not to tell Miller she'd been pregnant as "an act of compassion."

If Mary, who lives in Connecticut, had known about Weber's past, however, she would never have let him near her. A year earlier, his license had been revoked in New York for his inept care of 10 other women.

Only a few states automatically revoke a doctor's license when it has been lifted elsewhere. According to Arthur Levin, director of the Center for Medical Consumers, thousands of doctors who have lost their licenses or gotten in trouble for being drug-addicted, senile or otherwise incompetent simply move across state lines. Others just go on treating patients without a license.

According to the most conservative estimates, 5 to 10 percent of doctors-- or at least 30,000 to 60,000 in the United States—could be hazardous to your health. A recent study by Public Citizen's Health Research Group concludes that medical negligence in hospitals alone injures or kills 150,000 to 300,000 Americans each year.

Why are some doctors dangerous? Experts cite two major reasons: They've become physically or mentally impaired, or they were poorly trained or simply incompetent to begin with.

HOW GOOD DOCTORS BECOME IMPAIRED

According to Charles Inlander, president of the People's Medical Society, impairment is the number-one reason doctors are deadly. It can take many forms, but these are the most common.

■ Alcohol and Drug Abuse. According to David I. Canavan, M.D., medical director of New Jersey's Impaired Physician's Program, 10 percent of physicians are alcoholic and another 3 percent are drug-addicted. That translates to at least 78,000 doctors nationwide. In a recent Los Angeles case, Ashley Hughes, 4, won a $21 million verdict against Neil Jouvenat, M.D., who negligently used forceps during her delivery, twisting her spinal cord and leaving her a quadriplegic. In a pretrial deposition, the obstetrician admitted to abusing alcohol, cocaine and other drugs before Ashley's birth.

■ Mental Illness. According to a 1989 New Jersey report on impaired and incompetent physicians, 1 percent—or 6,000 in the U.S.—are mentally unbalanced. One internist began behaving erratically in a hospital and was found later that night walking naked on a railroad track. Diagnosed as having "acute and paranoid psychosis," he agreed to stop working in the hospital. Yet he continued treating patients in his office.

■ Senility. Long after growing too old to practice, some doctors continue. Sandra K. Perfater, a nurse from Charleston, West Virginia, won a malpractice suit against an elderly pathologist whose mistaken diagnosis of breast cancer had led to the unnecessary removal of both her breasts. "I was outraged," Sandra recalls. Even after losing the case, the pathologist continued to work in a lab until he died last year at 81.

■ Ignorance. Doctors who are mentally and physically healthy can still be impaired if they fail to keep up with medical research. According to Harvard psychiatrist Steven Locke, M.D., modern medicine changes so rapidly that 4 in 10 doctors in one survey admitted they could no longer keep pace with developments in their own fields. This can have fatal results. A recent federal survey showed that 37 percent of premenopausal breast-cancer patients and 60 percent of rectal-cancer patients were not getting the most effective, up-to-date treatments. Herbert H. Keyser, M.D., author of Women Under the Knife, estimates that of the 45 million operations done in the U.S. each year, at least 10 million are inappropriate or unnecessary.

DOCTORS WHO LACK BASIC SKILLS

The most common causes of incompetence include:

■ Poor Training. While some foreign medical schools provide excellent training, others do not. Students who can't qualify for admission to American medical schools often attend unaccredited schools in the Caribbean.

■ Fraud. Those who can't get a medical license sometimes practice without one. In one Virginia case, Raymond Norris Lecraw pleaded guilty to two felony counts and six misdemeanors after he was found treating patients in the Crystal City health clinic he directed—even though he'd failed in five attempts to get a medical license.

Other so-called doctors have fraudulent degrees. "A school in the Dominican Republic was selling medical degrees several years ago," says Dale Breadon, associate executive vice president of the Federation of State Medical Boards. "A nurse or a chiropractor who spent thousands of dollars to go to the school could do very little and still get an M.D."

■ Lack of appropriate skills. Even doctors who start with good credentials can become dangerous if they practice beyond their area of expertise. "As long as you have a medical license," says Charles Inlander, 'you can call yourself a psychiatrist, a cardiologist, a plastic surgeon—anything We have cardiologists doing family medicine to keep patients and gynecologists doing liposuction because it pays so well."

■ Greed. As Inlander suggests, some dangerous doctors are driven by greed. One New Jersey doctor did so many needless surgeries he lost his malpractice insurance, yet he kept treating patients. After one unnecessary hysterectomy, a woman required numerous follow-up surgeries. Asked why he had done the hysterectomy, the surgeon replied, "I needed money at the time."

WHY AREN'T DANGEROUS DOCTORS STOPPED?

It's not always easy to tell who they are. Even the best doctors sometimes make honest mistakes. Medical science can't guarantee perfect results, either. A doctor who does nothing wrong may still be sued because a patient was disapppointed in the outcome (a baby was born imperfect, for example). According to the American Medical Association (AMA), 39 percent of all physicians—and 65 percent of obstetricians—have been sued for malpractice at least once; yet in 57 percent of those cases, the doctor was found innocent of any wrongdoing. Still, some doctors continually make mistakes that endanger patients' health and lives.

The state medical boards set up to police bad doctors offer far too little protection. According to a recent survey by the Health Research Group, only 3,034 disciplinary actions were taken against 585,000 doctors in 1991. Sidney Wolfe, M.D., Public Citizen's health research director, says, "The agencies chartered to protect us from unfit practitioners have themselves fallen down on the job."

Often understaffed and underfunded, state medical boards move at such a snail's pace that even after incompetence, negligence or abuse has been proved in court, hearings on lifting a doctor's license can drag on for years. Family doctor Aaron Cottle, M.D., was convicted of three counts of child sexual abuse in 1989. Yet he continued to practice in West Virginia until his license was finally surrendered in 1991.

Patient advocates also charge that bad doctors stay in business because colleagues refuse to expose them. According to the New Jersey report, doctors who witness a colleague's negligence often keep quiet because they don't want to ruin a friend's career or they fear the inept doctor will sue them for slander. After Ashley Hughes' botched forceps delivery, for example, two doctors who knew of the blunder could have immediately treated the infant to minimize her spinal-cord injury. Instead, they told the family the baby had a hereditary disease and would probably die in a few months.

In another case, a nurse reported a physician to her state medical board for not sterilizing needles before reusing them on other patients. The complaint was simply filed, with no action taken. Why? The key investigator (also a doctor) explained, "We [only] had the one allegation from the nurse."

Unlike some other professionals, such as certified public accountants, doctors who obtain a medical license never have to be retrained or retested to prove competency. As Inlander notes, a medical-school graduate only has to "pass one licensing exam (with an average passing score as low as 75 out of 100), successfully complete an internship somewhere and 'possess acceptable personal attributes,' whatever that means. And that's it—a job for life."

HOW TO AVOID DEADLY DOCTORS

According to John H. Renner, M.D., president of the Consumer Health Information Research Institute in Kansas City, the best ways to protect yourself are to stay alert and become an informed consumer. The best ways to do that:

■ Check Credentials. Find out where your doctor went to medical school and received internship training. Also ask about licensing and board certification, but be cautious. According to Dr. J. Lee Dockery of the American Board of Medical Specialties (ABMS), more than 100 boards have been set up in the U.S. to make doctors appear accomplished. To be "certified" by such a board, a doctor may only have to pay dues. To be certified by an ABMS medical board, on the other hand, he or she must complete three to seven years of accredited training and pass a series of exams. Only 24 boards* have been approved by ABMS and the American Medical Association. To verify a doctor's status, call 800-776-CERT. To find out about a doctor's track record, call your state medical board or check Questionable Doctors, a guide listing thousands who've been disciplined. (For a copy, contact Public Citizen, 202-833-3000, ext. 298.)

■ Look for "red flags." A doctor who continually cancels appointments may be busy, but he could also be abusing alcohol or drugs. A disheveled office, resentful nurses and bizarre behavior are all warning signs.

■ Be wary of fad diagnoses. "If a doctor tells you within thirty seconds

---

* The 24 ABMS member boards are the American Boards of: Allergy and Immunology; Anesthesiology; Colon and Rectal Surgery; Dermatology; Emergency Medicine; Family Practice; Internal Medicine; Medical Genetics; Neurological Surgery; Nuclear Medicine; Obstetrics and Gynecology; Ophthalmology; Orthopedic Surgery; Otolaryngology; Pathology; Pediatrics; Physical Medicine and Rehabilitation; Plastic Surgery; Preventive Medicine; Psychiatry and Neurology; Radiology; Surgery; Thoracic Surgery; and Urology.

that you've got hypoglycemia or yeast hypersensitivity, ask tough questions," Dr. Renner advises. "You need to keep your garbage detector on high." Ask the basis of the diagnosis and insist on being tested before—undergoing treatment.

■ Take a friend along. When you're really sick, it's hard to judge a doctor's advice or spot danger signs. It helps to have a knowledgable friend or relative act as your advocate in the doctor's office. Lawrence C. Horowitz, M.D., author of Taking Charge of Your Medical Fate, advises choosing "someone you trust...who will make the effort to take charge on your behalf."

■ Distrust doctors who "know it all." Be wary of those who claim they can cure every ill. Dr. Renner says, "I would rather go to a doctor who admits he doesn't have all the answers than to some yo-yo who never says 'I don't know.'"

■ Become an expert on your illness. If you have a chronic condition like diabetes or arthritis, spend a few hours at the library reading up on the latest treatments. The National Health Information Center (800-336-4797) can also send you information or direct you to an organization that can. "Know the range of opinion on your disease and go with middle-of-the-road treatments," Dr. Renner advises. "Don't be the first one to die from taking a new pill, but don't be the last one to try it, either."

■ Ask questions before taking medication. Has this drug been tested on women? What were the results? What possible side effects can you expect?

■ Look beyond a warm bedside manner. Many women who'd been

medically harmed told us they'd trusted their doctors because they seemed so "understanding" and "caring." But as Dr. Renner observes, "The nicest guy I ever knew was a con man. The most important qualities in a doctor are competence and integrity. Beware of one who tells you only what you want to hear; a good doctor tells you the truth— even when it hurts."

■ Know your family history. Jean Strode of Tacoma, Washington, found it hard to believe the doctor who said her newborn grandson might have a rare, incurable form of anemia called thalassemia. An amateur genealogist, Jean knew thalassemia tends to run only in families of Mediterranean descent, yet the baby's ancestors were all English and Scotch-Irish. The baby was retested and found healthy after all.

■ Discuss your doctor with friends. Even after her baby was born dead, Terry McBride, 33, says, "I was so naive I didn't blame my doctor. I was planning to go back to him." But when Terry began talking to other women, she learned her doctor had been been linked to many infant deaths, unnecessary hysterectomies and botched surgeries in her town. Friends had avoided telling her about his unsavory reputation because "we didn't want to worry you." It's kinder to spread the word about bad doctors.

HOW TO FIND DR. RIGHT

Experts offer these tips for finding the best doctor:

■ Ask other health professionals—a nurse, dentist or hospital pathologist— which doctor they or their loved ones see. In small towns, a pharmacist is also a good bet. As one doctor pointed out, "Pharmacists in small communities know what is going on. They know who the drug addicts are."

■ Choose a doctor affiliated with the best hospital in town. In general, university teaching hospitals are the best. And hospitals are required by federal law to check the National Practitioner Data Bank every two years to see if a doctor has lost malpractice suits or been disciplined by a hospital, professional society or state medical board. Although patient-advocacy groups want this taxpayer-funded data bank opened to consumers, only hospitals, health clinics and licensing boards now have access.

■ Schedule an interview. Check the diplomas on the wall and ask questions: Are you board-certified (and by what board)? What hospitals are you affiliated with? What medical societies do you belong to? If the doctor is well-trained, ask additional questions about work habits. For example: How much time do you allow for your appointments? Do you give simple advice over the phone? How can I reach you in an emergency? Even the most skillful physician can't protect your health if he or she is not readily available when needed.

HOW TO REPORT MEDICAL MALPRACTICE

Report bad doctoring first to your state medical board. Check directory assistance in your state capital for the phone number or contact the People's Medical Society (462 Walnut Street, Allentown, PA 18102, 215-770- 1670). When you file a written grievance, send copies to the grievance committee of your county or state medical society, the hospital where your doctor practices and your state health department. Report suspected drug or alcohol abuse to your state medical society.

You may also want to contact one of the growing number of patients'-rights groups that keep track of dangerous doctors and try to warn people before they get hurt. Three such organizations: The Center for Patients' Rights, Box 4064, Charleston, WV 25364-4064, 304-925-8794; The National Center for Patients' Rights, 666 Broadway, Suite 410, New York, NY 10012, 212-979-6670; and Safe Medicine for Consumers, Box 878, San Andreas, CA 95249, 209-754-4408.

9

There's A Lot Of Money To Be Made In Poverty

"THE POVERTY INDUSTRY,"
By Mike Hudson, Eric Bates,
Barry Yeoman, and Adam Feuerstein;
Southern Exposure, Fall, 1993

Across the South, big corporations are making billions of dollars in profits by targeting the region's most economically vulnerable citizens. Poor and working-class people. African-Americans, Hispanics, and other minorities. Middle-class consumers who suddenly find themselves jobless or overwhelmed by bills.

Each year, millions of Southerners are swindled, ripped off, or gouged by exorbitant prices for loans and basic financial services. They are targeted because they lack the income, credit history, or skin color to qualify for the fair-market rates and above-board treatment offered to more affluent—and mostly white—consumers.

They are people like Deborah James.

Deborah James shushed her baby as he cried and wriggled in her arms. She was worried. She was in debt and could see no way out.

"Stop Adrian," she told her son. "Quit, quit, get up."

Across the table, a loan officer with ITT Financial Services in Jacksonville, Florida was oozing concern.

"He's just tired, that is what his problem is," the loan officer said. "I'll get you out of here buddy, just give me a little time. He can smile, give me a smile."

He pushed some papers in front of James.

"Look at that. OK, then this one right here. And this one right there. And this one right there."

She signed a few more, and it was over.

"If you've got any problems at all don't hesitate to call me," he said. "I'll give you my card, so don't get behind that eight-ball anymore. You can always call me and I am sure that we got a solution."

James thought ITT was helping her climb out of debts to a waterbed store and health spa. She was wrong. It was digging her in deeper.

Once the finance company took over her debts, it rewrote her loan con-

tract five times over two years—
lending her $2,669 to pay off bills.

James has paid back more than that
in monthly installments, but her debt
now totals more than $4,000. Why?
Because ITT charged her interest rates
between 21 percent and 30 percent,
tacked on fees each time it rewrote the
loan, and billed her more than $1,600
for credit insurance, an item consumer
advocates say is virtually worthless to
borrowers.

When James couldn't keep up with
her payments, collectors working for
the company called her home.
Sometimes late at night. They called
her at work. They called her mom.

"It really and truly hurt me that
they would take advantage like that—
in such a disguise that everything they
were doing was for my benefit," James
says.

Other ITT customers report the
same mistreatment. The company
charged Art Wrightson, a restaurant
manager in Tampa, more than $600 for
credit insurance on a loan of less than
$2,600. "They're flat-out slick," he says.
"They're taking advantage of a lot of
people."

Gertrude Stuckey, a cafeteria worker
in Jacksonville, ended up more than
$4,300 in debt after borrowing money
from ITT to pay a $500 dental bill.
When she couldn't pay, she says, the
company harassed her unceasingly.

"They laughed," she recalls. "They
thought it was funny when I said:
'You're violating my rights.'"

THE NEW LOAN SHARKS

Low-life leg-breakers and con men
operating from grimy storefronts aren't

the only ones preying on the vulnerable. These days, most of the profits
made from gouging disadvantaged consumers flow into the balance sheets of
big banks and major corporations like
ITT. They are well-known, respected,
insulated by the advice of powerful law
firms, oftentimes traded on Wall
Street.

Some break the law. But most
simply take advantage of harsh economic realities and lax government regulations that leave many consumers
with few choices and little clout in the
marketplace.

"Everybody is taking their pound of
flesh every time a poor person does a
transaction," says Gary Groesch, a
housing activist who now heads the
Alliance for Affordable Energy in New
Orleans. "If poor people got an even
deal, that would be a miracle."

The poverty industry begins at the
bank door, where poor and minority
consumers are shut out of mainstream
sources of credit. Government studies
and media investigations in recent
years have repeatedly demonstrated
that major banks systematically "red-
line" entire neighborhoods, refusing to
lend money to the people who need it
most. They also charge stiff fees for
small accounts and bounced checks,
making it tough for consumers with
modest incomes to get access to basic
financial services.

As a result, more and more
Americans find themselves living in a
financial ghetto, cut off from affordable credit. Yet the banks that put
them there still find a way to make
money from their discrimination.
Major financial institutions advance

money to front companies—trade schools and tin men, used-car dealers and pawn brokers, finance companies and second-mortgage lenders. These businesses then loan the money—often at sky-high interest rates—to people the banks won't do business with themselves.

"These scams have existed for a long time," says Marty Leary, research director of the Union Neighborhood Assistance Corp. (UNAC), which is investigating lending abuses across the nation. "What makes them different is the massive scale, the fact that they're very efficient profit generators for a very small number of people. It's a centralization of power and economic resources brought into communities on very predatory terms."

The result is a debtors economy where everybody profits—except the poor. They are trapped into a separate but far-from-equal banking system where they pay more for everything.

There is no way to calculate exactly how much consumers pay for unfair credit; consumer debt now totals $4 trillion, and many transactions go unreported. It is clear, however, that millions of Americans lose billions of dollars each year. Marty Leary of UNAC estimates that mortgage lenders and finance companies alone rob consumers of at least $70 billion a year.

The list of businesses that target the poor for profit is long. Among the biggest money gougers:

Second-mortgage companies work hand-in-hand with mainstream banks to target poor and African-American homeowners. Contractors and mortgage brokers prowl minority neighborhoods offering loans with interest as high as 30 percent to pay off bills or make home repairs. Big banks finance the operations—and then "buy" the loans to collect the interest themselves. Fleet Finance, the Atlanta-based subsidiary of the largest bank in New England, has been accused of fleecing more than 20,000 borrowers in Georgia.

Fringe banks—pawn shops and check-cashing outlets—make big profits by serving customers who have been locked out of mainstream banks. Check cashers typically charge two percent to 10 percent of a check's value to cash it. In many states, pawn shops charge interest as high as 240 percent.

Business is booming. The number of pawn shops has doubled in the past decade to an estimated 10,000. Since 1987, the number of check cashers has jumped from about 2,000 to an estimated 5,000.

Used-car dealers take in an estimated $50 billion a year, often working in tandem with banks and finance companies to set up low-income and credit-damaged customers for price gouging and loan schemes.

"For people who have bad credit, you're gonna have to take what they give you," says Rick Matysiak, special investigations coordinator for the Georgia Department of Insurance. "If you're gonna pawn off a car that has been cut in half and put back together, you put it to the people who have the least ability to fight back."

Finance companies like ITT Financial Services make huge profits by serving as high-interest lenders of last resort for borrowers with limited income or shaky credit. Consumer debts to finance companies now total more than $115 billion.

All but three Southern states allow finance companies to charge maximum interest rates of at least 36 percent a year—including 109 percent in Tennessee and 123 percent in Georgia.

Rent-to-own stores have become a $3.7 billion- a-year business by selling appliances and other household goods by the week or month to low-income customers—charging them as much as five times what they'd pay for the same items at traditional retailers. The industry has tripled in size in the past decade amid a frenzy of corporate buy-outs and increasing chain ownership. A third of its 7,500 outlets are in the South.

Trade schools use easy access to federal loan money and the promise of better jobs to take advantage of low-income students. The schools—and the banks that finance them—have left hundreds of thousands of students stuck with the bill for billions of dollars in fraud-tainted profits.

Debt collectors do the dirty work when consumers can't pay, using threats and manipulation to make sure lenders get their money. One consumer advocate told Congress that collection agencies and in-house bill collectors working for lenders have become "nothing more than terrorists" holding people hostage to their debts.

John Long, an Augusta attorney active in the Republican Party in Georgia, once represented big companies. Now he defends consumers. "I got tired of being the guy who had to go out and screw somebody," he recalls.

"You'd say: This is illegal, you can't do that. They'd say: We're gonna do it anyway."

Long says the small-time shysters that have long ripped off the unwary are nothing compared to the big corporations that now prey on the poor. "These guys that do it today—they've got it down to a science."

"THEY KEEP YOU POOR"

One reason getting cheated on a loan hurts so much is that it usually leads to a cycle of more and more debt. That's what happened to Audery Duncan after she signed up for classes at the Crown Business Institute, a trade school in Atlanta. She says school officials promised to teach her to read, but never did. She ended up stuck with a $2,500 student-loan debt to First American Savings.

Her credit was ruined, and Duncan had to go to a rent-to-own store when she needed bunk beds for her daughters. She pawned her engagement ring to pay for food and clothing. And because she cannot get a checking account, she now pays a $5 fee to cash her welfare check at a downtown Atlanta bank.

Bufford Magee, a New Orleans cabbie, pays $308 a month to three finance companies, including one that financed his bedroom furniture. "They've got two guys riding up and down the streets. They stopped me one day. I said, 'Man, I don't need no bedroom.'" But he finally relented. "Come to find out the bedroom ain't worth nothing. It was sheet material. They made it themselves."

Magee tried to get bank loans, but they refused him. "When the banks won't lend you money, what you gonna do? I try to live decent. I work seven days a week."

He held out an olive-green payment book from one of the finance companies. "You end up paying 40, 50 cents on the dollar," he said. "They keep you poor that way. You can't never get on your feet."

THE SEVEN DWARFS

For decades, one of the most profitable ways to keep poor people poor has been to go after the money they have invested in their home. Second-mortgage companies persuade homeowners who have been turned away by banks—especially African-Americans—to take out high-interest loans for bill consolidation or home repairs.

Over the past decade, however, a new innovation has fueled the rapid growth of this scam: A growing number of banks and S&Ls now buy these loans on the "secondary market." By purchasing the right to collect on these debts, bankers can earn money on the loans while claiming that they bear no fault if the deals turn out to be tainted by fraud. Companies hit with allegations of mortgage abuse include ITT, Citibank, Security Pacific (now owned by Bank America), and Chrysler First (recently purchased from Chrysler Corp. by NationsBank).

In Georgia, Fleet Finance has been sued for buying thousands of mortgages from a group of loan brokers nicknamed the "Seven Dwarfs." Almost all the loans had high fees and interest rates—especially for blacks. A state judge determined that black homeowners held 60 percent of the Fleet loans with the highest interest rates. Blacks also paid upfront fees of 11 percent, while whites paid eight percent. Homeowners nationwide averaged less than two percent.

Fleet officials deny they ever had control over the brokers. But court records show that four of the companies sold more than 96 percent of their loans to Fleet, and Fleet admits it "preapproved" many of the loans before the brokers closed the deals.

Last summer, the Georgia Supreme Court ruled that Fleet has not violated the Georgia loan-sharking limit of 60 percent annual interest. But the justices said the bank's practices "are widely viewed as exorbitant, unethical, and perhaps even immoral" and urged state lawmakers to put stricter limits on second-mortgage rates.

Fleet has meanwhile profited handsomely from the absence of real regulation. In 1990, the finance company made $60 million on its national portfolio of 71,000 high-interest loans, at a time when many of its parent company's mainstream banking operations were losing money. Those profits—along with money from the student-loan business—gave Fleet the clout it needed to take over the Bank of New England in 1991. Thanks to that deal, company assets now total $45 billion.

FROM WHISPERS TO WALL STREET

Banks not only shut off credit to poor consumers, they also make it expensive to maintain a checking account. According to a survey of 300 large banks by the Consumer Federation of

America and the U.S. Public Interest Research Group, the average annual cost of a regular checking account hit $184 this year—up 18.5 percent since 1990, nearly double the rate of inflation.

Such price hikes have left many consumers unable to afford a bank account. According to the Federal Reserve, the portion of American families without an account has increased from 9 percent to 14 percent in the past 15 years.

That's where "fringe bankers" come in. Pawn brokers and check cashers offer themselves as one-stop financial centers for the bank-less. They sell money orders and lottery tickets, make wire transfers, take payments for utility bills, distribute food stamps under government contract, and make high-priced "fast tax loans" to customers who can't wait for their IRS refunds.

The "non-bank" market is being tapped by entrepreneurs like Jack Daugherty. Daugherty started small: Ten years ago he owned a single pawn shop in Irving, Texas. If he said "pawn shop" at a country club, people would turn away and whisper. If he had gone to an investment banker for a loan, they'd have shown him the door. Corporate America believed it was somehow *above* pawn shops and check-cashing outlets.

But thanks in large part to Daugherty, all that has changed. Back in 1983, after years of dabbling in night clubs and dry oil wells, Daugherty had an idea. The pawn business could boom, he thought, if it could overcome its shady image. His plan was simple: Give customers self-esteem. Make sure things look nice and the employees are friendly and fair, so people won't have to feel like they have to slink into a pawn shop. Daugherty poured money into advertising, public relations, and charity drives, and soon found his Cash America chain of pawn shops on *Inc.* magazine's list of the nation's fastest growing companies.

Cash America is now traded on the New York Stock Exchange. Its symbol: "PWN." It's the largest of four publicly traded pawn chains based in Texas. All but a handful of its 245 pawn shops are located in the South. Last year, Cash America reported nearly $13 million in profits on $186 million in revenues.

With profits high, the rest of Corporate America is now rushing to cash in on fringe banking. A five-bank syndicate led by NationsBank Texas recently extended a $125 million line of credit to help Cash America expand. Western Union and American Express are diving into the check-cashing business, which collected about $790 million in fees in 1990.

But despite their image-polishing and new corporate look, there is one thing about the business that Cash America and other fringe-bank conglomerates have not tried to change: the prices. The average loan rate at Cash American hovers over 200 percent. Indeed, the chain makes no attempt to undercut the competition, charging the highest finance fees allowed wherever its stores are located.

"The reason for that," Daugherty explains, "is we don't want to alienate the industry." If his prices were unfair, he adds, his customers would go elsewhere.

But many don't have much of a choice. When Pacquin Davis, a public-housing resident in Atlanta, decided she wanted to break away from pawn shops and check cashers, she had to try three different banks before she found one that was willing to give her a checking account. The first two she visited, First American and Georgia Federal, turned her away because a furniture store had left a bad mark on her credit history. Georgia Federal refused to even allow her to open a savings account, she says.

Her Legal Aid attorney, Dennis Goldstein, says at least a dozen of his clients have been turned down for savings accounts at Atlanta banks because they have bad credit. That makes no sense, he says, because there's no chance of bounced checks with savings.

Snubbing credit-damaged customers is one more way banks drive the poor away. "They just put that fear in your heart," Davis says. "It kinda scares you to walk in that door."

"DEAD IN THE WATER"

Customers like Davis who get turned down for bank accounts wind up paying more for access to their own money. John Caskey, a Swarthmore College economist who monitors fringe banks, estimates that a bank-less family earning $16,500 spends nearly $300 a year on check cashing and money orders.

Some check cashers take even bigger cuts. Last year, when the federal government sent checks to thousands of poor families whose children had been wrongly denied disability benefits, a big chunk of the settlement went directly into the hands of check cashers.

Delores Hagler, director of Social Security in New Orleans, says one parent reported that a check casher charged her 50 percent to cash a $16,000 government check—an $8,000 fee—because she didn't have an ID. Other parents reported paying from three to 10 percent—often hundreds of dollars—to cash their settlement checks.

Such abuses are widespread. In Florida and Texas, dozens of check cashers have been accused of loan-sharking. In Virginia, the attorney general has sued five check-cashing companies that lend customers money in exchange for post-dated checks. In a typical transaction, a check casher loans a customer $200 in exchange for a $260 check that can be cashed on the customer's next payday. The interest bite on these brief loans can equal annual rates of 2,000 percent.

Pawn brokers across the South, meanwhile, have been bilking the poor by pawning car titles. Customers sign over their title, pocket a loan, and drive away. If they can't repay the money, the pawn broker gets the car. Interest rates can reach 1,000 percent.

One 66-year-old customer in Atlanta pawned his 1979 Mercury Cougar for $300. He agreed to pay back $545 over 12 weeks. When he fell behind toward the end, the pawn broker tacked on late charges and threatened to put him in jail. So he went to Legal Aid for help. His attorney found the loan contract listed the annual interest rate at 24 percent, even though the real rate was 550 percent.

"These people exist on people like myself who are stuck and broke," says the man, who asked not to be identified. "If I haven't got a car, it means I'm dead in the water. So they knew that and it means they can charge most anything they want."

REPO MEN

As the number of people who are "stuck and broke" has risen over the past decade, so have efforts to make money off them. Jack Daugherty, the pawn shop king, estimates the "non-bank" market includes 60 million Americans. So far, he says, pawn brokers and check cashers have tapped only 10 million to 15 million of those.

That leaves lots of room for expansion for the pawn industry—and for other businesses that serve the bank-less. So it was no surprise when Daugherty and his chief financial officer at Cash America decided to open a chain of used-car lots for people who couldn't get bank loans.

Urcarco opened in a big way. In 1989, it raised $43 million from investors across the U.S. and Europe. It became the nation's first publicly traded chain of used-car lots.

Loan rates were high—18 percent to 27 percent—but the company promised low down payments and better-quality cars. Its TV ads parodied its competitors by featuring a cowboy-fied salesman named "Bubba." When he slapped the hood of a car, its fender fell off. Urcarco sales soon hit $38 million a year.

Then the bottom dropped out. So many loans were going into default, the company's repossession rate hit 50 percent. Urcarco lost $24 million in three months. Company officials blamed overexpansion and the recession.

But were there other reasons why so many people were having trouble paying? In Houston, a class-action lawsuit accused the company of slipping hidden finance charges into its contracts and selling credit insurance at illegal rates to customers with shaky credit. One salesman told *Forbes* magazine that a customer needed just one thing to pass a credit check at Urcarco: "a down payment."

"I did a lot of deals that I was told, 'I don't care what you do, but make it look like that guy can afford the car,'" a former Urcarco collector told the *Dallas Morning News*, "They try to act totally professional, but if you sit behind the doors at the lot, you find it's not."

A company spokesman denied any wrongdoing. In the end, however, Urcarco settled the class-action suit for $100,000. Late last year, the company sold off its inventory, changed its name to AmeriCredit, and shifted to the consumer-loan business.

Michael O'Connor, a Houston consumer attorney who won the settlement from Urcarco, says he's seen lenders all over Texas tacking on extra charges—especially for customers who have been denied bank credit and have to rely on "second-chance" financing. "That's when they turn the screws up," O'Connor says.

In Tampa, Florida, one of the nation's largest car dealers ran newspaper ads urging people with bad credit to call and ask for "Betty Moses," a made-up name. Royal Buick and a loan officer at Florida National Bank then falsified paperwork to secure loans from the bank. Many buyers defaulted within weeks, losing their cars and their downpayments. The banker and more than 20 Royal Buick employees were convicted of fraud.

INSURANCE RIP-OFFS

Perhaps the most lucrative way that car dealers and lenders cheat customers is by selling credit insurance. Studies by the Consumer Federation of America and the National Insurance Consumers Organization show that borrowers are overcharged between $500 million and $1 billion a year on credit insurance.

Credit insurance is supposed to pay off a loan if the borrower becomes sick, dies, or loses the items put up for collateral. But consumer advocates say it's overpriced and usually worthless, since borrowers rarely collect on their claims.

The law says borrowers cannot be forced to buy credit insurance. But the commissions that lenders earn from selling it are so generous, it's hard to resist sneaking it into a loan.

ClayDesta National—a Texas bank controlled by Clayton Williams, the unsuccessful Republican candidate for governor in 1990—has admitted it broke the law by forcing low-income, black, and Hispanic car buyers to buy credit insurance. The bank came up with $1.3 million to repay the victims.

A prosecutor said the scheme targeted people who had been denied auto loans, because it was easier to get them to "take it or leave it." ClayDesta had been losing money since the mid-1980s and was ranked as one of the worst banks in the nation. But the illegal insurance sales brought in $500,000 a year and helped put the bank in the black.

A former loan broker said in a sworn statement that he had warned ClayDesta's consumer lending chief it was illegal to force borrowers to buy insurance.

The banker's only response, he said, was a smile.

Bankers aren't the only ones smiling about credit insurance. Finance companies make much of their money from such deals, often by refinancing loans for the same borrowers over and over so they can collect new fees and more commissions. A national survey by First National Bank of Chicago found that two-thirds of finance company loans are made to existing customers, either through refinancings or add-ons to earlier loans.

What do consumers get in return? Not much. While other types of insurance typically pay 70 cents in claims for every dollar collected in premiums, credit insurers pay an average of only 42 cents. In 1991, the credit insurance subsidiary of ITT Financial Services paid only 29 cents on the dollar. That same year, one Georgia company, First Franklin Financial, sold $10 million worth of credit insurance—and paid out just 8.5 cents on the dollar.

All this adds up to incredible profits for lenders. In 1991, the small-loan subsidiary of Fleet Finance in Georgia pulled in $6.7 million and posted a profit margin of 75 percent, thanks mostly to credit insurance. ITT's Georgia subsidiary did even better—

taking in $9.7 million with a profit margin of 82 percent.

Last year the Georgia insurance commission fined Fleet $325,000 for overcharging borrowers for credit insurance. Court documents and statements by borrowers across the nation also show that ITT has aggressively packed credit insurance onto consumer loans—despite repeated warnings from state regulators that it was breaking the law.

Insurance abuses and other questionable practices push many borrowers into debt they cannot escape. By 1990, ITT had 100,000 customers in bankruptcy—about a tenth of the annual number of personal bankruptcies in the entire nation. The company also found itself facing a tidal wave of lawsuits in Florida, Alabama, and other states. It settled a class-action suit in Minnesota for nearly $49 million and an attorney general's probe in California for $30 million.

Deborah James is one of hundreds of borrowers in the Florida case. She paid as much as $895 for insurance on a single loan. On her first few loans, James says, ITT added in credit insurance without asking whether she needed it. She didn't. She already had all the insurance she needed through her job at Sears.

As ITT came under fire across the nation over its insurance sales, it began tape-recording its loan closings. Transcripts of James' last two closings show that ITT did tell her insurance was optional on those loans. By then, James says, it seemed to be a regular part of the loan. She thought it was for her own good.

But when she tried to make a claim for jewelry and a TV that had been stolen from her home, the insurance company said no. The same thing happened when she made claims for medical complications after two pregnancies.

Kristie Greve, a spokeswoman for ITT, denies charges that the company has systematically cheated borrowers. "To have a few people stand up and say things like that . . . I think that's a real slap in the face."

Swimming in $600 million in red ink, ITT announced earlier this year that it was selling its portfolio of consumer loans as part of a "strategic refocus." It plans to concentrate on second- mortgages—an area where it is also facing lawsuits in several states.

RENTING THE DREAM

Global conglomerates, intent on creating new markets beyond paper loans, have taken to peddling dinette sets and color TVs to the poor. Thorn EMI, a recording and electronics company based in the United Kingdom, pocketed $443 million in profits last year thanks to assets like music superstars Garth Brooks and Tina Turner. In 1987, it jumped into a whole new venture, buying the Rent-A-Center chain for $594 million. Since then, Thorn has expanded its empire to 1,200 stores nationwide and now controls one-fourth of the nation's rent-to-own market.

Why is the business booming? A trip to a Rent-A-Center in Roanoke, Virginia gives a hint: There you can buy metal bunk beds for $16.99 a week for 78 weeks—a total of $1,325. Across town at Sears, a comparable bed set can be had on sale for $405.

That, in essence, is the story of rent-to-own: selling on time at markups that are astounding. Three million customers a year pay the price. Nearly 60 percent of Rent-A-Center customers earn less than $20,000 a year. Just four percent earn $45,000 or more.

The rent-to-own business got its start in the 1960s as a way to skirt new laws designed to limit interest rates that inner-city merchants were charging customers who bought on credit. By redefining such transactions as rentals with "the option to buy," rent-to-own dealers are free to charge interest rates of 100, 200, even 300 percent a year.

Rent-to-own dealers say their prices are higher because their repair costs are high, and because customers can return items at any time with no penalty. Bill Keese, a former Texas state legislator who leads the industry's trade association, says rent-to-own helps people who have been shunned by banks and department stores. "Our customers have as much right to the American Dream as anyone else," Keese says.

But behind the red-white-and-blue sales pitch is an industry that cannot break away from the crude habits of the old-time ghetto merchants it has replaced. Legal Aid attorneys say many rent-to-own dealers still sell used goods as new, break into homes to repossess merchandise, charge unfair insurance and late fees, and threaten late-paying customers with criminal charges. A West Virginia rent-to-own company paid cash settlements last year to four customers jailed on bogus theft charges sworn out by the dealer.

Several Southern states have laws that make "failure to return rental merchandise" a crime. Rent-to-own stores frequently use these statutes—aimed at people who steal rented cars or video tapes—as a powerful collection tool.

Donna Smalley, an attorney and law professor in Alabama who represents the rent-to-own industry, says many people who work in the business simply don't understand that it's not a crime to owe money. "You would be amazed at how many managers I have who say: 'I can't wait to pick that sucker up and put him in jail.'"

COLLECTORS AND PALLBEARERS

That sort of attitude is common among businesses that profit from the poor. Whether renting furniture to low-income consumers or getting debt-ridden homeowners to pay a second mortgage, many lenders use take-no-prisoners collection tactics to squeeze payments out of financially strapped customers.

Deborah James says ITT telephoned her at work so often she was afraid she was going to lose her job. An ITT office file on James dated June 16, 1988 contains a brief notation: "Pull File—Call all relatives. Ph POE [Phone place of employment] & get dept she work in— Call at home late at night."

Although she had no money in the bank, James says, company agents asked her to write post-dated checks that they could cash as soon as she got her hands on any money. "I told them I did not do that," James says. "But sometimes I'd do it just to get them off my back. I said: OK, I'll do that and they'll leave me alone—'til the next time."

Consumer attorneys and government regulators in several states say ITT has routinely harassed borrowers who have fallen behind. Last year the company paid $1.3 million to settle charges of collection abuses in Wisconsin.

Many creditors hire bill collectors to put the squeeze on debtors, and consumer advocates say collectors routinely use psychological torture to terrorize people.

Payco American Corp.—one of the biggest debt collectors in the nation—goes after $3 billion in debts each year. In August, federal officials accused the publicly traded company of threatening debtors with jail, misrepresenting collectors as attorneys, using obscene language, and other illegal tactics.

Carleton Fish of the American Collectors Association says reports of serious wrongdoing are "aberrations." But government regulators report a growing number of protests about collection hassles. Complaints to the Federal Trade Commission about collection agencies have doubled since 1990—to 2,000 a year. The FTC gets another 1,000 complaints a year about lenders who do their own collecting.

Many more abuses go unreported because victims are afraid to complain. A study by the Wisconsin attorney general estimates that only one in 100 people harassed by bill collectors ever complain to authorities.

The FTC has gone after individual collectors, but state and federal agencies have yet to tackle the industry in a systematic way. Lone consumers often feel they have nowhere to turn.

Carver Jones was living the American Dream: a home in an exclusive neighborhood in Houston, two BMWs, a generous line of credit. Then he hurt his back in a car wreck and lost his job.

His creditors sicked a New York-based collection agency on him. "They yelled and screamed at me," Jones says. "It was unbelievable." The calls were so vicious he thought about killing himself. "I pounded on my bed, cried, got a pistol out, made a list of pallbearers."

When Jones complained to the New York attorney general, however, he was told the state could take no action "because your complaint basically involves a disagreement between you and the merchant regarding what occurred."

THE COMPANY STORE

The modern poverty industry exercises awesome power over the lives of working-class and minority borrowers. It may not control the poor as completely as the company store once dominated coal miners, or wealthy planters tyrannized sharecroppers. But the principle is the same: The company makes money while those who work for a living sink deeper and deeper in debt.

Activists agree that fighting big businesses that profit from the cycle of debt will take intense research and organizing. "It's not local slum lords that are doing the damage," explains Marty Leary, research director of Union Neighborhood Assistance Corp. "It's corporations that are unaccountable, mysterious—and somewhere else."

And growing bigger every day. Many now reach across the nation—and around the globe. Jack Daugherty of Cash America intends to use Wall Street respectability and bank financing to expand his Southern pawn empire to every state in the union. Beyond that, he dreams of adding more international holdings to the 27 pawn shops his company already owns in Great Britain.

"We're looking at Europe," Daugherty says, his voice rising with excitement. "Canada. Australia. New Zealand. Russia. South Africa. It's the *world*—worldwide."

BANKING ON DEBT

As the United States has become the largest debtor nation in the world over the past decade, household and business debt have also soared to record levels. Consumer credit alone is now a $4 trillion business.

To cash in on the debt frenzy and evade regulations that govern the nation's 11,300 commercial banks, a diverse range of new businesses have started performing banking functions. The result has been the rapid rise of a "parallel" financial system. Giant corporations—including Ford, General Motors, General Electric, Westinghouse, Sears, and American Express—all have huge financial service businesses that are not subject to the same federal regulations as big banks or small-town S&Ls.

These unregulated companies are not covered by federal laws that require banks to disclose financial transactions, maintain healthy reserves, limit interstate wheeling and dealing, end racial discrimination in lending, and serve the needs of the entire community, rich and poor alike.

Banks have cried foul. Ironically, however, they themselves have nurtured the growth of their unregulated rivals—and increased their own financial risk—by issuing credit lines to finance companies. The companies obtain most of their funds by issuing commercial paper—a sort of short-term corporate IOU. Banks support the process by issuing huge lines of credit to back up the debts, or by creating their own consumer-finance subsidiaries.

According to a study conducted for the Economic Policy Institute, a Washington-based think tank, banks currently guarantee 90 percent—$112 billion—of the commercial paper sold by the 15 largest finance companies. Westinghouse, for example, draws on a $6 billion line of credit issued by 49 banks.

This leaves the banks in what the study calls "a classic Catch-22 position." If the finance companies prosper, they will lure more borrowers away from banks. If they continue to run into financial trouble—as several have done in the past year—the banks will inherit the risk.

Taxpayers and communities also suffer the consequences. Since the Federal Reserve System backs up the banks, taxpayers will ultimately be expected to foot the bill if finance companies default on the money they have borrowed. What's more, such short-term speculation ties up billions of dollars in paper-swapping deals—leaving the entire economy thirsting for the kind of productive investments in people, factories, research, and infrastructure that would create jobs and promote stability.

Banks have responded by lobbying for less regulation, saying they want to be free to compete with the new companies. But Tom Schlesinger and Jane D'Arista, the authors of the study for the Economic Policy Institute, argue for the opposite. They say that all financial institutions should operate under bank-type regulations. They propose a Financial Industry Licensing Act that would put all financial firms operating with the public's money and trust under a similar set of standards for soundness.

"Since soundness regulation clearly is needed for banks, it should be extended as well to institutions that have assumed many of the functions of banks," they write. "In an increasingly integrated marketplace, single-industry fixes cannot succeed. It's time to level the financial playing field by raising—not lowering—standards of prudence and public responsibility."

"THEY WON'T GIVE YOU A CHANCE"

One homeowner who testified before Congress last year described how a major bank profits from shady home-repair deals. The following is excerpted from her testimony before the U.S. Senate Committee on Banking, Housing and Urban Affairs.

My name is Annie Diggs. I have lived in the same house on Blakley Street in Augusta, Georgia since 1936. On January 17, I celebrated my 78th birthday.

I was born in 1915 in Macon and was raised in Shady Dale. My father was born in the West Indies, but drowned six months before I was born.

My grandparents were born as slaves. My mother was forced to work for the fair, so she left me to be raised by a great aunt, who is my namesake, Annie Virginia Coleman. The Colemans were originally farmers in Georgia, but had to give up farming after the boll weevils invaded.

When I was 14 years old, I married Will Diggs, who worked as a fireman for the Georgia railroad. My husband and I was blessed to have 10 children.

After I became a widow in '46, I worked as a maid at University Hospital, a clerk at a grocery store, and I worked in a food processing plant known as Castleberry. For the last 27 years of my working life, I was employed as a domestic at Elliott's Funeral Home.

I stopped working in 1979. Since that time, my only source of income is my late husband's railroad retirement, which is now $515 a month. I also receive food stamps worth $60 per month. Frequently, I have to go without food.

In 1987, my home needed major repairs due to a leaky roof. I went to a bank. I had a $343 balance on my existing mortgage. The bank turned me down.

Later, I was contacted by a woman working for a local loan company. She looked at my house and contacted a company that agreed to do repairs for $3,300.

The manager of the loan company told me I should pay off several other little bills so I wouldn't have nothing to pay but my loan and so I could get some extra money to buy a washer and dryer, too.

They never told me the rate or how long the loan would last.

When I went to sign the papers for my loan, I was asked to sign a stack of papers I did not understand. Instead of the $3,300 which I originally needed, I ended with a note to Tower Financial for $15,000 at an interest rate of 18.9 percent. My house is pledged security. My monthly payments are $251 a month, almost half of my total monthly income.

I was charged $2,595 in fees. My loan documents show that I received $4,328 at closing, but I didn't receive that. I don't know why they got me charged. I never had this money.

The home repair work was very poor, the paint peeled off, and my roof continued to leak. I learned my loan had been sold to Fleet Finance. I complained to Fleet about the sorry repair work.

They said that was my problem. All they was interested in was getting the monthly payment on time.

My ceiling finally fell in. For more than five years, I have lived in my house with the roof still leaking. All the while, I have paid Fleet.

I have paid more than $13,000 on my loan since 1987, but Fleet Finance tells me I still owe more than $16,000 on my loan. How can that be? I cannot understand how I could owe $16,000 on a loan that was originally only $15,000.

I am scared of losing my home; I really am. I go to bed and get up in the morning looking for the mailman thinking I'm going to get a letter telling me to move. Every time I turn around,

they badger me and badger me. They won't give you a chance.

ON ADVICE OF COUNSEL

It's an old pitch: Escape the frigid Northeast and come to the Florida sun. Oranges right from the tree. Easy Financing. Own your dream home at bargain prices.

The homes-in-Florida hustle has been around for decades. But during the 1980s, one of the state's biggest developers found a new way to profit from an old scam: tricking disadvantaged buyers into taking out loans that were sometimes double the actual value of the homes.

Prosecutors say General Development Corporation used slick salesmanship to lure more than 100,000 unsophisticated buyers of modest means—most of them minorities and recent immigrants—and then rigged appraisals to overstate the value of the homes by as much as 100 percent. The company provided financing through a subsidiary, and then sold the fraud-inflated loans on the "secondary market" to banks and S&Ls.

GDC was no fly-by-night operation. Its board included such powerful figures as ex-Governor Reubin Askew and Howard Clark Jr., former chief financial officer for American Express.

Banks and corporate officials weren't the only ones to profit from the fraud. Cravath, Swaine & Moore, one of the most respected and richest law firms in the nation, reviewed every step of the home sales program and advised GDC on sales tactics. In 1989, Cravath took $5 million in fees from the developer.

In August 1992 a federal jury in Miami convicted four top company executives—including former Cravath associate and GDC board chairman David Brown—of conspiracy for their roles in the scheme.

THE DEBT MASSACRE

Three years ago, James Pough walked into the General Motors Acceptance Corp. office in Jacksonville, Florida and opened fire. He killed nine people before he took his own life.

At first, the worst mass murder in Florida history looked like just another example of a gun nut gone mad. But now court documents charge that predatory credit and collection practices by the loan company helped push Pough to the breaking point.

Pough bought a 1988 Grand Am from a local Pontiac dealer. According to WJKS-TV in Jacksonville, the dealer valued the car at $9,125, but warranties and other tacked-on costs increased the price to $15,300. On top of that, GMAC financed the loan at 19.8 percent interest. Payments were $392 a month. Pough, a laborer earning about $400 a week, paid $3,500 before he couldn't pay anymore.

GMAC took back the car and auctioned it off—and then informed Pough he still owed $6,394. Yvonne Mitchell of the city Consumer Affairs Division says Pough complained to her that GMAC collectors were arrogant and nasty. "I remember him telling me he offered to make a payment, and they refused it," Mitchell told the *Florida Times-Union* Instead, she says, GMAC wanted the whole amount—right away.

After Pough's rampage, husbands of two of the victims sued GMAC, saying officials had endangered workers by making loans "to people that they knew couldn't pay." As far back as the early 1980s, a top company executive had similar concerns. He wrote branch offices to ask, "Are we buying marginal or poor risk paper knowing that extremely difficult collection measures are going to be necessary? Are undue pressures being exerted on field employees and credit employees to conclude assignments, at any cost?"

The lawsuit has yet to go to trial. GMAC denies it did anything to put employees at risk. It has asked a judge that documents in the case be sealed as "trade secrets."

THE GREAT MOBILE HOME RIP-OFF

For many Southerners with modest incomes, mobile homes have long afforded the best hope of having a place of their own. "Manufactured homes" are the fastest growing form of housing in the nation—with sales jumping 60 percent during the 1980s and 23 percent last year alone. The $6 billion-a-year industry also holds another distinction: It's been riddled with more fraud in recent years than just about any other business in America.

In the mid-1980s, manufacturers representing more than half the mobile-home market were indicted for padding factory invoices in order to inflate profits they earned through loan programs run by federal housing and veterans agencies. Investigators said the scheme gouged more than $100 million from low- and moderate-income borrowers. Veterans officials estimated manufacturers padded invoices on at least 80 percent of the 295,000 mobile homes shipped in 1984.

Such corruption was widespread. "I'm glad everybody else has been told to stop," said former-First Brother Billy Carter, a top executive with Scott Housing Systems in Waycross, Georgia. "It would have been hard to stop if everybody else hadn't stopped." Scott paid a $50,000 fine.

Many who were cheated were unable to repay their federally guaranteed loans. In 1990, federal officials estimated that veteran and housing programs had lost more than $650 million on bad mobile-home loans. Federal investigators urged—without success—that the loan programs be scrapped because of widespread mismanagement and fraud.

Michael Calhoun, a Durham, North Carolina attorney who has represented more than 5,000 mobile home owners, says new buyers often pay interest rates of 14 percent, and many earlier buyers are still locked into through-the-ceiling rates from the 1980s. Mobile homes drop so quickly in value, Calhoun adds, that it's almost impossible to refinance and get lower interest rates.

"I've got people paying over 20 percent on a 15-year mobile-home loan," Calhoun says, "and they're still paying it today."

"A BRUTAL BUNCH"

Richard Bell worked as a bill collector in Texas for over a decade before quitting to become a consumer advocate. In this excerpt from his testimony before the House Subcommittee on Consumer Affairs, he describes how the industry operates.

One day at work, I was doing the usual, making phone calls and screaming at the mother of a person who owed money to my client. After I repeatedly slammed the phone on my desk, I looked up and saw my 18-month-old son staring at me. I had brought him to my office, and he was stunned at what he saw his father doing. I will never forget the look of terror on his face. My son wouldn't talk to me for a long time after that. It was two days before he would sit on my lap again.

After that day, every time I got back on the phone and started yelling at a consumer, I saw the image of my son's face filled with terror. My son and my conscience got to me. I left the industry and vowed to help clean it up.

This nation's bill collectors are a brutal bunch. I know. I worked for over 19 different agencies. At some, I held management positions or trained collectors. I have worked for some of the largest companies in the industry, including American Creditors Bureau, Debt Collectors Incorporated, and G.C. Services.

While I worked in Texas, the consumers in 90 to 95 percent of my accounts were out of state. Texas has no licensing for bill collectors, and creditors from all over the country use bill collectors from states with little regulation or enforcement.

Initially, when you get a file from the creditor showing that someone owes them money, you call the consumer. If you cannot get ahold of the consumer, you call the references the consumers provided in their application and frighten them into divulging the whereabouts of the consumer.

Parents are the first line of attack. They always know where their kids are, and they are often listed as references. Since they are usually reluctant to divulge information about their children, bill collectors say something like:

"I'm with the investigations unit of Walter County, we are investigating a gang of thieves and I do not know what this is about Ma'am but your son has been implicated. And, by the way Ma'am, if that stereo that is missing is in your home, you may be aiding and abetting a crime. Like I say, I don't have all the information but this is urgent! Have him call me right away."

After being frightened like that, it's easy to get the elderly to pay their children's bills. But since so many elderly are on a fixed income, they often do without needed medical care, heat, or food as a result of paying collection agencies.

When I would get called back, I would answer the phone: "Investigations" or "Law Office" or "Legal Department." Then I would likely say:

"Hello, Mr. Smith? You live at 500 Elm Street don't you? The client has placed a deliquent account with a collection agency. The agency has forwarded me the affidavit requesting criminal investigations, as well as capital gains tax fraud. Charges will be filed, according to federal and state codes. The bond has not been set, the warrants have not been issued. At this point, I believe the client is willing to forgo this procedure provided you're prepared to send the balance of your account by Western Union or overnight delivery to the collection agency. If I receive a call by 1700 hours tomorrow and find out you have paid this bill, I will go to the courthouse and have the judge sign a Stay of Execution Order and your criminal record be expunged."

The trick that bill collectors have mastered is sounding helpful yet threatening at the same time. This technique silences those who would likely complain about a collector who screamed and insulted them.

One of the biggest myths is that people who don't pay their bill are deadbeats. Approximately 96 to 98 percent of consumers truly want to pay their bills. Every consumer tries to work out something with their collector, some form of monthly payment. This is not profitable for the collector. Collectors are only interested in immediate payment in full.

The philosophy of the vicious bill collector is that the more trouble he creates in the consumer's family, the quicker the bill will be paid. We would tell kids their father was having an affair, or tell the consumer that they could lose their children to local child welfare agencies. This is especially successful when used against single mothers.

Collectors who turn to illegal and predatory tactics to collect debts have the clear consent of agency management—and more than likely the consent of the creditor. My research shows that many of the creditors do not check with the Federal Trade Commission or state attorney general about the agencies they use. Why? Because the most brutal collectors provide creditors with the greatest return They are interested only in the bottom line.

"THE PERFECT JOB FOR YOU"

Juanita Shorter looked on as her classmates plunged used, contaminated needles into each other's arms. Their teacher stood by silently.

Shorter had come to Connecticut Academy, a private trade school in downtown Atlanta, to train as a medical assistant. The school's recruiter had promised her a free, government-funded education that would prepare her to work in a hospital or doctor's office.

Instead, she found a school where needle-sharing was common and waste disposal was cavalier at best. "We was fooling around with needles, blood," she says. "We could throw the blood in the garbage cans. We could discard urine anywhere. I wouldn't let them inject me with the same needle, though. I knew that needle was contaminated."

Despite her revulsion, Shorter stuck with the seven-month program. The school, after all, was accredited. And with the prospect of a good job to support her two children, "I wasn't ready to give up." So she sat up nights in her trailer memorizing medical terms until she cried. She bought colored markers and wrote the words over and over until she learned them. She even brought home clean needles to practice on her boyfriend.

It wasn't until she graduated that Shorter realized the training was useless. No hospital would hire graduates with Connecticut Academy diplomas. One doctor "told me he could not hire me with that," she recalls. "He said they'd throw him a malpractice suit quick."

During the past decade, thousands of poor and working-class Southerners like Shorter have been defrauded by private trade schools that lure them with promises of jobs—and then saddle them with big debts. In the process, the schools function as cash machines for big banks, enabling them to pocket billions of dollars in student loans guaranteed by the federal government.

Less than a month after Shorter graduated, a woman from First American Savings called her and ordered her to begin repaying more than $5,000 in student loans "What loan?" Shorter replied. "I didn't make a loan. I filed for a grant."

The bank said otherwise. Without telling her what she was signing, Shorter learned, Connecticut Academy had tricked her into applying for a student loan.

Before long, the lender turned her account over to a collection agency, which called her four or five times a day, sometimes as late as 11:30 p.m., threatening to sue. Living on food stamps and $235 a month in federal aid, Shorter couldn't repay. The collection agent persisted. "She would ask me, do I have a car, do I own my house, how much furniture did I have?"

Shorter continues to look for work, without success. "To be honest, my future is at a standstill," she says. "I wanted to show my kids that you can always better yourself. But you look at my situation. What I'm showing them is: Your mama went out there and did the stupidest thing in her life. She listened to someone who was supposed to be trustworthy. She worked hard to get a diploma, and she can't even stick it up on the wall because it makes her so mad, because it's no good whatsoever."

HOLE IN THE WALL

With public job training programs slashed and jobs hard to come by, private trade schools have become a big business. As of 1990, the last year for which the U.S. Department of Education has figures, more than 4,500 accredited for-profit trade schools enrolled 1.4 million students. The schools promised them careers as beauticians, bookkeepers, medical assistants, computer operators, truck drivers, secretaries, and security guards.

The schools take credit for training an entire class of workers. "If these schools were to come to a halt, so would America," says Stephen Blair, president of the Career College Association, an industry trade group.

Whatever their value, the schools have flourished on government handouts: More than 80 percent of their students get federal grants or guaranteed loans. In fact, trade schools collect almost 20 percent of all federal student loans—some $2.5 billion in 1991 alone.

Some trade schools do offer solid training and good job prospects. But many have used shady salesmanship and outright fraud to exploit the dreams of the poor.

The trade school swindle is relatively simple. Across the South, hundreds of schools advertise on daytime television, and their recruiters comb poor neighborhoods and welfare lines looking for new students.

"Do you love money—the feel of it, the smell of it, the way it sounds when you crunch it up?" asks one TV commercial. "If green is your favorite color, we have a perfect job for you. Become a bank teller and get paid to work with money... You'll be rolling in the dough before you know it."

Lured by promises of a free education and a guaranteed job, students come to the school, take a token admissions test, and sign some financial aid forms. It is only when they get to class that they realize it's a sham.

In Miami, a respiratory-therapy school was equipped with broken machines; students had to enter through a hole in the wall of an X-rated tape store. In Albany, Georgia, a school charged more than $4,000 to train students as low-wage nursing-home aides—while a nearby public school offered the same course for $20. In Florida, a chain of schools for travel agents spent more than half its budget on recruiters—and less than two percent on teachers and classroom materials.

Confronted by such scams, some students drop out. Others graduate, only to discover that their school has no job placement service. Many are hounded by banks and collection agencies to repay their student loans. They cannot get a job because their diplomas are worthless; they cannot go back to school because they have defaulted on one student loan and can't get another. The disasters start spiraling.

When Kathy Walbert graduated from Connecticut Academy and found herself unemployable, she and her disabled husband needed money to eat. But with their wrecked credit, they couldn't take out a loan against the modest house they own in East Atlanta. So Walbert hocked her wedding ring and a pistol at a pawnshop, and now she pays $12.50 a month—at 150 percent annual interest—to keep them from being sold.

"We don't even have money to buy groceries with. We can't even afford nitty-gritty. We've got $3 in the bank," says Walbert. "I'll tell you the truth: I wish I never went to the school. It really messed up my life."

Phil Mebane attended a training session the school held for its recruiters. In a sworn affidavit, Mebane said the director of admissions "made it clear that the school's sole purpose was to make money by obtaining federal financial aid funds. It appeared that the school's teachers were employed simply to keep the students entertained so that they would stay in school for at least six days—until the student loan check came in."

According to Mebane, the admissions officer "said that the school did not care if the students learned anything."

Michael Sykes, the director of the now-defunct Connecticut Academy, insists that he ran a legitimate school. The teachers, he said in a court deposition, "were dedicated to what they did and had backgrounds important to the fields."

Sykes acknowledges that health inspectors had cited the school for unsterile conditions and improper handling of medical waste. "It's possible," he said, "that someone got a little lax."

THE TRUCK MAN

Trade school officials like Sykes aren't the only ones who profit from the fraud. According to the Department of Education, banks make $1 billion a year processing student loans—earning a higher rate of return than what they make on auto loans, home mortgages, and government securities.

Typically, a school bundles up batches of loan applications and sends them to a lender. Since the government guarantees the loans, the bank has no incentive to check out a student's credit or a school's reputation. The lenders advance money to the school, confident they'll get their money back, no matter what.

Even when students get cheated, banks make money. Lenders accused of profiting from trade school fraud include Florida Federal Savings and Loan, Crestar Bank of Virginia, Wachovia Bank of North Carolina, and Charleston National Bank of West Virginia.

The banks like it that way. "It's very hard for a banker, operating at arm's length in making loans, to assess just how good or bad a particular academic program is," says David Hardesty, an attorney for the West Virginia Bankers Association.

For years, the federal government made at least nominal attempts to ferret out the swindlers. But when Ronald Reagan became president in 1981, he began his crusade to dismantle the Department of Education. Over the next six years, the number of government reviews of trade schools dropped from 1,058 to 372. At the same time, the amount of federal aid skyrocketed.

"It was like throwing money into an open field," says Brian Thompson, a spokesman for the Career College Association.

The abuses skyrocketed too. In Nashville, Tennessee, a beauty-school owner named Tommy Wayne Downs applied for—and received—$175,000 in loans for imaginary students. He got caught only when his secretary accidentally tipped off the federal government.

Downs began his career as a recruiter for a home-study course in truck driving. He was so eager to recruit students that he would take them to pawn shops to sell their belongings for tuition down payments.

"I focused my attention on welfare offices, unemployment lines, and housing projects, where I became so familiar that some of the residents referred to me as the 'truck man,'" he told a U.S. Senate panel. "My approach to a prospective student was that if he could breathe, scribble his name, had a driver's license, and was over 18 years of age, he was qualified."

"What you sell is basically one thing," Downs added. "You sell dreams. And so 99 percent of my sales were made in poor black areas."

Many schools began accepting students who couldn't possibly finish the course work—but who could help rake in guaranteed loan money. In Durham, North Carolina, Rutledge College lured a mentally retarded man named Tilton Thompson away from a Goodwill Industries training program with promises of special tutoring and a guaranteed job. He received neither.

Thompson got his loan canceled only after a Legal Services attorney threatened to sue.

Like many trade schools, Rutledge College was no fly-by-night operation. For years it was part of a nationwide chain of 27 schools owned by George Shinn, owner of the Charlotte Hornets pro basketball team and a major donor to political candidates like South Carolina Senator Ernest Hollings and former North Carolina Governor Jim Martin. Banks like Manufacturers Hanover Trust were pleased to do business with his trade schools—even though they boasted a student dropout rate of 20 percent every six weeks.

"It's a rip-off for poor people," Rutledge graduate Vivian Green told *The Charlotte Observer*. "It feeds poor people's dreams—people who want to do better."

"FRAUD AND ABUSE"

Although trade school fraud occurs nationwide, widespread poverty in the South has made the region a particularly fertile territory for the scam artists. In Virginia this past May, the attorney general charged Commonwealth Educational Systems with encouraging students at five business schools to forge spouses' signatures on loan documents, falsifying records to collect loans from dropouts, inflating the credentials of instructors—even telling prospective students that the eight-year-old school was founded in 1889.

"Where the most vulnerable exists, that's where there seems to be the most ripoffs," says Jon Sheldon, an attorney with the National Consumer Law Center.

As early as 1985, the U.S. Government Accounting Office charged that two thirds of trade schools were lying to students—overstating job placement rates for graduates, for example, or offering "free scholarships" that did not reduce tuition.

It took Congress until 1990 to do anything about it. That year, more than 40 percent of all trade school students defaulted on their loans. "Usually it's the students who have not gotten an education who are most likely to default," says Darlene Graham, a North Carolina assistant attorney general. All told, unpaid loans cost taxpayers $2.9 billion last year—or 44 cents out of every dollar spent on federal student loans.

A Senate subcommittee chaired by Georgia Democrat Sam Nunn investigated and found "fraud and abuse at every level" of the student loan program—particularly among trade schools. In response, the Department of Education cut off aid to 828 schools with high default rates, forcing many to close. And Congress passed a law toughening accreditation standards and forgiving loans to some defrauded students.

Brian Thompson of the Career College Association insists the new measures have eliminated abuse by forcing the worst offenders to shut down. "Granted, there were abuses in the past," he says. "All of that has been changed. All of that has been corrected."

But while the feds can now cut off aid to outlaw schools, it may take years to shut them down. "That's a slow way of getting at fraud," says Sheldon of the National Consumer Law Center. "You need day-to-day policing." What's more, thousands of students still owe money for the worthless education they were sold before the new law took effect.

LANDMARK CASE

Tim Tipton wanted to spend his life doing more than working in a tool-and-die shop. He saw his future in his hometown paper in West Virginia.

There, in an advertisement, Northeastern Business College promised to train students in computer-aided drafting. It seemed like a perfect career move: "I figured with my background, working with blueprints, I shouldn't be bad off."

But once he signed the papers for a $3,500 student loan, he learned the school didn't even have computers. "When we went in, they gave me shit that I could have bought for 30 or 40 bucks at any bookstore," he says. The only equipment was a "very basic manual drafting kit," and the textbooks were outdated. "Any kid in the eighth grade can get into any vo-tech school and get those books or better," he says.

Tipton tried to stick with the program. When he complained about the poor equipment, school officials claimed new machines were coming. It didn't take him long to figure out the computers would never arrive, he says, and three months after enrolling, Tipton dropped out. Soon after, Northeastern Business College closed down.

When Charleston National Bank started hounding Tipton, he contacted the Appalachian Research and Defense

Fund, a legal-aid group based in Charleston. That's how he became the lead plaintiff in a landmark case involving trade schools.

"A lot of people have a misconception of West Virginians being hillbillies," Tipton says. "I wasn't one of them. I knew right off I was defrauded, I was misled, I was fried."

Since the school had already closed, it couldn't be sued. So Tipton's attorney, Dan Hedges, took on some even more powerful institutions. He sued a slew of banks and S&Ls for ignoring the fraud while raking in profits. He charged the Department of Education with slacking off on inspections and allowing schools to regulate themselves. And he accused the Higher Education Assistance Foundation (HEAF), a private group that insures student loans, of collecting fees without supervising schools or banks.

"It's not just the ripoff artists," Hedges says, "it's the government that sanctions it."

The banks and their insurer contended they shouldn't be expected to check out the schools. "I am not about to defend certain of these schools. There may have been fraud going on. I don't know," says HEAF attorney Wendie Doyle. "The fact is, the borrower made the choice to go to the school. If we were to be subject every time a borrower is dissatisfied with his education, I don't think there'd be much of a loan industry."

But a federal court in West Virginia ruled that banks can be held liable for acting in partnership with fraudulent businesses. The suit was eventually settled out of court. Tipton and three of his classmates got their debts canceled, and Hedges plans to file suits on behalf of 100 other students from Northeastern Business College.

PROFITS VS. TRAINING

Students in other states, including Virginia, Georgia, Texas, and Florida, have filed similar lawsuits. Juanita Shorter has become the lead plaintiff in a class-action suit involving former Connecticut Academy students.

LaRonda Barnes, the Atlanta Legal Aid attorney who filed the suit, hopes the spate of lawsuits will give pause to educational predators. But she knows that court cases alone won't end the scams as long as the loan system offers easy money instead of adult education.

"Once you put the profit element in there," Barnes says, "you're running the risk that people will be doing this only to make money."

Others agree. "It's a ridiculous system to take kids who are very unsophisticated about a lot of things and give them a sea of loan papers from people who pull them off a welfare line," says Jon Sheldon of the National Consumer Law Center. "Why is the federal government juicing this as a way of training people?"

Sheldon and other consumer advocates say the government needs to establish uniform accreditation standards for trade schools and perform the type of surprise inspections that restaurants and other businesses routinely face. The government should also encourage real job training by contracting with businesses or non-profit groups to provide training in targeted fields where jobs will be available, supporting community colleges that hold classes in housing projects, and providing counseling to assist students in making the right career choices.

Without such community alternatives and tougher regulation, trade schools and the banks that finance them will continue to profit from fraud. "Were I released from prison tomorrow, I could go out and do the very same thing again," says Tommy Lee Downs, the Nashville beauty-school operator serving time for fraud. "I mean, you are talking about the ability to steal unfathomable amounts of money."

REFORMING HIGH FINANCE

It was a rare sight under the gold dome of the Georgia state capitol, where white lawmakers and business lobbyists are used to being in the majority. Last February, hundreds of black citizens packed a committee room and choked the hallway outside. They came to support a bill to cap the huge interest rates that poor and minority homeowners pay on second mortgages.

With millions of dollars in bank profits on the line, Loyce Turner—chair of the Georgia Senate banking committee and a banker himself—moved to squelch the uprising. Turner warned the audience not to clap or shout support as the bill's sponsor, State Senator David Scott, made his plea for the rate caps. He also said that because the meeting was not a public hearing, the assembled citizens had no right to speak to the committee. "We are not trying to railroad or stop anything," Turner said.

Scott didn't try to hide his anger. "If this committee isn't going to represent the people, I don't want to serve on it," he said. "This is a strong miscarriage of justice. If this room was full of white people, this wouldn't happen. The banks run this committee."

The committee put the bill aside, but continued pressure from citizens and the media paid off. After Scott agreed to raise the rate cap by three percentage points, the committee passed the bill on to the full Senate, which approved it by a vote of 44-11.

It seemed like a great victory for consumers. In the end, however, the banks won. When a House panel—also chaired by a banker—took up the bill, the pockets of its five members had already been lined with nearly $8,000 in campaign contributions from lenders. With industry lobbyists packing the meeting room, the subcommittee killed the rate-cap legislation. "They don't want this bill *whichever* way we write it," Scott lamented.

It's an old story in Georgia and in statehouses across the South, where consumers have won few victories over the past decade and a half. Consumer laws in the region remain weak and ineffective—thanks to the predominance of free-market-at-any- cost rhetoric, confusion at the grassroots, and generous campaign contributions from banks and other financial businesses.

The result is a patchwork system of state and federal regulations that effectively exempts low-income and working-class consumers from government protections that more affluent consumers take for granted when they enter a bank or S&L. Across the region, predatory lenders operate virtually unchecked. No Southern state except Georgia regulates fees charged by check-cashing outlets. All but two allow pawn shops to charge interest rates of 240 percent or more. Most put no limits—or extremely high ones—on the interest and fees charged by finance companies and second-mortgage lenders. And government regulators have only recently shown much interest in making banks obey fair-lending laws.

Jean Ann Fox, president of the Consumer Federation of America and its Virginia affiliate, says the message to disadvantaged consumers is simple: "You're on your own, and we're not going to protect you. We're putting our trust blindly in competition—even though competition doesn't work when consumers don't have a real choice."

STOP THE SHARK

But as the turnout for the Georgia hearings indicates, things are beginning to change. More and more, consumers who have been gouged and ripped off are pressuring their lawmakers to clean up the financial system.

In Atlanta, a grassroots group called Citizens for Fair Housing has sprung from experiences with Fleet Finance and other lenders that prowl the second-mortgage market. In nearby Augusta, a similar coalition, Citizens Addressing Public Service, has marched on Fleet headquarters wearing bright yellow t-shirts that say, "Stop the Fleet Loan Shark." Members of CAPS have taken the bus north to lobby Congress and the Federal Reserve Bank.

Union Neighborhood Assistance Corporation, an offshoot of a Boston hotel workers union, is coordinating a national grassroots campaign against Fleet and other predatory lenders. UNAC has set up a toll-free consumer hotline—1-800-96-SHARK—and has pressured corporations that own shares in Fleet to sell their stock.

Community-reinvestment advocates like ACORN—Association of Community Organizations for Reform Now—are stepping up the pressure on banks to lend money and provide services to low-income and minority neighborhoods. The second-mortgage scandal across the South has provided them new ammunition in their fight against lending discrimination by bringing forward people who can attest, in a very personal way, to its effects.

Dorothy Thrasher, a 61-year-old homeowner in northwest Atlanta, told state legislators how two vinyl siding salesmen pressured her for weeks with an offer to make her home a low-cost demonstration model. She finally gave in, and ended up with an $18,000 home-repair loan at 23 percent interest. Fleet Finance purchased the loan and began collecting the monthly payments of $335, leaving Thrasher only $90 from her government pension check to buy food, utilities, and medicine.

"When I testified, I just told the truth about what those people had done to me," Thrasher says. "The whole place was filled with so many sad folks, most worse off than me. I felt like we was going to get some response, but I was disappointed. It looks like Fleet has too much control. They got the money, and all we got is our stories."

MONEY AND VOTES

Why weren't those stories enough to sway the legislature? An examination of campaign finance reports indicates why lawmakers remain deaf to the voices of disadvantaged consumers—and why legislation to protect consumers is so often subverted in Georgia and other Southern states.

The banking industry is a patron of most key members of the Georgia legislature:

The 10 members of the Senate banking committee received a total of more than $22,000 from the lending industry last year. On the House side, the 25 members of the banking panel—including those who killed the rate-cap bill—pocketed over $29,000 in contributions from the banking industry.

Turner, chair of the Senate bank committee, has received nearly $7,000 from the banking industry since 1990, including $1,000 from NationsBank. The Charlotte-based banking giant has drawn criticism for its recent purchase of Chrysler First, a huge mortgage company accused of predatory lending against low-income borrowers.

Senator Chuck Clay, the committee vice chair, took in more than $3,000 from banks last year, including $500 from NationsBank. He is also representing Fleet Finance in a class-action suit charging the company with racketeering and fraud.

The Georgia Mortgage Bankers Association funneled more than $18,000 in campaign contributions to Georgia lawmakers last year through its Good Government Fund.

Three key members of the House and Senate banking panels are bankers themselves. Turner chairs First Bank and Trust Co. of Valdosta and is a director of its holding company, Synovus Financial Corp.

Other Georgia politicians also enjoy close ties to the industry. Governor Zell Miller received $9,600 from Fleet's PAC during his 1990 campaign. Fleet said Miller gave a motivational speech at a company management meeting a few years ago.

With industry money in their pockets, legislators replaced the rate-cap bill sponsored by Senator Scott with one requiring licenses for mortgage brokers. Legislative leaders say licensing will stop "99 percent" of mortgage abuses. Consumer advocates say it's a minor reform designed to head off real regulation. Second-mortgage lenders can currently charge annual interest rates of 60 percent; Scott's bill would have capped interest at 11 points over the prime rate.

GUARDING THE HENHOUSE

Like other Southern legislatures, the Georgia assembly has always been hostile to regulations on business. Culver Kidd, a Georgia slumlord and president of a string of small-loan companies, fought fiercely against business regulation during his 45 years as a state legislator. "He would let nothing come through that looked like consumer protection," recalls Donald Coleman, an Atlanta Legal Aid attorney.

Kidd also helped his silent business partner win appointment as a judge in Baldwin County, where he ruled on collection actions against their tenants and borrowers. Before Kidd was voted out of office last year, the powerful Democrat—known around the Capitol as the "Silver Fox"—sponsored a bill that would have discouraged his customers and other small borrowers from filing bankruptcy.

Despite Kidd's loss, good-old-boy politics and corporate power maintain a stranglehold in Georgia. Across the region, a number of trends over the past decade have left disadvantaged consumers even more vulnerable:

Budget cuts have forced many consumer-protection agencies to curtail their already modest efforts. In Virginia, the state Office of Consumer Affairs has laid off workers and eliminated its toll-free hotline for citizen complaints. Reagan-era budget cuts and growing caseloads have also forced many Legal Aid programs—which provide legal advice to the poor—to cut back on their consumer efforts.

Many newspapers and TV stations have given up hard-edged consumer reporting in deference to advertisers, and to owners who increasingly value profits over public service. In North Carolina, for example, the *Raleigh News and Observer* transferred its auto and real estate editor to the advertising department. The reason? Executive Editor Frank Daniels III says the paper does little real reporting on the car business because "it doesn't make much sense to piss off advertisers."

Government cutbacks and increasing poverty in many communities have forced advocates for the poor to concentrate on providing for immediate needs like homeless shelters and food. In the midst of a lingering recession,

the fight for better finance laws and long-term reforms has often taken a back seat.

The Revered Minnie Davis, chair of the newly formed citizen coalition in Augusta, says that many people assume that financial reform has "been taken care of, somebody's handling it. They find out it's really not being taken care of—and we're really in a stew."

With consumer attention diverted over the past decade, many states passed "deregulation" bills that reduced protections for consumers—often with little or no opposition. In 1983, Georgia lawmakers opened the flood gates to second-mortgage abuses by eliminating a 16-percent interest cap. The proposal to kill the cap passed the House that year by a vote of 156-0. "The votes were lined up in favor of that bill long before the opposition even heard of it," former State Senator Todd Evans remembers.

MASSIVE RESOURCES

Such obvious pro-business maneuvers will be harder to pull off in the future, however. The statewide scandal over second mortgages has sparked a sense of sustained outrage among low-income consumers and their allies. Grassroots advocates, attorneys, government regulators, and Atlanta newspapers have joined forces to put heat on lenders who profit from the poor—and on the lawmakers who support them.

But citizens fighting for reform face an uphill battle against the massive resources of predatory lenders like Fleet. The bank—the 14th-largest in the nation—has hired the Atlanta law firm of former U.S. attorney general

Griffin Bell, who represents George Bush in the Iraqgate scandal. It set up a $30 million fund to repay borrowers who have been wronged, hoping to stave off criminal investigations in other states. It held a press conference with Atlanta Mayor Maynard Jackson to announce an $8 million donation to revive minority neighborhoods. And it has tried to shore up its image by joining with the National Consumer League, a respected non-profit group, to start a financial-education program for high school students.

Other lenders have tried different methods for ducking lawsuits and government investigations. After it was hit with millions of dollars in lawsuits, ITT Financial Services began having borrowers sign agreements requiring that most disputes be decided by a private arbitration firm called Equilaw.

Equilaw tells creditors like ITT that arbitration puts an end to "excessive jury verdicts." But a California judge has ruled that the arbitration program illegally denies borrowers the right to sue, and a Florida lawsuit says the arbitration clause is unfair because it imposes a $750 hearing fee on consumers and suggests they must travel to Minnesota for a hearing.

"Basically you can create a collection agency with ultimate powers if you call it an arbitration organization," says Gloria Einstein, a Legal Aid attorney in Jacksonville, Florida.

Consumer advocates have had some success in exposing abusive practices at Fleet and ITT. But things remain business as usual for most companies that profit from the poor. Even as the second-mortgage industry has come under siege in Georgia, small-loan companies in the state continue to operate under some of the worst lending laws in the nation.

With the help of sympathetic legislator-businessmen like Culver Kidd, the small-loan industry has blocked attempts to improve fair-lending laws. The industry PAC, Consumer Credit People for Responsible Government, tells members that campaign contributions are crucial to their profits, because the industry is "a creature of the General Assembly." Last year, the industry dished out more than $28,000 to state lawmakers.

Such influence-buying has paid off. Georgia law allows small-loan companies to collect stunning interest rates: from 123 percent on a $50 loan to 45 percent on a $1,000 loan.

The rent-to-own industry also enjoys legislative sponsorship for price-gouging, thanks to a strategy of pre-emptive regulation. In state after state over the past decade, rent-to-own lobbyists have persuaded lawmakers to introduce industry-sponsored bills that include token protections for consumers, such as requiring that stores be honest about whether an item is new or used. More important, the legislation exempts rent-to-own stores from retail credit laws and traditional interest-rate caps.

Legal Aid attorneys call it "disclose and anything goes." So far, at least 35 states—including 11 in the South—have passed such laws. And the industry is now lobbying Congress to pass a similar federal law.

When it cannot head off regulation early, the industry attacks. In 1983,

North Carolina legislator Jeanne Fenner introduced a bill to limit what rent-to-own stores could charge. The measure was gutted, but the industry still took revenge. During Fenner's next two campaigns, rent-to-own dealers from as far away as Texas gave more than $20,000 to her opponents. Fenner, who spent a fraction of that, lost both races. Since then, there has been no serious attempt in North Carolina to pass a law to limit finance charges at rent-to-own stores.

FOOD AT CHRISTMAS

Consumer advocates say changing the economic patterns that allow rent-to-own dealers and the rest of the poverty industry to thrive won't be easy. They call for a comprehensive range of steps to reform the system, citing the need to:

■ educate consumers about their rights and create effective organizations to ensure that grassroots voices are heard at the local and state levels.

■ pass immediate regulations to limit the usurious interest and fees charged by pawn shops, check cashers, finance companies, second-mortgage lenders, and used-car dealers.

■ create a unified system of federal regulation that puts the entire financial industry under one set of standards, requiring all lenders to disclose financial transactions, end racial discrimination, and provide loans in poor neighborhoods.

■ expand non-profit, consumer-based alternatives such as community credit unions and empower people to create their own economic development initiatives from the bottom up.

Ultimately, consumer advocates say, real reform depends on shifting the control of credit from huge corporations to local communities. Backed by current fair-lending laws governing mainstream banks, grassroots groups have already forced some commercial lenders to promise millions in loans for credit-starved neighborhoods. But so far, critics say, most pledges of community reinvestment are just so much public relations.

In Atlanta, Carrie Copeland has been trying for years to get downtown banks to open up to her fellow public housing residents. Copeland wants banks to lower the minimum balance they require for checking accounts—which run as high as $200—to $25.

"The banks are good at everything except banking," Copeland says. "Other things, helping us in the community, they're very good at that. They give food at Christmastime. They never turn us down on good things like that. But we want to go a step further. We want to save a little money."

Other activists are starting to make the connection between banking discrimination and predatory lending. In Augusta, CAPS has gone from raising hell about Fleet to pressuring local banks to lend money in redlined neighborhoods and appoint minorities and women to their boards of directors.

The group started early this year. Its first meeting drew 60 people. The next, more than 300. They marched on Fleet, on the state Capitol, and on Washington.

"We have so many people in this area who have been hurt by Fleet," says

Davis, who chairs the group. "They're just hard-working people trying to make a living." But it took a while for them to get organized. Most thought they were all alone—that they had somehow brought their problems on themselves.

"They were ashamed at first, because nobody was saying anything," Davis says. "When other people start speaking out, they kinda overcome their shyness and say, 'That's happened to me, too. You need to do something to help these people.'"

Next year, when the Georgia assembly meets, CAPS will be there. So will Dorothy Thrasher and Citizens for Fair Housing in Atlanta. Working together, they will try again to overcome the financial power of the lending industry.

"I feel like one day some good will come out of it," Thrasher says. "You can't keep mistreating people and have the problem ignored forever. God doesn't let good people suffer and suffer without no justice."

LENDING SUPPORT

Consumer advocates say that shackling financial predators with tougher legislation won't be enough to stop lending abuses. Poor and working-class communities need alternative sources of affordable credit—ones that place people over profits and provide money to support grassroots economic development.

Across the South, citizens are working to create a variety of homegrown institutions that provide hope and economic stability to their members. Consumers who have been ripped off by credit scams are learning to stand up for their rights, creating grassroots groups to fight predatory lenders. Self-help groups are relying on sweat equity and creative financing to reverse years of apathy and decay. And "community development" credit unions are demonstrating how mainstream institutions—banks included—can serve impoverished communities without going bankrupt.

The Institute for Southern Studies is currently completing a year-long assessment of community-based economic development in the region, detailing the history and organizing strategies of the movement. We'll report on our findings in a future issue, profiling more of the many groups that are empowering ordinary citizens to take control of their own lives and communities.

GRASSROOTS ORGANIZING
Coweta County, Ga.

Soon after Lora Kling moved her family into a new home in Coweta County, Georgia, their neighbors started calling them "the people with the lake." That's because every time it rained, knee-high water flooded their yard.

Inside the house, the pipes and toilets gave off odors and bubbling noises. Sewage from a bad septic line seeped into the basement.

The problems didn't end there. The builders, Jimmy and Dennis McDowell, financed the loan on the house and then sold it to Fleet Finance, the Atlanta-based mortgage giant. For years, Kling says, Fleet refused to provide an accounting of the loan—or even verify that payments had been credited toward the mortgage.

Kling fought back. She talked to hundreds of neighbors in the Peachtree Landing subdivisions that the McDowells helped build. Many had similar tales of brand-new homes with faulty construction and mortgages cloaked in mystery. She also confronted the McDowells, Fleet, and officials who supported them. Her grassroots hell-raising has sparked an uproar in this semi-rural county south of Atlanta—and has once again raised disturbing questions about one of the nation's biggest mortgage companies.

Attorneys for the homeowners are preparing a class-action lawsuit accusing Fleet and the developers of working hand-in-hand in a scheme to cheat buyers. The companies deny any wrongdoing.

Like the Klings, most of the homebuyers were blue-collar or middle-class people who had been denied conventional financing because of bad credit or a lack of credit history. They bought their homes through mortgages that were financed by the builders and then sold to Fleet.

When they fell behind on their payments, their homes were foreclosed and then resold—often to be foreclosed and resold again in a vicious cycle.

"The people who bought these homes were at great risk from the start," Kling says. "Most were grateful because under normal circumstances they would never have owned a home. It is clear that this was a willful scheme to force people to fail. Frequent foreclosures make way for more mortgages and more money for the developers and Fleet."

After two years of digging, Kling took her information to Diane Dawson, chair of the Coweta County Commission. Dawson says many homeowners told her that Fleet tacked on erroneous charges and late fees and made it nearly impossible for them to get information about their loans. Meanwhile, Dawson says, the builders refused to fix construction problems. Many buyers were forced to spend thousands of dollars for repairs, pushing them deeper into a financial hole—and often into foreclosure.

Fleet officials say they owned about 400 McDowell mortgages, but sold many of them back to the developer because of incomplete paperwork. Fleet says it no longer does business with McDowell.

William Brennen, an Atlanta Legal Aid attorney who has been investigating Fleet for years, says the Coweta County case mirrors others across the nation. "Every time Fleet gets caught doing something illegal, they say they're stopping," he says. "But that's like saying Charles Manson has stopped killing people—it doesn't do the victims any good. Fleet only stops after they get caught."

The efforts by Kling and Dawson have prompted the Georgia Office of Consumer Affairs and the U.S. Justice Department to investigate. The two women wrote a 40-page report to federal officials that includes charges that county inspectors were paid off by the developers to overlook building-code violations in the subdivisions.

In response, 23 people named in the report filed a $50 million lawsuit accusing Kling and Dawson of libel, invasion of privacy, and stalking. The women say the lawsuit is simply an attempt to silence them.

But they won't be quiet. The problems with her home have transformed Kling from a private woman to a public figure. She has helped bring together hundreds of other homeowners who are pushing for justice. She ran for county commissioner, losing with a respectable 46 percent of the vote.

As Kling sees it, the choice facing her and other homeowners is simple: walk away and lose everything, or stay and fight.

"I'm too proud a person to allow someone to control my life," she says. "I'm not going anywhere, so we decided to fight."

CONSUMER EDUCATION
Columbia, S.C.

Dorothy Garrick became interested in consumer issues after she lost her job and went into debt to pay her bills. She is now Southern regional director of the National African-American Consumer Education Organization and president of its local chapter in Columbia, South Carolina.

It's hard to get help in hard times. Around 1985 I was terminated at the telephone company, and while my case was being arbitrated I was unemployed. It put me in a financial bind. So I had to try to get assistance with my utility bills and it was hard to find. Well, where would you go?

I was one of those consumers, I didn't get involved. When you're working, making a good salary, you think everything is okay until you hit rock-bottom. Then you go to these agencies and the people that they have at the front desk, they treat you like you're less than a person.

The company didn't have cause to terminate me, so I was rehired back to my same salary. But by then I had ruined my credit, because I didn't know how to handle a creditor. It's always hard to catch up. That's why I feel that I'll always be active in the consumer arena: I know what it feels like to be treated *less than*, because you don't have.

I can see how easy it would be to get caught up in it, if you need to make a mortgage payment, or a car payment, and they say, "Okay, we'll lend you money." You know you're paying almost 25 cents on the dollar in interest, but you feel the need is so great you have nowhere else to go. So you will borrow, borrow, borrow 'til you can't borrow any more. Some of the scam artists, that's a way for them to take your homes and your cars, and to own you where you never get out of debt. That's why consumer education is so important.

I became interested in consumer issues and started attending conferences in Washington, D.C. with Florence Rice, who is now president of our national organization. There were times we went to conferences and there were just maybe two or three blacks, including Florence and myself. So we noticed there was a need. We don't have enough people attending the conferences to spread the word in our communities.

Right now we're still in the organizing process. Mainly we're working out of our homes. We have about 20 members. We have people if you need 'em I can call on them. Some of them have been through the same thing I've been through.

We're grassroots people. I have a job: I work 10 hours a day, four days a week. But I can do a lot along with the other volunteers. We can network and provide information in our spare time. We can schedule workshops and seminars for different groups, just empowering people to find the information they need.

It's basically what we can afford out of our pockets, and friends who give money to help us with something. If we need some printing done someone will say, "I'll give you some money to help you with that." Or: "Give it to me and I'll take it to my office and make you some copies."

I'm also active in the Communications Workers union and the NAACP, so I can blend consumer education with other organizations I work with. My spare time is spent doing volunteer work. I was raised up with that—that you're supposed to put back what you can into the community. I'd rather go to a meeting or a seminar than go to a party.

LOCAL DEVELOPMENT
Four Corners, La.

Five years ago, Irma Lewis remembers, Four Corners was a dying community. The hamlet set among the sugar cane fields of southern Louisiana was full of decaying clapboard homes. Many of its 400 residents—whose average income fell below $10,000 a year—saw little hope for the future.

"Four Corners was a place forgotten," says Lewis. "But we're on the map now. People know Four Corners exists."

The people of Four Corners turned their community around by uniting to rebuild it. They've been inspired by a simple idea—neighbor helping neighbor to save their own homes.

The Southern Mutual Help Association, which has been fighting for the rights of sugar cane workers for more than two decades, came to Four Corners in 1989 with a proposition: It would bring in plumbers and other contractors to provide training. Residents, in turn, would pledge to pitch in and work until every house in town was renovated.

The 15 black women who attended that first meeting founded the Four Corners Self Help Housing Committee and began recruiting other residents. Together they pounded nails. They sliced through plywood with power saws. They sealed busted pipes. In all, they refurbished three dozen homes. Now the idea has spread to the neighboring communities of Sorrel and Glenco.

Lorna Bourg, assistant director of Southern Mutual Help, says that some Four Corners residents have been victimized by shoddy contractors. Although such abuse was not the impetus for the rebuilding campaign, Bourg says the self-help idea provides a grassroots model that could be transplanted to other towns and even urban neighborhoods as a way of heading off unscrupulous home-repair and second-mortgage companies.

To make it work, Bourg's group has helped secure more than $750,000 in federal support. It has also worked with Iberia Savings Bank to arrange loans at one percent interest for home repair. So far 28 of 30 applications have been approved, with loans ranging from $500 to $17,000. No borrower has defaulted.

And Four Corners shows no signs of turning back. When Hurricane Andrew swept into Louisiana last year and destroyed much of what it had taken residents three years to accomplish, they simply started over and rebuilt their homes better than ever.

The storm blew one woman's home off its piers. She was ready to call it a total loss and move away—until Irma Lewis told her to close her eyes. "I want you to visualize your house the way you want it," Lewis told her. "Think about how you want it painted. Think about how you want your porch." The woman closed her eyes. Soon she was smiling. Today, Lewis says, the house is back on its piers. "And it's beautiful."

COMMUNITY CREDIT
Mt. Vernon, Ky.

Dwight and Shana Mahaffey have been paying the Beneficial Mortgage Company $230 every month for four years to buy a mobile home and three-acre lot near Mount Vernon, Kentucky. Beneficial, a subsidiary of one of the largest consumer-finance companies in America, charges them 16.5 percent interest.

The Mahaffeys borrowed $15,000 from Beneficial in April 1989. Come next spring, the five-year note comes due—and they'll still owe a final "balloon payment" of $13,713.

Fortunately, the couple has a better deal waiting for them: Central Appalachian People's Federal Credit Union has promised to write them a loan at 10 percent interest. Central Appalachian will refinance some small consumer loans the Mahaffeys already have with the credit union and add them into a loan to pay off Beneficial. In all, the Mahaffey's monthly debts will be cut in half.

Across the region, Central Appalachian and other "community development credit unions" are providing an alternative to hard-working people like the Mahaffeys who are often shut out by banks and charged painful prices by finance companies, pawn shops, and other lenders of last resort.

Community credit unions loan money to factory workers, the elderly, and welfare recipients at affordable rates—without tacking on insurance charges and other hidden fees. In the process, they have established themselves as grassroots centers of community pride, economic development, and consumer education.

There are an estimated 300 credit unions nationwide serving limited-income borrowers. Nearly half are in the South, and all are non-profit institutions owned and run by their depositors.

In many ways, these credit unions are the mirror images of banks. Banks drain money out of low-income and minority communities by taking deposits from poor neighborhoods and using the money to make loans to people in more affluent areas. By contrast, credit unions funnel money into low-income communities by making loans only to their members, and by attracting "non-member" deposits from corporations, foundations, churches, and other non-profits.

Bankers say loaning money to low-income and minority people is too risky. Credit unions across the region are proving them wrong:

Throughout North Carolina, the Self-Help Credit Union offers mortgages to low-income home buyers and provides credit to non-profit groups, employee-owned businesses, and other agents of social change. Founded in Durham a decade ago with bake-sale proceeds, Self-Help now manages $40 million in assets. It was recently touted on Capitol Hill as a model that could help President Clinton live up to his campaign promise to create 100 "community development banks."

In the northwestern panhandle of Florida, the North East Jackson Area Federal Credit Union sits in a trailer in Pearl Long's side yard, surrounded by fields of peanuts. Its members—many of them independent African-American farmers—pool their money for crop loans and used-car financing.

For hundreds of miles around Berea, Kentucky, Central Appalachian People's Federal Credit Union lends out $1.2 million a year to poor and working-class borrowers. It has 1,500 individual members, as well as more than 40 member organizations that serve as branch offices, including schools, housing projects, and even a plastics factory.

"THEY WORK SO WELL"

Despite their successes, such "limited-income" credit unions represent barely two percent of the 13,000-plus credit unions nationwide. "It amazes me there aren't more of these, because they work so very well," says Mike Eichler, a community organizer in New Orleans for the non-profit Local Initiatives Support Corp.

They also remain tiny compared to banks and employer-based credit unions. In 1991, these poor people's institutions averaged less than $2 million in assets, compared to $17 million for all credit unions.

History—and government intransigence—have something to do with why there are so few of them. Grassroots credit unions first emerged in Southern black communities during the 1940s, enabling those cut off by mainstream banks to pool resources and borrow money. The federal government copied the idea during the 1960s, creating at least 400 as part of the War On Poverty.

The feds invested lots of money in setting them up, but did little to ensure training and stability. "By 1967 or 1968, they pulled the rug out completely," says John Isbister, an economist at the University of California in Santa Barbara who has studied credit unions. "They just stopped funding them—and most of them just failed."

One hundred or so survived, but the casualty rate from that haphazard effort provided a ready excuse for Republican-appointed regulators who didn't care much for the idea of credit unions for the poor. During the 1980s, Isbister says, federal officials repeatedly held back federal loans to grassroots credit unions and limited the amount of "non-member" deposits they could take in. In the late 1980s, the savings and loan debacle—created largely by Reagan-era deregulation—offered yet another rationale for hindering the growth of community credit unions.

Many have had a tough time of it. Federal regulators have repeatedly threatened to shut down the North East Jackson credit union in Greenwood, Florida. Created during the 1960s to support civil rights activists denied credit by the local white power structure, the credit union earned only 35 cents in interest during its first year. By 1980, its loan delinquency rate had soared to 30 percent. But under the leadership of Pearl Long, a retired teacher whose equipment shed housed the credit union for a while, the lender has squeezed its late-payment rate to 2.5 percent—close to the national average of 1.6 percent.

In Kentucky, Central Appalachian has also cut its late-payment rate in recent years and now writes off barely three percent of its loans as a loss. Marcus Bordelon, a former banker and VISTA volunteer who manages the credit union, says the lender works with borrowers who fall behind, stretching out payments and helping them get on their feet.

Bordelon says the credit union is also there for anyone who gets into trouble with for-profit lenders. One member who didn't know Central Appalachian offered loans in addition to savings accounts went to Kentucky Finance Company to borrow $500. The lender made him put up his car as collateral, and then added on $300 in insurance, car club membership, and other fees. At 36 percent interest, the borrower would have owed more than $1,000. He escaped by refinancing with the credit union at 16 percent—with free credit insurance and no collateral required.

Another credit union member signed up to "rent to own" a TV and stereo from Curtis Mathis for $37 a week. After three months, she realized she was going to pay $4,000 for items priced at $1,700. When her phone and cable hookup were cut off, she went to the credit union and borrowed money to buy the things outright.

Dwight and Shana Mahaffey have used loans from Central Appalachian to cover hospital bills for their children and repay a student loan that put Shana through business school. "Anytime I want anything," Dwight says, "all I have to do is go to the credit union."

Dwight, who works as a manager at a McDonald's and helps run his parents' sporting goods store, is also using the credit union to get out of the 16.5-percent mortgage on the trailer and land he and Shana bought from her parents. His in-laws already had a mortgage from Beneficial, and the Mahaffeys thought it would be convenient to stick with the same lender.

"The thing with finance companies, they make it so easy," Dwight says. "Somebody needs some money real fast, they go into Kentucky Finance or Beneficial and in 30 minutes walk out with a check. They don't care what the interest rate is."

To educate consumers about their financial options, Central Appalachian holds workshops and includes "scam alerts" in its newsletter. Credit union advocates also hope federal officials will expand access to affordable credit by providing seed money and fairer rules governing financial institutions. President Clinton, they point out, could have been talking about grass-roots credit unions when he said before the election: "I think every major urban area and every poor rural area ought to have access to a bank that operates on the radical idea that they ought to make loans to people who deposit in their bank."

Mike Eichler, the New Orleans-based activist, says credit unions don't cost much to run, especially when other non-profits and churches donate office space and staff. Most of the time and money goes into start-up—investing the leg work needed to drum up community support. Such effort, he emphasizes, brings results.

"I don't think there's apathy about the fact that people are stuck with having to pay 30 percent for a loan," Eichler says. "It's just a matter of convincing them through organizing that there is an alternative."

10 CENSORED

Haiti: Drugs, Thugs, The CIA, And The Deterrence Of Democracy

"WHAT'S BEHIND WASHINGTON'S SILENCE ON HAITI DRUG CONNECTION?,"
by Dennis Bernstein;
Pacific News Service, 10/20/93

At stake in the U.S. confrontation with the Haitian military regime is a cocaine smuggling operation that earns millions of dollars for Haitian military officials while dumping tons of the deadly white powder on American streets. Yet while the country debates the merits of armed intervention in Haiti, the Clinton administration has remained mum on the Haitian "drug connection."

A confidential report by the Drug Enforcement Agency obtained by Pacific News Service describes Haiti as "a major transshipment point for cocaine traffickers" funnelling drugs from Colombia and the Dominican Republic into the U.S.—with the knowledge and active involvement of high military officials and business elites.

The corruption of the Haitian military "is substantial enough to hamper any significant drug investigation attempting to dismantle" illicit drug operations inside Haiti, the report states. Echoing the report's findings, exiled Haitian President Jean Bertrand Aristide recently blamed the military's role in the drug trade for his ouster.

Despite extensive DEA intelligence documenting Haiti's drug role, neither the Clinton administration, nor the Bush administration before it, have ever raised that role publicly. Now critics of U.S. policy on Haiti, including one Congressman, are questioning that silence, suggesting it reflects de facto U.S. support for the Haitian military and a reluctance to offer unqualified support for Aristide.

"I've been amazed that our government has never talked about the drug trafficking...even though it is obviously one of the major reasons why these people drove their president out of the country and why they are determined not to let him back in. We're talking hundreds of millions of dollars of illegal profits that are having disastrous consequences for the American people," says Rep. John Conyers (D-MI).

Larry Burns, head of the Washington, D.C.-based Council on Hemispheric Affairs, claims, "From the moment Aristide was overthrown two years ago, Washington has equivocated on whether it wanted him back or not..." To secure the military "as an anchor to Aristide's sail," Burns charges, Washington "turned a blind eye to the corruption charges, and pretended that it could be reformed through professionalization and U.S. training."

A senior administration official at the National Security Council dismisses the charge but when asked why the administration has failed to publicize DEA allegations of drug trafficking, the spokesman had no comment.

The DEA first established a Country Office (CO) in Port-au-Prince to assist the Haitian government with its anti-narcotics activities in November 1987. Throughout Aristide's brief tenure in office, DEA agents worked closely with Haitian military narcotics services, investigating an illegal cocaine network estimated to be moving some $300-$500 million worth of cocaine into the U.S. per year. Although the DEA office was shut down after the 1991 coup, it reopened in the fall of 1992. But soon after DEA intelligence prompted the arrest of a member of Haiti's CIA-linked National Intelligence, DEA local agent Tony Greco received death threats from a man identifying himself as the National Intelligence member's boss.

A Congressional source familiar with the DEA's history in Haiti told PNS that Greco had also "connected (Lt. Colonel Michel) Francois to the drug trafficking operations in Haiti." Francois, the current chief of police, is alleged to be behind the current campaign of terror.

What disturbs Rep. Conyers is that none of this information ever reached the public. "By turning a deaf ear to what is obviously a prime force behind Aristide's ouster, we raise questions about our own involvement in drug activities," Conyers says. He is currently investigating how it is that the ships and aircraft necessary to sustain such a large operation evade detection and interdiction, while the U.S. government has managed to spot, stop and turn back almost every ramshackle boat carrying refugees.

Indeed the DEA report shows that after the 1991 coup sent Aristide into exile, there were virtually no major seizures of cocaine from Haiti as compared to nearly 4,000 pounds seized in 1990.

Michael Levine, author of "Deep Cover" and a decorated DEA agent with 25 years of experience fighting drugs overseas, says what's going on in Haiti is "just another example of elements of the U.S. government protecting killers, drug dealers and dictators for the sake of some political end that's going to cost a whole bunch of kids in this country their lives.

"I saw the drug traffickers take over the government of Bolivia in 1980, ironically with the assistance of the CIA, and we (the DEA) just packed up our office and went home."

"THE CIA'S HAITIAN CONNECTION,"
by Dennis Bernstein and
Howard Levine;
San Francisco Bay Guardian, 11/3/93

Although the Clinton administration insists it is making every effort to return ousted Haitian president Jean-Bertrand Aristide to power, covert connections between Haiti's military junta and the CIA may be helping to keep the regime in place.

Confidential government documents obtained by the Bay Guardian show that the CIA helped establish and finance Haiti's powerful National Intelligence Service, which played a key role in the 1991 coup and continues to

provide paramilitary muscle for the anti-Aristide dictatorship. As recently as February 1993, a confidential congressional report described the NIS as "working closely" with the CIA.

The documents—along with interviews with members of Congress, senior administration sources, and a high-ranking member of Aristide's cabinet-in-exile—raise troubling questions about Clinton's policy toward the tiny, impoverished Caribbean nation and provide strong evidence to support critics who claim the United States is giving little more than lip service to the cause of Haitian democracy.

Among other things, the Bay Guardian has learned:

Haitian Lt. Col. Joseph Michel François—the reputed kingpin behind the military junta—was trained at a clandestine U.S. Army combat facility known as the "coup school," whose alumni also include jailed Panamanian dictator Manuel Noriega and former Salvadoran president Roberto d'Aubuisson.

Paramilitary death squads controlled by François and Frank Romain, the former mayor of Port-au-Prince, are carrying out what some critics call a systematic attempt to wipe out Aristide's base of support, making it difficult if not impossible for the ousted president to reclaim political power. The death squads, known as *attachés* have been linked to roughly 4,000 murders since the coup.

Former Haitian officials and congressional sources link François and the NIS to a massive drug-smuggling and money-laundering operation that sends at least a billion dollars worth of cocaine a year to the United States. Aristide's attempt to crack down on the drug ring may have helped spark the coup—and since the military junta took power, cocaine exports have soared.

In fact, a U.S. Drug Enforcement Agency operative who was investigating an NIS officer allegedly involved in drug smuggling had to flee Haiti in 1992 after receiving death threats on a private telephone line with a secret number known only to a few top government officials.

At least two senior members of Congress, Rep. Charles Rangel and Rep. Major Owens, both New York Democrats, told the Bay Guardian they have enough reason to suspect CIA involvement in the Aristide coup that they are calling for a full congressional investigation.

HALF-HEARTED EFFORTS

As the crisis in Haiti drags on and the military junta refuses to relinquish power, critics have charged that the United States is making only token efforts to restore Aristide to office.

Larry Burns, an analyst at the Washington, D.C.-based Council on Hemispheric Relations, pointed out that the United States has not fully participated in the United Nations embargo of Haiti (unlike most other countries, the U.S. has exempted its own companies in Haiti from the embargo). It's also curious, he told the Bay Guardian, that the Clinton administration has failed to make a public issue of the military regime's role in drug trafficking—a tactic that the Bush administration used extensively to dis-

credit Panama's Manuel Noriega.

"You would think that the White House would want, as one of its major points, to pin the drug tail on the military donkey in Haiti," Burns said. "It would be their best opportunity to rally the American people to a pro-Aristide position. Yet they never used it."

White House Deputy Press Secretary Don Steinberg told the Bay Guardian that "there's nothing half-hearted about our administration's commitment to returning democracy to Haiti and Aristide to power."

"We sent military trainers to Haiti, we've supported the embargo, and we've fully supported the Governor's Island accords," which were supposed to lead to Aristide's return, Steinberg said. "This administration has not for a second coddled François or Cédras." Lt. Gen. Raoul Cédras heads the military junta.

But Rep. John Conyers (D-Mich.) said he was worried that the administration's silence on the military's connection to the drug trade would only embolden the junta and tighten its grip on power.

"We have turned a very deaf ear to what is obviously a moving force," he said. "It leads you to wonder if our silence is because we knew this was going on and that our complicity in drug activity may parallel the accusations that were raised about our involvement in drug activities—that is, our government and the Central Intelligence Agency's—during the Vietnam conflict."

Although they admit they have no hard evidence, both Rangel and Aristide's exiled interior minister,

Patrick Elie, told the Bay Guardian they see shadows of the CIA's hidden hand behind the September 1991 coup, which overthrew Aristide after only seven months in office.

"I don't have a specific answer as to whether the CIA was involved," Rangel said. "But I do know that our feelings against Aristide were made pretty clear before the coup."

Rangel was referring to the Bush administration's open backing of former World Bank official Marc Bizan against Aristide. But in a show of popular support that caught the Bush administration by surprise, Aristide received 67.5 percent of the vote, while Bizan captured only 13 percent.

Elie told the Bay Guardian that the relationship between the CIA and Haiti's National Intelligence Service went far beyond mere cooperation.

"In fact," he said "the NIS was created by the Central Intelligence Agency. It was created by it and funded by it."

Elie, whose job included oversight of the NIS, launched an investigation shortly after taking office that revealed that the CIA had covertly given the NIS $500,000—twice what the U.S. government was providing Haiti overtly for drug interdiction.

He said that although the NIS was supposed to be used to combat drug smugglers, "in fact, all the NIS has done has been political repression and spying on Haitians."

Records of the Drug Enforcement Administration confirm that the NIS operates with CIA assistance. According to a confidential DEA document titled "Drug Trafficking in Haiti," presented to members of Congress in February 1993 and obtained by the Bay Guardian, the NIS "is a covert counter-narcotics intelligence unit which often works in unison with the CIA."

On Sept. 26, 1992, the report states, the DEA itself was driven from Haiti when its main agent was forced to flee the country after receiving death threats. DEA attaché Tony Greco received the threats on his private line in the U.S. embassy, "given out to only a few trusted individuals," the memo says, within a week of his providing information that led to the arrest of a NIS officer for drug trafficking. "The unidentified threat," the report states, "came from an individual who claims to control many Haitian soldiers in the narcotics distribution trade."

Rep. Major Owens (D-N.Y.), who chairs the Congressional Black Caucus task force on Haiti, told the Bay Guardian: "I worry about the CIA having had a role in the overthrow of the Aristide government. The Congressional Black Caucus has joined with congressman Joseph Kennedy (D-Mass.) in calling for a full-scale investigation."

Bay Guardian phone calls to the CIA headquarters in Langley, Va., were not returned. Steinberg said he knew nothing about possible CIA involvement in the coup and was "hearing about it for the first time." He refused to comment on the allegations of drug smuggling.

THE SCHOOL OF COUPS

Rangel, who has traveled several times to Haiti and is close to the deposed administration of Aristide, told the Bay

Guardian that although Cédras heads the junta, François, who is also Port-au-Prince's chief of police, wields the real power.

François, Rangel said, "has been targeted as being directly responsible for the recent murder of [Justice Minister] Guy Malary," who was dragged out of church, beaten, and killed on Oct. 14.

Michel François learned some of his skills right here in the United States. He is a graduate of the U.S. Army's School of the Americas (SOA), which Father Roy Bourgeois, founder of SOA Watch in Columbus Georgia, described as a "combat and counter-insurgency training facility for soldiers from Central and South America and the Caribbean."

White House spokesperson Steinberg didn't deny that François had attended the Army training school. "But just because he graduated from SOA doesn't mean he has U.S. government intelligence connections," Steinberg said. "A lot of people graduate from that school."

Bourgeois said SOA was founded in 1946 and operated in Panama until it was kicked out in 1984 as part of the canal treaty. It was reestablished in Ft. Benning, Ga.

"In Latin America," he said, "it's known as La Escuela de Golpes, the school of coups," because of the achievements of some of its 55,000 graduates, including d'Aubuisson; Noriega, who is serving 40 years in federal prison for drug trafficking; Gen. Hugo Banzer, who ruled as Bolivia's dictator from 1971 to 1978; and Hector Gramajo, Guatemala's former defense minister who helped oversee years of brutal repression in that country and was the guest speaker at SOA's graduation in December 1991.

On March 15, 1993, the United Nations Truth Commission released its report on El Salvador and, Bourgeois said, "about 75 percent of the officers cited in the most serious massacres, including the killing of six Jesuit priests, the assassination of Archbishop Oscar Romero, and the rape and murder of four U.S. nuns, were SOA graduates."

Bay Guardian calls to SOA were not returned.

DRUG MONEY

The coup and resulting embargo may have left thousands of Haitians dead and created terrible hardship for many thousands more, but it's apparently been quite profitable for the drug traffickers.

According to a Feb. 10, 1993, memo from one of Conyers' congressional staffers, a copy of which was obtained by the Bay Guardian, "the wholesale value of Haiti's drug industry on the U.S. market is now equal to $1 billion a year, which equals the entire revenue of Haiti's population of six million.

"Haiti has become the second most important transshipment point, after the Bahamas, for cocaine shipments from Colombia to the U.S.," the memo states.

The DEA's "Drug Trafficking in Haiti" document also says that Haiti is believed to be a main center for laundering of drug money.

One of Elie's key tasks was to have been overseeing the drug interdiction efforts, and he had developed an extensive program that included close cooperation with U.S. agencies. But the program was barely off the ground when the coup drove him into hiding in Haiti—and five months later, into the United States. (He has since fled the U.S., fearing for his life, and called the Bay Guardian from an undisclosed location because he was told there is a $750,000 contract on his head. Three pro-Aristide radio broadcasters have been murdered in Florida.)

"While I was in hiding," he said, "I monitored Michel François over the airwaves directing the landing of a [drug smuggling] plane right in the middle of Port-au-Prince. I immediately notified the U.S. embassy in Port-au-Prince. I was in touch with the CIA main agent there at the time, and I gave him the time and date of that landing.

"I don't know if he did anything with it. Since the coup, despite our repeated attempts to continue this collaboration with the U.S. as the legitimate government of Haiti, we were met with stonewalling."

Elie's account is supported by the memo to Conyers, which stated that after the coup, "all those jailed for drug-trafficking have been released and...Michel François has personally supervised the landing of planes carrying drugs and weapons."

And a September 1992 State Department report titled "International Narcotics Control Strategy Report: Mid-Year Update" noted that "although President Jean-Bertrand Aristide was planning new policies and institutions to combat narcotics traf-

ficking, his ouster...crippled narcotics control efforts in Haiti."

Meanwhile, observers say, the violence continues—targeted largely at the popular organizations that helped bring Aristide to power. As part of the reign of terror, death lists are being posted in small Haitian villages, Liam Mahoney, an independent human rights monitor in Haiti, told the Bay Guardian by phone on Nov. 3.

The military regime so far has ignored the Governor's Island accords that on Oct. 30 called for Aristide's return to power, leading some to speculate that the junta wants to completely destroy Aristide's power base before they allow him to return—if they allow him to return at all.

"If something is not done soon, there will be no Aristide supporters left," said Rep. Owens. "They will all be destroyed."

Dennis Bernstein is coproducer of KPFA's *Flashpoints* and an associate editor at Pacific News Service. Additional reporting by Greg Saatkamp and Julie Light.

How To Nominate a Censored Story

Some of the most interesting nominations Project Censored has received are from people who spot something in the back pages of their newspaper or in a small-circulation magazine they subscribe to and wonder why they haven't seen anything reported about it elsewhere. In the same way, you can help the public learn more about what is happening in our society by nominating stories that you feel should have received more coverage from the national news media. The story should be current and of national or international significance. It may have received no media attention at all, appeared in your local newspaper or some special interest trade magazine, or been the subject of a radio or television documentary which received little exposure or follow-up. Your nominations, input, and suggestions are important to the success of Project Censored and we appreciate them. To nominate a *Censored* story of the year, just send us a copy of the story, including the source and date. The annual deadline is October 15. Please send nominations to:

NOMINATION
PROJECT CENSORED
Sonoma State University
Rohnert Park, CA 94928

INDEX

Energy Policy Act of 1992, 59
Environmental Protection Agency
(EPA), 63, 90, 127, 128, 129, 130,
131
and carpet health risks, 107-109
and Waste Technologies Industries
(WTI), 116-120
Ernst, Morris, 167, 191
Espionage Act, 162
Executive Order 12356, 183
Exxon, 97, 116, 253
Fairness & Accuracy in Reporting
(FAIR), 95, 133, 184, 200, 208, 222,
270, 278, 290, 295
Faludi, Susan, as judge, 11, comments
of, 36
First Amendment, 148, 155, 157, 171-
172, 178, 180, 182, 184, 185, 187,
188
Freedom of Information Act (FOIA),
99, 141, 174, 183
fringe banks, and corporate fraud, 75,
267, 271
Gerbner, George, as judge, 11
Government Patent Policy Act, 58
Grieder, William, 32, 86
Haiti, 40
censorship of, CIA connection, 79-
81, 302-308
Haitian National Intelligence Service
(NIS), 80, 304-306
Hazelwood decision, 24, 156, 185, 187
Herman, Edward, as judge, 12, com-
ments of, 36-37
Hill & Knowlton,
censorship of, influence of, 91-93,
House Un-American Activities Com-
mittee (HUAC), 167
immune deficiency disease, from
Chernobyl accident, 62, 248, 250
Jensen, Carl, 8, 181, biography of, 311-
312

Jhally, Sut, as judge, 12, comments of,
37
judges,
for 1994 edition, 11-12
for previous, 26
comments of, 34-39
Jungle, The, 18, 35
"Junk Food News," 28-29, 45, 139-149
top subjects of, 140-144
news ombudsmen explain, 145-148
Karpatkin, Rhoda, as judge, 12, comments of, 37-38
Kesterson National Wildlife Refuge,
68, 256
Klaas, Polly, 51-52
Klotzer, Charles, as judge, 12
Krug, Judith, 12, 227
labor, 182
and Silicon Valley, 82-83,
and NAFTA, 87, 89
Lady Chatterley's Lover, 14, 172
Lappe, Frances Moore, as judge, 12,
comments of, 38
Licensing Act, 155-156
Lippmann, Walter, 164
Liverpool, Ohio,
and hazardous waste incineration,
116-120
Lutz, William, as judge, 12, comments
of, 38
MacKinnon, Catherine, 13-14
Madame Bovary, 158
Madison Avenue, 22-23, 91
malnutrition, and Cuba,
censorship of, 93-95
Mapplethorpe, Robert, 186
Marx, Karl, 141, 158
McCarthy, Joseph, 169
media,
1993 trends in, 41-47
heroes of, 45-47
merger trend in, 41-42

and Federal Emergency Management Agency, 125
and Iran-Contra, 137
and Commission on Pornography, 184
and corporate assistance, 245, 285
Reno, Janet, 113, 120
rent-to-own industry, 78, 275, 293
"Resource Guide," 195-217
Rockwell International, 34, 84, 86
Rocky Flats hazardous waste disposal censorship of, 84-86
Roth-Memoirs Test, 171
Sandia Report on Education, optimistic findings and censorship of, 55-58
Sanger, Margaret, 162
Satanic Verses, The, 185
Schenck v. United States, 163
Schiller, Herbert, as judge, 12, comments of, 39
school choice, 56-57
Scopes, John T., 164
"Seasonal News," see "Junk Food News"
Sedition Act, 162
Seldes, George, 160-161, 163, 167, 170, 193
selenium poisoning, censorship of, 67-71
"Selling of the Pentagon, The," 179
"Sex News," see "Junk Food News"
Shame of the Cities, The, 18
Silicon Valley, 81-83
Sinclair, Upton, 18, 35, 160, 164
Socrates, 152
Somalia, censorship of, 52-55, 234-239

Sports Illustrated, 67, 69-71, 253
Steffens, Lincoln, 18, 160, 311
Stone, I.F., 160, 170, 179, 193
Tarbell, Ida, 18, 160
Texaco, 97
Tomorrow, Tom, 1, 11
"Top 10 Censored! Reprints," 231-308
Trial Lawyers for Public Justice (TLPJ), 103
tribal people, 101
Tyndall Report, 50, 210
U.S. Office of Censorship, 168
U.S. Philips, 103
Ulysses, 165, 172
Uniform Correction, 189
unions, labor,
    and Chapter 11, 59
    and Silicon Valley, 82-83,
    and carpet toxicity, 108,
    and the House Un-American Activities Committee (HUAC), 167
United Nations Children's Fund, 50-51, 231
vacatur process,
    censorship of, 102-104
Wall Street Journal, The, 89-90, 92, 122
Washington Post, The, 53, 84, 86, 107, 122, 133-134, 145, 179, 188
Waste Technologies Industries (WTI), censorship of, 117-120
Watergate, 179-180
Weidenfeld, Sheila Rabb, as judge, 12, comments of, 39
Windmere, 103
youth,
    high mortality rate of, 50-52
"Yo-Yo News," see "Junk Food News"

About the Author

Dr. Carl Jensen is a professor of Communication Studies at Sonoma State University and Director of Project Censored, an internationally recognized media research project. Founded by Jensen in 1976, Project Censored is America's longest-running research project which annually explores news media censorship.

Jensen has been involved with the media for more than 40 years as a daily newspaper reporter, weekly newspaper publisher, public relations practitioner, advertising executive, and educator. He spent 15 years with Batten, Barton, Durstine, and Osborn, the international advertising agency, where he was an award-winning copywriter, account supervisor, and vice president.

Specializing in mass communications, Jensen received his B.A., M.A., and Ph.D. degrees in Sociology from the University of California, Santa Barbara, in 1971, 1972, and 1977, respectively.

Since 1973, he has been teaching media, sociology, and journalism courses at Sonoma State University, where he developed Sonoma State University's B.A. degree in Communication Studies and the University's Journalism Certificate Program.

Jensen founded the Lincoln Steffens Journalism Award for Investigative Reporting in Northern California in 1981. He also participated in the development of the Bay Area Censored awards program by the Media Alliance in San Francisco in 1989 and in the development of Project Censored Canada in 1993.

He has written and lectured extensively about press censorship, the First Amendment, and the mass media.

Jensen has been cited by the national Association for Education in Journalism and Mass Communication for his "innovative approach to constructive media criticism and for providing a new model for media criticism." The Giraffe Project honored Jensen "for sticking his neck out for the common good" and for being a "role model for a caring society." The Media Alliance presented Jensen with the Media Alliance Meritorious Achievement Award in the "Unimpeachable Source" category. The Society of Professional Journalists in Los Angeles awarded him its 1990 Freedom of Information Award.

In 1992, Jensen was named the outstanding university professor of journalism in California by the California Newspaper Publishers Association and was awarded the 1992 Hugh M. Hefner First Amendment Award in education from the Playboy Foundation for his achievement in defending the First Amendment.

He has been a guest on many radio/television news and talk shows including a Bill Moyers PBS television documentary on Project Censored.

Jensen is married and has four children and three grandchildren. He, wife Sandra, and Danske, their great Great Dane, live in downtown Cotati, in Northern California.